MONICA'S STORY

All these—all the meanness and agony without end, I sitting look out upon,
See, hear, and am silent.

WALT WHITMAN
from *Leaves of Grass*

Monica's Story

Andrew Morton

St. Martin's Press ❧ New York

Monica's Story

Copyright © 1999 by Andrew Morton and Prufrock LLC

All rights reserved.

Printed in the United States of America.

For information address St. Martin's Press,
175 Fifth Avenue, New York, N.Y. 10010

Library of Congress Cataloging-in-Publication Data
available upon request

ISBN 0-312-24091-0

Published in Great Britain by Michael O'Mara Books Limited
First U.S. Edition: 1999

10 9 8 7 6 5

Contents

Contents

Author's Acknowledgments

It took a leap of faith and trust for Monica Lewinsky to sit down with a relative stranger from another country and culture to discuss every detail of her short but eventful life. That by the end she only saw me as the irritating elder brother she never had is a testimony to her patience and endurance after days of probing and sometimes pointless questions.

Her mother, Marcia Lewis, and her father, Dr. Bernie Lewinsky, showed similar fortitude, particularly when talking about the pain and humiliation their family have faced over the last year.

My heartfelt thanks to them as well as to Barbara Lewinsky, Peter Straus, Michael Lewinsky and Debra Finerman; all their memories of a young woman they love and know so well have greatly enriched the text.

Just as her family have sustained Monica during her ordeal, so too her friends have been a source of comfort and support. Catherine Allday Davis, Neysa DeMann Erbland, Linda Estergard, Carly Henderson, Leonore Reese, Nancy Krasne and Dale Young all spoke openly and affectionately about Monica, her many virtues and her imperfections. My appreciation too, to the Lewinsky legal team, Jake Stein, Plato Cacheris, Sydney Hoffmann, Preston Burton and, of course, Billy Martin, for their insights.

As ever, thanks to my publisher Michael O'Mara who was with me from the moment I started this journey to the end, as well as the publishing team, Jacquie Wines, Toby Buchan, Emma Haynes, Martin Bristow, Helen Simpson and Hope Dellon, who worked tirelessly to finish the book against tight deadlines.

Finally, thanks to my wife Lynne and daughters Alexandra and Lydia who kept their cool while I was losing mine.

ANDREW MORTON
London,
February 1999

Photograph Acknowledgments

The majority of photographs in this book have kindly been provided by Monica Lewinsky, her father, Dr. Bernie Lewinsky, her uncle, Dr. Bill Finerman, Jr., and friends. Otherwise, the picture credits are as follows:

Page 15 (*below*) PA News; Page 20 (*both*) AP; Page 21 (*above*) PA News, (*below*) AP; Page 22 (*left*) AP, (*right*) PA News; (*below*) Rex Features; Page 23 (*below*) AP; Page 24 (*below*) AP.

Foreword

I AM DRINKING WATER from a glass engraved with the seal of the President of the United States, in a room on the tenth floor of a smart apartment building in Beverly Hills. The late November sun glints on the glossy high-rise offices of downtown Los Angeles a few miles south.

The apartment is blandly sophisticated in a slightly Middle Eastern manner; the living room has one long mirrored wall, white carpeting and the other walls white, with doors leading off to a white, modern open-plan kitchen and a featureless bedroom. All around is evidence of the unfinished business of moving, an untidy sea of half-empty packing boxes, discarded wrapping paper, unread newspapers, unopened parcels.

The new occupant has tried to impose her more homelike and, as she would call it, "shabby-chic," taste on this unprepossessing setting; an antique armoire decorated with roses, lamps with rose-covered shades and pink rose fabrics intrude into the insipid decoration, while numerous paintings of the ubiquitous roses in antique frames—one she bought from the Portobello Road market in London for thirty dollars—adorn the white walls. This girl likes roses a lot, just as she enjoys rummaging through flea markets for antiques.

This is the new home of Monica Samille Lewinsky, the young woman whose affair with Bill Clinton has resulted in the first impeachment trial of an elected President in American history. Yet the girl in question seems the very antithesis of a sophisticated courtesan as she sits in an armchair covered in cream fabric that she has just bought on discount, knitting a teal and gray scarf as a Christmas present for a friend. She is of medium height, around five foot six inches, with a luxuriant helmet of dark brown hair, and is dressed for comfort in a dark blue Old Navy jogging suit, her bare feet tucked under her thighs. Her lips are full, her hands small but expressive in their movements, her voice light and young, and when she laughs a dimple appears on her right cheek.

In the background, the television relays live coverage of Special Prosecutor Kenneth Starr, the man who has made her life an utter misery for the last year, giving evidence before the House Judiciary Committee. As he presents his detailed account as to whether President William

Jefferson Clinton should face impeachment and removal from office, Monica talks about her childhood, her needles clicking as she chats. It is a scene as surreal as it is incongruously domestic. While Starr speaks—for a total of twelve hours—to this august Congressional body about impeaching the President, the name Lewinsky never far from his thin lips, Monica worries about changing to smaller needles to make her scarf less bulky.

She only becomes animated when Starr is cross-examined by the President's counsel, David Kendall, about the worst day of her young life when, in January 1998, she was confronted by armed FBI agents, taken to a hotel room, and held for twelve hours while Starr's deputies questioned her. When, on television, Starr repeatedly denies that she was held during this "sting operation," Monica puts down her knitting and shouts at the screen, "How on earth would you know? You weren't even there!"

First impressions of Monica, then, are of a feisty, self-possessed young woman who, as she talks in detail about her life to date, reveals her remarkable capacity to remember times, places and dates with precision and accuracy. Her wit, too, is as nimble as her small knitting fingers; "Why don't you ask Linda Tripp?" is her tart response when I mention a problem with the tape recorder which we are using during our conversations. Monica's anger towards the woman who betrayed her by recording their phone conversations is never far beneath the surface.

It is also easy to see why Starr's deputy prosecutors found her such a compelling and convincing witness when, in twenty-two lengthy interviews, she talked about her affair with the President. All her family respect her photographic memory, often telling me, in response to some question of mine, "Ask Monica about when that happened, she will know." Like the President, she enjoys solving logical puzzles and games although she is no intellectual; ironically, she also displays little interest in political issues, apart from education.

Yet leafing through her school and college essays, which display lucid lines of thought and argument, it takes little imagination to realize that she was the author of the famous "Talking Points," a memo she wrote advising Linda Tripp as to how she should structure her affidavit in the sexual harassment case brought against the President by Paula Jones.

While Monica's mind is ferociously orderly and logical, the organization of her day-to-day life is chaotic, a constant searching for keys, shopping lists and the other essential paraphernalia of existence. She is one of the untidiest people I have ever met, a quality which she airily dismisses as being the result of her upbringing, the family having always had a maid to do the tidying up. Monica is the kind of girl who finds it easier to discuss the merits of exculpatory evidence in a law case than to boil an egg.

If she is a woman certain of her own mind, she is less sure about her own heart. As we leaf through family photograph albums, this emotional uncertainty quickly becomes apparent: "God, I look so fat in that picture"; "Look how much weight I put on over this summer"; "I'd lost twenty pounds here"; and so on. Such photos are early evidence of her insecurity, and her low sense of self-esteem, as well as a record of her unhappy family background—her parents divorced when she was a teenager—all translated into her fluctuating weight and her continuing worries about it. Moreover, it is clear, after even a few days of knowing Monica, that her disorderly routine and her neurotic behavior over her weight perfectly explain why she never cleaned the notorious blue Gap dress that was stained with the President's semen.

Indeed, it was the gulf between the real Monica Lewinsky and her image as a Beverly Hills playgirl who stalked the President that brought us together. I had met her the previous week in the offices of her New York attorney, Richard Hofstetter. I would like to be able to boast that she thought me her ideal biographer because I had written about Diana, Princess of Wales, and that she loved my prose style, leading her to insist that I tell her story. In fact, she had never read my book, *Diana, Her True Story*, or ever thought much about the late Princess. The reason was more prosaic, but also rather more amusing.

One wet and windy Saturday morning in early November 1998, a reporter from a British Sunday newspaper arrived on my doorstep in North London and told me that his paper had a cast-iron story which said that I was writing a book about Monica Lewinsky. This was news to me and I said so, but the Sunday paper in question, living by the Fleet Street motto, "Never let the facts get in the way of a good story," duly printed it the next day as true. This false story then winged its way across the Atlantic and onto the radar screen of Monica's lawyer, Richard Hofstetter, who, out of the blue, the following Friday night contacted Michael O'Mara, my publisher, at his London offices and asked if I was indeed interested in meeting Monica. It is one of the more delightful ironies of this entire project that it began as a result of a complete myth.

Mike and I managed to stop laughing long enough to book a pair of airline tickets to New York to meet the lady in question. On the airplane, over a couple of glasses of in-flight champagne we mapped out a complex and cunning strategy—if Monica was as unpleasant as everyone said, we resolved that we would make our excuses and spend a day or two on a little light Christmas shopping.

So it was that, in a rather claustrophobic conference room in her attorney's office, we first met Monica, a demure, polite young woman who was a far cry from the brassy Beverly Hills babe of media mythology. The Monica I discovered is a bright, lively and witty young woman who, while she bears the scars of her continuing public shaming, remains undefeated. She is a well-educated girl who likes singing, shopping and poetry—T.S. Eliot is her favorite poet—and has seen her life measured out, not in coffee spoons, but in the contents of her e-mails, her computer hard-disk drive and her closet. Strong-willed and determined, she exhibited a degree of courage and trust to allow me to delve into the inner recesses of her heart without any editorial control—apart from being given the chance to check the facts.

With these editorial provisos in place, it was obvious that here was a fascinating human story of love, betrayal and obsession, and one that had been obscured by the legal debate about impeaching the President. At heart, it is the tale of how an immature and emotionally vulnerable young woman came to Washington and fell for the world's most powerful man, himself a flawed individual riddled with doubt and desire. Their secret affair was certainly more than a passing sexual fling, their twenty or so meetings over more than two years sustained by countless late-night phone calls, all of them made by the President. Neither faced up to the truth of their relationship, nor to their mutual obsession; both have paid a high and continuing price, she for her loyalty and her love, he for his desires and his lies. Reflecting on the affair today, Monica admits, "We were both responsible, we both wanted it. It was wrong because he was married, but I was young. It was a mistake, but it happened. I realize that I put myself in a situation where I had no control. He had control over when he talked to me. He had control over when he saw me. He had control over the relationship . . ."

How heavy a price she has paid for that mistake became clear when we took her, her mother Marcia Lewis and her stepfather Peter Straus, among others, to an Italian restaurant facing Central Park. The conversation was light and lively, Peter Straus, a former Assistant Secretary of State for Africa in the Kennedy administration, was interested in my latest book on the President of Kenya, Daniel T. arap Moi, while Mike O'Mara chatted about opera with Monica's mother, herself the author of a book about the Three Tenors.

The jolly mood instantly evaporated, however, when Monica, her mother and stepfather left the restaurant early, only to be ambushed in a hail of flashlights and abuse by waiting photographers supplying New York tabloids. As they snapped away, they shouted foul abuse at Monica in the hopes of provoking a reaction. Next morning her photo was on the front page of the *New York Daily News*, complete with a wholly fabricated story, under the headline "Monica's Big Fit," of how she had thrown a tantrum in another restaurant, as well as the almost obligatory unflattering comments about her weight. (The story brought her an unlikely protector. A homeless man living in a doorway near her hotel to whom she took food and drink every day promised that he would chase away any paparazzi who bothered her.)

Unpleasant as this incident was, its saddest feature was that it indicated that Monica has reached a point where she simply accepts it as part of her daily life; she has become a piece of meat to be chewed on by the mass media, the Special Prosecutor and the White House. "It's a good thing you guys didn't take me to a cigar bar," she joked wickedly afterwards, a reference to her behavior with one of the President's cigars, an episode lovingly chronicled by Judge Kenneth Starr in his famous report.

In fact, that rather dark, self-deprecating sense of humor has enabled her to survive the crisis, lightening the blackest moments in her constant fight to avoid becoming the sacrificial lamb in a battle between two powerful men. She tells "Monica-and-Bill" jokes herself, and when, after Thanksgiving last year, she stayed with her father in Los Angeles, she was entertained by an amusing parody of the entire scandal written by a family friend, Paul Horner, a TV-comedy scriptwriter.

Indeed, through the dark days of the last year, the love and support of her family and friends, above all, have sustained her as every intimate detail of her relationship with the President has been revealed in withering and humiliating detail by the Special Prosecutor and the media. Her mother, a quietly spoken, self-effacing woman who lives for her family, has been Monica's sounding board and emotional punching bag during that time, accepting her tantrums, her tears and her torment. Not altogether uncritically, however: "No matter how much we love Monica, no matter how we defend her," Marcia admits, "we do recognize that she bore responsibility for what happened." There is, too, something of the weariness of defeat in that remark, for although she supported Monica tirelessly, Marcia Lewis's own spirit was broken when Kenneth Starr effectively pitted mother against daughter in court as he labored to snare the President. It has left an indelible scar, just as Monica's father, Dr. Bernie Lewinsky, still has nightmares about his daughter going to jail. If nothing else, the story of the intern and the President illustrates how easily the modern high-tech state can dissect and destroy not only individuals, but the basic building block of society, the family.

The one positive outcome of a year which has seen Monica and her family tested almost to emotional annihilation, has been the fact that she has come much closer to her father, from whom she was estranged during her teenage years when he and Marcia divorced. Since the scandal erupted, Monica has spent much time with him and her stepmother Barbara in their Los Angeles home, renewing her emotional bond. When she is with him she is noticeably quieter, more deferential and more careful than she is with her mother, with whom she has an intensely loving but sometimes explosive relationship.

Just as the scandal has both destroyed and renewed the Lewinsky family, so too it has brought Monica much closer to her friends who supported her during her worst moments. In order to maintain those links, and thus her sanity, however, she has to plan visits to them like a military operation. Her stepfather Peter Straus explains the estranging effects of worldwide, twenty-four-hour media attention, most of it hostile: "She's been bruised and isolated so she can't go flying around, seeing people. It's been very lonely." Thus, when in November last year, Monica and I flew to Portland, Oregon, to visit her friends from her days there at Lewis and Clark College, we behaved like a pair of fugitives— false names, heads down, baseball caps on, no eye contact—to make sure she was not recognized.

It proved to be a weekend of renewal for Monica, for she was able to relax and be herself with those who knew the real person behind the head-lines, the unadorned friend with all her faults and weaknesses, but all her many virtues, too. She found it truly energizing to commune with friends like Catherine Allday Davis, Linda Estergard and Carly Henderson, join-ing in the laughter and singing in the back of the car as they drove to a restaurant for a Thai meal. As Catherine says, "She's mature, she's thought-ful and she's caring, but she makes mistakes, big mistakes. But the human being is really very different than the person portrayed in this scandal."

The girl who caught the eye of President Bill Clinton, a man of acknowledged sexual charisma and more than twice her age, is a person of endless contrasts: sure of her own mind yet unsure of herself; possessed of a high sense of entitlement but a low sense of self-worth; a girl with a fierce and sometimes perverse loyalty to others but little regard for her own survival. She leads not only with her chin, but with her heart, desper-ate to find a meaningful relationship yet impatient of the modern mating ritual. It is no coincidence that her two serious adult affairs have both been with married men.

For someone who appears, on meeting her, to be worldly and sophisti-cated, she remains rather naive, achingly honest and trusting, the Beverly Hills gloss masking a vulnerable human being. Her close friend from school-days, Neysa DeMann Erbland, observes, "She is a flawed but good woman," adding that Monica has "endured the public ravaging of the most personal parts of her life." In public, too, she is always sunny, almost too solicitous and helpful; on her own she is prone to pessimism and despair.

It was, however, the public face of Monica, the bright, lively, entertain-ing and rather pushy twenty-two-year-old, that first caught the eye of the President in the summer of 1995, when an extraordinary set of circum-stances brought them together at the White House. Today, she remembers that moment with almost painful clarity: "There was an intense flirtation, an intense chemistry between us, but I don't think it was that much differ-ent to the other women he's flirted with, or seen or been attracted to. I think it was a combination of mutual attraction and the timing being right."

If "right" is the correct adjective, then Monica Lewinsky was the right girl in the right place at the wrong time. The rest, as they say, made history.

● ●

Betrayal at Pentagon City

 $\mathcal{S}$ TIFLING A YAWN, Monica Lewinsky pulled on black leggings and a gray T-shirt, then made for the door, negotiating her way around the half-filled packing boxes that littered her ground-floor apartment in the Watergate Building in downtown Washington. Once outside, she climbed into her brother's Jeep Cherokee and nursed it through the morning traffic for the fifteen-minute journey to her new gym on fashionable Connecticut Avenue.

Conscious, as ever, of her weight, she wanted to get in shape for her new job, working in the Public Relations Division of Revlon, the cosmetics company, in New York. Yet while it was an exciting and enticing prospect, her anticipation of this new life was tinged with regret. She was leaving the person she loved, the one man who had occupied her every waking moment and invaded her restless nights for the last two years— the President of the United States.

There was another and more pressing worry. As she took part in the morning aerobics class, her mind was occupied with more than a sentimental reverie for the man she had loved and now seemed destined to lose. She had been ordered to make a sworn statement in a civil case brought by Paula Jones, a clerical worker from the President's home state of Arkansas, who claimed that, in May 1991, when he had been state Governor, he had sexually harassed and assaulted her. But while she had complied with the order, Monica had lied in her affidavit. As far as she was concerned, the fact that she had had an affair with a married man, even if he was the most powerful individual in the free world, was nobody's business but her own.

As the disco beat pounded through the mirror-walled exercise room, Monica knew she had a major problem, a predicament that had been gnawing at her soul for nearly a month. She had told a girlfriend, a middle-aged secretary at her office in the Pentagon, about her affair. Now that friend was threatening to go public. For the last month Monica had tried everything to ensure her silence, even offering her a condominium in Australia.

What she did not know then, however, was that her friend, Linda Tripp, had in fact been bent on betraying her for almost a year. She had even taped Monica's phone calls to her, planning to use the girl's indiscreet remarks in a "kiss-and-tell book" she proposed to write; worse still, she had plotted with a right-wing political spy, a magazine reporter and Paula Jones's lawyers to expose her. In the last couple of days Tripp had made a Faustian pact with the Special Prosecutor, Kenneth Starr, a former Bible salesman turned lawyer who had been zealously pursuing Monica's lover, the President, for the last four years. Starr would guarantee Tripp's immunity from prosecution for illegally taping her friend's calls if she told him everything, a deal that would leave Monica facing jail for having sworn a false statement.

Monica knew none of this, however, as she stopped off at the Starbucks coffee shop for her usual brew, a large latte, skimmed, with sweetener and a shake of chocolate and cinnamon. As she sipped her coffee and read the *Washington Post* for that Friday, January 16, she was paged on her beeper by "Mary," the code name Tripp was now using in their increasingly fraught communications.

She immediately called back, hoping that the older woman had at last seen sense and agreed to file an affidavit that would leave both of them in the clear. In her nasal New Jersey drawl, Tripp told her that she was planning to see her new lawyer later that day, and wanted to meet with Monica before that critical meeting to discuss what she should say in her affidavit. Monica readily agreed and arranged to see her at the shopping mall in Pentagon City at eleven o'clock. Relieved, she resumed her reading of the paper, only to be interrupted by another page from "Mary," who now pushed the meeting back to a quarter to one. Again she agreed.

That was not the only page she received that fateful morning. Next there was a call from "Kay"—the code name used by the President's Personal Secretary, Betty Currie. She told Monica that she had spoken to the President about inquiries from the media, and particularly from Michael Isikoff of *Newsweek* magazine, whose questions seemed to indicate a level of knowledge about the illicit affair. The President's message was to say nothing. Monica asked Betty to wish the President "Good luck," knowing that he was due to give his sworn statement in the Paula Jones case on the following day.

Finishing her coffee, she decided that, rather than return to her apartment, she would pick up a few more packing boxes for her move to New York. She hoped that, if Tripp held firm in her affidavit and the President did the same in his deposition on the following day, then at last she would be able to wake up from this silly nightmare and the ridiculous Paula Jones case would drift out of her life.

Having killed some time, Monica still arrived early at the Pentagon mall, and therefore stood by the sushi bar reading a women's magazine. By now, however, she had begun to feel sick—seriously nauseous, in fact, as an awful sense of dread dragged at the pit of her stomach. She had lost all faith in Tripp, whose behavior and disposition had altered dramatically over the last few months. Indeed, she now seemed a different person from the friend to whom Monica, one fateful day just over a year before, had reluctantly confided her love for the President.

In truth, she was tired of Linda Tripp, sick of her prevarication and her lies; she hated, too, the fact that she was now beholden to a woman she no longer liked, let alone trusted. A three-hour lunch a couple of days earlier had been a dragging ordeal, Monica forced to be pleasant as she listened to the other woman's evasions and her sly excuses. Now, to cap it all, Tripp was late.

It crossed Monica's mind that she should leave the mall and go home to finish her packing. She delayed, worried about the look on the face of her "Handsome"—her affectionate nickname for the President—if he were ever to discover that she had revealed their intimate secret. And he certainly would find that out if Linda Tripp were to swear an affidavit expressing what she knew of Monica's affair with him.

Then, as she continued to loaf by the sushi bar, she at last spotted the lumpy figure of Tripp, dressed in a dun-brown business suit, slowly descending the escalator. Lowering her magazine, Monica walked towards her, hiding her irritation behind a mask of friendship, preparing to greet her one-time friend while hoping that their meeting would be as short as it would be successful. "Hi," she said, reaching out to hug Tripp. The other was stiff and unresponsive, however; worse, she gestured with her eyes to two cold-faced men in dark suits and white shirts who had followed her down the escalator.

As they approached, an overwhelming sense of fear seized the base of Monica's throat, almost choking her. They introduced themselves as agents of the Federal Bureau of Investigation, extending their shiny steel badges rather than their hands to confirm their identities. Then, in clipped sentences that she could barely hear above the hubbub of the lunchtime throng, they told her that they were sanctioned by the United States Attorney General, Janet Reno, to investigate crimes committed in relation to the Paula Jones lawsuit.

"Ma'am, you are in serious trouble," they told her ominously, before adding, "But we would like to give you an opportunity to save yourself." Gasping for air, she looked plaintively at the two agents and then at Linda Tripp. *How could she have done this to me? How could I ever have trusted her, and trusted her for so long?* Hardly able to breathe, her heart pounding harder than she had ever thought possible, she managed to blurt out the one sentence she had heard in almost every crime movie she had ever seen: "I'm not talking to you without my attorney."

They barely missed a beat, replying with practiced certainty, "That's fine. But if you do that you may not be able to help yourself so much. We

[17]

just want to talk to you. You are free to leave when you want." Monica's token defiance barely lasted the time it took for them to say the words; shocked and frightened, she burst into a flood of tears. Tripp now spoke for the first time. In her rasping voice she told her young friend, "Trust me, Monica, this is for your own good. Just listen to them. They did the same thing to me." Then she reached forward and, like a latter-day Judas, tried to embrace her. Monica pulled away in revulsion.

The FBI men made it clear that if she cooperated she might not be in so much trouble, and it took Monica a few seconds before she grasped the meaning of what they were saying. Her every instinct told her to walk away; equally, however, she calculated that if she did so she would not find out what was going on, and would not therefore be able to help either her case, or the President. She therefore agreed to accompany the FBI agents to their room in the Ritz-Carlton Hotel, which is adjacent to the concourse. At this point she had one overwhelming thought in her mind—she must warn the President.

As this unlikely group now ascended the escalators Monica was screaming in her head to the passing parade, "Help! These monsters have me. Please, somebody save me. Dear God, please help me." But the shoppers passed by without a glance, without offering a helping hand, without even having a clue about the calamity that had just overtaken the silently pleading girl.

She was in shock and she was panicking, but most of all she was in deep, deep trouble. As the lift took Monica, her treacherous friend and the two cold-eyed FBI men to the Ritz-Carlton's Room 1012, she found herself thinking,

"How did I get here?"

● ●

CHAPTER ONE

"My Little Farfel"

O N A HOT SUMMER'S DAY—July 23—in 1973, after an interminable labor in the same San Francisco children's hospital where she herself had been born, Marcia Lewinsky gave birth to her first child, Monica Samille. As the proud father, Bernie, himself a doctor, looked on, the nurses who had helped Marcia through her longest day marveled at the beautiful long eyelashes of her seven-and-a-half-pound daughter. Bernie called her "My little Farfel," *farfel* meaning "noodle."

Bernie Lewinsky's parents had both fled Germany in the 1920s to escape the increased harassment of the Jews by the emerging Nazi Party. His father, George, sought a new life in El Salvador in Central America, where he worked as an accountant for a coffee import–export business. During a trip to London in 1939, on the eve of World War Two, he met Susi, a young German teacher who had left her home in Hamburg after the Gestapo took away her entire class of Jewish children during a raid on the school where she taught Hebrew. Two weeks later George and Susi married. They settled in El Salvador, where they enjoyed an affluent lifestyle, far removed from the horrors of the war that was to devastate Europe. Yet even though their homeland was thousands of miles away, they instilled in their son Bernie, who was born in 1943, the archetypal Teutonic virtues of hard work, self-discipline and respect for the rule of law. When Bernie was fourteen, the family immigrated to California, where, after high school, he went on to study medicine at the University of California in Berkeley and Irvine. It was while he was at medical school that he first met Marcia Vilensky, then aged twenty to his twenty-five.

Like George Lewinsky, Marcia's father, Samuel, had fled his native land—in his case, Lithuania, then suffering under Stalin's purges of the 1930s. Samuel Vilensky first settled in San Francisco, where Marcia was born in 1948. When she was four, the family moved to Tokyo, her father having decided that there were exciting business opportunities in postwar Japan. Samuel developed a successful import–export business in Tokyo, and the Vilenskys enjoyed a life as affluent as it was cosmopolitan, given their Russian roots, expatriate social circle and Japanese friends. Marcia and her sister Debra, who was born three years after the family had left America, wanted for nothing: the house was staffed by a bevy of servants, including a chauffeur. The two girls integrated well into the local community, both becoming fluent in Japanese. This idyll was, however, to be abruptly shattered.

In 1964, Samuel Vilensky died suddenly of a heart attack. With his death the family business fell in ruins, and Marcia, Debra and their mother, Bernice, had to return to California, where they stayed with Bernice's mother, Olga Polack, in Sonoma County, just outside San Francisco. To support the family, Bernice took a job as a legal secretary, although it barely paid enough to make ends meet. The days of a large house and lavish lifestyle were consigned to history. It was, Marcia recalls, a bitter wrench, "a huge change, to move out of the country you have grown up in."

With the family coffers suddenly empty, Marcia enrolled for study at a community college. After two years one of her uncles stepped in, undertaking to pay the fees for her to attend California State University, Northridge, where she majored in urban studies, aiming to become a town planner once she had graduated. These dreams were shelved for good when, at Easter 1968, she met Bernie Lewinsky, a quietly spoken, self-effacing medical student five years her senior. "The bond that drew us together was the fact that we had both lived abroad," says Marcia, although she concedes that after the trauma of her father's death she was looking for emotional security.

With Bernie facing the stressful prospect of a medical internship, both families agreed that it would be better if the couple, young as they were, married before he began this time of long hours and little sleep, so that they could, at least for a while, enjoy a normal married life. In the commotion and excitement surrounding the wedding, the differences in their characters—she charming, biddable, shy, unconventional and creative, he undemonstrative, down to earth, practical and hard-working—were set aside, and they were married in a Jewish ceremony at San Francisco's Fairmont Hotel in February 1969.

Shortly after their wedding they moved to London, where Bernie worked for a year as a registrar (the British term for resident) at the Royal Marsden Hospital, concentrating on his specialist field, oncological cancer. Both look back on that period with fond memories; Marcia, an Anglophile to her fingertips, loved the country's history and tradition, while Bernie enjoyed the challenges he faced at one of the world's leading cancer hospitals. It was during this time that Monica was conceived. Marcia, who returned to San Francisco near the end of Bernie's time at the Royal Marsden in London, excitedly sent a telegram to her husband at the hospital: "Dear Bernard, We're having a baby. Love, Marcia."

For Marcia, the arrival of Monica signaled a fulfillment of a kind. As she says, "Like many women of my generation, I never really assigned myself a career. Being a mother was my goal. My kids are precious to me—you could say too important."

It was clear from early on that Monica was a bright child; she could talk before she could walk, and was speaking fluently before her second birthday. Marcia doted on her baby daughter, but she soon discovered who was the boss: "Monica," she says, with a smile of weary acceptance. "She was a strong-willed child who always knew her own mind. Yet her strong will and determination have never been to control others. It is all about Monica knowing what is right for Monica."

Both her mother and her Aunt Debra remember numerous examples of Monica's utter certainty about her own decisions, even as a small child. When she was two years old, Debra took her to the park near her home in San Francisco to play on the swings. When it was time to leave, Monica refused to get off her swing and, although she adored her aunt—who throughout Monica's life has been a close confidante and staunch friend—ignored all attempts to persuade her to go home. Eventually, Debra tried to trick her by calling out, "Bye," and walking away, thinking the little girl would run and catch up to her. She was wrong. Although it was getting dark, Monica remained glued to her swing. It was only when she had at last had enough that she agreed to leave. "To me," says Debra, "that isn't necessarily bad—she knew her own mind even at two years old. I think she is an exceptional person, quite fascinating. She was then like she is now, charming, sweet, extremely bright and difficult, very strong-willed."

Her strength of will, which some might call obstinacy in one so young, surfaced again when Debra was due to marry her fiancé, Bill Finerman, a cardiologist, at his grandmother's home in Beverly Hills in 1976. Monica, then three, was to be the flowergirl. Just twenty minutes before the service, she decided that her light-blue dress, which had long sleeves, would look better if it was sleeveless—she already had an eye for fashion. With the bride putting the finishing touches to her own dress, there was no time for argument or persuasion. Marcia decided that the only solution was to do as her daughter wanted, and she reached for her scissors. The offending sleeves removed, Monica happily put on her dress and, her aunt says, "stole the show."

Marcia also admits that the combination of her daughter's tenacious yet emotionally needy nature and her own readiness to avoid a fuss, at almost any cost, probably influenced Monica's behavior in adulthood. "I'm by nature non-confrontational; Bernie was very autocratic, very stern, because of his upbringing so you can see the dynamics of the family."

In 1976, after Bernie had finished a two-year stint at the Letterman Hospital in San Francisco, the family left their three-bedroom home there

[21]

for Los Angeles, where he had secured a well-paid position in private practice. A year later, Marcia gave birth again, this time to a boy, whom they named Michael. Monica was thrilled. The four-year age gap was deliberate, designed to prevent sibling rivalry, but Monica adored her baby brother from the first, and immediately nicknamed him "Jo Jo." When mother and son returned to the family's Spanish-style house in Beverly Hills they found, stretched across the front door, ribbons and a huge banner saying: "Welcome Home Jo Jo." She was so taken with her brother that she would often hide in a closet until his nanny, who liked a regimented routine, put him to bed for the night. Then she would squeeze from her hiding place and play with him until they were discovered. "She mothered him to death," recalls Marcia, who, significantly, also observes that, unlike his elder sister, Michael has a relaxed, shrug-of-the-shoulders approach to life's decisions and difficulties.

In general, Michael remembers, Monica was "overly thoughtful" and "always concerned about me," though he adds that she was "a great sister." For his part, he agrees that he is much the more level-headed of the two: "Monica can run the spectrum of emotions in a very short amount of time," he says diplomatically. So while he remembers their three-bedroom house on North Hillcrest Drive with affection, recalling days splashing about in their own pool with their father, Monica remembers the fact that the suburb was plagued by raccoons coming into the houses.

Although some people have portrayed Marcia as a flighty socialite, perhaps because under her pen name "Marcia Lewis" she wrote a monthly column for the *Hollywood Reporter Magazine*, in reality she was a homebody, happy to devote her time and energies to her children. Which was just as well because besides Michael's arrival, there was another significant change for Monica: at the age of six, she first went to school. The John Thomas Dye School in Bel Air is a well-established private school with a daunting academic and social reputation. With its immaculate buildings and grounds, high-caliber teaching staff and a roll-call of former students who have reached the political and economic summits of the country, it is a quintessential example of WASP culture. Its alumni include political friends of former President Ronald Reagan and his wife, Nancy, the son of Katharine Graham, owner of the *Washington Post*, and also a number of California congressmen and senators.

For a time, this bright, lively Jewish girl fit in well. She excelled at mathematics, her written work regularly earned top grades, and her love of poetry was recognized early on. The fact that both her parents read to her a lot as a child and encouraged her own reading was a significant factor in her early intellectual growth. In the hothouse atmosphere of John Thomas Dye it was perhaps no surprise that her stated ambition was to become

President of the United States. She had other, less daunting, dreams, however. When she was seven she wrote that she wanted "to be a teacher and help other people to learn . . . I would be nice but strict," she stated.

Nancy Krasne, a family friend who was in the same school car pool as the Lewinskys, and who has known them for twenty years, remembers Monica as a "very special girl" among a high-powered group. "I always thought that she was the one who was going to be successful," Nancy says. "Monica was very bright, bordering on the brilliant, and very expressive. She was hard-working, conscientious, very much the little adult in some ways, but in others, emotionally very immature. The problem was that she didn't fit the Beverly Hills mold, even though she was so eager to please, to join in with the others." As an example of this driving wish not to be set apart from her fellows or, worse, excluded by them, Monica once spent an entire weekend at home learning how to jump rope so that she could join in with the other girls on schooldays. For a girl who confesses that she is hopeless at sports, nothing could better demonstrate her overwhelming desire to be one of the crowd. She certainly made the grade academically, regularly winning commendations for her work, and invariably bringing home excellent report cards. She remembers it as "a really terrific school . . . very challenging and mind-opening."

But there were drawbacks. The fact that she lived some way from the school in Bel Air meant that it was difficult for her schoolfriends to drop by to play—at that time Barbie dolls and Olivia Newton-John, star of the film musical *Grease*, were all the rage. When she was nine and entering third grade, there were incidents at school, if not of physical bullying, at least of the casual cattiness and cliquishness of children, particularly girls, which often remain as a canker in the psyche well into adult life. Nor was her cause helped by the fact that she was beginning to get a little overweight. She was dubbed "Big Mac" by one of her classmates, Matthew Spaulding, a gibe made all the more painful because at the time she was harboring a schoolgirl crush on him.

Monica also vividly remembers the time when Tori Spelling, the daughter of the Hollywood film mogul Aaron Spelling, held a birthday party at her parents' palatial home. Pop superstar Michael Jackson and the world's smallest pony were expected to be two of the competing attractions at this most glittering of occasions, and everyone in Tori's class was invited—except Monica. Not knowing if the omission was a casual oversight or a deliberate snub, Marcia rang the Spellings' social secretary to check. As a result, an invitation was duly sent out, even though Monica had not been on the original guest list.

Marcia, not surprisingly, concealed this fact from her daughter, and Monica only discovered that she had not been invited as a matter of course when two classmates taunted her about the late invitation. Monica had no idea why Tori should choose to exclude her, especially as they were in Brownies together. However, once she realized the truth of the situation she refused, as a matter of principle, to attend. It was a tough decision for a girl so eager to please and so desperate to belong, but it was also an early sign of one of Monica's most formidable characteristics, her unshakable resolve. She says of the incident, "My mom always taught me to do unto others as you would want done to you. So you should invite everyone to your birthday parties, you should give everyone in your class a Valentine's card. You shouldn't exclude people. Not only is it bad manners, it is very hurtful."

That emphasis on good manners and proper form, something which in part reflected the European influences of her parents, was noticed by those who visited her Beverly Hills home. A friend from her schooldays, Michelle Glazov, recalls that Monica was expected to behave with "almost Victorian decorum" at home, in marked contrast to most of their contemporaries. Moreover, while Bernie and Marcia were not overtly religious, they followed Jewish cultural traditions, sending Monica to Hebrew school at the strict Sinai Temple—a source of resentment in their daughter, who wanted to attend a less orthodox synagogue with her schoolfriends.

At the same time, the high sense of entitlement that comes with living in Beverly Hills led to frequent family clashes, particularly between Monica and her father. For example, when her best friend got her own phone line and Snoopy telephone, Monica asked if she could have the same, and there were tears and tantrums when her father said no. There were similar quarrels when he wouldn't buy her a Minnie Mouse dress during a visit to Disneyland. "I guess growing up it seemed that Mom was the yes one and Dad was the no one," says Monica, "which is not uncommon in a lot of families." Bernie agrees: "Oh yes, I was called 'Dr. No' by my kids, all that kind of stuff."

The focus on materialism, on owning the latest designer clothes and gadgets, was an inevitable corollary of growing up in Beverly Hills, a place where surface and show form the fabric of social life, where to be willowy, blonde and driving the latest BMW is for many people the standard. This obsession with status and money became too much for Monica's beloved Aunt Debra, who decided to move east with her husband and son Alex for a less status-conscious life. "It's a great place for people in their twenties but not good to raise children," she says. "Monica never really fit in. If she had been very thin and in with the fast crowd she would have been OK. But it really wasn't her."

With hindsight, Marcia too regrets the years spent in Beverly Hills, recognizing that her children, particularly Monica, were not suited to the lifestyle. "I myself was never happy in LA. I felt that it wasn't the right place, and I'm sure that was communicated—perhaps unwittingly—to my children."

Monica is more pragmatic, recognizing that if children are raised in a certain environment, their parents have to accept the consequences of that upbringing. She accepts, too, that there is a streak of acquisitiveness in her character that she might not have had if she had been raised in a different city, a different culture. "I don't think I'm a spoiled brat. I don't fit into the Beverly Hills stereotype—in fact that was one of my problems growing up there. However, I do have a certain level of expectation about what I deserve, both from the way in which I was brought up, and from the environment in which I was brought up."

Her high sense of expectation gave rise to a classic confrontation between father and daughter when she asked for a Bat-mitzvah to celebrate her coming-of-age. It is customary in Beverly Hills for Jewish children to have very elaborate Bar/Bat-mitzvah parties at the age of thirteen, usually held in a ballroom or the reception room of the temple with friends and parents' friends: "Like a wedding for one," recalls Monica. Sometimes the reception would be themed with a main attraction, such as a magician. Wanting to be like all the other kids, Monica anticipated a big celebration. Instead, Bernie offered to spend $500 on a party in the backyard of the family home. A full-scale party was not beyond his means but he believed that that was quite sufficient to celebrate an event that was supposed to be religious. Monica, knowing well how this would fail to impress her peers, let it be known in no uncertain terms that it most certainly was not sufficient, nor was it what she wanted. When her mother took her side, the result was a hurtful family argument, in which, inevitably, things were said that would have been much better left unsaid. In the end she did have a birthday party, complete with a DJ and a hot-dog stand, and admits that "it was fun."

Yet the relationship between Monica and her father was by no means characterized by an endless locking of horns. Monica recalls spending hours watching him work at his hobby—woodworking—although she was never allowed to help. She remembers, too, with much pleasure the day when he gave her her first bike—a pink contraption with a banana seat—and then took her to the movie *E.T.*, after which he cooked a special picnic supper of barbecue chicken.

Certainly Bernie seemed atypical of the disengaged Beverly Hills professional concerned more with with his career than with his children. He often woke Monica late at night or at dawn to watch important events on TV like the first launch of the space shuttle or the wedding of the Prince and Princess of Wales. At other times they would sit out in the warm California night and he would point out and identify for her the stars and planets and constellations. When she was eleven she wrote him a touching

Father's Day tribute: "My dad is the best in the West. He is very kind and considerate twenty-four hours of the day. Maybe some fathers don't deserve to be treated specially but my dad really does deserve it."

Monica fondly recalls wearing a pink T-shirt emblazoned with the words "Daddy's Little Girl," and says, "I always wanted to *be* Daddy's little girl." She also says, though, that she was always trying to gain his approval but never really felt that she won it, taking very much to heart her father's slightest criticism or adverse comment. In his own quiet fashion Bernie did and does love her dearly, but in Monica's eyes he was never quite as expressive or demonstrative as she would have wished.

Thus it is not difficult to see how this emotionally needy child—a child, moreover, who had such high expectations of those she cared for— often felt disappointed or rejected when her desires were not met. "I always remember getting into fights with Dad, usually at mealtimes, and I would usually leave the table crying," she remembers. While her childhood memories are of her father coming home from work tired and irascible, she now concedes that the draining emotional strains of a demanding job, where every day he was dealing with seriously ill patients, contributed to their increasingly fractious relationship. "Monica so wanted to be Daddy's little girl," says Marcia. "She had these very high expecta-tions and her father was not like that. It's not that he's a bad man; it's just that he's not the sort to say: 'Come and sit on my knee, you pretty little girl.' It was not his way."

While her relationship with her father was, and continues to be, tricky, Monica forged a close and affectionate bond with her mother, who almost invariably sided with her in family quarrels. "My mom and I are so simi-lar," she says. "We talk very similarly and have the same intonations." Yet, while Monica seemed to be the dominant partner in the relationship, beneath the bluster and argument she needed her mother much more than she cared to admit, even to herself. Aunt Debra comments, "I think it is a typical mother-daughter relationship, very loving but with conflicts of opinion."

Monica wrote of her deep emotional bond with her mother in a school essay about the Hungarian-born Jewish poet Hannah Senesh, a World War Two agent of British Intelligence; in 1944 she was captured in Hungary by the Nazis, tortured and shot. The young Monica got the story a bit mud-dled after seeing the 1988 movie *Hanna's War*, and thought the Nazis had told Senesh that her mother would be killed unless she, Hannah, revealed details of the British spy network. In a telling passage in her essay, Monica wrote: "I wish that I had the inner conviction that Hannah Senesh had. I am not nearly half as brave as she was. However, what I have in common with Hannah is that I too share a very close relationship with my mother. Hannah and her mother had a bond that could not be broken by anything and that is the same with me." As a result of seeing the film she may have got parts of the story wrong—when Senesh was arrested, her mother was in fact living not in Hungary but in Palestine—but the love and loyalty illustrated in her version of it affected her deeply. It became even more important to her on the day her "friend" Linda Tripp betrayed her.

Even so, although the deep emotional dynamics of the inter-dependence between herself, her mother and her father contain the key to understanding Monica's personality, it would be a mistake to seat all her actions in those relationships. The craving to be respected and liked by her peers and, linked to that, her anxiety about her weight should not be overlooked as influences upon her character and behavior.

Whatever her emotional problems, there was no questioning her intel-lectual ability. By the time she left the elementary school in Beverly Hills, it had become clear that she had a photographic memory, particularly for numbers, while her logical mind—a quality she ascribes to her father's side of the family—and eloquence made her a formidable student. Nancy Krasne believes that "she was definitely Ivy League material."

When, aged ten, Monica transferred from John Thomas Dye to Hawthorne Elementary School, also in Beverly Hills, she soon proved her academic gifts. But fourth and fifth grade were to be difficult for Monica. Whilst she made friends she became increasingly hampered by her feel-ings of inadequacy and, like many teenage girls, these feelings became focused on her weight. In a world where to be thin corresponds to a high sense of personal worth and status, Monica's unathletic build, coupled with the fact that she reached puberty earlier than her contemporaries, disturbed her. She desperately wanted to belong, yet her chubby figure made her feel like an outsider, contributing to her emotional burden.

However, it was around this time that Monica started to become inter-ested in boys. Mark Streams, a classmate, gave her a chocolate-covered, heart-shaped lollipop and she considered him to be her "boyfriend."

By sixth grade Monica had become popular with her schoolfellows and a growing spurt the summer before had resulted in a slimmed-down figure. However, the weight problems were to continue and Monica was thrilled, when, the summer before eighth grade, her mother allowed her to attend a "fat camp" in Santa Barbara, a summer school for overweight youngsters which offers a regime of healthy diet and regular exercise. "I wouldn't say it was fun," recalls Monica, "but of course I was dying to go. My mom really wanted me to go too because she had had her own battles with her weight in her life and so could empathize. Living in LA it was really important how you looked. It was upsetting to me because I didn't want to be fat." She arrived at Hawthorne for the fall term feeling leaner, fitter and much more confident. "It was the start of a great year for me," she recalls.

That year, Monica was voted Vice-President of her class by her schoolfellows. It was then that the first President came into her life. It was not Bill Clinton, of course, but the President of her class, Danny Shabani. As President and Vice-President, he and Monica, then thirteen, spent a lot of time together, organizing events and chatting regularly on the telephone. They became close friends. "He was smart, cute and had a tender side to him, not something you saw all the time," says Monica. Although she had had a crush on him the year before, Monica valued her friendship with Danny and the only time they came close to a date was in the summer of her fourteenth birthday when he invited her to the movies. When he brought her home, she found that, ever the gentleman, he had secretly arranged for the delivery of a bouquet of a dozen red roses, her favorite flowers. "It was," she says, "one of the most romantic things anyone has ever done for me. It was so sweet." The only thing which spoiled the moment was the fact that Michael, who idolized Danny, hung around the couple spoiling Monica's hopes of a kiss.

While her relationship with Danny remained platonic, Monica began dating a teenager who became her first real boyfriend, Adam Dave. "Adam was very, very smart. I've always been attracted to intelligent men," she says. At the same time, to begin with, the relationship was fun. When he played baseball Monica was there to cheer him on, and she would spend hours in the evenings chatting to him on the telephone. Some nights she would even hide in her clothes closet whispering down the line because it was past the time she was supposed to be using the phone. However, their teenage romance went on to anticipate the pattern of all her relationships, an emotional roller coaster characterized by angry partings followed in turn by affectionate longing.

This behavior was to characterize her relationships with the two married men in her life. Monica explains it thus: "I am a very emotional and romantic person, but also pragmatic and logical. The combination of those elements means that I want to be in love and enjoy the perfect relationship, yet I only believe the relationship is 'real' if a man gets mad at me when I do something wrong. If a man is never upset with me or something I did, then he is not being honest about his feelings or honest with me—and so I feel that he is being a phony. I also feel this way about men who always agree with me." So she had a fight with Adam Dave because—as illogical as it may seem—he refused to argue with her and thus confirm to her that their romance was real and therefore "true." The result was that she ended their relationship, and then spent months pining for Adam when he refused to kiss and make up. It was another early sign that, though Monica knew her own mind, she had little control over her heart.

As Monica was grappling with the trials and tribulations of adolescence, her parents were trying to come to terms with the disintegration of their marriage. For many years their friends had seen the divide both in their characters and in their aspirations. "They should never have got married in the first place, they just weren't suited to each other," observes one family friend. Monica, who admits she literally internalized the family stresses and strains by eating, says of that time: "My family life was not pleasant. My father worked a lot and the stress of his job, dealing with sick and dying people, was toll taking. It did not help his mood to come home to a relationship that was not right for either of my parents. We always ate dinner together but they were often unpleasant. My parents fought, but not necessarily in front of us. They weren't very affectionate or loving towards each other. We did things, the four of us, but we weren't the quintessential family. I think that was hard for me because I really wanted that. I love the idea of a family Thanksgiving and family Christmas. I am very family-oriented, I grew up watching the *Brady Bunch* TV show and had ideals about how I wanted my family to be. It's one of the things I would most like to change about myself—I have a tendency to write the script and to decide in my own mind how other people should act and what they should say and feel. Then I get disappointed when inevitably they don't follow the script because it is an impossible scenario."

Though Monica saw almost every moment of the drama unfolding in her parents' marriage, she didn't realize that its final curtain was about to fall. Nor, for that matter, did Bernie.

In September 1987 he was in his office, gently explaining to a woman patient that she was suffering from lung cancer, and that it might prove to be terminal. Suddenly his receptionist interrupted the consultation, telling him that there was someone to see him, and that it was urgent. As he walked out into the lobby a small man scurried up to him, shouted, "Divorce papers!" and threw a package at him—it hit him on the chest—before scuttling away.

Bernie's comment on the incident is as understated as it is literal. "It came like a bolt from the blue."

CHAPTER TWO

• •

Tremors at Home

*I*T WAS SUPPOSED TO BE a quiet and happy evening out, but it ended as the saddest day of Monica's young life. On September 21, 1987, Marcia Lewinsky took Monica and Michael to their favorite restaurant, Hamburger Hamlet on Sunset Boulevard in Beverly Hills. Over shakes and fries she told them that she and their father were divorcing. It was, Marcia thought, news that her children would welcome. She believed that what she saw as their jagged relationship with their father meant that they didn't love him and so they would not be upset by his departure, but instead would see it as the end of their unhappy family life and the beginning of a new era, an idyll starring just the three of them. She had thought they would be pleased. She was badly mistaken.

Michael burst into tears, and Monica ran to the rest room, where she was promptly sick. When, pale and shaken, she returned to their table, she vented her anger and shock upon her mother, who was stunned by the vehemence of her daughter's tirade. As they were leaving, Marcia, stung by Monica's criticism, took her to one side and said that the reason why she and her father were divorcing was Bernie's infidelity with a nurse at his practice. Marcia recognizes now that if she had not been so upset, so thrown off balance, by her daughter's reaction, she would never have spoken so plainly. But the damage was done.

Numb with shock and disbelief, Monica and her brother came home to find their father waiting in the family den. As Monica sat with him, for the first time in her life she saw him cry, shedding tears of regret for a failed marriage, and for his children. "It was really sad," she remembers. "It was shocking, it was shattering, a really painful moment and one of the saddest days of my life."

A few days later, on October 1, Los Angeles was rocked by an earthquake which left six dead and a hundred injured. To Monica, it seemed as though nature itself was mirroring her life. "It was symbolic," she says.

Ever the romantic, Monica had cherished a fond hope that, though her parents were not getting along, and had not done so for some time, they might one day become the kind of idealized family she dreamed of.

Indeed, she still has vivid dreams that her parents are still together, and that the pain of the past has become just a distant memory. "One of the hardest things for me was shattering this fantasy that I had of a family life," she says, acknowledging that even now she has much to resolve about that trauma in her life, especially her relationship with her father.

Under California law a couple must be legally separated for a year before a divorce can be finalized. So Bernie, after sleeping in Michael's room for a couple of nights, moved out of the house and took an apartment on Wilshire Boulevard. As Monica and Michael struggled to adjust to his absence, the anxiety and tension at home inevitably unsettled them. "The divorce was very difficult for Michael and me. For many years, and even sometimes today, we have been in the middle of their disagreements. I often feel like I am taking sides. I look back on this period of my life and see anger, confusion, and disappointment," says Monica. Not surprisingly, given the differences not only in their ages but in their characters, Michael's memories of his parents' marriage and the divorce differ somewhat from Monica's. "In the beginning there were a lot of difficulties between my parents," he remembers, "and I found myself in the middle as Monica tended to side with her mother. That made me even more kid in the middle." "It was an emotionally complex and confusing time for Michael, as he spent the week with Mom and every other weekend with Dad, having to adjust quickly to their different personalities," Monica adds. They were a family divided, and Michael, now a student at Carnegie Mellon College, admits that he found it difficult to accept the change, especially as Marcia and the children moved to a different apartment every year. At the same time, he sees the optimistic, rather than pessimistic, side of their life together, unlike his sister. While he sees his childhood as having been happy and relatively uneventful, Monica, for all her outwardly smiling and ebullient character, always broods on the darker side.

Coinciding with the family breakup, Monica had started her first year at Beverly Hills High School—the setting for the long-running teenage soap drama *Beverly Hills 90210*, a zip code synonymous with the beautiful and the bland. Already nervous and apprehensive about starting at a school with a roll call of old alumni straight out of central casting, and notorious for the emphasis its pupils placed on status and glamour, Monica found her self-esteem plummeting. As her friend Lenore Reese, daughter of a US Army Engineers officer, observes, "Beverly Hills is a relentless place. It is very unkind to heavy people."

For Monica, those stresses, coupled with the nightmare of her parents' divorce, proved almost unbearable. Michael remembers her as being often upset and sometimes in tears after the divorce, the sweet elder sister now morose and taciturn. It was not just the family's trauma that depressed her, however, but also the elitist, snobbish atmosphere at Beverly Hills High.

She skipped class and ignored her homework assignments, either going to the houses of friends who lived nearby or spending whole days at the movies. She ate for comfort, putting on more than fifty pounds in less than a year. As the weight piled on, her unhappiness with herself and her life increased. Her misery was complete when she got a "D" grade in English, a humiliating experience for a teenager long thought of as an intellectual high achiever.

Once the divorce was finalized in 1988 and the family home, on Hillcrest Road, sold—at the time it was valued at $1.2 million—Marcia and the two children lived in a series of rented apartments in Beverly Hills, a further unsettling experience, particularly for Michael, who wanted to live in a house. "It was devastating for Michael," recalls Monica. "He was very distressed when we moved out" after the divorce.

Now that the children lived permanently with Marcia, it was perhaps inevitable that they should find themselves siding with her in the emotional battle between their estranged parents. Monica's growing hostility towards her father was strengthened when she read the divorce papers which her mother had inadvertently left on the kitchen table. As she studied the documents, she was both confused and deeply shocked by the bitter words said about each other by two people whom she loved so dearly. For example, Marcia accused Bernie of having a violent temper and of belittling the children, and compounded these charges by making lavish financial claims against him. In her inventory she asked for $720 a month for tennis lessons for Monica and Michael—neither is athletic—as well as $720 to pay for therapy for the two children, anticipating the need for counseling during the divorce and after. What with claims of $20,000 a year for holidays, $100 a month for Monica's hair and $2,400 a month for the family's clothes and shoes, Marcia was asking for $25,000 a month in maintenance. Bernie countered by saying that his wife was a spendthrift who had talked him into leasing a new Mercedes for her and buying her a $3,000 fur coat only days before serving the divorce papers.

Today, both parents independently agree that the divorce papers which became so embarrassingly public after the scandal about their daughter broke in 1998, were drafted by lawyers as nothing more than bargaining chips in the financial discussions. They did not reflect the reality of the Lewinskys' lives, nor the fact that their divorce, though painful, was not as acrimonious as many believe. Nevertheless, the whole affair was a classic example of how not to handle a divorce. As Marcia admits, "It's nothing to be proud of, and I wish I had known then what I know now about how much children suffer. At the time I thought kids were adaptable. I was very wrong."

The effect on Monica, especially after she had read the harsh sentiments in the divorce papers, was profound. Increasingly angry, as well as confused and saddened, she directed her fury at her father, blaming him for the breakdown of the marriage and refusing to see him on the weekends when he had custody of the children. She says, "I had this secret hostility towards my dad. He didn't know that I knew he had had an affair and that I was angry with him about it. He wanted to see me a lot more but I didn't want it. We didn't really spend much time together. I was angry with him—very angry with him. At the time I was very supportive of my mother; she was the good guy and my dad was the bad guy. I see things differently now, though—there were faults on both sides."

Her animosity towards her father was, and remains, a source of sadness for him. Dr. Lewinsky remembers that at the time of the divorce he wrote two letters, one to each of his children, expressing his thoughts about his marriage, and his feelings toward and love for Monica and Michael. He has kept them, waiting for the day when his children will read what he had to say about their lives together. Although they know about them, they have yet to open them. Bernie himself takes up the tale: "After the divorce Michael came every other weekend and sometimes during the week, but not Monica. She was angry. I felt the way to deal with it was to let her work out her own feelings and hope she would come around and discuss the issues with me. But she elected not to."

Michael, unaware of his father's infidelity, developed a very strong bond with him, whereas, angry, unhappy and hurt, Monica found solace in food. She explains her feelings thus: "One thing about food for me is that it's very reliable. You always know what your favorite cookie is going to taste like. You always know it's going to be good and it's very easily obtainable. There's a security about it."

When she skipped her ninth grade classes, she would also hang out in the Drama Department at Beverly Hills High. It was here that she discovered a source of renewal, throwing herself into costume-making, learning to design and sew costumes for the school shows. In her first year she won a third prize for an Elizabethan dress which she had designed and which was used in the school's Shakespeare Festival. As to acting, in a showpiece department which could boast actors like Nicolas Cage and Richard Dreyfuss as graduates, competition for acting roles was of course fierce. As a freshman, Monica was not allowed to audition, so she was thrilled when in her sophomore year, she was chosen for a small role in the musical *The Music Man*. "That was a really terrific experience for me," she recalls.

Inevitably, Monica's circle of schoolfriends—which included Michelle Glazov, Natalie Ungvari (who would later be forced to testify against her friend before the Grand Jury), Pamela Revel and Susie Morris—was drawn from those who took an active part in the work of the Drama Department. "I had a full life in drama," recalls Monica. "It was like a family. People would hang out together in Room 181 for lunch, after school and the weekends were often spent in rehearsal—no matter what side of the foot-lights you were working. It was one of the places at Beverly where freshmen really intermingled with sophomores, juniors, and seniors."

But while she felt at home in the world of drama and make-believe, Monica "hated"—her word—the social side of Beverly Hills High. "A 'normal' High School girl was thin, a cheerleader, had lots of boyfriends and went to endless parties. That wasn't me. Everybody looked great, everyone was very conscious of how they looked there and so being over-weight was not acceptable. The pressure was horrid," she says. It has been widely noted that two of her contemporaries were the now notorious Menendez brothers, Erik and Lyle, who in 1989 murdered their rich parents for their money.

By now, Monica's weight had become an overriding concern, blighting her attitude towards boys, school and herself. Her schoolfriend Michelle Glazov observed at the time, "I think often Monica was insecure in her physicality. She didn't necessarily think she was as pretty as other girls, or as wanted by boys as other girls." Nothing seemed to work, however, for as Monica entered her junior year at Beverly Hills High her weight continued to spiral upwards. At last her mother, seeing her daughter's unhappiness and deepening depression, suggested a solution.

The Rice House in North Carolina is a specialist eating-disorders insti-tution where students are placed on a strict rice-only diet, aiming to lose thirty pounds in a month. If Monica enrolled for a few weeks, Marcia argued, and took extension courses from the University of California at Los Angeles (UCLA), it would help her to recover both physically and academically. Much to Monica's fury and dismay, her father disagreed with the plan, even though it was clear that she needed professional help and guidance to come to terms with an emotional burden that was souring her teenage years. She and her parents therefore went to see a therapist at UCLA, at Bernie's insistence, who recommended that the troubled sixteen-year-old be admitted to an eating-disorder unit at the Rader Clinic in Culver City, Los Angeles.

It was a turning point. She spent a month in the clinic, discussing her problems each day with professional therapists as well as attending a self-help group called "Overeaters Anonymous." It was a stormy road to recovery as Monica, argumentative to the last, fought a daily battle of wills with her eating-disorders counselor, Lisa Ladin—although the latter's insistence on setting limits and on strict discipline earned her patient's lasting respect.

During her stay at Rader, Monica explored her feelings about her parents and the divorce which had so deeply scarred her. In one essay, in which she touched on her innermost longings, she wrote that a witch had cast a spell on her father, and this explained why he had been so

[34]

indifferent toward her. In her story the spell was broken so that now he was free to love her, and at last to show her he did. As painful as some of this therapy must have been, Monica emerged from her course not only much slimmer, but with a newfound determination to get on with her life. "I felt energized and elevated," she says, although she continued to see a therapist for some time afterwards.

An essential part of her rehabilitation was the decision in 1989 to transfer her away from the hothouse atmosphere of Beverly Hills High to a school where she would find it easier to fit in. Her mother chose Bel Air Prep, a much smaller, private school where the emphasis was on one-to-one tuition. Besides the academic advantages, the importance attached to looks and slimness, as well as to wealth and status, was not quite so pronounced as it had been at her previous school.

In this atmosphere, Monica, then sixteen, flourished. Her English teacher, Everol Butterworth, rekindled her love of language, enthusing her with an interest in poetry. She read widely and avidly, finding the poetry of, among others, Walt Whitman, Ezra Pound, Robert Frost, and particularly T.S. Eliot—whose "The Love Song of J. Alfred Prufrock" is her favorite poem—and others a source of inspiration for her own musings. "It was life-changing for me," she says.

In a compilation she made of her favorite poetry and poets, she interspersed their work with her own offerings. One of her poems in particular, which she called "The War of Emotions," gives an insight into the turmoil in her adolescent soul.

> I crouch in a corner all by myself fighting the war of emotions,
> Battling against FEAR, ENVY, DEPRESSION, and REJECTION,
> I struggle.
>
> I am trying to survive but they tug and yank me.
> The more they pull, the weaker I become.
> I hope and pray for my survival.

Poetry appealed to the eternal romantic in Monica's character, itself a part of her endless search for a white knight who would gallop up on his charger and sweep her off her feet. She is a sentimental young woman who loves antiques, roses, and very feminine decorations, and admits, "I cry very easily."

She put her expressive nature to good effect when she won a school talent show, singing "On My Own" from the hit musical *Les Misérables*. Indeed, her fine singing voice led one of her contemporaries to comment that she was the girl most likely to see her name in lights.

In spite of the confusion in her life, Monica, always a strong-minded girl, was never slow to voice her opinions about matters she held dear. One incident highlights a quality that emerges time and again: her readiness to prove her loyalty. In May 1991, not long before her eighteenth birthday, she sent an emotional petition to the principal of the Bel Air school, urging him to reconsider his decision to expel (for brawling) a classmate who came from a deprived background. "I am begging you to have compassion in your decision and allow him to graduate so he can experience Life, not life on the streets," she wrote, arguing that he had always been a good student and that she herself had learned much from him.

Yet in spite of this veneer of self-confidence and her renewed academic vigor, anxiety about her weight remained close to the surface of her life. Her friend Neysa DeMann Erbland, who joined her at Bel Air from Beverly Hills recalls, "She was always upset about her weight, she was a little chubbette, an emotional eater. When she was upset she comforted herself by eating. She was distressed that she didn't have a boyfriend and so ate more, becoming less attractive, and so it was a vicious circle."

Monica's romantic spirit, her search for security and love, for emotional nourishment, led her into a series of inconclusive relationships. At Beverly Hills High she had developed a hopeless crush on a teenager four years her senior, while another young man who caught her eye eventually preferred one of her friends. The girl in question was typically willowy, but the fact that she was Monica's friend made his rejection even more difficult to bear.

This disappointment in starting a relationship led her back to her pursuit of a rekindled romance with Adam Dave, whom she had kept in contact with since Hawthorne Elementary School. In part she saw in him a window into her previous life, a time when her parents were still married, when she was thinner and doing well at school. Beyond that, however, she enjoyed his company and regularly sent him small gifts as well as poems she had written. "I thought I was in love with him, I pined over him," she says.

For his part, he made an unreliable friend, one moment allowing Monica to feel close to him, the next shutting her out. Certainly Monica's romantic feelings remained unrequited and Adam treated her with the casual cruelty of the uninterested young man, knowing that no matter how badly he behaved she would forgive him. For Monica, insecure, overweight, and with a negligible sense of self-worth combined with a desperate thirst for approval, the relationship was as humiliating as it was futile. In short, as she herself says, "It was just yucky." It continued throughout high school and Monica's first year of college, and eventually petered out when she and Adam went their separate ways.

While this personal drama was being played out, Monica, despite now being at college, was still active in the theatrical group at Beverly Hills High. As she was no longer a pupil at the school, she was now paid when she helped out making costumes for upcoming shows. Sometime earlier, the school had taken on a new drama technician when the previous incumbent, a dependable, middle-aged man of many years' service, left. Andy Bleiler, a slim, light-haired young man, then aged twenty-five, soon got a name for flirting with the students, even though it was known that he was in a long-term relationship with Kate Nason, a divorcée eight years his senior with a daughter. During Monica's junior year at Beverly Hills, she had only known him because of his secret romance with one of her friends.

After she had left the school, Monica found that she was no exception when it came to Bleiler's flirtations with the teenage students. On her visits to the Drama Department she was flattered by his attention but, knowing his reputation, thought little of it. Then on a spring night in May 1991, after a performance of one of the shows, he walked her back to her car. Encouraged by his manner, she talked about the difficult issues in her life, finding him a sympathetic listener. As she was about to leave he kissed her goodnight and then, as she says, "We made out," though they never came close to having sex at this point; Monica remained a virgin until she was nineteen.

Andy Bleiler was not married, nor did he even give the impression that he was engaged to Kate, as was in fact the case. Despite the fact that she was eight years younger than he was, during that summer he continued to flirt with Monica, asked her for her phone number and paid her flattering attention—surprising behavior in a soon-to-be-married man. So far as Monica was concerned, however, his flirtatious attentions were a welcome relief as her own life once again lurched into crisis. Not only was her friendship with Adam Dave hitting the skids, but her relationship with her father had reached an all-time low.

The tension in the family had already been exposed at Michael's Barmitzvah in 1991, during Monica's final year at Bel Air. Even though the rabbi had recommended that the family should sit together in the temple for the ceremony, her father preferred to sit in the row behind his ex-wife and children with his new girlfriend, Barbara Lerner, who later became his second wife. Harsh words were spoken in the temple, and the animosity felt by Marcia from the extended Lewinsky family was almost palpable. Monica sang at the synagogue, and, says her mother, "Her voice was so hauntingly beautiful grown men at the service were weeping." Monica herself remembers the whole occasion with pain: "It was so embarrassing—I was just so upset. It was really crushing to me and very, very traumatic." At the same time she did not resent the fact that Michael had his own Bar-mitzvah; as she says, "I don't begrudge Michael anything that he's ever gotten. I've never felt like, 'You shouldn't have given to Michael, you should have given to me instead'."

Worse was to come. When she graduated from Bel Air Prep—she gave the graduation speech before the audience of parents, students and staff—

she had assumed that her father would pay for her to go on to college (university) for the requisite four years. Without consulting him, she applied to various colleges both in California and in other states, only to learn later that, despite doing very well at Bel Air, because she had scored a "D" grade in English in her freshman year at high school—the year of her parents' divorce—she was not eligible for University of California schools as they prohibit admissions with a "D" in any main subject. She was admitted to Boston University, but her father, considering that the state colleges of California provided a good enough education, declined to pay her fees. "It was one of the most devastating experiences for me. It was just so frustrating and I was so very bitter," she says.

Instead, they came to a mutual agreement that the only option, other than to take out a student loan, was to go for two years to the less prestigious local community college at Santa Monica (a junior college, that is, an institution offering two years' study equivalent to the first two years at a university), where the fees would be significantly lower. She hoped to be able to save enough to pay her tuition fees for the last two years at a university. She had already been encouraged by her parents to take on part-time work—she was working at a tie store called the Knot Shop to pay off a loan on the Jeep her mother had leased in Monica's senior years in High School and which she wanted to keep on.

Her time at Santa Monica College, from 1991 to 1993, was as unhappy as it was frustrating. She felt that junior college was not academically challenging enough for her, and envied her friends who had gone to four-year schools. Depressed yet volatile, Monica was in a fragile state, literally at the end of her tether.

Eventually the inevitable happened and she broke down, collapsing in floods of tears over something as trivial as another driver occupying her college parking space. She returned home in torment and her mother, seeing her overreaction to such a minor incident, realized that her daughter needed professional counseling. Monica's association with her previous therapist had ended when she was eighteen, but Marcia had heard of a psychotherapist, Dr. Irene Kassorla, who had a reputation for giving patients the sort of practical help that would allow them to get on with their lives rather than continue to indulge in long-term psychotherapy. Marcia says, "It was my decision and I take full responsibility for the subsequent publicity. While she [Dr. Kassorla] turned out to be glitzier and more shallow than I had thought, she did three good things—she got Monica focused on studies, helped repair the relationship with Bernie and helped her lose weight." Monica continued to consult Dr. Kassorla, both in person and by phone, for five years from 1992, discussing her affair with the President in detail.

At about the same time—when Monica was going through a humiliating and unfulfilling relationship with Adam Dave, and when her relationship with her father was at its nadir, she was miserable at Santa Monica College and was once more putting on weight—the flirtatious Andy Bleiler began to enter her life with increased frequency.

Bleiler had married Kate Nason in October 1991, and just a few months later, in February the following year, he and Monica met again at a performance of *West Side Story* at Beverly Hills High. He began flirting and Monica, even though she knew he was now married, found his attentions flattering, greatly boosting her confidence and her morale. "It was great because he thought I was so sexy and, I mean, for a fat girl, for a guy to find you really attractive, it was really rewarding for me," she recalls. Lenore Reese remembers her friend making constant self-deprecating comments about her weight. "She really battled with her weight and for a man like Andy Bleiler to find her beautiful was such a compliment. He was her first love and he totally took advantage of her. He was an adult with many years' experience and she was a young, insecure girl."

The newly married drama technician continued to flatter and flirt with her, on one occasion asking her to leave her panties for him. Besides the sexual chemistry, she found him very bright, witty and creative, a combination that both attracted and intrigued her. They spent stolen afternoons together in local motels, talking and making out, though still stopping short of full intercourse. At the same time Monica's work on the costumes at Beverly Hills High gave them a perfectly innocent reason to spend time together. Gradually she began to fall for him, finding his attentions more fulfilling than the worthless and in any case doomed relationship with Adam Dave. "The more times we were together the more I cared about him," Monica says of Bleiler. There was, however, one immovable stumbling block—his marital status.

Perhaps surprisingly, given the strength of her feelings for him, it was not until December 1992 that they became lovers, Monica losing her virginity to a man whose wife had recently become pregnant. She was much older than her contemporaries had been when they first had sex; indeed, she had deliberately waited until she was a little more mature, knowing that her friends had not really enjoyed the experience when they were younger. (A few years later, in February 1996, during a conversation about teenage sex, she told the President that she was glad she had waited because she was, as a result, much more comfortable with herself, and much more familiar with her body's responses. He said he, too, had been a late starter.)

The relationship with Bleiler epitomizes the clash between Monica's dream of romance and the compromising reality, the contradiction at the heart of her emotional needs. She wanted the perfect relationship with a man who was hers alone, who would shower her with love and affection. Instead, and despite the fact that she is a self-confessed control freak, she began her adult love life with an unattainable man in a situation over which she had little control, let alone mastery. "Looking back it was just a lack of self-worth, of thinking that I did not deserve anything better. Deep inside I didn't think I was good enough to have a full relationship. It was a very painful and raw time for me. I think too that a lot of women go through this kind of relationship at some time in their lives," she observes.

It is one of the many ironies of Monica Lewinsky's young life that, while she was to go on to study psychology at college and to form a profound intellectual understanding of the human mind and condition, she was unable to apply that knowledge to her own life and decisions. For without a doubt one of her most endearing yet infuriating characteristics is that, while her head may tell her to take one course of action, her unruly heart will drag her in the opposite direction. The result is that her feelings of loyalty, however perverse, invariably triumph over her sense of self-preservation.

It has always been Monica's tendency, which became her tragedy, to confide, in varying degrees, about her love life to her family and close friends. Soon enough there were voices raised, counseling her against becoming involved with a married man. Dr. Kassorla cautioned her charge against continuing the affair, more for her own good than out of any moral judgment, but did not suggest that she break it off. Her father was much more forthright: "I told her in no uncertain terms that it was wrong and to cease the relationship forthwith. I had absolutely no idea that it had continued."

Her mother, by contrast, struggled to weigh her duty as a parent against her love for her daughter, watching helplessly as Monica embarked on a "destructive" affair with a man Marcia describes as a "piece of garbage," a man who romanced teenage students while his wife was pregnant. She does not spare herself, either, commenting, "I think I could be criticized for not going to the school and reporting him. As a parent at the school, it was, in a way, my responsibility. But you don't want your daughter's name bandied about, you don't want to make a big fuss. It would have caused our family embarrassment.

"I figured that the damage is done, now let's privately pull her away. It's ironic that that situation was repeated a few years later in a much more horrendous way. I searched my soul whether there was a lesson to be learned from the Bleiler affair. If Monica had seen her mother confront this man, made a public protest of what happened, whether this wouldn't have given her a better message than, very lovingly and with care, pulling her away, taking a gentler approach."

Monica's earlier discussion with her father, which had started out as a frank conversation about her life, and had ended with Bernie commanding her to give up Bleiler, severely jolted her. She was torn between her attraction to the man and the hopelessness of the situation. In early February 1993, when Bleiler's wife was four months pregnant, she decided to end their affair, admitting, "I felt bad about it, but at the same time when I spoke to him a few days later he said that he was feeling better because he didn't feel guilty anymore. Perversely, that made me feel depressed."

The parting was short-lived. Later that February, just before Bleiler's twenty-seventh birthday, he and Monica were working together on the musical *Oliver!* at Beverly Hills High. During a break in the production he once again made a pass at her. The relationship resumed almost as though it had never been ended. For his birthday party, which was held at the school, Monica organized a surprise cake in the shape of an iguana, his favorite reptile. Later, they had sex in the light booth of the auditorium and, afterwards, Monica said "Happy birthday, Andy" in the same breathy tones as Marilyn Monroe. Andy joked that she should have said "Happy Birthday, Mr. President"—and she duly did.

In the spring of 1993, as Monica prepared to take her final exams at Santa Monica College, she and Bleiler were seeing each other a couple of times a week. By now, however, it was very much an on-off affair, and as her friends became increasingly aware of the man in her life, they could see how hurt and upset she was becoming. They both cared and worried about her, and regularly advised her to end the relationship for her own good. Her high-school friend Neysa DeMann Erbland, who herself admits to having been something of a "wild child," recalls that the relationship was invariably tumultuous, Monica swinging between angry tears and sentimental forgiveness in her attitude toward her married lover. Neysa had a low opinion of Monica's choice in men. "I thought he was an asshole and told her so. He behaved more like a boy, not an older man," she says.

Monica's mother was also "appalled" that her daughter had resumed the affair against the wishes of both her parents, and likens trying to wean her off her obsession with Bleiler to trying to bring her off drugs, adding, "If you've ever tried to help a person through a bad romance, you know it's not so easy."

Shortly before the birth of Andy and Kate Bleiler's son in July 1993, he and Monica broke up again, this time at his behest. He told her that he felt guilty about the relationship and wanted to be a good father. Perhaps unsurprisingly, his resolve did not last long. Only weeks later, he approached her again and their affair resumed. From this she learned a lesson which she was to remember during her affair with the President. "I came to learn with married men that they feel guilty, say they want to stop it and then succumb to temptation anyway. So they always come back."

By now, however, Monica knew—for once—that she had a way of ending this unsatisfactory affair for good. Even though she had loathed her time at Santa Monica College, she had earned good grades in the honors program, with the result that she had been accepted at a number of California universities, including Berkeley, her father's alma mater. At the same time, Bernie had now agreed that she could study in the neighboring state of Oregon if she chose. The college she liked the look of was Lewis and Clark in Portland, Oregon, as it reminded her of Bel Air Prep. It was small, intimate and friendly, whereas Berkeley was large and anonymous, its sheer size sparking unhappy memories of her days at Beverly Hills High.

Academic preference aside—she intended to major in psychology—there was a more personal reason for choosing Lewis and Clark. "I wanted to get away from Los Angeles," she says, "and part of that was getting away from Andy. It was not that I didn't have feelings for him, or didn't want to be involved with him but I felt that I wasn't going to get over him while I was still in Los Angeles. It was going to be too hard. I wanted to make a fresh start and make a new life for myself."

That fall she headed north.

CHAPTER THREE

· ·

Grunge, Granola and Andy

$\mathcal{P}$ORTLAND, the largest city in the state of Oregon, on the north-west coast of the United States, is a jeans-and-sneakers kind of place, which is perhaps as it should be, given that the worldwide head-quarters of Nike is just down the road. It boasts the highest concentration of coffee bars and bookstores in America—including Powells, the world's largest bookshop, which takes up a whole block downtown.

Beverly Hills it is not. With forty-four inches of rainfall every year, rub-ber boots rather than designer sunglasses are the vital fashion accessory. Plastic surgeons are thin on the ground here, and so too are men's Armani jackets—only two of the city's restaurants insist on formal attire. It is not a great surprise to learn that Portland is the birthplace of the late Kurt Cobain, legendary lead singer of Nirvana, the quintessential grunge band.

It's a casual, laid-back place, where recycling is more than just a long word, and Rodeo Drive involves horses rather than clothes-horses. In Portland a crowd will meet to mourn the axing of a favorite tree, whereas in downtown Los Angeles only a particularly gruesome murder attracts a street gathering.

In her first few weeks there, in the fall of 1993, Monica could have been excused for thinking that she had arrived on the moon. The collision between LA chic and Oregon grunge did not make for the easiest of tran-sitions. For example, when it was her turn to do housework in the house she shared, she phoned her mother in a panic for instructions on how to clean the bathroom.

While her mother gave her much-needed domestic advice, her father helped with other arrangements. He and Barbara, whom he married in 1991, Monica singing at the ceremony, traveled with Monica to her new home, buying her a bed as well as pots and pans and other essential household items. She had decided to share with Kurt Carpenter and Karl Fulmer after spotting their ad asking for roommates on a bulletin board on the college campus. The three of them decided to rent an attractive four-bedroom clapboard house which, unbeknownst to Monica, was by an odd coincidence just a few blocks away from the home of Andy Bleiler's uncle.

When Monica moved in, the mismatch in lifestyles was immediately apparent. While her roommates led a hippie-style existence, picking up cast-off furniture from church sales and playing rock music late into the night, Monica, a non-smoker, decorated her room in the then fashionable shabby-chic style, dominated by her love of color, roses, floral decorations and embroidered cushions. "It was my safe haven," she says, although her room was chaotically messy. "She was a slob like the rest of us," recalls her friend Lenore Reese, who was at Lewis and Clark with her, "although she always tidied up, and had her hair done and legs waxed when her mother visited." But if Monica didn't fit in with her roommates, it was not long before the ethos of the college and the city captured her heart. During the next two years she enjoyed some of the happiest and most stimulating days of her life.

The changes in her soon became obvious. While she had lost twenty pounds before she went to Portland, her physique changed dramatically once she got into the swing of the city. She was living apart from her parents for the first time; besides that, she had escaped the pressures of Beverly Hills and said farewell to an unsatisfactory love affair. "Growing up in Beverly Hills was not great and it was something I could have done without," she says.

She joined an all-women gym, exercised regularly and lived on a diet of salads and lemon chicken pasta, her specialty dish. In short order she had lost a further twenty pounds. "I was feeling much better about myself," she recalls. A bonus was that the Knot Shop in Los Angeles, where she had worked, had just opened a new branch in Portland when she arrived, and they were happy to hire her for part-time work. She augmented her allowance from her father by baby-sitting for neighbors. Her Aunt Debra was quick to notice the changes in her: "She began to grow as a person. She became more grounded and happier with herself."

Equally important was the fact that she was engaged and enthused by her psychology course in a way that lifted her spirits. While her emotional life till then had been chaotic and damaging, her mind was always focused, analytical and searching. The course at Lewis and Clark neatly fused her interest in the human condition with her logical, inquiring mind, although she had a tendency to come to forthright conclusions before assimilating all the relevant information. "In that first semester I realized I had made the right decision. I love to learn, and taking the course gave me a real high," she says. Indeed, so strong was the impression she made on her professors that several sent her touching letters of support when the scandal over her affair with the President became public.

As part of the course the students had to take part in a practicum, which in Monica's case meant working with the mentally ill during her junior year. She and a couple of other students helped out at the Phoenix Club in Portland, a meeting place for mentally ill clients, who learned essential social skills there. Besides arts and crafts, there were pool tables and other games as well as a snack bar. Monica found it "a very rewarding experience," as enriching as it was challenging, making her face up to her fears and prejudices about the mentally ill.

She found herself on a steep learning curve. She worked in the kitchen, using razor-sharp knives alongside mental patients with a history of violence, calmed down a woman who became hysterical, and dealt tactfully with a male patient who made untoward and inappropriate sexual advances to her and a fellow female student. Her interest in the theater led her to organize a visit by the Phoenix Club members to see a local performance of Gilbert and Sullivan's *HMS Pinafore*. Although this was primarily intended to be an enjoyable evening out, it was also a way of helping her charges to understand that in society there are all kinds of unwritten rules—such as not talking during a performance—which have to be followed if people are to be accepted in that society.

The theater visit was a success, but Monica's enthusiasm overcame her ability when she volunteered to make matzo-ball soup for the eighty or so club members. Even though she asked her mother for guidance, Monica, who does not list cooking among her interests, admits that the matzo balls were virtually inedible. As befits one brought up in Beverly Hills, she says, in her typically self-deprecating way, "I make one thing really well for dinner . . . reservations."

Indeed, while you could take the girl out of Los Angeles, it was more difficult to take Los Angeles out of the girl. Fellow students remember that their first impressions of her were of someone disarmingly frank and open, particularly about her weight and about sex, forthright in discussion, flirtatious but genuinely good-hearted. She was a larger-than-life character, who was too brash and loud for some tastes. Lenore Reese comments, "She is articulate, very quick and intelligent and very comfortable with her sexuality, which some people found a little forward."

Others saw that behind the noisy chatter and sexual banter was a loyal, sensitive and genuinely kind human being. "She is the kind of woman who brought you chicken soup if you were ever sick," says Linda Estergard, who met Monica during her first semester at Lewis and Clark. "She is one of my top three angels in the world. She will do anything for you, so very giving and nurturing."

Linda, who was married, had enrolled at Lewis and Clark as a mature student. She fondly recalls their first meeting, in a lecture theater. Monica was seated next to Jason Lesner, a student from Los Angeles whom she was close to for a time, and was quite hostile when first introduced to Linda, fearing that she was going to make a move on him. She visibly relaxed when she realized that Linda was married. That encounter said much about Monica's insecurity and low self-esteem. It was something Linda came to understand further during a two-hour heart-to-heart in the college parking lot, during which Monica frankly discussed her lifelong struggle with her weight. Given this mutual trust, it is no surprise that the two became firm friends, Linda acting as a kind of mother figure to a tightly knit circle of confidantes which eventually included, as well as Monica, Catherine Allday Davis, Carly Henderson, Moana Kruschwitz, Zach Isenberg, Bradford Duvall, Jason Lesner and Lenore Reese.

Monica gradually began to widen her social circle although she did not date any of her fellow students. She did go on a few casual dates with local men but the encounters amounted to very little. Inevitably there were times when she felt lonely, leading her to reach for the telephone to hear a familiar voice from back home. One of those voices was Andy Bleiler's. Against her better judgment she kept in touch, and they met for a few stolen hours when she returned to Los Angeles to join her family for Thanksgiving in November 1993.

They stayed in contact during the winter and she saw him again in the spring vacation the following year. During that meeting her female intuition led her to suspect that he was seeing another woman—that is, besides his wife, Kate. It was a tempestuous and tearful reunion, especially as her instincts proved to be correct. She later discovered he had indeed formed an intimate relationship with a girl whom she knew from her days in Los Angeles. That secret relationship would soon stretch Monica's loyalty to him to the limit.

Shortly after that meeting, Bleiler phoned Monica and told her that he too was thinking about moving to Portland, giving as his reason that he didn't want to raise his son in Los Angeles, which he found too expensive. But whatever was behind that decision, it was news that Monica greeted with a mixture of eagerness and dread; with exhilaration at the prospect of seeing her erstwhile lover, but fear that she would be even more frequently driven back into the extra-marital routine of stolen moments, scratchy arguments, bitter betrayal, tearful reconciliation and guilty excitement.

Linda Estergard remembers talking to Monica shortly after she heard Bleiler's news. "The day she found out that he was moving here she was very upset," Linda said. "She is a very emotional girl and she was upset because she didn't want him to come. One of the reasons for her leaving Los Angeles was to get out of his clutches. Now he was coming back to haunt her. She knew that if he moved she would be too emotionally weak to resist restarting the relationship."

Monica confided her worries to other close friends. Fellow psychology student Carly Henderson recalls, "She didn't want him to come because she knew in her heart that if he did she would start sleeping with him again." It is a refrain echoed by Neysa DeMann Erbland: "She was anxious about him coming up. I remember her saying, 'Oh my God, he's going to be back.' She knew that if he made a move she would fall right back into it. Monica was so worried about him coming up." Other college contemporaries like Lenore Reese tell a similar story, testimony which is in stark contrast to Bleiler's own version of events, a version he made public shortly after the Clinton–Lewinsky scandal broke.

In June 1994 Bleiler, leaving his wife and children behind in Los Angeles, arrived in Portland to look for work and accommodation. The inevitable happened—the moment he arrived he visited Monica. "He was all over me, and for the first time he told me that he was in love with me—I was a wonderful person, he really cared about me and he loved me. It was incredible—he was sweet and romantic the whole time." Then, after five "wonderful" days, he returned to Los Angeles, where Kate was involved in a protracted legal battle with her ex-husband over custody of their daughter. A few weeks later, however, he returned to Portland, resolved to spend the summer looking for work while Kate dealt with her legal affairs in Los Angeles.

Those summer months were the most tempestuous, intense and hurtful of Monica's five-year relationship with Andy Bleiler, a time she remembers with a mixture of tenderness, sorrow, anger and bitterness. She thought this interlude would be a rerun of the weekend they had spent together earlier in June. It was not to be. "I look back on it now and it was such a horrible summer. It was so painful and damaging for me. It was so volatile—Andy would be very hot and cold, one minute all over me and then he would ignore me."

His presence that summer also caused her to neglect her studies. She had planned to take a graduate course in forensic psychology, and in order to do so needed to get a high score on the GRE (Graduate Record Examination), a preliminary qualification test. With her mind on Bleiler she could not apply herself as she ought to have done, and in consequence received a very disappointing score on the exam. Those of her friends who saw the telltale signs in her behavior were quick to warn her off him. "When she started seeing him again I told her she was nuts," says Neysa Erbland. "At times she was happy as a clam, at others consumed with guilt. It was not good for her."

Once Kate and her children joined Bleiler in the fall of that year, 1994, the dynamics of the relationship changed significantly, in a way that Monica's friends found difficult to accept, or even to understand. Although she and Bleiler split up again—this time at his prompting—she began to become friendly with his wife, and often baby-sat for the couple as she also did for Andy's uncle. Before long, Monica's affections were as much for Bleiler's family as they were for Andy himself. Knowing that they had little money, she regularly bought clothes for the children and helped the family out in other ways. She was seen almost as part of the family, while she in turn liked Kate and adored the children.

Her mother, who was increasingly anxious about her daughter's obsession, explains her behavior thus: "She was able to compartmentalize her sexual relationship with this man and her love for the wife and the children. She really did love those kids, she would baby-sit for them because she adored them and she saw no dichotomy in that. In the grown-up, adult world that split is obvious, but at her stage of development she did not see it."

Not unnaturally, Monica's view does not altogether chime with Marcia's, although she does not spare herself, reflecting, "In the first year Kate was almost non-existent because my initial attraction to Andy came before he was married. It was very different to if I had met them as a couple and started having an affair with the husband. We didn't become close friends until she moved to Portland. I have to confess that the relationship with her was sick because I came to care about her a lot as a person, and came to care about her, too, because I loved Andy so much."

Her friendship with Kate, her affection for the children, and the continual conflict between herself and Bleiler—though they were not lovers at this point—eventually hardened Monica's resolve. In November 1994, shortly before she left Portland to spend the Christmas vacation with her family, she wrote him a long letter saying that she didn't want him in her life anymore, or even to be friends with him. After yet another tempestuous meeting they agreed to remain friends, but Monica left for her family feeling that the affair was finally over. She was to be sadly disillusioned. The moment she returned in the New Year, the phone rang. It was Andy Bleiler, pleading, begging, beseeching her to be his friend, saying that his wife hated Portland and that he couldn't live without Monica. "He manipulated me, he played on my weakness, knowing that I had a soft spot for him," she says.

Their relationship resumed in a halfhearted way, but Monica still had a nagging feeling that he was seeing someone else. Finally, acting on that instinct, she called the girl in question in Los Angeles and the full story came spilling out. Much younger and even more naive than Monica, the girl felt abused; Bleiler, she believed, had taken advantage of her. Worse still, the girl was seriously thinking about telling Kate about the whole tawdry business.

Horrified, Monica called Bleiler and arranged to see him. When they met, in February 1995, she told him in no uncertain terms what she thought about his behavior, at which he started crying "like a baby," asking not only for her forgiveness but for her help. Monica recalls that he was in tears. He knew that his girlfriend was young, and he was desperately worried about the very real danger that she would tell his wife. "I am going to kill myself," he told Monica. "So here I am," she says, "brokenhearted because he had cheated on me and his wife with her [the girlfriend] and yet again he pulls on my heartstrings and I am faced with this dilemma: 'Do I honor Andy or do I honor myself?' So I honored him and his feelings. He just took advantage of me."

As a result of that meeting Monica agreed to speak to the teenage girl and duly did so, managing to get her to agree to maintain her silence. Furthermore, with only three months left until she finished college, Monica decided that the only way she would continue to have anything to do with Bleiler was if he saw her regularly, as though theirs was a "normal" relationship. She also took a perverse satisfaction in paying him back for his treachery by having a fling with his younger brother Chris who, Bleiler said, "would never like me because he only liked tall, skinny women." Monica felt that she had showed him otherwise.

Looking back today over the whole history of her relationship with Andy Bleiler, Monica admits, "This is where the conflict in me lies, having deep feelings for someone as if I were in a proper relationship while the reality is so very different, full of compromises and lies." She acknowledges the full irony of the fact that, while she was seeing Andy Bleiler, she had studied, as part of her psychology course, François Truffaut's 1975 movie *The Story of Adèle H*, based on the tragedy of Victor Hugo's daughter, who traveled halfway across the world to be with a man who shunned her. Monica found that the portrayal of the woman's obsession and how it drove her to madness carried echoes of her own emotional predicament. "It was," she says, "a very telling movie."

One of her closest friends, Catherine Allday Davis, who came to know her well during her final year at college and who spoke to her regularly during her affair with President Clinton, explains Monica's behavior in this way: "Her relationship with Andy was damaging to her in the same way as her affair with the President. She was involving herself with a man who was never going to be hers and it was stopping her from being a normal woman and going on normal dates. In some ways she thought that she wasn't good enough to be loved.

"Monica is a bright girl and she can vocalize what is going on but she can't act on it. In her defense it's not as though she is the only woman out there who has these issues in dealing with men. It's a case of smart women, stupid choices."

One of those foolish choices nearly cost Monica her college degree. It resulted from a series of decisions which, taken individually, were a testament to her generous heart and loyalty; when they were examined in the light of the presidential scandal, however, they seemed far more sinister.

A constant problem for the lovers was that Bleiler was always having to find an excuse to be away from the family home so that he could see Monica. When he had first arrived in Portland, Monica had introduced him to David Bliss, the Shop Foreman of the Lewis and Clark Theater Department, as a way of helping him to secure work or at least job contacts, and Bliss did occasionally offer Bleiler work. For a time, therefore, Bleiler told Kate that while she was out David Bliss had phoned, and that he had some extra work for him, a lie that enabled Bleiler secretly to meet Monica. When this excuse began to wear thin, Monica took a sheet of headed notepaper from the Theater Department and wrote a note to Bleiler saying that he was wanted for three dates in April and May 1995. She forged David Bliss's signature at the foot of the letter and mailed it to Bleiler, believing that he would now have a cast-iron excuse as a cover for meeting her.

Unfortunately, for some reason the letter was never delivered, and in due course it was returned to its ostensible sender, David Bliss, who threatened to have Monica expelled when he discovered that she was the culprit. Knowing that Bliss was about to contact Bleiler about the matter, which would have meant Kate learning the truth, Monica tried to protect Bleiler by telling another lie. She told Bliss that her lover had known nothing about the letter, and Bliss accepted her written apology.

Only her closest girlfriends—and, of course, Andy Bleiler, who subsequently twisted the facts of their affair at a now notorious press conference—were aware of the real story. Interestingly, the episode prefigures the aftermath of her affair with President Clinton, in particular the fact that she was prepared to sacrifice herself by signing a false affidavit to keep her ex-lover out of trouble. It was, too, another example of her readiness to put her loyalty to those she cared about over and above her desire to protect her own interests, invariably to her disadvantage.

Her affair with Bleiler is important in explaining the psychology of her relationship with the President, but it would be wrong to think that her life was totally consumed with thoughts of him. There were long periods when she didn't see him, and other times when their relationship reverted to one of just friendship. Indeed, after settling down at Lewis and Clark during her first year, she considers her second, final, year to have been the happiest and most fulfilling period of her life.

For the most part her house-sharing experiment was a success, and she enjoyed the company of close, supportive and loyal friends with whom she spent weekends of barbecues, parties and trips to the movies or local restaurants. On one occasion their group spent a wintry weekend at Timberline, two hours' drive from Portland, making snowmen, having snowball fights—in short, having a good time.

Just how far Monica had developed since leaving Los Angeles was revealed the day after she graduated in May 1995. The new psychology graduate, who hates heights and describes herself as a "scaredy cat," decided to watch her friend Zach Isenberg and his brother Josh make a bungee jump over the Lewis River in Washington state. The organizer convinced Monica to give it a try, and much against her better judgment she heard herself say "OK." It was, she says, "the most unbelievable experience"; it was also something she would never have dreamed of doing during her Beverly Hills days. Nor would she ever have dreamed that she would have needed guidance on how to find a boyfriend. During a conversation with a fellow female student the talk turned to men, both women despairing of ever finding a mate. So they attended an evening lecture, each paying $40 for the privilege, to hear a woman explain how to find a partner. The audience, who were mainly middle-aged, were told that it was much more difficult to find a companion in later life—unlike when one was young and at college. Laughing, Monica and her friend described themselves as a couple of real losers and headed for the nearest bar. They ended up chatting to a group of guys, drinking too much and dancing in a club until the early hours. "It was one of the funniest evenings ever," recalls her fellow student.

Although Monica went on a number of dates during her time at college, she remained almost perversely faithful to Andy Bleiler—apart from the revenge fling with his brother. "In fact she is a very faithful person," notes Linda Estergard, now a social worker. "She just makes the wrong choices."

Certainly academically she had begun to realize her potential. She had taken and thoroughly enjoyed numerous additional classes, and had built up a strong and affectionate rapport with her teachers, notably Tom Schoeneman and Nancy King Hunt. Indeed, as she talks about her life, she is at her most animated and enthused when describing her final year at Lewis and Clark.

As a teaching assistant in Psychology of Sex, she led group discussions in a "sex lab" where students explored the relationship between sexuality, individualism and society. The other students were reticent in offering their ideas and opinions, so Monica broke the ice, giving her own frank views, culled from her unhappy experiences, on the links between physical appearance, weight and sexuality, views which impressed many of those present.

Though Monica has been painted as a "scarlet woman"—or worse—in the course of the whole Clinton scandal, she remains firm in her conviction that one's sexuality is nothing to be afraid of. "I don't see sexuality as being something to hide away in the dark or be ashamed of. I think our sexuality is something to be honored, cherished and valued. In part it is a difference in generations. I come from a generation whose mothers burned their bras and said, 'Make love, not war.' Yet ours is the same generation who have grown up with the fear of AIDS, where caution and protection are an integral part of our sex lives."

[51]

One of her other courses, The Social Construction of Madness, had a profound effect on Monica. This dealt with the notion of "the Other," and primarily with the way in which society labels people, which conveniently allows them to ignore the fact that they may be like each other. It is a theory used extensively by the military as a means of demeaning an enemy and denying his basic humanity, on the principle that soldiers will be prepared to kill those who have thus been demonized.

A year after completing that course, Monica found herself discussing those self-same theories with President Clinton himself, and suggesting that he add a psychologist to a panel of experts who were, at the President's much-publicized behest, examining how to improve race relations in America. She even gave him a book, *Disease and Misrepresentation*, in case he wanted to explore the matter further. It is a bitter irony that, since the Clinton–Lewinsky scandal broke, Monica herself has been made to reflect further on the concept of "the Other," painfully observing the way that she has been demonized and mythologized in and by the mass media, scorned and ridiculed as someone beyond the normal boundaries of American family life.

It is clear from her suggestion to the President that Monica, while relishing the intellectual challenges of her degree course, also enjoyed the practical application of psychology in society. As she considered life after Lewis and Clark, she once more thought about going on to graduate school to get a Ph.D. in forensic psychology and jurisprudence.

For her practicum during her senior year she had worked in the Public Defender's Office in Portland under Marsha Gruehler, an experience which focused her mind on the possibilities of making a career in this field. During her time there she had analyzed the impact of new legislation, relating to juveniles, on the work of court psychologists, and had devised a questionnaire to help assess the costs involved in implementing this measure. This was practical, intellectually challenging work which harnessed her analytical skills effectively. Her father, who with his wife, Barbara, had traveled to watch Monica receive her Bachelor of Science degree in psychology at the graduation ceremony in May 1995, encouraged her thoughts about a career in the Public Defender's Office, arguing that she should try to get a full-time job there. Besides the satisfaction she would gain from working in a fulfilling career, she already had a house and friends in Portland; even more importantly, she seemed much more settled and at peace with herself.

What Dr. Lewinsky did not know, though, was that Andy Bleiler had moved to the same city as Monica and was still seeing her. Her mother did know and, aware of the pain and damage the relationship caused her daughter, had tried unsuccessfully to get her to give him up. The truth was that the "Bleiler effect" was uppermost in Monica's mind as she wrestled with her future options. "I loved Andy dearly but the relationship was tumultuous, emotionally damaging and clearly immoral. Leaving Portland seemed to be the only way to begin to put him behind me," she recalls. Added to this were other factors: many of her friends were leaving Portland; she needed a higher score on her GREs if she wished to take postgraduate courses and would have to take them again; she did not want to go back to Los Angeles; and she missed her mother, Michael, and Aunt Debra.

As it happened, the fateful decision to move to Washington originated not with Monica, or her father, or even with Andy Bleiler, but with her mother. During a conversation with her daughter, Marcia told her that the grandson of her friend Walter Kaye, a wealthy Manhattan insurance mogul, donor to the Democratic Party and an acquaintance of the First Lady, had been an intern at the White House—White House internships are prestigious, highly selective, unpaid temporary jobs—and had much enjoyed his time there. If the idea appealed to Monica, Marcia said, she would talk to Kaye and see if he could put in a good word for her. Help came from another quarter as well. One of her customers at the Knot Shop, Jay Footlik, now worked at the White House and promised to speak up for her when the candidates were being assessed.

The more Monica thought about her mother's suggestion, the more excited she became. It made sense to work in the White House for six weeks during the summer, as it would allow her a short break before resuming her academic studies, as well as giving her a chance to spend time with her mother. Marcia had long wished to leave Los Angeles, but in the turbulent aftermath of the divorce Monica and Michael had, in Marcia's words, "wanted to stay where they felt 'at home,' and they were right." However, when Debra and Bill Finerman moved to Virginia, Monica was at college in Portland and Michael "had recovered somewhat from the divorce, and this time, when I suggested moving, the kids were enthusiastic." In order to be near her sister, Marcia had moved to Washington and taken an apartment in the Watergate building, where Debra and Bill had a pied à terre which they used for overnight stays and at weekends. While working at the White House, Monica would be able to live with her mother, and would also be able to see Aunt Debra often.

Monica duly applied, completing an essay section where she discussed the need for psychologists to work in government to understand better the "human dimension" in society— and was delighted to be accepted as one of the class of two hundred young interns that year. Before she left Portland, she took a long, tearful farewell of Andy Bleiler. Proud and excited that she was going to Washington, he wished her well. For her part, though she still loved him, she had little expectation of seeing him again soon—if ever. "I bawled my eyes out at the airport and cried all the way to San Francisco," she admits. "I was so sad to be leaving him. It was really hard for me—I told him that after we had said goodbye I didn't want to see him again."

On the long flight to Washington she was mournful at leaving her old life behind, yet could not suppress her feelings of anticipation as new horizons beckoned her. Contemplating her days to come at the White House, she thought, "It's a great addition to my résumé. It will be exciting. It's only for a short time, and it can't hurt."

With a rueful smile, she now says, "How wrong I was."

Arguably, her mother has even more reason to regret that fateful decision, for it was she who encouraged Monica to come to Washington not only to get away from Portland and Andy Bleiler, but also to live with her. Yet there was another, secret, motive that informed all Marcia's thinking about her daughter's future.

"Like all mothers tend to do," she confesses, "I thought she would meet a nice young man."

CHAPTER FOUR

• •

Monica Goes to Washington

*I*T WAS THE SMELL of eucalyptus wafting along the powder-blue-carpeted corridors that first seduced Monica. Then the sight of a slightly bored-looking Secret Service agent standing by a heavy-framed mahogany door made her heart skip a beat. For behind that door was the hallowed Oval Office.

Her supervisor, Tracey Beckett, who accompanied the young intern on her first ever visit to the West Wing of the White House, explained that the reason why the door to the Oval Office was closed was that the President was inside, working, and that was also why a Secret Service agent was stationed outside the door. "I was in awe," Monica remembers. "All I could think of was 'Wow!' My excitement wasn't because it was President Clinton on the other side of the door, but because it was *the* President." Wide-eyed with excitement, she naturally couldn't wait to tell her friends that, after just two weeks working as an intern at the White House, only the thickness of a door separated her from the world's most powerful man.

On July 10, 1995, Monica had joined two hundred other young graduates making nervously light-hearted conversation in Room 450 of the Old Executive Office Building (OEOB), as they waited to be told their assignments as unpaid interns for the next six weeks. Most of her anxious colleagues had degrees in politics or related subjects; Monica, however, had often joked with her college friends that a degree in psychology was the one really essential requirement in the febrile atmosphere of Washington.

After the new group of interns had listened to a series of lectures they received their assignments. Monica was detailed to work in the correspondence section of the office of the White House Chief of Staff, Leon Panetta. She was delighted to learn that she would have her own desk and computer in Room 93 of the OEOB and that, because she had written an excellent essay, her duties were to be much more than simply answering the phone and copying documents; she would also from time to time deliver sorted mail to the West Wing, where the Oval Office is. Nevertheless, the pink pass around her neck—all interns have to wear one—signified that she was definitely at the bottom of the White House hierarchy, and could not move around the building unless accompanied by a White House supervisor. In the White House an orange pass gave access to the OEOB but not to the East or West Wings, while an administrator with a blue pass could go anywhere. Typically Monica, always feeling entitled to the best of what was on offer, immediately set her heart on getting a blue pass. It is worth noting that this was before she had even seen, let alone met, the President.

Unlike other interns, Monica had no political ambitions—indeed, she wasn't even interested in politics—and certainly hadn't brought with her to Washington an agenda, sexual or otherwise. In a buttoned-down, secretive community in which every move is calculated, she was a little too willing, too open and too straightforward for her own good. When, in her characteristic eagerness to please, she made coffee for her colleagues, or gave them small gifts, she failed to notice the quizzically raised eyebrow or the suspicious glance questioning the motivation behind her unbidden generosity. "I didn't know it was a crime in Washington to be nice to people," she says.

Monica flirted innocently with a couple of the other interns, and joined in games and picnics, but found that, although she was enjoying her time at the White House, she was not really a Washington type. Despite being bright, lively and motivated, she never fitted into the mold of a White House worker.

In a world where every action, however trivial-seeming, is considered and controlled, she was too reckless with her heart, too vulnerable to criticism and too prone to self-doubt, while patience and self-restraint have never formed part of her repertoire. Above all, she lacked worldly wisdom, as her mother observes: "While the two years she had spent in Portland had been good for her, she knew very little of the real world. She was an innocent abroad in a very sophisticated and cynical town."

When Monica arrived in Washington that summer of 1995, she was too preoccupied to notice or even consider the social and political undercurrents swirling around the White House. Before she started work she, Marcia and Michael had spent a few weeks in Virginia, staying with Aunt Debra and her husband. Monica spent much of that time pining for Andy Bleiler and her friends in Portland. Indeed, during the Fourth of July weekend, only days before she took up her post at the White House, she had returned to Oregon to see her chums and to spend a few hours with her lover. The visit resolved nothing, save that Monica returned to Washington determined to throw herself into her summer job before resuming her studies for a retake of the GRE so that she could take a postgraduate degree.

Although for the most part she found the work stimulating and exciting, it didn't take her long to realize that the White House gossip factory went into overdrive whenever one subject came up in conversation: Bill Clinton. The President had a reputation as a flirt and a womanizer, and his large circle of female admirers shared gossip, making knowing remarks about certain women in the White House who may or may not have been among his many alleged mistresses.

Monica was mystified. "I had only ever seen him on TV and I never thought of him as attractive," she says. "With his big red nose and coarse, wiry-looking gray hair, he's an old guy. There were tons and tons of women in the White House with crushes on him and I thought, 'These people are just crazy. They have really bad taste in men.' I mean, girls my own age were saying that this old guy was cute, that he was sexy. I thought, 'Gee, this place is weird. What's wrong with Washington?'"

That July, however, she first saw President Clinton in the flesh and came to realize exactly what the "tons and tons of women" were talking about. Her mother's friend Walter Kaye had invited Monica and Marcia to watch an arrival ceremony for the President of South Korea on the South Lawn of the White House. It was an intensely hot and humid day. As they stood behind the gold ropes in the VIP section, Monica, in a sundress and wide-brimmed straw hat, was more concerned about not passing out than about watching the passing parade.

Suddenly the public-address system came to life and a voice announced, "Ladies and gentlemen, the President of the United States accompanied by the First Lady." As the military band struck up "Hail to the Chief," there he was on stage. "I remember being very taken aback. My heart skipped a beat, my breathing came a little faster and there were butterflies fluttering in my tummy," Monica says. "He had a glow about him that was magnetic. He exudes a sexual energy. I thought to myself: 'Now I see what all the girls are talking about.'"

She was now eager to have a closer look at the man who was, ultimately, her boss. Her chance came towards the end of July, when a supervisor gave the interns permission to attend a departure ceremony. During one of these functions, which are held whenever the President leaves the White House for more than a few hours, he walks along a roped-off path between two lines of people, shaking hands as he goes, and then climbs aboard a gleaming navy-blue military helicopter, Marine One, which whisks him away, usually to the presidential retreat, Camp David in Maryland.

After her first sight of President Clinton, Monica found her second view of him a real letdown. As he made his way along the line of people pressing against the ropes, it was clear that he was on autopilot, merely going through the motions of meeting and greeting without engaging with his well-wishers. When he reached Monica's section he looked straight through her. "It was disappointing because he seemed nothing up close," she recalls.

Knowing she was due to attend another departure ceremony on Wednesday, August 9, Monica decided to give him another chance, to see if the man she had at first sight nearly swooned over was really so vibrant in person. She decided to wear a new sage-green suit her mother had just bought her from J. Crew. Most important of all, her new suit gave her a sense of confidence and self-assurance.

As the President moved down the roped-off line of guests, he stopped to chat to a fellow intern and her father, who were standing just in front of Monica. While talking to them, he suddenly spotted her and, as she says, "gave me the full Bill Clinton . . . It was this look, it's the way he flirts with women. When it was time to shake my hand, the smile disappeared, the rest of the crowd disappeared and we shared an intense but brief sexual exchange. He undressed me with his eyes." This was no juvenile fantasy. Later, during their affair, the President was to tell Monica that he remembered that moment vividly. "I knew that one day I would kiss you," he said to her as they sat in his office.

The moment over, she turned away and bumped into her friend Jay Footlik, who had recommended her for the internship. While they stood talking, she noticed that the President was still looking her way.

Next day, still exhilarated by her silent exchange with the President, Monica was thrilled to learn that, at the last minute, the interns had been invited to attend a surprise forty-ninth birthday party for the President, which was to be held that afternoon on the South Lawn of the White House. Thinking that he might recognize her if she wore the same outfit, Monica drove home, ironed her "lucky green suit," and returned to the White House.

It was a relaxed and light-hearted occasion with a Wild West theme, the two hundred or so interns and the permanent White House staff amused by the comic antics of their bosses, who had organized a series of skits in honor of "the Chief." Vice-President Al Gore arrived for the party in a beat-up station wagon, while a number of other senior advisors, including Leon Panetta and Harold Ickes, made their entrance on horseback. Even the President was dressed in cowboy gear, while, appropriately enough, country and western singer Jimmy Buffett was the musical highlight of the event.

During the birthday show, the President spotted Monica early on and kept looking her way and smiling—although she was not the only one to get the "full Bill Clinton." When it was time for him to walk along the line of well-wishers, Monica was, this time, at the front and in due course was rewarded with a presidential handshake as she told him, "Happy birthday, Mr. President." In response, "He looked deep into my eyes and I was hooked," she remembers. As he moved off, his arm, casually but unnecessarily, brushed against her breast. Continuing to walk on down the line, he looked back at Monica and tried to identify her from the plastic pass hanging on its cord from her neck. Noticing this, she saw that the pass was the wrong way around. She quickly untwisted it, knowing that he would see from its color—pink—she was an intern. The President smirked at her.

Flattered and excited by his attention, Monica decided to join a male colleague and go to the end of the line of people behind the ropes, hoping to get a picture of him (many of the guests had brought cameras). When the President arrived he spotted Tom Campbell, an old friend from his college days in Washington. They talked about old times for around twenty minutes, Monica and her friend part of a dozen-strong group listening to the two men reminisce. By now the party was over and most of the guests had departed, leaving only Monica and a few others on the lawn. As the President headed back to the White House, he turned around and caught Monica's eye. In the exuberance of the moment, she blew him a kiss, at which he threw back his head in laughter.

When she got home to her mother's apartment she excitedly told her mother and Aunt Debra about the day's events, then spent most of the evening reading the autobiography of Gennifer Flowers, a nightclub singer with whom Clinton had had a long affair while he was Governor of Arkansas. "At the time there were so many other women who found him attractive that I didn't see anything wrong in feeling the same way," she says. "I was still consumed by Andy and this was just teasing—it was fun and made me feel good."

Certainly both the older women saw it that way—nothing more than a giddy flirtation, a welcome respite for Monica as she licked her emotional wounds over Andy Bleiler. "It was very flattering to her but it seemed like high-school stuff," says Debra Finerman. "It wasn't taken seriously because everyone knew President Clinton was a flirt and had lots of women. I remember thinking to myself, 'I can't believe this middle-aged man is engaging in such immature behavior.'"

The following day saw Monica—exercising to the full both her penchant for the dramatic and her tendency to see life as an unfolding movie script—fondly expecting the Secret Service to call her discreetly with the news that the President wanted to see her, in the same way that Clinton's hero, John F. Kennedy, used the Secret Service to bring women to him during his presidency. Every time the phone rang her nerves jangled. The day passed, however, without the dramatic presidential request for her company.

These brief flirtations with the President were good for her ego, but what was more important was that she was enjoying the mechanics of the job. Her remarkable facility for remembering numbers, dates and people's names ensured that she pulled her weight in spite of her inexperience, and her conscientiousness and enthusiasm for her work were soon noticed by her superiors. Monica was now thinking in terms of working at the White House permanently, despite her belief that she was not a "Washington type." After a conversation with her supervisor, Tracey Beckett, who was encouraging and told her that she could use the help, she decided to stay on for a second internship in the hope of securing a full-time position after that had ended.

With this in mind, in mid-August she attended another departure ceremony, during which the President stopped to chat to a group of interns who were about to finish their six-week stint. Summoning up all her courage, Monica introduced herself, carefully making the point that she was staying on for a second term. Then, after he had joined them for a group picture, he left for his summer vacation. A few weeks later, Monica and several other interns were enjoying a picnic and soaking up the last of the summer sunshine on West Executive Avenue, which lies between the Old Executive Office Building and the West Wing, when the President suddenly walked out of the White House. The interns, disconcerted by his unexpected arrival, stood up in a gesture of respect. As he passed, he grinned at Monica and they waved to each other.

By now she had told several of her friends, including her former Beverly Hills classmate Natalie Ungvari, who visited her in Washington in September 1995, that she harbored a crush on the President. She had even written him a poem for National Bosses' Day, which she had had printed on a card and signed by all the interns. When the Director of the Intern Program, Karin Abramson, suggested that she take it over and give it to the President, Monica suffered a rare attack of shyness and insisted that Abramson accompany her. In the end the poem was given to a presidential aide, and in due course she received an autopen letter of thanks in response.

She was in luck, however, during Natalie Ungvari's visit. Monica arranged for her friend to be given a VIP tour of the West Wing, but since she was still an intern, Monica herself was not allowed in that area. She therefore left Natalie to make the tour, returning forty minutes later to wait for her friend in the basement lobby of the West Wing. While she waited she chatted to Lewis Fox, a uniformed Secret Service officer, who told her that the President would shortly be passing by. Sure enough, a couple of minutes later he walked into the lobby, where he began to talk to two women guests. Then he turned to Monica. As soon as she announced her name, the President, with a twinkle in his eye, said, "I know." They had their picture taken together and as they made small talk, Monica couldn't help noticing that he was giving her the once-over. While she found his attention flattering, she worried, typically, that she might appear too fat, and therefore tried to suck in her stomach as she chatted to him. She also thanked her lucky stars that she was wearing black, a slimming color. The incident, as insignificant as it may have been, is almost a paradigm of Monica's nature—the hopeful, apparently self-confident, almost brash young intern silently constrained by her lack of self-esteem.

However much fun Monica found the flirtation with the President, like any twenty-two-year-old she had to think of her long-term future. She took two weeks' leave in October 1995 to retake her GRE, fully intending to pursue graduate school the following year. She wanted to keep her options open if the White House job did not transpire. Yet, even though her mind was focused on her future, no matter how hard she tried, she could not forget Andy Bleiler—her heart once more overruling her head. It was a pattern she just could not seem to break. Throwing caution to the winds, she returned briefly to Oregon to see him. It did not take her long to realize that she had made a terrible mistake.

Immediately on being reunited with him, she sensed that Bleiler, who had found a permanent job at Canby High School in Portland, had returned to his familiar pattern of behavior and was seeing another girl now that Monica was no longer around. Her suspicions were to be proved horribly accurate some months later. At the time, however, in order to disguise the fact that he had a new mistress, Bleiler went into the tried and trusted routine which he had used before to end their relationship. Once again, he told Monica that he felt guilty about the affair, and that he wanted to focus on his wife and their children. Devastated by the rebuff, Monica dissolved into hysterical, inconsolable tears, and set off back to Washington downcast and depressed. It was the last time she would see Andy Bleiler for more than a year.

Her gloomy mood was dispelled the moment she arrived back at her mother's apartment, however. On her answering machine was a message from Jennifer Palmieri, Special Assistant to the Chief of Staff, who had known of Monica's job search thanks to her immediate supervisor, Tracey Beckett. She said that there was a job opening in Legislative Affairs and that she had recommended Monica to Tim Keating, one of the President's Special Assistants and Staff Director for Legislative Affairs, who was in charge of hiring and firing. A short while later she was interviewed over coffee by Keating, who was concerned that if Monica, who was one of several candidates, was offered the position, she should make a commitment to stay on past the election scheduled for November 1996. For her part, Monica's only caveat was that she planned to enroll for graduate school in the fall of 1996, but Keating told her they could deal with that nearer the time. A few days later, she was asked to meet two senior officials in Legislative Affairs, a sign that her preliminary interview had gone well.

On Friday, November 1, 1995, a national holiday celebrating Veterans Day, Monica was in her room, mooning over Andy Bleiler, when she received a phone call that changed her life, and possibly the course of

American history. It was from Tim Keating, who told her that he had some good news and some bad. The good news was that she had got the job, and would be working in the correspondence section of the Office of Legislative Affairs in the White House; her salary would be $25,000 per year. The bad news was that he didn't know when she could start, because a government shutdown was in the offing.

Monica could hardly contain her joy. Putting the phone down she first screamed with excitement, then wasted no time in calling her friends and family. "I was thrilled," she remembers. "Here I was, just a few months out of college, and I have got my first full-time paying job at the White House. What is more, I would have a coveted blue pass. I was so proud of myself."

The only problem was the forthcoming government shutdown or "furlough," which was the result of a budgetary impasse between Congress and the President. Effectively, this meant that the government was not voted the money to pay for the administration, leaving the White House to be run by only a skeleton staff of key advisors until such time as the matter was resolved. Because Monica was still technically an unpaid intern, however, she could be employed to fill in the gaps left by senior staff who were forced to go home.

It was in this atmosphere of crisis that Monica Lewinsky started her first day in her temporary job, working shoulder to shoulder with the most powerful men and women in the country, including the President. It was a highly unusual—indeed, extraordinary—state of affairs, whereby a junior White House employee came to be closely involved with the movers and shakers of the nation, working from early morning until very late at night.

On her first morning, Wednesday, November 15, 1995, Monica spotted the President as he walked by the door to the Chief of Staff's office, where she was working. She mouthed "Hi," and he smiled back a "Hi" before returning to the Oval Office.

What was particularly unusual that day was that the President, who normally visited the Chief of Staff's office once a week, dropped by four or five times. On one of these visits Monica, who knew that her mother's friend Walter Kaye had been due to give the President some handmade shirts that day, asked whether he liked the new shirts. The President seemed nonplussed by the question, leaving Monica thinking ruefully, "You blew it—he probably thinks you're an idiot."

Later that day the tightly knit group of office workers planned to celebrate the birthday of Jennifer Palmieri, who had been instrumental in getting Monica her job. Surprisingly, the President joined the impromptu party, where he spent a good deal of the time smiling and looking at Monica; she was, in White House parlance, getting a lot of presidential "face time." For some time she was kept busy answering the phones, a controversial radio talk-show host having given out Leon Panetta's telephone number and encouraged his listeners to ring the Chief of Staff and complain about the government shutdown. So while the President was grinning at Monica, she was placating irate callers bent on heaping abuse upon his head.

After a while, the President went into the Chief of Staff's inner office. Seeing this, and now free of angry callers, Monica, who was wearing a smart navy-blue pantsuit, decided to raise the stakes in their flirting ritual. She was standing with her back to the office door, and when he returned she put her hands on her hips and with her thumbs lifted the back of her jacket, allowing him a fleeting glimpse of her thong underwear where it showed above the waistline of her suit's pants. This incident, now infamous, was, as far as she was concerned, merely one step further in their flirtation. It was over in an instant, although she was rewarded with an appreciative look as the President walked past.

It was a calculated gamble, and one which might have had immediately calamitous consequences for her. Her friend Neysa DeMann Erbland observes, "When she told me about the thong thing I was shocked. She is sexual and playful [by nature], but that was a lot for her to do. By doing that she must have instinctively known that he wanted her. If she had read the signals wrong, then she would have been fired, no doubt about it. So she was sure that he was into this and her instincts proved to be correct."

As the evening wore on the President came more frequently to the office Monica was working in; he asked for people who weren't even in the White House, since all the senior presidential aides were in the Capitol building, negotiating with Congress for a solution to the impasse. Later she passed the office of George Stephanopoulos, the Senior Advisor for Policy and Strategy, and, glancing in, saw the President was in there alone. He gestured to her and said, "Come on in here for a second." When she went in, she found herself alone in an otherwise empty office with the President of the United States. Then, incongruously, he asked where had she gone to school? Nervously struggling to make conversation, Monica blurted out, "You know, I have a really big crush on you." Laughing, he hesitated for a moment before replying, "Come into the back office."

Monica's recollection of the next few moments is vivid, if romantically colored. In the inner office, the President stood close to her before wrapping his arms around her and holding her tightly. "I remember looking at him and seeing such a different person than the one I had expected to see. There was such a softness and tenderness about him, his eyes were very soul-searching, very wanting, very needing and very loving. There was, too, a sadness about him that I hadn't expected to see."

[63]

There were other thoughts racing through her mind: "Oh my goodness, he's so gorgeous—and I can't believe I am here, standing here alone with the President of the United States." They talked about her schooldays and where she was from, and he told her that she was beautiful and that her energy lit up a room. "He probably says that to everybody but at the time he made me feel incredibly special. Then he was just holding me, taking in my worth and my energy as a woman and a human being. He asked if he could kiss me and when he did, it was soft, deep, romantic. It was wonderful. At the same time as kissing him I'm thinking, 'I can't believe this is happening,' as well as 'What an incredible, sensual kisser!'"

Then, while he stroked her face and hair, Monica said to him teasingly that she had done this before, meaning that she knew the rules about having an affair with a married man. "I didn't want him to be worried, I wanted him to feel comfortable with me," she says. "I wanted him to trust me." She was enough of a realist, however, to believe that his regular White House girlfriend must have been "furloughed" and that as soon as the political crisis was resolved he would return to this other mistress. This assumption said less about the situation than it did about Monica's low self-esteem—she always saw herself as second best in her relations with men. Just as at school and college, at the White House she assumed that any man who took the slightest interest in her did so out of pity or because there was no one else available. She therefore simply enjoyed the moment, experiencing the thrill of kissing the President of the United States, knowing that there was little realistic chance that the relationship would go any further.

The President and the newly promoted intern chatted for a short time before one of them said that they should get back to work. It was not to be long, however, before they enjoyed a more intimate physical encounter. A couple of hours later, by which time it was about ten P.M., he appeared in the doorway of the Chief of Staff's office, then walked in, having first made sure that they were alone. She had already written down her name and telephone number, and now passed the note over to him. He looked at it, smiled and said, "If you want to meet me back in George's office in five or ten minutes you can." She agreed. After waiting nervously for a few minutes, Monica was relieved when the President opened the door to Stephanopoulos's inner office, which was dark, and gestured her inside. They smiled at each other, and immediately kissed. Soon, in the intensity of the moment, the encounter had become a good deal more intimate, their clothing unbuttoned, their hands exploring each other. Then, in the unlovely and degrading language of Kenneth Starr's report, "she performed oral sex on him."

During that time the President took a call from a Congressman as Monica continued to pleasure him. The American public were subsequently to be especially shocked by this behavior, but what impressed Monica at the time was her realization that Bill Clinton was her sexual soulmate. As she says, "We clicked at an incredible level. People have made it seem so demeaning for me but it wasn't, it was exciting and the irony is that I had the first orgasm of the relationship." Later they talked for a while, and before she left the office, the President noticed her pink intern's pass—she was still not officially on the staff—commenting, "This could be a problem."

As it happened, Monica was to see him again later that night, though this time in the presence of his personal secretary, Betty Currie and other staff—a curious transformation from the intimacy of earlier to the more usual White House formality. She arrived home on cloud nine, still floating on the smell of his cologne and the intoxication of their first evening alone together. She woke both her mother and her aunt, telling them that the President had kissed her. Both women, thinking that she was referring to no more than an old-fashioned kiss on the cheek, were none too pleased to have been woken from their slumbers for such an apparently tame piece of news.

Next day, it was an anxious Monica who arrived at work, nervously watching the President's body language. At first he ignored her when he came to the Chief of Staff's office; then, when she in turn feigned indifference towards him, he became much more interested, so much so that at the end of the day one of the interns who was working in the office said to Monica, "I think the President has a crush on you." That immediately set the alarms bells ringing: "It startled me and made me nervous," she recalls.

She felt a certain relief, therefore, as well as anxiety, when the President didn't visit the office at all on November 17, and as the day wore on she became reconciled to the fact that it had been fun while it lasted. That night the office staff worked late, and Monica ordered pizza for those who were still there burning the midnight oil. Unfortunately, coworker Barry Toiv knocked into her with his pizza and Monica had to rush to the bathroom to clean the new red jacket she was wearing. It seems that the President had spotted her in the corridor, for when she emerged he was standing in the doorway of Betty Currie's office. As she passed him he said, "Here, you can go out this way."

For the first time, Monica entered the holy of holies, the Oval Office. Then they walked through into the President's back office, where they talked and "fooled around." "I was just freaking out, thinking, 'Oh my goodness I'm walking through the Oval Office. This is so unbelievable.'"

Again they talked for a while, and Monica asked him about calling her at home. When he replied that he was anxious about her parents she reassured him: "It's OK, I have my own line so you don't have to worry about that." Then, insecure as ever, she told him, "I bet you don't even remember my name," to which he answered, "What kind of a name is Lewinsky, anyway?" "Jewish" was her immediate riposte.

She left to get him a couple of slices of vegetarian pizza, an errand which enabled her to be alone with him again once she had navigated her way back past Betty Currie. In the latter's hearing the President then told Monica that she could use the exit through his private quarters back into the main corridor, which meant that she would not be seen leaving by his secretary.

The couple "fooled around" in his bathroom, and it was during that encounter that she first unbuttoned his shirt. "It was such a sweet moment. It was the first time I had seen him without a shirt, and he sucked in his stomach. I thought it was the cutest thing. I said, 'Oh, you don't have to do that—I like your tummy.' It was very endearing and sweet—it made him seem a more real person to me." It was then, too, that the President took the relationship onto another level by telling Monica that he was usually around at weekends, when the White House was relatively quiet. "You can come and see me then," he told her, albeit without spelling out how such a clandestine meeting could be organized. "I can hardly come and knock on the door of the White House," she remembers thinking.

A little later that evening he accepted her suggestion that he join her and the other staff in her office for pizza and conversation, and while he was there she asked to have her picture taken with him. As the photograph shows, Monica, who is adept at putting on a bright public face to mask private unhappiness, for once smiled for the camera and meant it. Already the heady exhilaration of this new relationship, however temporary, was smothering the black moods of depression about her former lover, Andy Bleiler. The affair had come as a welcome pick-me-up, although certainly she had no idea whether it would last for any length of time. Indeed, she was by no means sure that he remembered her first name. She was strengthened in this suspicion after the furlough crisis had ended and she had begun her new job at Legislative Affairs. She passed him in the corridors a couple of times, and while he always acknowledged her, he also invariably called her "Kiddo."

She did not find that oversight too much of a heartbreaker, however, for, as she says, "There was this real excitement for me of not thinking about Andy. It was, like, 'There is some other guy to like me now.' I'm not unusual this way, a lot of girls get over one guy with another. It's just how it is—except that the other guy isn't usually the President of the United States."

Indeed, after that second private evening encounter on November 17, Monica was beginning to see Bill Clinton as a man rather than as the

President of the United States, appreciating his human vulnerabilities and foibles rather than being in awe of the office. Furthermore, and again typically, the girl who sees herself as a one-woman fashion patrol now took it upon herself to spruce up Clinton's image. This is by no means unusual where Monica is concerned. Her brother, father, and assorted boyfriends have all come under her gimlet eye for style.

In November, towards the end of the furlough, Monica asked Betty Currie whose office is adjacent to the Oval Office, if she would pass along a tie to the President for her. Monica explained that she had sold neckties all throughout college and would love to pick one out for Bill Clinton. Betty said of course. In her mind's eye Monica saw a tie that was "classy and presidential," yet at the same time "young, a little kicky, with pizzazz." She also, of course, wanted it to remind him of her each time he wore it. After hours of searching she finally picked out a hand-stitched silk Zegna tie from Italy and took it to Betty Currie, who assured her that she would give it to the President. Monica was thrilled when, a few days later, she bumped into Currie, who told her that the President, who was then visiting Ireland, had not only said that he "loved" the tie but had had a picture taken of himself wearing it, which he wanted to give to Monica.

Early in December, shortly after the President had returned from Ireland, Monica was walking through the West Wing when she came across him talking to a group of visitors with whom he was having a meeting. Spotting Monica, he turned from the group and asked, "Did you get the picture of me in the tie?" Disconcerted and rather embarrassed that he had broken off discussions to talk to her, she replied that she hadn't, and passed by. Later that day, however, Betty Currie called and asked her to come over. When she arrived, Currie told her to go see the President as he wanted to sign the picture for her. She went into his office, and he duly wrote on the photo, "To Monica Lewinsky, Thanks for the nice tie, Bill Clinton." It seemed he knew her name after all.

For Monica, their meeting that afternoon was a very human encounter. Knowing from their earlier conversations how sensitive she was about her weight, Clinton complimented her on how much she had lost since he had last seen her: "You look really skinny." "He could be so adorable," she says. "The sweet, little-boy side to him was the part I fell in love with." They went into his back study, where he fetched her a Diet Coke; they kissed and then began to talk.

Monica says: "He was such a real person, he was much gentler and nicer than Andy . . . That was how I saw him and that was the part that I fell in love with." Before they parted that afternoon, she told him, "I'm probably the only person in the whole world who wishes you weren't President."

[67]

CHAPTER FIVE

• •

"He Was Like Rays of Sunshine"

THE MERCURY in the thermometer was well below zero. Snow billowing in from the west ensured that the Sunday-morning streets remained empty and the highways almost deserted. On TV, the weathermen were predicting that the blizzard hitting Washington that day, Sunday, January 7, 1996, was going to last for a few days—"Stay indoors and stay warm" was the gloomy refrain.

At her mother's apartment in the Watergate building, Monica was lying on her bed, alternately gazing out at the falling snow and idly flicking through a book, when the phone rang. She reached out to answer it, but the caller hung up. A couple of minutes later the phone rang again, but before she could pick it up the answering machine cut in. As she pushed the button to override the message, a male voice said, "Ahhh—so I guess you are there." Monica thought it was her college friend Jason Lesner. "Yeah, I am. How are you? What's going on," she replied as she snuggled down on her bed, getting comfortable for a long, cozy chat.

Suddenly she realized the truth. She could hardly believe her ears—the President had called her at home! "Oh my goodness," she said, "it's you . . . Oh, hi. I'm so sorry I didn't recognize your voice." After a few minutes of small talk, he told her that he was going in to work in about forty-five minutes. Taking the hint, Monica asked if he would like company. "That would be great," he replied. She told him her office phone extension and they arranged to speak again in an hour or so.

As she hastily dressed and then cajoled her reluctant brother into driving her to the White House, on a Sunday afternoon and through the relentless snow, she reflected that here she was, going on her first date with the new man in her life. "It was a pretty cheap date, I guess," she now jokes. Yet the phone call from the President did in fact represent a genuine breakthrough in their relationship. Their first encounters during the furlough could have been dismissed as simply the result of her having been in the right place at the right time. "I don't think it was different, I'm sure, from the millions of other women that he's been with or flirted with or seemed to be attracted to. I think it was a combination of the attraction being there and the situation, the timing being right. The situation just happening with the furlough that there was this possibility for us to be alone," says Monica.

After she had started her new job at Legislative Affairs, on the odd occasions when she had seen the President he had usually called her "Kiddo." It was a habit that made Monica, who almost invariably looks on the gloomy side of things, think he had forgotten her name. She had even teased him about this when, on New Year's Eve 1995, a couple of weeks after the affectionate meeting at which he had given her the signed photograph of him wearing the tie she had sent him, they had a chance encounter in the inner study of the Oval Office. One of the White House stewards, Bayani Nelvis, was getting her a Davidoff cigar from the President's private store as a treat when Clinton himself walked in unexpectedly.

He sent Nelvis on an errand, leaving them alone together, whereupon Monica said to him as though making an introduction, "Monica Lewinsky, President Kiddo." He reacted defensively, saying that he had looked for her but had lost her phone number; he had, he said, tried to find her number in the book, but it wasn't listed. His little-boy-lost tone really touched a chord—"It was so cute," she recalls. Before long they were kissing, and matters advanced from there, although they yet again stopped short of actually making love. Afterwards the President said again that she could see him on weekends. Once more she gave him her unlisted phone number, telling him playfully that it was the last time she was going to let him have it. After he had wished her Happy New Year and given her a lingering goodbye kiss, Monica went home in a mood of high elation.

While that meeting had been fun, it had also been unplanned. On January 7, however, he had made it clear that he wanted to see her. As her brother drove her to the White House, Monica now knew for certain that the President was really interested in her. After Michael had dropped her off, she went to her office; then, as was to become a feature of their affair, she waited for the phone to ring. He was as good as his word. The display on her telephone receiver blinked with the word "POTUS"—the acronym for "President of the United States." They arranged that she should pass by his office carrying papers, while he would make sure he was in the vicinity, thus engineering a "chance encounter." Both were acutely aware of the need to be careful, a subject that peppered their private conversations throughout the relationship. At one point the President had mentioned to her that people were saying he had a crush on an intern, a worry that made them doubly cautious.

Carrying her papers, Monica duly walked past the Oval Office, but to her horror the door was closed and Special Agent Lew Fox was standing guard outside. She chatted with him briefly before the President opened the door, greeted Monica, and made an excuse to invite her inside, telling Fox that she would be there for a while.

A "first date" in the Oval Office was as irresistible as it was bizarre. "On the one hand I was excited to see him at just a boy-and-girl level," she says. "On the other, here am I sitting on a sofa in the Oval Office. It was cuckoo."

The President asked her if she wanted a drink, which was their cue to go into the inner office and from there to the bathroom, the most secluded area of his private quarters, where, according to Monica's testimony, they were "intimate" for about half an hour. "It was," she says now, "getting more intense and passionate." Afterwards they chatted for a long time in the Oval Office, he at his desk, Monica in what they called "her chair" to his right. She made a suggestive joke about the cigar he was chewing—a precursor, perhaps, of the "cigar incident" later that year.

The report by Judge Kenneth Starr, the Independent Counsel who investigated the Clinton–Lewinsky scandal, focused in humiliating detail on the sexual aspects of their affair, but to Monica what mattered most was the emotional side of the relationship. "There was such a little-boy, a childish, quality about him that I found very attractive. I once told him that he was like rays of sunshine, but sunshine that made plants grow faster and that made colors more vibrant.

"At the same time I liked being with him; he made me feel attractive, but I didn't think I would fall in love with him. It was just fun and I would be lying if part of the excitement was not that it was the President." Besides that, the more she focused on the President, the less she thought about Andy Bleiler.

Though Monica was now seeing Bill Clinton more as a man than as the President, her nagging insecurity made her constantly doubt her own worth to him, gauging the character of the man she was beginning to know against the constant undercurrent of chatter about his womanizing. "I had a double way of looking at him," she says. "On the one hand, there was this sensitive, loving, tender person, a needy man who was not getting the kind of love and nurturing he desired, and then there was his reputation as a philanderer with a different woman every day."

This emotional uncertainty colored her feelings towards him. So when he promised that he would call or that they could meet, and then neither came about, these failures fed both her insecurity about the relationship and her existing anxieties about her appearance or weight. A midnight phone call in mid-January from the President to Monica at home played upon those fears. He chatted to her for a while, and then initiated phone sex for the first time. Monica was nervous, uncertain whether or not he had liked what she had said; afterwards, knowing his reputation and always anxious to please, she worried that if the conversation had not gone well he might never see or speak to her again, and would all too soon forget about her. Even so, he ended the conversation in a way that was to become familiar: "Sweet dreams," he told her.

In spite of his words, these underlying worries preyed on Monica's mind, especially as he had failed to keep an earlier promise to call her. The following Sunday, January 21, as she was leaving work to meet her mother in order to buy her a coat, she saw the President, accompanied by a bodyguard, in the Residence hallway. They talked together amiably as they walked along the corridor; then, as she was about to leave, he told her that she could go out through the Oval Office, at the same time dismissing the Special Agent. Once inside, however, Monica stood firm when he indicated that they should go to the inner office, where most of their intimate encounters had taken place.

Before their affair went any further, she was determined to have a showdown with him, and where better than the Oval Office?—especially as she was wearing a black military-style beret because she was having a "bad-hair day." She complained that she hadn't heard from him, and that she had little indication about how he felt towards her. As she reproached him, all her fears and anxieties came spilling out, and she told him that if he wanted her to be shy, to stand on ceremony and treat him purely as the President, she would do so. If, however, he wanted her to treat him like a man, there had to be a little give-and-take.

Smiling gently, he put his arm round her and took her into the inner office, where he gave her a hug, complimenting her on her beret because it framed her "cute little face" so well. He was in pain not only physically—he suffers from chronic back problems—but emotionally: that day, he had received news of the first killing of an American serviceman in Bosnia. So while he and Monica once more indulged in their form of making out, it was an emotional occasion for both of them, particularly for the President, who, as Commander-in-Chief of all US forces, was feeling his heavy responsibilities especially keenly.

"You have no idea what a gift it is to me to get to spend time with you and talk to you," he told her. "I cherish that time we spend together. It's very lonely here and people don't really understand that." Misty-eyed with emotion, and with the news of the American soldier's death fresh in his mind, he went on to tell her about the difficult decisions he had to make. "I've been sick about it," he said. "It's really hard to know that someone died because of your executive order."

His distress touched Monica deeply. "At that moment I thought we were so lucky as a country to have such a caring and sympathetic man as the President, and I felt much closer to him. Our relationship, which had started as a physical attraction, was now becoming a genuine emotional bond. That day was a milestone, in that it brought me one step further to falling in love with him."

Certainly the President did little to discourage the process, calling her at the office and at home every few days, arranging to meet her at a going-away party for a White House staffer, and flirting with her at public events. At times he acted more like a lovesick teenager than the President of the United States, constantly telling Monica that she made him feel twenty-five again. He frequently complimented her on her beauty, her energy and her mind, and was sometimes amused by remarks of hers that she found mundane or commonplace.

There were numerous examples of the President's newfound, almost boyish ardor. On one occasion she was returning from the staff mess when he started waving to her from the Oval Office. Other visitors, thinking it was them he was targeting, waved back. Shortly after she got back to her desk he called her—a risky act as her phone might have been answered by one of the other staffers—and told her, "I saw you in the hall today. You looked really skinny."

What had started as a flirtation, little more than a bit of fun between Monica and the man she now called "Handsome," seemed to be developing into something altogether more serious. On the first Sunday in February they again met in his office, having once more engineered a casual encounter outside. Although, as was by now almost a matter of course, the meeting had its intimate side, for most of the time they chatted about a great variety of topics, serious, sexual and funny. They talked about when they had lost their virginity, about her combat boots—"Just like Chelsea's," he noted, referring to his teenage daughter—and about Monica's unhappy relationship with Andy Bleiler. "He's such a jerk," the President opined.

Monica even felt confident enough to voice her unspoken fear about the foundations of their affair, asking him in a lighthearted way if his only interest in her was because of the sexual side of their relationship. The President seemed genuinely shocked that she could think such a thing. With tears filling his eyes, he told her emphatically, "I don't ever want you to feel that way. That's not what this is."

Certainly both the tenor of that meeting and the tempo of their relationship had begun to suggest otherwise. Monica now felt so affectionate and comfortable with the President that, as she prepared to leave, she put her arm around him as he sat at his desk and gave him a hug. He kissed her arm and said that he would call her. When she asked if he had her numbers he reeled off both her home number and her work extension without missing a beat. "OK, you pass," she said gaily as she left to return to her office. Just a few minutes later he called her to say that he had really enjoyed seeing her, describing her as a "neat" person. "I was elated, just elated," she recalls. "In the beginning it was this very raw, sexual connection, which had now developed into romance and tenderness as well."

While the physical encounters and the telephone calls were important, equally sustaining was the private communication they developed when they were on public parade. Because she knew his daily schedule, she was able regularly to engineer matters so that they could pass each other in the corridor simply to say "Hi." On public occasions such as an arrival ceremony, they would make sly eye contact and smile. Such behavior is by no means unique. During her affair with Captain James Hewitt, Diana, Princess of Wales, used to wear red nail polish as a signal to her lover that she was thinking of him, and herself found a certain bleak amusement in watching Prince Charles and his mistress, Camilla Parker Bowles, making eye contact at public events.

For Monica Lewinsky and Bill Clinton, it was the neckties she bought for him that formed a running commentary on their relationship. She often said to him, "I love it when you wear one of my ties because then I know that I am close to your heart." Invariably he would wear one of them on the days after they had been together or for significant events. On one occasion Monica gave him a multi-colored (bright blue, black and white) Hugo Boss tie a couple of days before he was scheduled to have his picture taken with White House Legislative Affairs office workers, herself included. She asked him to wear it for the occasion, and when he did she acknowledged to herself that he had passed a private test. "I wondered if he was thinking of me that morning of the office picture, and lo and behold, he was," she says. Unfortunately—and ironically—the photo call itself was canceled.

He too was aware of the importance of her ties. On October 26, 1996, at a public rally in Virginia, he answered a joshing question she put to him about where he had got that tie, with the words "A girl with a lot of style gave it to me." Monica believes that he once deliberately cut a tie she had sent him, telling Betty Currie that it had been ripped in the mail. The ruse gave him a reason to summon Monica to his office, and thus to be alone with her for a while without anyone suspecting.

So when his steward, Bayani Nelvis, testified before the Grand Jury wearing one of her ties, Monica took it as a significant sign, just as she did when the President himself sported one of her ties on the day she appeared before the Grand Jury in August 1998. She felt that it was a gesture of support and, while in his own Grand Jury testimony he denied attaching significance to the ties, Monica is unshakable in her belief that he knew exactly what he was doing. "I will go to my grave, in spite of what he said, knowing that he wore my tie on that day for a reason."

[73]

Back in February 1996, such eventualities were unthinkable. Even so, sooner or later the sentimental bubble surrounding what was to become the world's most famous office romance was inevitably going to burst. Monica sensed the change of mood almost immediately after that last phone call on February 7, when the President stopped calling her. She hoped that he might call her on Valentine's Day but it wasn't until February 19, President's Day, that she heard from him again. He called her at home—the first time she had spoken to him in fifteen days. He was hesitant when she asked if she could see him, and so for the first and only time she went to the Oval Office uninvited.

Leaving her mother's Watergate apartment, Monica made her way to the White House (President's Day being a public holiday, she had not gone to work that Monday), arriving sometime after noon. Once there, she armed herself with a sheaf of papers, ostensibly for the President to sign, made her way to the Oval Office, and was admitted by the ever-present Secret Service agent on duty outside the door. Already anxious and near tears, she realized immediately that something was wrong. Sitting at his desk, the President told her that while he liked her as a person he felt really guilty about their affair: he didn't want to hurt Hillary and Chelsea, and he wanted to work at his marriage. "I don't want to be like that schmuck [Andy Bleiler] up in Oregon," he added.

He brushed aside her pleadings, saying, "You know, if I were twenty-five years old [in fact, he would be fifty that year] and not married, I would have you on the floor back there in three seconds right now. But you will understand when you get older." Indeed, the theme of the difference in their ages and of how she would see life differently when she was older ran throughout their relationship. He gave her a farewell hug and told her that they could still be friends. Monica tried to put a brave face on it, but she was distraught. On the way home, as a fitting end to a day of tears and depression, she had a flat tire.

She shed bitter tears that night. For her mother and Aunt Debra, though, the ending of the affair came as an enormous relief. They had watched Monica's involvement with the President first with mild amusement and then with mounting concern and anxiety. Initially, when she had placed a picture of him in her bedroom and talked about his wonderful eyes and how handsome he was, they had dismissed her chatter as the result of a harmless infatuation. Over the next few weeks, however, like blood seeping out from under a closed door, the awful truth began to dawn. Now, they felt a gut-wrenching fear, made up of anxiety for Monica's well-being, concern that she was once again involved with a married man, and above all a nagging dread that this affair was too big for any of them to comprehend, let alone to deal with sensibly.

Marcia says, "It took months before I realized that her admiration for him had changed to something personal. You have to remember that she never talked to me about the sexual side of their relationship and I shut my eyes to that aspect of it. When I realized that something not good was happening I was disappointed and demoralized.

"I felt it was wrong, not so much in a biblical sense, but wrong for her as a young woman. It was such a dead-end relationship and it frightened me because of the enormity of it. It was a terrible secret to bear.

"She knew how concerned I was, but part of me was hoping that it would blow over. In reality, though, what do you do? March down to the White House, say I'm Monica's mom and I'm here to see the President, and shake my finger at him? Tell him to leave my little girl alone? That's absurd."

In December 1995, Monica had told her closest friend, Catherine Allday Davis, about her fling with the President. At first Catherine had seen the relationship as a wild, exciting but short-lived experience that would help her friend get Andy Bleiler out of her system. However, knowing Monica's capacity for acting as her own worst enemy, Catherine grew more and more concerned as the weeks went by. "I started getting upset for her. I was afraid it was becoming another relationship like she had with Andy, that it would monopolize her emotions and energy and that she would end up falling in love with him.

"What really horrified me was that this wasn't the relationship she needed or wanted at that stage in her life. She needed someone's undivided attention. She ended up with the world's most unavailable man."

Inevitably, Monica didn't see it that way, whatever Clinton might have said when he ended their affair. Tearful, sad and depressed, she mooned over what might have been, dreaming of her "Handsome." She continued to do her work, but the fact that his smiling picture beamed down on her from the White House walls only made matters worse. While she saw him as the President, with the most important job in the world and all the difficulties that a packed schedule entailed, she had never really considered that he was a married man until that fateful meeting on February 19. Apart from seeing Hillary Clinton at the White House staff Christmas ball, the First Lady was, for Monica, a marginal figure, and in consequence her feelings towards her lover's wife were confused and contradictory.

On the one hand, she subscribed to the commonly held belief that the Clinton marriage was purely a business arrangement, and one, moreover, that would end once his presidency came to a close. On the other, she acknowledged that the President and First Lady were two intellectually "brilliant" people who connected on a level which mere mortals had difficulty comprehending. Moreover, any feelings of guilt Monica may have had were muted by the exhilaration of the affair, as well as by the occasional idle daydream of the future. "At this point," she says, "I wasn't thinking that we had a future together. There were days when I thought that maybe they [the Clintons] won't be together when his term ends and he will be free. Other times I just accepted that they would be married forever." In the midst of her despair, she nursed a dim hope that, as had happened with Andy Bleiler, she would one day find herself back in Bill Clinton's arms. This hope was rekindled soon enough.

A week or so after the breakup she chanced upon the President walking through the west basement lobby with a number of senior aides. Abruptly turning on her heel, she beat a hasty retreat, not wishing to be seen in his company by Evelyn Lieberman, then Deputy Chief of Staff, who was known for her sharp tongue and irascible temper and who she suspected was growing suspicious about her behavior. That night, however, he phoned her at home to say that he had seen her, and that he had in fact called her in her office because he wanted her to visit. She offered to return to the White House but he declined, saying something about helping Chelsea over her homework. Monica was bemused, if elated. "I thought this was odd behavior for someone who had just ended a relationship. That phone call made me think that he was still interested. But I wasn't sure."

For the next few days she used the well-worn feminine tactic of feigning lack of interest to stimulate attention. So if, for example, she saw the President in the corridor, she would greet him with formal reserve. On one occasion she deliberately turned her head away when he passed by. This gesture had the desired effect—he subsequently called her and complimented her on the fact that she had lost weight, a comment, whether true or not, he knew she would find flattering.

There were a couple of occasions during that period, in March 1996, when she and her erstwhile lover met by chance. One Sunday Monica was showing her friend Natalie Ungvari, who was again visiting with her, around her section of the White House when she spotted a familiar figure dressed in blue jeans, blue shirt and baseball hat walking back to the private movie theater, where he was watching a film with his wife. Monica shouted "Hey!" and the President stopped and turned around. She introduced Natalie to him, although her friend, whose head was spinning with the names of all the people she had met, didn't immediately recognize the man holding out his hand in greeting. As Monica affectionately picked out a piece of popcorn that was lodged in his shirt, Natalie was astonished to discover that the President already knew where she was from—the result of earlier conversations with Monica. The latter was inclined to be proprietorial, for, she says, "During our time apart I realized that I had developed very strong feelings for him. Absence had truly made my heart grow fonder." Although the President soon returned to the theater,

Monica found that she felt somewhat irritated by Natalie's interpretation of their conversation with him.

Monica and the President soon bumped into each other again, this time during office hours. She had grazed her hand and knee one night, and had been to see Dr. Mariano, the White House doctor. The next morning as she crossed the hall she encountered the doctor with the President. He had been out jogging and was feeling unwell. As Monica passed them, Dr. Mariano asked her how she was doing and the President asked what had happened. Afterwards, when he went upstairs to dress for work, he donned one of Monica's ties (the tie that his steward, Bayani Nelvis, later wore when testifying before the Grand Jury). Monica saw this when she passed him that evening in the hall. The President was with Harold Ickes but he stopped her to say hello. Around eight o'clock that night, he called her in her office and when she answered said, "I'm sorry you hurt your hand." In the ensuing conversation he invited her to join him and his guests to watch a movie in the White House Theater, but when she learned that senior staff would be present, she declined his invitation and asked if she could take a raincheck on that one. However, she did ask if she could see him on the weekend.

Thus, on Sunday, March 31, just six weeks after the President had ended their affair because of his sense of guilt, they were back in the old routine: Monica went to his office at lunchtime, carrying a folder of papers. In the past she had brought pictures of herself as a child, the President commenting of one of them that she looked rather too pensive for a two-year-old. This time she hid a Hugo Boss tie and a silly erotic poem among her batch of papers. It was after this encounter, which led inevitably to kissing and sexual caresses during which Monica—famously, thanks to the Starr Report—moistened one of the President's cigars in a most intimate fashion, that she realized that she had fallen in love.

She couldn't allow herself even to think that her feelings might be reciprocated. In many ways it was easier and safer to believe either that he had forgotten about her, though he clearly hadn't, or that he didn't really care about her. Those thoughts stopped her from thinking the unthinkable: that he truly cared about her. There were many signals—from the romantic metaphor of him wearing ties she had given him to the way he would thoughtfully compliment her and remembered so much about her life, for they talked often about her childhood and schooldays—that suggested he did care. But Monica, nursing her insecurities, simply couldn't bring herself to believe it.

Nor, for that matter, could anyone at the White House. A handful of Monica's closest friends, and her mother and aunt, had an insight into the true nature of her relationship with the President, but her colleagues could be excused for seeing only a young woman who seemed to spend too much time around the West Wing and the President. That young women staffers seemed to want to get too close to the President was a well-recognized syndrome; the word "clutch" was used to describe them, and in some people's eyes Monica was a "clutch". For her part, Monica soon had a nickname for those she felt were criticizing her—"The Meanies." Even so, their remarks stung, not least because she genuinely *was* close to the President.

The behavior of senior White House staff at the time, and the subsequent "spin" they put on events once the scandal broke, were predicated on the assumption that Monica Lewinsky was a deluded, starstruck ingenue with a penchant for married men, who deliberately entrapped the President. Her Aunt Debra believes she knows why: "One of the most ludicrous and unfair things about this affair is that she is categorized as a stalker, that she chased him or followed him around. That's what people in the White House had to tell each other, because [to them] it wasn't possible that this man whom they revered could be having an emotional relationship with her."

Ever since, after Jennifer Palmieri's birthday party and her first intimate encounter with Clinton, a fellow intern had joked that the President had a crush on her, Monica's caution about the affair had verged on paranoia. Nevertheless, a combination of her own inexperience, the system under which the White House is run and the sheer practical difficulties of seeing the President alone quickly undermined those tactics. In an enclosed world where every minute of the President's time, every White House arrival and departure, is logged, and where every area of the White House complex is graded for access, Monica soon received a harsh lesson in territorial etiquette.

In part the problem lay with the nature of her work at Legislative Affairs in the East Wing, which, since she and her colleague Jocelyn Jolley were responsible for administering much of the routine correspondence between the White House and members of the Senate and Congress, involved a degree of trafficking within the White House.

When she started in her new post at Legislative Affairs after the furlough, on November 26, 1995, she was immediately faced with a huge backlog of work. This in turn meant that there was little time for on-the-job training, and none at all for a gentle introduction to the niceties of moving around the White House. One day that December she was walking past the Oval Office, the direct route from the East to the West Wing, when she was confronted in the corridor by Evelyn Lieberman who told Monica sternly that as an intern she was not allowed in the area. The unexpected rebuke brought the girl to the verge of tears and she went to the bathroom to compose herself. Then, with her self-possession restored and determined to make clear that she was no longer an intern but the

[78]

holder of a blue pass, which gave her carte blanche to move around the building, she went to Lieberman's office to clarify the situation. "They hired you?" the Deputy Chief of Staff asked caustically, before telling Monica the correct procedure for getting from the East to the West Wing without passing the Oval Office.

Other minor incidents added to Monica's edginess. Once, when she was visiting the West basement lobby, she overheard a senior official asking Bayani Nelvis, "What were you doing talking to that East Wing girl?" On another occasion, when she was with a male colleague, the President himself caused her embarrassment. As he passed her in the corridor he offered a cheery "Hi, Monica." Her colleague asked how the President knew her name, and said that he himself had worked at the White House for two years, but the President did not know who he was. Monica made light of the incident, saying that she had met the President through a family friend who was a Democratic Party donor.

Her Aunt Debra says an atmosphere of jealousy and mistrust pervades the White House. "Everyone is so jealous and stabbing each other in the back. They will step on each other, they'll kill each other to get time with him [the President]. That's how they are. So these people were already starting to gossip and if we had been more sophisticated the alarm bells would have gone off. We would have said to Monica, 'Oh no, you've got to stop this affair right now,' because of all the backstabbing. That place is dripping with evil."

Undoubtedly the criticism that most irks Monica is that she wore "inappropriate" clothing such as short skirts and low-cut blouses during her time at the White House. In fact, as befits someone who prides herself on her fashion sense and on her well-developed notions of what is appropriate, she almost invariably wore long skirts or pantsuits to work, not least because she tends to be self-conscious about her heavy legs. She also angrily refutes suggestions that she was a presidential "hanger-on" who went to events at the White House and elsewhere uninvited. Correct form matters to Monica—a case in point being her decision as a youngster not to go to Tori Spelling's birthday party because she had not been properly invited.

Conscious of the whispering campaign about her, and worried about what the ever-present Secret Service agents were saying, Monica sometimes dampened the President's enthusiasm for seeing her. (She was right to be wary, as Secret Service agents regularly took bets that the President would arrive from the Residential Wing within ten minutes of Monica being admitted to the White House.) On one occasion he phoned to find out if she was going to the good-bye party of White House staffer Pat Griffin, and asked her to meet him later. Monica told him that people were talking and that they shouldn't make eye contact or talk at the party.

On the occasion of the movie invite—just two days before their affair resumed—it was Monica who had had the sense to see how this would have been received by senior staff. "I tried so hard to be careful and still got into trouble," she recalls. "I should have just done what I wanted."

At her prompting, the President worked out how he could use a phone which didn't make "POTUS" blink on her handset when he rang her, thereby disguising the origin of the call. Given his boyish difficulty in mastering office technology, she was thrilled when he called her on a more anonymous line. Previously she had joshed him about his phone, saying, "Haven't any of your other girlfriends told you about that?" meaning the dangers of using his dedicated line. Offended, he replied, "I don't have any other girlfriends. Shut up about that."

Their use of the curtained inner office, her entrances and exits from his quarters by different doors, the engineered "accidental" meetings, and her avoidance of key White House officials, were all part of the precautions they took to keep the affair secret. She carried this caution with her even outside her place of work. When she was with her mother or aunt in public and they were discussing White House business, she always lowered her voice, and she invariably spoke cryptically about matters concerning the President.

Her efforts were in vain, however. Even as she shared private moments with the President in March, the ax was being sharpened. Evelyn Lieberman, who had spotted her around the President or his quarters once too often, told Monica's boss, Tim Keating, "I want her out of here." She cited Monica's "overfamiliarity" as the reason for removing her from the White House.

On Friday, April 5, 1996, Keating called Monica in and delivered the blow. He did not mention the real reason for her departure, saying instead that, as a result of problems in the Legislative Affairs correspondence section, the entire unit was being reorganized and that, rather than being fired, she was being transferred to the Pentagon. He sugared the pill by telling her that the job which had been earmarked for her was far "sexier" than her existing post, but his words fell on deaf ears. Monica was heartbroken. She went home and cried herself to sleep. "I was hysterical all weekend," she recalls. "All I did was cry and eat pizzas and sweets."

Monica's dismissal came just two days after Commerce Secretary Ron Brown, a trusted friend and aide of the President, was killed when the plane he was traveling in crashed during a trade mission to Bosnia and Croatia. That weekend, as Monica nursed her sorrow in her apartment, her bitter reverie was broken by a phone call from the President. Recovering her composure, she asked how he was coping with his loss. Then, as she was telling him her own news, she burst into tears and asked if she could see him. "Tell me what happened first," he replied. Between sobs she poured out her distressing news and when she had finished he said, "I bet this has something to do with me. OK, come over."

It was Easter Sunday, April 7. Monica had been crying all weekend, and when she arrived at his office that afternoon she looked "a wreck." For his part, the President seemed genuinely upset by and angry at the news of her departure, and not least by its imminence—her last day at the White House was to be Monday. "Why did they have to take you away from me? I trust you so much. I promise if I win in November I will bring you back here, just like that," he said, snapping his fingers to emphasize his resolve. "You can do anything you want to do here." Monica, her gallows sense of humor never far beneath the surface, made a saucy joke about the type of job that would win his approval.

Emotionally, however, it was a curious meeting. Although they made out after the fashion that had almost become an established routine, for once she felt she was "servicing" him, rather than joyfully sharing an intimate moment. She would have preferred for him to hold and comfort her; moreover, she was determined to tell him how she felt about him.

Monica's usual early-morning routine was to visit her local coffee shop, Starbucks, order a skimmed latte and sit and read the newspapers. As she sipped her coffee that morning she had read in her horoscope—her sign is Leo—that she should make known her feelings to someone she cared about. So as she and the President chatted she mentioned what she had seen in her horoscope and for the first time told him that she was in love with him. He hugged her and said, "That means a lot to me."

Their romantic reverie, which had been interrupted earlier by a phone call, was further disturbed by Deputy Chief of Staff Harold Ickes calling for the President. As he went into his office, Monica, worried about possible discovery, made a hasty exit through a back door. It was an unsatisfactory conclusion to a strange and unsettling day—even though, as she scurried out of his office, his words of comfort and his promises about her future return to the White House were already emblazoned on her heart.

In this whole sorry saga, here was perhaps the greatest irony of all. While Monica lost her post at the White House as a result of her affair with the President—whom she was not to see in private again for nearly a year—she was eventually to be accused of getting a job as a consequence of the very relationship which had blighted her career.

CHAPTER SIX

• •

The Waiting Game

*T*HE CONVERSATION WAS SERIOUS, intense and went on late into the night—as befitted the discourse of a twenty-four-year-old Rhodes scholar making his way among the dreaming spires of Oxford in 1970.

As a bearded Bill Clinton chatted to his friend Mandy Merck, the subject of sex and politics rose to the head of that evening's agenda. The focus of their discussion was the tragic death, in July of the previous year, 1969, of a young Democratic Party campaign worker, Mary Jo Kopechne. A passenger in a car driven by Edward Kennedy, the Massachusetts senator, widely regarded as the Democratic front-runner for the Presidency, she had drowned when the car swerved off a narrow bridge at Chappaquiddick Island and plummeted into the muddy water. The incident ended his presidential hopes.

Clinton, who had been to Capitol Hill as a student and had a keen sense of the double standards of the political world, meditated on the relationship between power and sex before giving his own verdict. He told his friend, "Politics gives guys so much power and such big egos they tend to behave badly toward women. I hope I never get into that."

This was a somewhat surprising comment from a young man who, according to his biographer David Maraniss, had played games of strip poker in which every other player was a woman, had suggestively dangled his hotel-room key at female musicians during a band contest, and was even said to have had an encounter with the maverick feminist Germaine Greer. He had attended one of her lectures, in which she argued that intellectual, brainy men were hopeless in bed and that, at least where sex was concerned, women should only pick relatively uneducated men, preferably working-class. Legend has it that Clinton smoothly asked her for her telephone number in case she ever changed her mind about intellectuals.

Once the law graduate had become established as a politician, the tales of his easygoing charm and charismatic effect on women multiplied. So when, in emotional disarray, Monica Lewinsky left the White House in April 1996, it would have been natural, if there is truth in the persistent rumors that he is a serial seducer, for him to have effortlessly closed the door on that episode in his life. With Monica banished to the Pentagon, Clinton could have suavely moved on to the next intern, or whoever, to take his fancy.

That he did not do so offers a different perspective on the character of the man and the nature of the relationship, an insight that echoes the sentiments he expressed that night in Oxford. For a further year and a half he continued to see Monica (though not privately for many months), to call her and to think of her. He accepted her gifts and her love, listened patiently to her gripes, deflected her anger and soothed her wounded pride. By turns obsessional, jealous and hysterical, Monica treated her illicit affair with the President of the United States as though it were a regular relationship; his tacit encouragement, together with her high sense of entitlement, at times bordering on the absurd, demanded no less. For example, she was furious when, on her birthday, he broke a promise and refused to play a tune for her on his saxophone over the phone from Los Angeles, where he was spending a couple of days.

It is one of the many ironies of the Clinton–Lewinsky scandal that, although the sexual side of their relationship was dwelt on in lovingly prurient detail in Kenneth Starr's report, that aspect of the affair proved ultimately unsatisfying, inconclusive and somewhat disheartening. True, the emotional affinity between them blossomed, yet they never achieved a mature and full sexual relationship, something that certainly Monica came to find frustrating.

Far from using her as a mere sexual plaything to be discarded at whim, the fifty-year-old President seemed to have a much deeper need for this girl in her early twenties. As the months went by, Monica came to know the man behind the public mask, a flawed figure riddled with doubt and wrestling with guilt, yet emotionally needy, vulnerable and ultimately alone. The politician who used to play his saxophone late into the night as a refuge against loneliness, would instead pick up the phone to call Monica Lewinsky.

He seemed to crave the company or conversation of this feisty, argumentative girl who called him "President Kiddo" to his face and the "Big Creep" when she was annoyed with him. She reminded him, he said, of his mother, Virginia Kelley, who sadly died from breast cancer in 1994 before he won his second term in office. "You're full of piss and vinegar, just like her," he told her once.

Aunt Debra remembers her niece confiding details of her conversations with the President: "He seemed to open up to her. He would tell her about his own sad childhood, his mother, and I remember once he told her, 'We are a lot alike because we've both had so much pain in our childhoods.'"

To Catherine Allday Davis, it seemed that Monica's attraction for the President emanated from her youth and her personality. "Monica is fun to be with, bubbly, lively, entertaining and interested," she says. "Clinton's political success lay in the fact that he tapped into the youth vote, so I can see why an outsider, particularly a young person, would hold a special appeal."

However great the attraction between them, throughout their affair and in its awful aftermath Monica paid a high price for the President's emotional and sexual angst. Bill Clinton controlled the relationship—inevitably, given his high office—and Monica was always there for him, hoping and yearning, just waiting for him to call. Under those circumstances, her love became an obsession, inhabiting her dreams as well as every waking hour. For a young woman who likes to feel in control, this was a relationship wholly and utterly out of her power, an all-consuming affair that underlined her immaturity and exacerbated her existing insecurities and neuroses. Her aunt also describes the relationship as an "obsession" for Monica: "She was infatuated with him. But given who he is, her age and emotional background, it was understandable. She was Cinderella waiting for her Prince Charming to come along."

The truth, however, is that there was no magic in the world powerful enough to help her. For while the Starr Report paints a picture of a sexually precocious woman, in reality Monica Lewinsky is wholly unfitted to coping with a romance of this nature; indeed, her very inexperience and immaturity contributed significantly to the ensuing calamity. As her mother says, "While Monica was comfortable with her sexuality, as many women of her generation are, she was very naive in her relations with men. She was very credulous and unworldly."

Upon reflection, Monica agrees with her mother, and hints, too, at the indiscretion that brought about disaster. "I feel that he should have shown more restraint and left it as a flirtation and as an unacted-upon fantasy," she says. "I'm not blaming him for what happened, but it was just too much. It was too much of an emotional burden for someone my age. If I had really understood everything I would have seen him more as a President than a man, and I would have realized the ramifications of ever telling anybody about it."

The bleak realization of the negligible prospects of sustaining her illicit romance dawned on her the moment she walked into the Pentagon on April 16, 1996. It was a stark and depressing contrast to the White House. Her first impressions were of cheap, shabby furniture, dun-colored walls, crew cuts and severe faces above unfamiliar uniforms—very different from the White House, with its pristine decoration and overriding sense of style.

As ever she put on a sunny smile as she met her new colleagues. After some discussion she had been assigned the job of confidential assistant to the Assistant Secretary of Defense for Public Affairs, Kenneth Bacon. Her new post brought her a $3,000 raise to $28,000 a year, plus generous overtime, and the prospect of a good deal of foreign travel, but Monica knew from the moment she sat down at her desk that this was not the job for her. If she had little interest in politics, she had no interest in defense policy, the work—endlessly transcribing tapes—was mundane and boring, and the people were neither her type nor from her age group. Gritting her teeth, she grinned and bore her next six months in purgatory, waiting for the moment when the President would call to say that a new job was waiting for her at the White House as he had promised.

The only consolation during that desolate time were repeated phone calls that first week at the Pentagon from "Handsome," who told her that the reason she had been moved was because Evelyn Lieberman felt that he and Monica were paying too much attention to each other, and that "everyone needed to be careful" as it was a presidential election year. (Lieberman's own account before the Grand Jury was rather more terse: the President had asked her who had fired an intern. She said that she was responsible, to which he replied, "Oh, OK.") At least, Monica comforted herself, she hadn't been moved because her work was poor. The President also told her that if she didn't like the Pentagon he would get her a job on the presidential campaign team, but Monica was concerned that the very people who were hostile to her at the White House would also be organizing the campaign.

It was, her mother remembers, a desperate time for her. "When she moved to the Pentagon, that's when the true, *true*, blackest, darkest, worst of it began. She was miserable. She would sit by the phone and count the days and stay in her room and cry. She didn't go out because she was afraid she'd miss a call."

In terms of the rhythm of their relationship, Monica was right to attach so much importance to the President's calls. For the first few months after her departure from the White House he called every four to seven days, the calls becoming less frequent only when he hit the campaign trail in the weeks before the November election. He seemed as acutely aware of her timetable as she was of his, often calling the day after she had returned home from one of the frequent trips abroad she was required to make with her new boss, Kenneth Bacon—in the spring of 1996, in short order, she visited Bosnia, Australia, Russia and Scandinavia.

Monica came to expect the President to call a day or so after he had returned from a foreign trip, or if he had spotted her at a public event— and she was usually rewarded. It seemed that he missed her as much as she missed him. When he called and left a brief message on the answering machine she saved it, just so that she could replay the tapes to hear his "wonderful" voice. "He was so good about calling," she says. "He was always worried about me, always saying things like, 'Don't worry, I'm going to take care of you. I don't want you to be unhappy.'"

At times she was taken aback by just how much he remembered about their conversations, and by how careful he was of her susceptibilities. It was almost as if not seeing her in person made it easier for the President to be himself. As she says, "The reason why those phone conversations were so important and nourishing to the relationship was because they were safe—neither of us worried that someone would walk in. At the same time we were as passionate as we could be." Certainly the phone sex was as intense, if not more so, than when they met.

During one conversation in early May 1996, she mentioned that her father and stepmother were flying to Washington for her brother Michael's graduation, and that she was trying to arrange for them to attend a radio address, a regular event during which the President tapes his weekly "fireside chat" before an invited audience in the Roosevelt Room of the White House. A few days later he called and asked, with some puzzlement, why her family had not been at the radio address. Monica told him that he had mixed the dates up, and gave him the correct date when her family would be coming. Then, only a couple of days after that, Betty Currie called Monica at work and said that she understood that her parents were coming to town and wanted to go to the radio address. Surprised, Monica asked herself, "How on earth does she know? This is cuckoo." Obviously the President had taken time out from his hectic schedule to brief his secretary. Currie went on to explain that there might not be a radio address that week, but that the President had asked her to give Monica's family a tour of the White House and had said that he would try to see them then.

In the meantime, Monica had already arranged for her family to be at Fort Meyer, Virginia, to watch the arrival ceremony for the Irish President, Mary Robinson, on June 13. As Clinton walked past the crowd he spotted Monica, who was wearing a straw hat decorated with flowers. "I like your hat, Monica," he said to her, a comment that astonished her father, who had no idea the President even recognized his daughter, let alone knew her name.

At the radio address the next day, the President was solicitous towards Monica's family, carefully arranging the group for the standard, albeit greatly treasured, photo with him in the Oval Office. Even though there were many other guests, he made time to talk to them, chatting to Michael, who had just reached voting age, and eliciting from him the fact that he intended to vote for Clinton in the forthcoming election. Barbara Lewinsky, though she had not the slightest inkling of the real nature of her stepdaughter's relationship with the President, sensed the chemistry between them. At one point during their tour of the White House she noticed how he kept staring at Monica. She nudged her and whispered, "Girl, the President sure has your number—he just keeps looking at you."

[86]

While the phone calls from the President enabled them to engineer occasional, apparently innocent, meetings at more-or-less public events, their conversations were the umbilical cord which sustained—indeed strengthened—their relationship. He sometimes called several times a day, frequently calling back if he was interrupted by official meetings or other business. As Monica says, "A lot of emotion and passion with the President, and the depth of feeling between us, developed when our relationship was mainly on the phone. We spent hours talking about family things and our past. We were being real about each other. It certainly wasn't just about phone sex."

When he called in mid-July Monica asked if she could see him even though it was still in the middle of the campaign season. He told her he would see what was going on and then get back to her to let her know if that was possible. However, when he did get back to her, very early one morning, it was to say that things were just too busy. Despite her disappointment, Monica took comfort from the call. "It meant that he woke up thinking of me. That meant a lot," she says.

There were times when he spoke to her for comfort and consolation, and others when he called just to hear her voice. For example, and significantly, he called her on the night of May 16, 1996 when he learned that one of his closest friends, Admiral Jeremy "Mike" Boorda, had committed suicide. He was in a doleful mood, and felt very much alone. "I wish you were here to give me a big hug," he told her sadly. It was noticeable, too, that on the following day he wore one of the ties she had given him.

On other occasions they swapped jokes—Monica regaling him with the latest scuttlebutt from the Internet—talked about their families, the forthcoming election, in fact, according to Monica, "everything under the sun." During one chat she asked if the campaign was difficult for him, as this was the first he had undertaken without the help and support of his mother. He appreciated her sensitivity in recognizing that his mother's death had left a gap in his life. "She would have liked you," he told her. "You are very much alike."

Doubtless Virginia Clinton (later Kelley) would have recognized in Monica a drive and ambition similar to her own. While Virginia's energies had been directed to seeing her son make his mark in the world, Monica worked hard simply to see the President. To her mind, if she was seen by him, she hoped that a personal encounter, however brief and public, would prompt a phone call, a hope usually fulfilled.

One Sunday, she and her mother were driving to their apartment when she saw the President's motorcade and realized that he was on his way to church nearby. Monica was tanned, had lost weight thanks to a new slimming drug, and thought it would be fun to see him. Hastily, she got her mother to stop the car and let her out; then she found a place from which she would get a good view of the slow-moving line of cars. The ploy worked. As the motorcade passed by, the President saw Monica on the sidewalk and started waving furiously at her. That afternoon, still convinced that seeing her had been a happy accident, he called and was effusive in his compliments. "You looked stunning," he said. She did not tell him she had stage-managed the encounter.

On another occasion, she told him that she would be at a ritzy public function at Radio City Music Hall in New York in August 1996, which was being held to celebrate his fiftieth birthday. "Look for me, I'll be wearing a sexy red dress," she added. At the party they enjoyed a secret erotic encounter, for in the crush of people around him she was able briefly to brush his crotch with her hand as he was greeting wellwishers. She stayed in the same hotel as the President and First Lady, later joking with him that this was the first time that they had spent the night under the same roof. Next day she hung around, waiting for him to pass in the motorcade. Again he saw her, and he later remarked that she reminded him of a female character in the TV detective series, *Mike Hammer*, who always seemed to turn up unexpectedly. She did nothing to shatter his illusion that their chance encounters were anything other than serendipitous.

However, Monica strongly repudiates the notion that somehow she was stalking the President, arguing that they were in a genuine relationship, but that communication was, by the very nature of his position, an entirely one-way traffic. It was not possible, nor would it have been sensible, for her simply to pick up the phone and call him to say that she wanted to talk. At the same time, however sustaining any one particular conversation or meeting—even the briefest of meetings—might have been, the familiar anxieties, the sense of slights, real or imagined, soon kicked in when he was not on the line to soothe her. That summer, as his campaign to win a second term in office got into full swing, he was often too busy to call regularly, much to her chagrin. As an aside, during the long hours of waiting that inevitably accompanied the election campaign, she would play Billie Holiday's soulful "I'll Be Seeing You" when she was missing him and feeling blue. "It kind of sustained me," she says. "My favorite line that reminded me of us and our situation so much was 'I'll be seeing you, in all the old familiar places that this heart of mine embraces.'"

Inevitably the relationship, already hamstrung by his high position and the need for secrecy, suffered, although Monica admits that she had a hand in the process. She recalls: "I would sit by my phone every weekend, waiting, because I didn't know when he was going to call. I worried, too, that if he called and I wasn't there he would forget about me and speak to someone else. So often my insecurity got the better of me." In late April, for instance, soon after she had moved to the Pentagon, she decided to go to a public function, a fund-raising event in Washington, in the hope of seeing him there. It was the first public event, apart from arrival and departure ceremonies at the White House, that she had attended, and she waited patiently behind the ropes to shake his hand and say "Hi." While she achieved that objective, she left the event in a temper because he had embraced an attractive Russian woman standing nearby, who was, as it happened, a good friend of his. He could see that Monica was upset, however, and on the following morning he called her. The message he left on her machine simply said "No answer"; then, as he hung up the phone, he added in a whisper, "Shucks."

He called again a couple of days later, and this time they got into a fight, Monica tearfully asking him why he had embraced his friend and not her, all the pent-up anxieties of the last few weeks spilling out. "I was just trying to be careful," he told her. "The cameras were there and she's a big donor."

However, the next time they met, at a Saxophone Club event in May 1996, when he saw her he gave her a huge hug; later, as he was leaving the room, he pointed over to her and mouthed "I miss you." Amusingly, the man standing next to Monica, a former White House staffer, thought the President was saying it to him.

Yet as much as Bill Clinton cajoled her or tried to placate her, in her heightened emotional state it took very little for Monica to take offense. Just as, in July, she cried herself to sleep when he broke his promise to play the saxophone for her twenty-third birthday, so she became upset when she heard that, during a visit to Los Angeles, he had been out carousing with actress and singer Barbra Streisand and TV reporter Eleanor Mondale. Such childish spats were, however, but a drop in the ocean compared with the single overriding obstacle that ran as a counterpoint to the relationship. Above everything else, the usual tensions and misunderstandings generated by the dynamics of a secret affair with a married man were multiplied a thousand times by the fact that her lover was the President.

Her friends tried in vain to stop Monica from torturing herself. "When she hadn't heard from him for several days she became insane and crazy," recalls Catherine Allday Davis. "She would say, 'I'm so angry at him because I can't see him.' My response would be on the lines of 'I'm glad he can't see you.'"

On one occasion in September, the President phoned Monica from Florida during the election campaign, and she asked him when they were going to consummate their relationship properly. When he said that he was not going to have sex with her, she voiced her disappointment and anger. He never properly explained why, but Monica and her friends believe that he felt that to consummate their relationship fully would be dangerous. This time, however, she overstepped the mark. "If you don't want me to call you anymore, just say so," he answered curtly, an ultimatum that immediately chastened her.

Even when they met and were able to talk, it was never quite enough, Monica finding it difficult to conceal her frustration at the barriers raised by the briefness of their encounters and the ever-present need for caution. As a reaction to this, in October, after they had enjoyed a really intense and highly erotic phone conversation, they fell to discussing her possible return to the White House. The President also talked about her visiting him that week, when, he promised, they would share a kiss. The following night she went to a public function at which he was present. Once again he was warm and affectionate, publicly embracing her. Yet despite his efforts, she felt that he was not paying her enough attention and stormed out. "I was upset," she says now, "and it was not fair to him, but everything seemed to come to a head." That night when he called her again, she vented all the mounting disappointments of the last few months. "Oh come on now," he told her, "I'm too tired for you to be mad at me." About their proposed meeting, he went on to suggest that she come to his secretary's office so that he could see her, since he knew that Monica was visiting the White House to see Billie Shaddix about some photographs. Betty Currie duly contacted Monica and asked her to come to her office. In the end, however, she was kept waiting for nearly an hour in the West Wing reception area. When Currie finally arrived she told Monica that the President had already left, and explained that she was afraid to bring the younger woman into her office because Evelyn Lieberman, the woman who had had Monica moved from the White House, was in the vicinity.

Monica's ill-disguised disappointment, and her general sense of frustration, were matched only by the increasing concern of the tightly knit circle of friends and family who watched the drama unfold from the sidelines. As Neysa DeMann Erbland recalls: "I was worried about her in the same kind of way as [I was about] her relationship with Andy Bleiler. I was not worried that America would find out about it, but that he [Clinton] would splatter her heart. I told her that so she would get out of there, get a life outside of him."

It was easier said than done. The less Monica socialized, the lonelier she became and the more she focused on the affair, circumstances which inevitably became a vicious circle. A naturally gregarious and outgoing personality, she had made some new friends in Washington, in particular Ashley Raines, a young woman from Clinton's hometown of Little Rock, Arkansas, who had been a coworker at the White House, where she was Director of Office and Policy Development Operations and Special Liaison. The two of them went shopping or to the movies or restaurants together, becoming firm friends. Even though they talked about everything under the sun, Monica's mind was constantly on the President. On at least one occasion Ashley, who had learned of the affair in the summer of 1996, asked her to change the subject.

It would be wrong to think that, when it came to other men, Monica's life during these months was entirely monastic, turned over wholly to her devotion to the President. Even when she had a regular boyfriend, however, she always kept one eye on the clock, like Cinderella racing to get home before midnight just in case Prince Charming might call. On one occasion, for example, she was dating a man whom she names only as Thomas, a Pentagon worker, a charming, craggy-faced, older man whom she had met on a trip to Bosnia in July 1996. Just after she returned from that tour she saw him on a date, and he invited her to stay the night at his house. She decided against it, thinking that the President might call. Her instincts proved unerring, as they usually did, and they chatted away far into the night, the President enthralled, actually sexually aroused, by her excited description of the Bosnia visit. She told him how proud she was to be an American when she saw how the US troops had helped to restore sanity and give hope to this war-torn land.

That evening encapsulated the emotional contradiction in her heart and mind. She yearned for a normal relationship, but when offered the chance of attaining her goal she seemed to shrink back. It is as though she felt unworthy of enjoying a typical romance, and as though the deep scars left by her parents' divorce had made her afraid of approaching genuine commitment. So she clung to a romantic vision of love at once unattainable and unrealistic, the pain she felt somehow corresponding to her sense of worthlessness. Better the anguished fairytale than the genuine but flawed reality.

Even though, in the early days of her romance with Thomas, Monica began to feel good about herself, she was constantly distracted by the thought that she might be missing a telephone call from the President. She also couldn't resist teasing the President, saying that he now had competition.

In the fall of 1996, she ended her three-month fling with Thomas—because, ironically, he was seeing other women. When the affair began, her friends had been delighted: here was a single guy who might take her mind off the President. But it soon became clear that Thomas was never going to be the new love of her life. Then, in early October 1996, just as the relationship was ending, Monica discovered that she was pregnant.

She was convinced that she did not want to be a single parent, not least because she wished to be in a full relationship before having children, and so, with the greatest reluctance, she decided to have an abortion. She had problems finding a suitable doctor on the East Coast, and she and Thomas fell out over sharing the costs of the procedure, which meant she had to borrow the money from Aunt Debra. Originally Thomas had promised to accompany her to the hospital but, with relations between them strained, she decided to go through with it alone. Monica had thought that, being a sassy, liberal-minded West Coast girl, she would sail through the operation. In the event, it proved to be noisy, painful and distressing, leaving her traumatized and deeply scarred. "I was not emotionally prepared for the experience," she says, "It was just horrible and very depressing." Her friends were anxious and concerned for her. Neysa DeMann Erbland says, "It was very difficult time emotionally for her, especially as she wants kids so desperately."

She did not realize at the time just how profoundly affected she would be in the long term. Her mother did, though, and virtually forced her to undergo counseling at the medical center in Virginia where Monica attended a weight-loss clinic. There, in November 1996, Monica first saw therapist Kathleen Estep, to whom she talked at length about the trauma of her abortion.

Estep found Monica anxious and depressed, with a very low sense of self-esteem. At only their second meeting, she confessed to her affair with the President, talking rapidly for the whole ninety-minute session about their clandestine liaison. During her counseling sessions Monica discussed her fear of her relationships failing or not lasting, focusing in particular on those with Clinton and with her father. Most unhappily, just as she was beginning to make progress, Kathleen Estep moved away, leaving Monica without professional guidance at this critical juncture in her life.

The abortion, coupled with Monica's anxieties over her job, her hopes about returning to the White House, her troubled relationship with the President and her loneliness in Washington, sent her into a downward spiral. Then, at this time of desolation, isolation and depression, the unlovely figure of Linda Tripp began to take control of Monica's life.

It is difficult to believe, now, that there was a time when most of America—not to say most of the world—had never heard of Linda Tripp. Everyone knows today that it was her machinations that exposed Monica's affair with Bill Clinton and ultimately brought the President to impeachment; what is much more difficult to discern is her motivation. Yet the plain fact is that the roots of the veteran government secretary's Machiavellian scheming lay in the complex and contradictory matrix of her character.

Born in 1950, as a youngster growing up in New Jersey Linda Tripp suffered much the same misery about her physical appearance as Monica did about her weight. By the age of fourteen she had grown to be five foot eight inches tall. Her height, her broad shoulders and unfortunate nose, led to her being given the cruel nickname "Gus," after the basketball star

Gus Johnson, by her contemporaries. It was something she bitterly resented; "Don't call me that," she complained in one yearbook of her school in East Hanover, New Jersey, while another year she complained about "a certain fairweather friend"—words which she would have cause to reflect on. Like Monica, she went through the trauma of her parents divorcing; her father, a science teacher whom she remembers as a strict disciplinarian, left the family home when she was in her senior year of high school. She spoke to him for the first time in thirty years after the Clinton–Lewinsky scandal broke.

As if that in itself were not enough, she also resented, not unreasonably, the fact that, while her younger sister was able to go to college as a result of the financial settlement from the divorce, the money came too late for her. Instead Linda, who in any case achieved only mediocre grades at school, settled for secretarial college, shortly afterwards marrying a soldier, Bruce Tripp, by whom she had two children, Ryan and Alison, both now in their twenties. While her husband was working his way up the promotion ladder, rising to the rank of lieutenant-colonel, Linda earned extra income by taking a job as a secretary on the Army base, trusted sufficiently to work with a top-secret commando unit, Delta Force.

Working on the covert side of defense gave her the vicarious thrill that being "in the know," working on the inside, gives to so many people. The girl known as "Gus" could now sneer at her former New Jersey schoolmates—she had a ringside seat from which to watch how America really worked. For four years from 1990 she was in the very front row, working as a secretary in the White House Press Office in the administration of Republican President George Bush, thriving on the gossip and the intrigue.

In January 1993, however, the Democrat Bill Clinton was inaugurated, and Tripp's world changed. Her disapproval of what she viewed as lapsed standards of dress, deportment and discipline at the White House once the Clintons took over was equaled only by her spiteful scheming and her skill at leaking information. Colleagues viewed her as superficially friendly but manipulative, with a vindictive streak that sometimes saw her threaten legal action against those who crossed her path. During the inquiry into the suicide in July 1993 of Deputy White House Counsel Vince Foster, she told investigators that a fellow secretary had a drink problem. As Tripp had been the last person to see Foster alive before he shot himself, she earned a certain minor fame. Indeed, on August 1, 1995, just a couple of weeks after Monica started as a White House intern, Linda Tripp testified before the grand jury considering the circumstances of Foster's death. The Counsel's links to the First Lady and the now notorious Whitewater land scheme soon had conspiracy theorists weaving their web of fact and fantasy, and his involvement was investigated by

Kenneth Starr. Tripp herself contributed to the rumor mill, whispering about dark forces in the government, people who had taken action against Foster because he knew too much and was too close to Hillary Clinton.

Her days working in defense had given Tripp, too, a taste for conspiracy theories, and her resentment at the course of her life—she and Colonel Tripp were divorced in the 1990s, after twenty years of marriage—made her a perfect recruit for right-wingers who hated Bill Clinton and all his works. At once self-serving, self-righteous and self-important, she had a highly developed sense of moral indignation. These characteristics were given an extra edge of bitterness when, in 1994, she was moved from the White House to the Pentagon on the resignation of her boss, White House Counsel Bernard Nussbaum. Tripp, who likes to be at the center of events, resented being moved to the Pentagon, even though, like Monica, she received an increase in her salary. It was said, too, that her move was welcomed by the new Counsel, who suspected her of leaking information and making trouble for her colleagues, several of whom she publicly criticized.

When she arrived at the Pentagon she soon started to throw her weight around, demanding her own parking space and private office so that she could prepare for her testimony in the Vince Foster investigation. By contrast, Monica, when she moved to the Pentagon in April 1996, had taken little interest in the Foster case. All she knew about Tripp was that she worked at the back of her section on the second floor and never answered her phones, obliging Monica to field the calls.

Though Tripp privately criticized the Clinton administration, in public she made a great show of loyalty, displaying outsize pictures of the President on her desk. It was this colorful show of loyalty to the President that first sparked conversation between her and Monica. Later, the fact that both women had been removed from posts at the White House drew them closer together.

Monica's initial impressions of Tripp were of a "cold, rather rough woman with a good heart." At work she was thorough, competent and professional, although she complained that her salary of $80,000 a year was not enough to fund her dreams of owning an antiques store and living on a property where she could keep horses. Indeed it was their shared interest in antiques, as well as the fact that they shared a similar sense of humor, that drew the two women together, in spite of the age gap of nearly a generation. Furthermore, Tripp already had, from her time at the White House Press Office, a reputation for taking young interns under her wing, thereby gaining their confidence, respect and allegiance. This friendship seemed to be following the familiar pattern.

Catherine Allday Davis says that Tripp plugged into a need in Monica, and that, with her insider's knowledge of the Washington scene, she was able to persuade the younger woman to act in ways which other friends were uncertain about because they had so little knowledge of the White House setup. "Tripp was like a gossipy coworker," Catherine says, "not a real friend. Monica really needed to talk about what was going on [that is, her affair with the President]. Ashley [Raines] didn't want to know and didn't approve, so Linda was the perfect person. She didn't judge her, but at the same time gave her absolutely no help."

At first they shared diet tips, in the course of a year Monica encouraging her new friend to lose sixty pounds, and offering her enthusiastic approval when Tripp joined Weight Watchers. They talked about antiques, about Tripp's difficulties with her ninety-minute bus commute from her home in the suburb of Columbia, across the border in Maryland, and about the problems of raising two children. Her divorce had been bitter, and although her son, Ryan, the elder of her children, was away at college, her relationship with her daughter, Alison, was so bad that at one stage she kicked the girl out of the house. Yet for all that Linda Tripp seemed a decent mother, and had a lovely home filled with the antiques she collected.

Despite her difficult relationship with her daughter, Tripp seemed fascinated by Monica's mother. She refused to meet Marcia before she herself had lost weight, a strange reason for hesitation, and constantly asked Monica what her mother thought about Tripp's various schemes and stratagems. In time, albeit too late, Monica came to realize that Linda Tripp had a secret addiction: she was trying to live her life through Monica. For some bizarre reason of her own she was stalking the girl—not physically, but attempting to invade her psyche. (This behavior continued even after Tripp had betrayed Monica to the Office of the Independent Counsel.)

At the time Marcia, who has never met Tripp and thought she was a contemporary of Monica's, considered her behavior weird, if harmless. Now she sees it as having been a form of entrapment. "She sought Monica out, a vulnerable easy target. Tripp has an obsession with Clinton—at one point she claimed that Hillary Clinton was jealous of her because she suspected that she was having an affair with the President. This woman is delusional and pops up everywhere Clinton has trouble. She seemed to insinuate herself in every situation that had a whiff of scandal. She is like a meddlesome witch, a praying mantis."

When Monica and Tripp talked, politics was rarely on the conversational menu, and the latter, sensing Monica's lack of interest in the subject, only spoke occasionally about Vince Foster. While she was inclined to make much of his friendship with the First Lady, Tripp's usual refrain was about the dire impact his death had had on her. She told Monica that she had become a compulsive eater on the return flight from Foster's funeral in Arkansas on board Air Force One, the President's personal plane.

During one conversation the topic of President Clinton arose, and Tripp told Monica that she was just the kind of girl he would like. "Oh, he would go crazy for you, I just know," she said. In her distressed and unhappy state, these words were balm to Monica's soul. They continued to be so, although to a lesser and lesser extent, for as the weeks went by, Tripp's belief that the President would love a girl like Monica became a kind of nagging mantra, as irritating as it was consoling. Just when those who loved and cared for Monica were urging her to end her unrequited love affair with the President and move on, there was one voice whispering in her ear, wheedling and flattering, urging her to continue with her pursuit of the romantic fairytale. Unknown to Monica, Tripp's honeyed words were uttered less out of friendship than from self-interest. She had the idea of writing a "tell-all" book about life in the White House.

In May 1996, after a call urging her to do so from a mutual friend, the conservative newspaper columnist Tony Snow, in Washington Tripp secretly met with the right-wing literary agent Lucianne Goldberg, a gravel-voiced New Yorker who was a political spy for President Richard Nixon during the 1972 election campaign. During the meeting, Tripp showed Goldberg notes and discussed a possible deal for a book focusing on the death of Foster and the shenanigans in the White House, and provisionally entitled *Behind Closed Doors: What I Saw In The Clinton White House.* In due course, a ghostwriter, Maggie Gallagher, wrote a proposal which included two pages about women Clinton had allegedly been involved with, referring to Debbie Schiff and Kathleen Willey (although at that time Willey was not named). After the proposal had been sent to Putnam, a leading New York publishing house, however, Tripp decided to drop the project, saying that she had little personal chemistry with her ghostwriter, and that she was afraid of losing her job. The book was only resurrected seriously in 1998, after Monica confessed to her relationship with the President.

Although she had abandoned the book, at least for the time being, where Monica was concerned Tripp now scented innocent blood. The older woman, who emerges as the wicked witch in this tragic fairy story, constantly dangled the rosy-skinned apple of romance in front of a trusting and gullible Monica Lewinsky. During the summer of 1996 Monica increasingly confided in Tripp. Although she never revealed the name of her lover, she did debate with her, among other subjects, the pros and cons of her plan to travel to New York to see the President at his fiftieth-birthday party. The older woman may well have made the connection between Monica and the President, something made easier by Monica's trusting nature. Unlike Marcia, Aunt Debra and her friends, Tripp told Monica exactly what she wanted to hear; her words carried extra weight because she was someone who gave the impression of knowing the Presi-

Previous page: Monica and her mother by San Francisco Bay just after she had started walking.

Above left: Monica aged two at her favorite park in San Francisco. She showed this picture to the President because she thought she looked too pensive for a two-year-old. He agreed.

Above right: The President preferred this picture, commenting that it looked much more like the Monica he knew.

Below: Monica with her brother Michael in the sandbox at Holmby Park, near their home in Westwood, Los Angeles. In the summer of 1998 they returned to that same park for an emotional heart-to-heart about the traumatic events of the past year.

Monica aged five, posing for her father, who is a keen
and very accomplished photographer.

Above: Monica with her father and a friend in September 1977.

Below: Second-grade school picture at John Thomas Dye. At that time Monica's ambition was "to be a teacher and help other people to learn . . . I would be nice but strict," she wrote then.

Facing page: Monica in third grade. She was a member of a local soccer team, The Cardinals, but was relegated to left fullback. "I was a hopeless athlete."

Above: In Santa Barbara with her mother, father and brother during visiting day at camp in the summer of 1986.

Facing page: Monica's first trip to New York, aged twelve.

Above: Monica with her escort for the Bel Air Prep Prom.

Below: Monica with her first boyfriend, Adam Dave, at Natalie Ungvari's 21st birthday party. Monica was upset when he discussed details of their relationship on tabloid TV.

dent's mind, who had worked with him, and who understood the workings of the White House and its key players.

Moreover, Tripp seemed convinced that Monica would return to the White House and that, once she was again ensconced there, the President would find her irresistible. "Being away from him, those words and sentiments were sustaining," Monica recalls. "It helped restore my confidence in the relationship, though at that time Linda did not know I was seeing the President."

As October turned into November and the election approached, Monica became more and more agitated, her days an ecstasy of anxiety and hope, dreaming of the moment when the President would call to end more than six months in purgatory at the Pentagon. Throughout the summer she had ticked off the days to the election on a calendar, knowing that it signified her return to the White House. "All she ever talked about was 'I can't wait to go back there, I can't wait to go back to the White House,'" recalls Aunt Debra. The night before the election Monica anticipated that the President would call her, and that she would then be able to wish him good luck. It didn't happen and she plunged back into despair.

On Tuesday, November 5, 1996, William Jefferson Clinton was reelected to the Presidency of the United States of America, convincingly defeating his Republican opponent, Senator Robert Dole. On the day after the victory the Clintons returned to the White House in triumph, the President and Vice-President greeted by politically appointed staff, including Monica, on the South Lawn. Knowing that "Handsome" liked her black beret, she decided to wear it for the reception. In the jubilant crush of advisors, Secret Service agents, well-wishers and hangers-on they were able to do no more than exchange meaningful looks, but Monica returned home fully expecting that the President would call that weekend and ask her to come to see him so that he could tell her what he had in mind for her when she returned to the White House.

"I got everything ready," she remembers. "I put out what I was going to wear and had my hair cut. Then I sat—and I sat and I sat. I waited all weekend for him to call and it didn't happen. I was beside myself, I was throwing things, I was crying uncontrollably. I was just so frustrated. I felt I had left the White House like a good girl, I hadn't made a fuss. A lot of women who had had a relationship with the President may not have been so compliant. So I felt so betrayed and so disappointed. I was just crushed."

Depressed and demoralized, Monica went through the motions of doing her work at the Pentagon, trying to come to terms with the fact that the dreams she had nursed for six months had been dashed. That point marked the most miserable period of her life up till then.

Not long after the election, in late November, Monica was walking into the cafeteria at the Pentagon when she saw Linda Tripp. Raw, miserable and forlorn, Monica simply couldn't bear the thought of having to listen to Tripp's nasal whine as she said yet again, as Monica knew she would, that now that the election was over Monica could go back to the White House, and that she was just the girl for the President. Sure enough, as soon as she sat down, Tripp launched into her familiar spiel. For once, Monica cut her short. "Look Linda, I'm going to tell you this and I hope you don't tell anyone. I already had an affair with him and it's over. Just leave it alone—it's not going to happen."

It was the cue Linda Tripp needed. "I knew it, I knew it! I knew you were the type of girl he would like. Now don't think I'm really weird, but my grandma and I get witchy psychic senses about things. I just get senses about people and I just knew it with you. Now, tell me what happened." And Monica, who had been cautious and secretive about the affair for so long, found herself reliving the events of the last year. As for Tripp, far from telling her young friend to forget Bill Clinton and move on, she could barely suppress her excitement. "It's not over," she said. "You have longevity. He's still talking to you after all this time, he'll call again—it's just that he's busy with the election. It's a crazy time."

Monica remembers that conversation vividly and with acute embarrassment. "It was like she was brainwashing me. I was so hurt, I was still so in love, I was so confused and I was so young. It was like my life was beginning and ending at such a young age and I didn't know what to do."

When she poured out her story to Tripp, Monica thought she was confiding in a friend. Instead, she was gently being lured into a trap, the unwitting bait with which to catch a president. According to Lucianne Goldberg's testimony, as early as May 1996, within weeks of first meeting Monica, Tripp had contacted Goldberg and told her about a "pretty girl" with whom she had become friendly and who had confided that she had a boyfriend in the White House, something which Monica, whose memory is first-rate, vehemently denies. Much later, presumably after Monica's November confession, Tripp spoke to Goldberg and told her that "the boyfriend" was in fact Clinton himself.

Looking back, Monica's mother realizes that it was from this time in November 1996 that Linda Tripp began to manipulate her daughter's life. "Here's this young woman who desperately wants to believe what you are saying. She wants to hear that there is hope, that there is true love. She was at the point where she had resigned herself to it being over when Tripp comes along and uses all these psychological tricks to play with her head—'Say you need a job—fight—I see it in the stars—don't give up.'

"Her real friends were telling her to move on and get over this, but Linda Tripp created false hope in someone very young, very vulnerable, in a depressed state where she could easily be influenced by someone so overbearing, strident and strong.

"Yet all this was building up to betrayal. It's horrible to contemplate and you have to wonder what kind of human being could do this. Presumably someone with no compassion, no humanity and no sense of moral responsibility."

All this lay in the future, however. Back in November of 1996, Monica continued to see Tripp and for a brief period talked about her relationship with the President, constantly hoping to be reassured, and equally constantly plagued by pessimism. Every time she doubted that the President would call and decided that the relationship was over, Tripp boosted her hopes. "He'll call, he'll call," said her friend with the "witchy" psychic powers, confident that he would call in the next couple of days.

Meanwhile, Monica had other things on her mind. She was taking a break from Washington to attend the wedding of her best friend, Catherine Allday Davis, in Hawaii. On the way she planned to see her father and stepmother in Los Angeles and then travel on to Portland to join up with Catherine before heading west.

She was due to fly out to LA on December 2, but then discovered that for the first time since the election the First Lady would be out of town. With Linda Tripp's words still fresh in her mind, she decided to change her airline ticket and give the President one more chance. "He gets this one night," she told herself, "and if he doesn't call I am changing my phone number."

With her bags packed ready for her trip, she sat in her room and waited. Once again her instincts proved true. That night the phone rang, and even before she answered it she knew it would be the President on the line.

"Hi, it's Bill. I have laryngitis," he told her in an unusually gruff voice. With those three words Monica sensed that her long wait was finally over. Moreover, any doubts she may have had about the virtues of her personal oracle, Linda Tripp, evaporated at the sound of his voice.

CHAPTER SEVEN

• •

Not Right in the Eyes of God

$\mathcal{F}$OR ONCE, Monica was feeling good about herself—her personal demons about the President, her weight, Andy Bleiler and her job prospects were for the moment laid to rest. She also had faith that her new confidante, Linda Tripp, whom she admired as a true Washington insider, would help find the key to unlock the door back to the White House and to a place in the President's heart. As the New Year, 1997, started, Monica looked forward to a new beginning. Her optimism did not last long.

Ironically, in the run-up to Christmas 1996 she had found contentment of sorts and had, by a combination of happenstance and absence, turned the tables on the men in her life. Unusually, she was in control. When the President called her in early December they had enjoyed a long and predominantly lighthearted exchange. She had even told him that her summer romance with Thomas, her lover from the Pentagon, had ended although she did not tell him about the abortion. "I wish I was there and I could put my arms around you," he said, and he was, she recalls, sweet and tender, telling her that he missed her and speaking as though the six-week gap since he had last called had been but the blink of an eye.

Again unusually, she had to turn him down when he invited her over to the White House. She told him of her LA–Portland–Hawaii trip and that she was due to fly out early the following morning. They joked that Monica would send him a postcard from Hawaii with a voluptuous girl in a bikini and that Monica should send it to Betty Currie to ensure that he got it. They talked long into the night, the President falling asleep during their final conversation. But though she could not make her date with the President, she had another assignation planned in Portland: a rendezvous with Andy Bleiler.

She had not seen Andy and Kate Bleiler for more than a year, but they had talked frequently on the telephone, Monica letting them have a steady stream of gossip. When she first joined the White House she had given them a rundown on the inside buzz, telling them about the women who were supposed to have had affairs with the President. On one occasion, she had mentioned to Kate that one senior White House staffer had the nickname "Kneepads" because of her alleged sexual liaison with the President. It was an off-the-cuff remark that would come to haunt her.

She had also sent the Bleilers a variety of presents from the Secret Service gift shop in the White House, including a picture of the President with his autopenned signature on it, and when Monica was working in the correspondence section of Legislative Affairs, she sent Andy Bleiler a photocopy of a letter of congratulations, signed by the President, which had originally been destined for a Congressman whose first name was also Andy. Bleiler enjoyed the joke and pinned the letter to his bulletin board at work. Monica's actions were silly rather than sinister, and her intentions harmless, if inappropriate, but once again these gestures were to backfire badly when the scandal broke.

While she prepared for her short stay in Portland, Bleiler phoned her constantly, anxious to know that she was definitely coming—a complete reversal of their established roles. At the same time, Monica had her own reasons for wanting to see him alone.

Ever since she had put herself through the emotional and physical pain of the abortion, Monica had worried about going to bed with another man. If she was to sleep with someone, she wanted it to be a lover who was familiar and safe, who would understand if she became distressed. For this reason, during her time in Portland she went to bed with Andy Bleiler for the last time. It was an emotional experience for Monica but she now knew that she could continue with her love life without any physical fears. Monica left Portland with very warm and romantic feelings towards Andy, but she also realized that he no longer had any hold over her.

Later, when they talked on the phone, he confessed that he had been seeing another woman for over a year, that his marriage to Kate was on the rocks, and that he was thinking of leaving her for his new lover—all of which merely confirmed what Monica had long suspected. Bleiler admitted, too, that he now recognized how much Monica had meant to him; he apologized for his behavior during their affair and told her that he truly valued her as a friend.

Hence, at this point, Monica was finally feeling good about her relationships. She also knew that she was looking good. She had picked up a tan in Hawaii, and had lost weight—in fact she was slimmer than she had ever been before, something that did not escape the President's notice. They met briefly when she attended the White House Christmas ball in mid-December, and he took time out from another reception the following evening to call and compliment her. "I just wanted to tell you that you looked really beautiful last night," he said, adding that he had bought her a Christmas gift—a hat pin—when he visited Albuquerque in New Mexico, and that he intended to give it to her before Christmas.

Monica was disappointed when they didn't meet, as they had planned, on the weekend before Christmas, but she did see him purely by chance when she and her mother attended a Washington performance of *The Nutcracker*, in which Chelsea Clinton was dancing. The President, who was with his wife, spotted Monica as he was about to leave and beamed at her. That brief encounter sustained her, as did other fragmentary connections such as the brief phone messages he left on her answering machine. There was, too, an encounter at the 53rd Inaugural Presidential Ball held at the Kennedy Center in Washington, DC, in January 1997, where she patiently waited for five hours behind the rope line so that she could see him on stage with the First Lady. Seeing her, he mouthed, "I like your dress," and kept smiling and looking at her.

Even though her contact with him in the New Year was minimal, Monica's confidence in herself remained high. "Normally," she says, "when I get ready to go to a hoity-toity event I become a basket case, down on myself, thinking that I look fat and ugly in everything. This was the first time in my entire life that I had ever got dressed for something and not thought about my weight for a moment. It was a very liberating feeling, a liberation from my personal demons."

Moreover, by early January her job prospects, as well as her relationship with the President, seemed to be very much on the rise. Before Christmas she had heard that her bête noire, Evelyn Lieberman, was leaving her post as Deputy Chief of Staff in the New Year to head the Voice of America radio network. This news gave Monica the sense that the main obstacle in her path back to the White House had been cleared. As a result, when the President called her in January and February she talked to him about her return to the White House. He was encouraging, and told her he would speak to Bob Nash, Director of Presidential Personnel, about the matter.

There were other indications that her hopes would be fulfilled. When she went to see Betty Currie after Christmas to drop off seasonal gifts— she bought Clinton, who was away from Washington at the time, a Sherlock Holmes game, knowing his penchant for puzzles—Monica had discussed with her a possible return to the White House. Currie seemed to know all about it, replying, "I know. The President said to me when you left the White House that we should bring you back after the election—that you were a good kid."

Monica now assumed that the wagons were rolling, an understanding bolstered not just by her conversations with the President and Betty Currie, but by the views of her new Svengali, Linda Tripp. "She became my personal diary, someone to confide in, bounce every idea and concern off," Monica recalls. "I came to need her approval for everything—and she came to control me. There were several times in the next few months when I said, 'Forget it. I've had enough. I give up.' But Linda would say, 'No, keep going,' and she was often right. It was a sick, sick relationship."

Looking back now, she explains her dependence on Tripp as the result of the combination of her youth, the after effects of her abortion, her hatred of her job at the Pentagon, and her lack of contact with the President. Furthermore, almost all the people who mattered to her—her mother, her aunt and her closest friends—were virtually insisting that she leave Washington and find a new life, neither of which she wanted to do. The one voice that encouraged her to persevere was that of Linda Tripp.

In February 1997, Tripp began to insist that Monica, who had compiled her own diary of dates when the President had called or seen her, should go over the affair in detail in order to try to work out a pattern to Clinton's behavior; she even encouraged her to make a spreadsheet of all her contacts with the President. Monica realizes now that Linda Tripp was letting her "ramble on and on" about her affair with the President for her own duplicitous purposes.

Very soon, the hope that had inspired her at the beginning of the year had evaporated, and Monica returned to the front seat on her personal roller coaster of optimism and despair. As the weeks without even the sight of a job at the White House turned into months, her frustration grew, especially as a variety of White House staffers, none of whom seemed to know anything about her desire for a job, kept fobbing her off. Marcia Lewis, worried as ever by her troubled daughter, perfectly described these tactics: "She was so sure that they were going to let her come back and let her work at the White House. No one ever told her that she wasn't coming back. They would just play her, month to month, speak to this one, speak to that one."

This policy of prevarication seemed to echo the President's own feelings about their affair. He would tell her that it was over, and then shortly afterwards would call her or even see her, his every action, however casual, perhaps unintentionally renewing her belief that they did, after all, have a future together. Catherine Allday Davis, who kept in close touch with Monica during these months, could see the harm this behavior did to her friend: "I used to respect him, and so couldn't work out why he couldn't see that he was destroying her. He would try to end it, which was fair and good. Then he would call her and he kept it up, he kept on stringing her along, a kind of Chinese water torture. He never drew a line and said, 'It's over, and if you call again you won't get through.'"

The ambivalence was well illustrated during February, as the President tried to end their affair yet found himself, both emotionally and physically, drawn back to Monica, his feelings of guilt wrestling with his desire for her; the politician and husband in conflict with the man and erstwhile lover.

Early in February they had a long conversation about their romance. Monica started brightly, telling him to look in the *Washington Post* on Valentine's Day; she had placed there a message for her "Handsome," headed by a quotation from Shakespeare's *Romeo and Juliet*:

With love's light wings did I o'er-perch these walls;
For stony limits cannot hold love out,
And what love can do, that dares love attempt.

Though the President appreciated the sentiments, he spoke to her again about ending the affair, this time saying that he didn't want to harm her. "You have been hurt so much by so many men. I don't want to hurt you like all the other men in your life have," he told her, sentiments which suggest that he was sensitive to her emotional vulnerability. Yet as the conversation continued they ended up having phone sex and he promised to call her again.

That Valentine's Day found Monica in London with her mother. However, when she returned, she was dropping something off at the White House when she saw Betty Currie, who told her that she had tried to get hold of her the week before. From this, Monica deduced that the President had been trying to get in touch while she was away. Then Currie called again to invite Monica to the radio address that week, on February 28; to which Monica wore the now notorious navy-blue dress from the Gap, which she had just got back from the dry cleaners.

There were only six other people present at the address, but throughout Monica nervously wondered if she was going to be alone with the President for that long-promised embrace. Once the recording was over they had their photograph taken together, after which the President told her to go to Betty Currie's office because he had something for her. Unfortunately, presidential aide Steve Goodin, who was very protective of his boss's time, was also present. As Monica learned from Betty Currie, Goodin had issued a warning that the former intern should not be left alone with the President. Monica was surprised, therefore, when, after waiting for some time, the President's secretary walked her through the Oval Office and into the private office with the President. Currie then excused herself, and left them alone.

For the first time in ten months Monica found herself alone with "Handsome." As they went into his little study she said, "Come here—just kiss me." He was, however, far more circumspect than usual, and instead of kissing her he said, "Wait, just wait. Be patient. Be patient," before handing her a small box decorated with gold stars. She opened it, and there was the blue glass hat pin he had promised her. Then, with a slightly embarrassed air, he gave her a book, which he put into her handbag with the words "This is for you." Monica, who enjoys the ceremony of giving and receiving presents, wanted to savor the moment and took out the beautifully bound volume, an edition of *Leaves of Grass* by the American poet Walt Whitman. "It was such a compliment as a gift," she says, "and meant the most of anything that he gave to me," not least because the sentiments expressed in the poetry spoke to her profoundly about the nature of her relationship with the President.

In that romantic mood, they moved to his bathroom, the most secluded area of his inner office, where they started to "fool around." After he had kissed her for the first time in nearly a year, he pulled away from her and said, "Listen, I have to tell you something really important. We have to be really careful."

Yet, their caresses continued, becoming more intimate, and this time, when in the middle of oral sex the President pushed her away, Monica told him that she wanted him to come to completion. He told her, "I don't want to get addicted to you and don't want you to get addicted to me." Whatever his own rationalizations, so far as Monica was concerned, it was much too late for that. She told him that she "cared about him so much" and they hugged. It was then that he agreed to go on with their embrace until, for the first time in their affair, the President found sexual completion in her presence, a tiny sample of his semen staining her Gap dress. For Monica, this marked a new chapter in their relationship, an intensity of feeling that would, she felt, bring them closer to the day when they would properly consummate their relationship. In the past he had always held himself in check, at first saying that he didn't know her well enough, and later arguing that he would feel guilty about it. That moment, on February 28, 1997, signaled to Monica that at last he truly trusted her.

Monica went out for dinner that night. Afterwards, being her typically messy self, she simply threw the blue dress in her closet. It was not until the next time that she went to wear it that she noticed the marks on it. While she was not absolutely sure that the tiny stains on the fabric were from the President, she did joke with Neysa and Catherine about it, saying that if he was responsible, he should pay the dry-cleaning bill.

Such thoughts were far from her mind, however, after her romantic interlude. She sent the President a Hugo Boss tie and an affectionate letter of thanks for his gifts. She genuinely believed that they had a future together, viewing the President's caution and physical hesitation as merely an echo of the relationship she had enjoyed with Andy Bleiler.

The President had other ideas. In his videotaped testimony to the Grand Jury on August 17, 1998, he said, "I was sick after it was over and I, I was pleased at that time that it had been nearly a year since any inappropriate contact had occurred with Ms. Lewinsky. I promised myself it wasn't going to happen again." Yet on March 12, a couple of weeks after their assignation in the Oval Office, Betty Currie called Monica at work and told her that the President wanted to speak to her, and that it was important. When she called, he said that there was a problem with the tie (this was the tie that Monica believes he cut with scissors) and asked whether she could come over before he went on a trip to Florida the next day. She agreed, and he then put her back in touch with Betty to make the necessary arrangements.

Sensing that he wanted to tell her something important, Monica became frustrated when Betty said merely that she would call in the morning and tell her at what time she should come to the White House. This phone call marked the point at which Betty Currie, a motherly figure, well liked in the White House, became the interface between the President and Monica. Since the latter no longer had a White House pass and the President did not want her visits to him entered in the log, from then on it was always Betty who coordinated their meetings. For Monica, the arrangement was a frequent source of unintended obstruction, and therefore of disappointment.

It seemed that fate had its own means of obstructing them, as well. Before they could meet, news of a terrorist outrage in Israel, a serious threat to the fragile peace between the Israelis and the Palestinians which Clinton had helped to broker, meant that the President had to make an immediate public statement; during this he was wearing one of Monica's ties—the tie which Bayani Nelvis would later wear before the Grand Jury. Monica's visit had to be canceled. That night, while "Handsome" was staying with the golfer Greg Norman in Florida, Monica had a vivid dream about him. She woke with a start, turned on the TV and discovered that he had badly injured his knee in a fall. It was a strange coincidence, which, in her elevated emotional state, seemed to her another sign that they shared a spiritual bond.

Monica soon moved into action. She assembled a get-well package of presents that included a card featuring a little girl saying to a frog, "Hi ya, Handsome," a magnet in the shape of the Presidential Seal of Office for his crutches, a license plate reading "Bill" for his wheelchair and a pair of "presidential" kneepads which she had adorned herself. Yet beneath the surface humor, she was troubled that he had not yet revealed what he had seemed to want to tell her on the telephone the day he had asked Betty Currie to arrange the now aborted meeting.

She finally got to see him on March 29, on the pretext of replacing the damaged tie. As well as the new tie, she brought a bagful of goodies including a copy of *Vox*, a novel about phone sex, a medallion with a heart cut out of it, and a framed copy of her Valentine's Day ad. Once again, Betty Currie showed her through the Oval Office into the President's back study and then returned to her own office, leaving them alone.

An initial, sudden kiss from the President swiftly developed into much greater intimacy, although, since he was still on crutches, the sight was as farcical as it was romantic. With a poetic flourish that goes rather beyond the legal necessities, the Starr Report describes the scene thus: "A ray of sunshine was shining directly on Lewinsky's face while she performed oral sex to completion on the President. The President remarked about Lewinsky's beauty." This description provoked much public mirth, but Monica stresses that the moment was a very private, intimate and romantic one, during which for the first time they enjoyed brief genital contact, "without penetration," as the Starr Report, less poetically, puts it.

As they sat in the dining room afterwards, Monica says, she felt very "mushy" towards the President. She told him that she had been thinking of him, and that she had this vision of them together as "Little Bill and Little Monica," walking hand in hand in the sunlight. In her sentimental way, she told him that their relationship really nurtured the little girl in her, making her life seem complete. She felt, too, that she brought out the "little boy lost" in the President. Today, she is rather more clear-eyed about her dreams: "When I first started the affair, it was the excitement and the fact that it was the President that was the attraction. That changed over time. By this time I wanted to marry him, wake up with him each day and grow old with him. At times it was more realistic than others. Looking back now, though, it was a pretty foolish dream."

The need to exercise caution was again stressed by the President as he and Monica talked. Throughout their affair she had always said that she would never tell anybody, and that she would always protect him. He told her that, if she were ever questioned about it, she should simply say they were friends. He also urged circumspection when they spoke over the phone, saying that he believed that a foreign embassy—he did not say which one—was listening in to his official phone calls.

Betty came to collect Monica from the back study. The President hobbled over to Betty's office with her, and, before she left, gave her a hug and a kiss on the forehead in front of his secretary, to signify that his relationship was paternal rather than intimate. Then he started singing the popular classic "Try a Little Tenderness," looking directly into her eyes when he got to the soulful line "She may be weary."

Also during this visit, when Monica handed over her résumé to the President, he mentioned that the matter of a job at the White House for her was being handled not only by Bob Nash, Director of Presidential Personnel, but also by Marsha Scott, Deputy Director of Personnel and a friend from his student days in Arkansas. It seemed that the Clinton cavalry was riding to the rescue—though none too soon.

She felt comforted after that conversation, as she always did, and yet the doubts soon crowded back in. Every day she faced the dilemma of

whether she should resign her job at the Pentagon and look for work elsewhere, or be patient, a virtue which is not high on her list of attributes.
Though she liked and respected her current boss, Ken Bacon, she hated
the long hours at the Pentagon and the dull, repetitive work. Even so,
she was a conscientious worker, gaining an outstanding achievement
award that year. A trip to Asia in April, which to some might have seemed
glamorous, in reality meant endless days of typing and nights spent in
anonymous hotel rooms. On the way home from that "nightmare" tour,
she told herself that the President would have to act quickly, or she would
go her own way.

The nightmare in Asia turned into family trauma the moment she
returned home in mid-April. She was greeted with the news that her
beloved brother, Michael, had been involved in a serious road accident.
He had fallen asleep at the wheel, and his car had left the road, turned
over and landed in a ditch. He had gotten out of the car only moments
before it burst into flames, miraculously sporting nothing more than a few
cuts and bruises. For Monica, whose sense of the dramatic is never far
from the surface, the event was probably more emotional than it was for
her unruffled younger brother.

Then, as she absorbed this misfortune, she was at the Pentagon one
day that same month when she received a frosty phone call from Kate
Bleiler, who angrily accused her of having had an affair with her husband.
Not wanting an angry conversation at work, Monica cut short the call.
Then, furious that Andy had not warned her that their secret had been
discovered, she called him at work. He told her that his current lover had
confronted Kate and told her that she was pregnant with his baby. In the
ensuing emotional drama, Bleiler had admitted sleeping with Monica—
but only while they had still been in Los Angeles. Monica continued the
lie, explaining to a distraught Kate that the relationship had only come
about because of her insecurity about her weight. The game was up soon
enough, however, when Kate discovered Valentine cards Monica had sent
her husband that year. She returned them to their sender with a terse and
angry letter.

It emerged that, when his wife had confronted him, Bleiler had put
most of the blame on Monica, saying that she had pursued him when they
moved to Portland and had pressured him into continuing the affair. His
story was a blatantly self-serving misrepresentation, and Monica was so
angry at his behavior that she told him never to speak to her again. Her
anger persists to this day: "Instead of taking responsibility and being a
man, he lied. It was very distressing."

All through this period, Monica had had Linda Tripp egging her on, at
times angry with her, at others annoyed with the President, but always
encouraging her to keep trying for a job at the White House, even when

she considered giving up. "Some people bring out the best in you; she brought out the worst. I was so negative about myself, so nasty, so catty . . ." Monica admits.

The much-dreaded uncovering of her affair with Bleiler stirred up afresh the turmoil in Monica's soul. To make matters worse, as she brooded day after day on her chances of getting a job, her friend and oracle Linda Tripp heated up her brew of paranoia and resentment, especially in helping to plan strategies whereby Monica would both win back the President and acquire a post at the White House. "She would excite and incite me, encourage me to be hard-headed and demanding, whereas my mother would always try and pull me back," Monica recalls. "Linda made me feel more entitled to things than the President thought I was. But I see now that those were my own actions, so I have to take responsibility for them."

In March, Tripp had told Monica that she had learned from a friend of hers, whom at the time she named only as Kate, that there was the possibility of an opening at the National Security Council office in the White House. Since no specific job was mentioned, Monica sent her résumé and a short covering letter expressing her interest in any opportunity which might become available.

The efforts she made in March to help Monica with her job search coincided with a meeting Tripp had with a *Newsweek* reporter, Michael Isikoff, known as "Spikey," who specialized in the case of Paula Jones, the Arkansas secretary who in May 1994 had filed a suit against President Clinton alleging that he had sexually harassed her in a Little Rock hotel three years earlier, when he was Governor of Arkansas. Clinton vehemently denied these allegations; further, he challenged the legal right of a private citizen to bring a lawsuit against a sitting President. The matter was being pursued by attorneys for both sides.

In a potential new twist, Jones's lawyers had tipped Isikoff off about a volunteer worker for the Democratic Party who alleged that she had been groped by Clinton in November 1993 when she went to see him in the Oval Office to ask for a job. The journalist tracked down the woman, Kathleen Willey, who told him during an off-the-record interview that the President had groped and kissed her against her will. She cited Linda Tripp as someone who would confirm that the incident had taken place.

Isikoff claims that when, in March 1997, he talked to Tripp about Willey, she told him that he had the "right idea" but steered him away from the White House volunteer. They met again a few weeks later in a bar near the White House where Tripp, who had come across Spikey Isikoff during her days at the White House Press Office, once more dangled the notion of a sexier story in front of him, a tale of the President and a young intern.

In a town where knowledge is power, Tripp seemed to be enjoying the excitement of toying with a senior *Newsweek* journalist. Isikoff was unimpressed, however. To him, a story about sex and the President was nothing more than that: the Willey angle added fuel to the still-tiny flames of the existing Paula Jones case, and indicated a pattern of behavior by the President as well as hinting at misuse of his position. At the same time, Lucianne Goldberg had earlier made it clear to Tripp that to have her book published, she must get details of what she knew published in a nationally known publication. So the pressure was on Tripp to ensure that the Willey story surfaced in the press, and with her name linked to it.

Unsurprisingly, the story Tripp told Monica was rather different. In their previous conversations, when she was encouraging her young and trusting friend to persevere in her efforts to woo and win the President, Tripp had often referred to another of Clinton's paramours who, as she put it, did not have "longevity." Though she had never mentioned the woman by name, she always contrasted what she alleged was the latter's short-lived fling with the fact that she, Tripp, knew Clinton loved Monica and would stick with her through thick and thin. The woman to whom she kept referring was in fact Kathleen Willey.

In March, an over-excited Linda Tripp told Monica that she had been approached in her office by a *Newsweek* journalist who had asked if she could corroborate claims that Kathleen Willey had been sexually harassed by the President. In her panicky state, Tripp said, she had tried to play down the issue of harassment but generally confirmed that there had been a relationship. The two friends discussed the matter further at the office, and later that night Tripp phoned Monica at home. She said that Willey had called her and that during the conversation Tripp had told the other woman that she was lying, that there had been no sexual harassment. Willey rebutted this, saying that Tripp was not remembering the incident properly. The issue in question was Willey's claim that Tripp had seen her shortly after she emerged from the Oval Office looking disheveled and upset, and could therefore provide corroboration of her physical state and her mental distress.

Months later that conversation was to take on greater significance when Monica and Tripp quarreled over whether Willey had phoned Tripp, or vice versa. By then Tripp was telling Monica a different story, and was claiming that it was she who had contacted Willey, a claim that altered the emphasis of the whole meeting with Isikoff. For Tripp to have called Willey, rather than the other way around, implied that she had warned her of Isikoff's interest, whereas if Willey had contacted her to see how the interview had gone, the clear implication was that the two of them were colluding on the story. Over the next few months Tripp changed her story about Willey so much that Monica didn't know what to believe.

By the time Tripp was approached by Isikoff in March 1997, Monica had learned, from her experience as "gatekeeper" for Ken Bacon, how to deal with journalists. She was therefore more than a little surprised that Linda Tripp, a woman with considerable experience of dealing with the media, should have apparently handled the encounter with Isikoff in such an amateurish fashion. "It seemed to me," Monica recalls, "that it was stupid for her to have said that the President messed around with someone and it wasn't sexual harassment."

Furthermore, she thought that, as a political appointee, Tripp should inform the White House of Isikoff's approach, so that they could take the appropriate action. Monica suggested that she contact either Nancy Hernreich, Director of Oval Office Operations, or one of the White House attorneys, Deputy Counsel Bruce Lindsey, with whom Tripp had previously claimed a close working relationship. Like her stories of her familiarity with the President, however, her closeness to Lindsey seemed to exist more in her imagination than in reality.

Eventually Tripp did page and then e-mail Lindsey, saying that she needed to speak to him about a media-related issue. As a result of her previous Grand Jury appearance over the Vince Foster affair, however, Tripp and Lindsey had been instructed not to contact one another. Lindsey therefore ignored her attempted contacts, a snub which deeply offended the prickly Ms. Tripp. As far as Monica was concerned, there the matter rested—at least for the time being.

In any case, Monica had something else on her mind—her career. When she arrived back in Washington in mid-April after her trip to Asia, she called Betty Currie and said that she needed to talk to the President. All weekend, the usual time for him to call, she waited, but he never phoned. It was the same the following weekend. Something was wrong, but she couldn't understand what.

Taking matters into her own hands, on April 28 she applied for a position in the White House Press Office, an action which her boss, Ken Bacon, facilitated by dropping a note to Lorrie McHugh, Deputy Assistant to the President, in which he praised her as "bright, energetic and imaginative." Monica considered contacting Betty Currie, so that she could let the President know of these plans, but Linda Tripp discouraged her from following this route, arguing that the President still had problems dealing with the idea of Monica returning to the White House. "It's really weird, I just understand him so well" was Tripp's constant refrain. Monica was granted an interview, which took place on May 1, 1997, but though it went well she was not offered the Press Office post.

At last, on the final Saturday in April, the 26th, the President spoke to her. When Monica voiced her disappointment that he had failed to call earlier, they got into a row, the President telling her that his knee was still giving him a lot of pain and that he didn't need her complaining as well. As with all their fights, they made up before the conversation ended, and yet again made plans to meet soon.

On May 17, the President, who was out of Washington for much of that month, managed to call her again, calling several times because he kept being interrupted by official business. He said he had been going to ask Betty Currie if she could come in the next day, a Sunday, so that he could see Monica, but as he couldn't reach his secretary, he called Monica at home. She told him about her unsuccessful efforts to land the job in the Press Office. The President, who frequently told her that her search for a job in the White House was "being worked on," seemed annoyed with her for not informing him of her application. "Why didn't you tell Betty? We could have tried to help you," he said. "Promise me that if you hear of something again you will let us know, OK?"

There were other matters on his mind, as became clear in the course of the conversation. As he had said during their meetings in February and March, he was worried about people knowing about their relationship. "This wasn't unusual," says Monica. "What was unusual was that he acted differently between March and May, and I couldn't figure out why." He then asked if she had told her mother about their affair, to which she replied, "Of course not. Why would you even say that?" She added that, so far as her mother knew, the reason why she had been transferred to the Pentagon was simply because of her friendship with the President.

In reality, of course, Monica's mother, aunt and closest friends had known about the affair for many months. When she talked to Catherine and Neysa on the phone, she had even played them the messages the President left on her answering machine. "This wasn't bragging to my friends about the relationship. It was more like just treating him and talking about him like a normal boy. I'm from a generation where women are sexually supportive of each other—I know all about my girlfriends' boyfriends, for example, and the President was no different. The information would never have gone beyond my friends."

The President went on to tell Monica that the Deputy Director of Personnel, Marsha Scott, whom Monica had yet to meet, had been checking into matters, and had gained the impression from Walter Kaye, her mother's friend who had helped Monica get her internship, that Marcia had spoken to him about the relationship.

This remark is intriguing, for in their respective Grand Jury testimonies neither Kaye nor Scott recalled ever having spoken to each other about Monica. In February 1997, however Monica's aunt, Debra Finerman, had had lunch with Kaye, who has the reputation of being a lovable but incorrigible gossip, and he alluded then to the fact that Monica had something of a name for being aggressive. Debra's angry response, according to Kaye, was to inform him that the President actually called Monica at home late at night. This set Kaye's mind racing, for he had been told independently by two New York Democrats that Monica was having an affair with the President.

It does seem possible, therefore, that Kaye, who was a great friend of Debra Schiff, a receptionist in the White House's West Wing lobby—she once complained to Evelyn Lieberman about Monica's "inappropriate attire"—had passed on what he knew, or thought he knew, about the relationship, to those around the President. That information had in turn filtered back to Clinton—hence his mentioning Kaye to Monica.

The matter was more serious than whether or not the President was mistaken in his use of Marsha Scott's name, or whether he was using it as a smokescreen to tease from Monica details of any indiscretion she may have made. It seemed obvious from what he was hearing that news about their affair had leaked, and he was worried about it.

It was an unsettling conversation and, even though they arranged to meet on the following Saturday, Monica felt that something else was amiss, something that went beyond the President's fear of discovery. At the same time, even though this would be only the third time she had seen him in private that year, their previous two encounters had been of such emotional and sexual intensity that she had high hopes that their relationship would reach even greater levels of intimacy.

On the Saturday they were due to meet, May 24, Monica arrived bearing gifts as she usually did—on this occasion a golf puzzle and a casual shirt from Banana Republic. In her straw hat she sported the pin he had given her during their last meeting. She was shown into the Oval Office and was greeted by the President, after which they moved to the dining room, where she gave him the gifts. They then went on into the back study, Monica fully expecting that they would begin to "fool around."

It was then that he dropped the bombshell. Her instinct that something was amiss had proved absolutely sure. The President told her that he no longer felt happy with their relationship, and that he wanted to end it. It was not right for him, or his family, nor did he believe it was right in the eyes of God. He went on to describe the pain and torment that having an extramarital affair gave him as a married man. Then, as his wife and daughter Chelsea played nearby in the White House swimming pool, he began to reveal the anguish in his soul.

For all his life, the President said, he had lived a secret existence, a life filled with lies and subterfuge. As a little boy he had lied to his parents, and, even though he was a smart kid and knew the consequences of his actions, he had maintained that hidden life, safe in the knowledge that no one knew about it, knew the true Bill Clinton. After he married in 1975, when he was twenty-nine, his secret life continued. The number of his affairs multiplied and Clinton became increasingly appalled at himself, at his capacity not only for deceiving others, but also for self-deception. By the time he reached the age of forty, he was unhappy in his marriage and hated what he was doing to himself and others, the struggle between his religious upbringing and his natural proclivities ever more pronounced. He had considered divorcing Hillary and leaving politics forever—at the time he had been re-elected for his fourth term as Governor of Arkansas. "If I had to become a gas-station attendant to live an honest life and be able to look myself in the mirror and be happy with who I am, that's what I was prepared to do," he confessed to Monica.

At that stage in his life, feeling miserable, downcast and directionless, he had made a momentous decision—it would, he believed, be better for his beloved daughter if he and Hillary stayed together and worked on their marriage. He said that since then he had tried to make his marriage work and had kept a calendar on which he marked off the days when he had been good.

Monica, who refers to that Saturday, May 24, 1997, as "D-Day" or "Dump Day," recalls, "I could see on that day and at that time that this was really a struggle for him and it was painful to talk about. It reminded me of my own struggles with my weight. Of course there was the usual flattery and bullshit when you break up, and it did make me feel better. But it was an incredibly intense meeting. I cried and he cried too." She recollects that the President went on to tell her that he still wanted her in his life, saying, "If you and I are just friends I can tell them to go to hell and you can come here and spend time and it won't matter what they think because nothing is going on. I want you to do whatever it is you want to do. I want you to be happy. I can be a very good friend for you and help you in a lot of ways that you don't even realize."

Monica, understandably, clutched at this straw. "When we finished our discussion I had the overall feeling that he still wanted me in his life, still wanted me to be a friend. He wanted to help and take care of me."

Even so, she felt, as everyone does when a relationship ends, utterly crushed and demoralized. Betty Currie came in to fetch her and, in her distress, Monica forgot to mention to the President the brewing Kathleen Willey situation as she understood it from Linda Tripp. She went with Currie out into her office, and when the secretary asked if she was all right, Monica burst into tears. Sympathetically, Betty told her, "You are like me, you just can't hide anything. Your face shows everything."

Monica walked home in a daze, her high-heeled sandals blistering her feet. "I was crying, I was distraught, I don't know how I got home without being hit by a car," she remembers. "I stayed in bed and cried all weekend. I was so upset and confused. It didn't make sense. When I look back

I was so young, so foolish, so trusting. How could he have messed with me so cruelly?"

Just three days after that emotional breakup the Supreme Court unanimously rejected Clinton's claim that he was "immunized" from civil lawsuits under the Constitution.

The Paula Jones case was now in play, big time.

CHAPTER EIGHT

● ●

"To Have Him in My Life"

*M*ONICA'S SPIRIT was almost broken after the President ended their eighteen-month affair, but her family and friends breathed an audible sigh of relief. At long last, they thought, she could move on.

For the last year Marcia had tried all kinds of tricks and ruses to wean her daughter off her improbable love affair. She signed her up for various social groups, sending away for brochures, in a vain attempt to widen her circle of acquaintances and enable her eventually to meet a decent single man. She even bought her a book on how to end an obsessive love affair. So she was pleasantly surprised when Monica started dating Doug Wiley, a thirty-five-year-old lobbyist. The romance, such as it was, soon faded, though.

Monica's emotional difficulties were compounded by loneliness. Her closest friend, Catherine Allday Davis, had moved to Tokyo, so that contact with her was now by e-mail; and Neysa DeMann Erbland, who had been living relatively close by in New York, was soon to return to Los Angeles. This meant that, apart from Ashley Raines, she had no close friends in Washington.

It was not only her friends who were leaving. That summer of 1997, her mother also decided to move—to New York—to be close to the new man in her life. Marcia had met Peter Straus, a wealthy and charming New York Democrat liberal, at the launch of her first book, *The Private Lives of Three Tenors*, a biography of José Carreras, Placido Domingo and Luciano Pavarotti. In early September, she moved to a studio apartment off Fifth Avenue; Monica stayed on alone in the Watergate apartment for the time being.

Monica could still turn to Aunt Debra, of course, but family and other commitments often kept Debra at home in Virginia. In any case, Debra saw her role not as that of advisor, or moral counselor, but as that of sounding board, someone in whom Monica could confide freely, knowing that her aunt would listen sympathetically and non-judgmentally. Further than that, Debra believed, she should not go. What Monica came to miss more and more was the advice, and the active involvement in her emotional welfare, of her mother and her closest friends.

Marcia knew how lonely Monica was and was deeply worried about her. "I kept trying other things, repeating a familiar pattern. So either geographically or emotionally we would move her, rather than confronting her problems. We tried to get her to move to New York, we asked friends if they knew any decent young men, and I tried to get her involved in other activities.

"Everything I did—typical of me—was in a non-confrontational, passive way, trying to pull the strings in the back. Let's go on a trip, visit a museum, join a group . . . and so it would go on. I would have given anything for her to have had a loving relationship between two equals."

In spite of all the warning signs, the rebuffs and disappointments, Monica still dreamed of securing a job—any job—back at the White House, in order to be near the man she adored. She said as much in her testimony to the Grand Jury on August 6, 1998, and also said that the President knew it: "I did make this clear to him, that it was always more important to me to have him in my life than to—than to get the job." If necessary, she was prepared to take a job at a lower grade and therefore a lower salary; by no means a minor matter for Monica, who has never had a great deal of money. It was a road which, over the next few months, inevitably led to frustration, anger and despair, not least because she continued to clutch at the forlorn hope that the President's rejection of her might not be final. After all, Andy Bleiler had more than once ended their affair, only to return to her soon afterwards. If she could just get back to the White House, where there was a good chance that Bill Clinton would see her from time to time, might he not do the same?

Late in May, just before Clinton had ended their affair, the job opportunity she had been waiting for arose. The post was in the National Security Office at the White House, and meant working for Sandy Berger, the National Security Advisor. Among other benefits, it brought the prospect of traveling on Air Force One. Monica was excited by the challenge and, at Tripp's urging, made sure she was considered for the post.

An interview was arranged for May 30, just a week after the President's sad farewell to her. She remembered his insistence that she should let him or Betty Currie know when she was applying for positions in the White House. And only a week earlier, he had said they could still maintain their friendship, even if she were again working at the White House. Not for a moment had she doubted that he had meant every bit of what he said— for her, his words, no matter how casual, were tantamount to promises, and could not have been more binding had they been carved on tablets of stone. Armed with these reassurances, she contacted his office, only to find that both the President and Betty Currie were away.

After her initial interview for the National Security Council (NSC) job, in the first week of June she contacted the Deputy Director of Personnel at the White House, Marsha Scott. She was shocked and upset when the latter's assistant told her that Scott, who, according to the President, had since March been handling Monica's transfer to the White House, had never heard of her.

Monica's insecurity and natural pessimism at once rose to the surface. Not only had she always believed implicitly in the President's promises, but she had not contacted Scott before precisely because she had believed that the President and Scott were in direct touch about a job for her. (Moreover, she was constrained by the fact that she did not know exactly how much Marsha Scott knew about her relationship with the President.) Now, faced with Scott's avowed ignorance of her NSC job application, Monica began to wonder if his promises were hollow, if he was merely fobbing her off in order to keep her quiet. The thought was almost unbearable.

Worn down by emotional strain, and believing that her adored "Handsome" was not trying to help her, Monica was near the end of her tether. Not surprisingly, in her uncertainty and unhappiness, which were made worse by her growing loneliness and feeling of isolation in Washington, she turned increasingly to the one person whom she could rely on to encourage and comfort her: Linda Tripp. During the summer of 1997, bereft of the companionship of her mother—who, naturally, was often away in New York, preparing for her move and visiting with Peter Straus—Monica became more and more in thrall to Tripp.

The two women endlessly discussed and dissected every word of the President's every phone call or message. Monica attached enormous importance to the President's smallest utterance. (He, as he later told her, had no inkling that she read so much into what he said—that she was, in effect, building up her hopes on the flimsiest of foundations.) Tripp encouraged her to blame the President for the long delay in her return to the White House, which Monica had thought would happen soon after the November 1996 election. Tripp said she simply could not understand why it had all dragged on for so long, and that it was "ridiculous" that a job had not yet been found for her, especially as the White House created jobs all the time.

Around June 9, 1997, after her rebuff from Marsha Scott's office, a furious Monica, aided and abetted by Tripp, wrote a terse note to the President saying that, if he were serious about her coming back to the White House, he should help her get a job. The note seemed to do the trick. A short time later Marsha Scott called Monica and apologized for what she called "the oversight," saying that she herself had only just returned to the office after having surgery.

It was a friendly conversation; Scott said that she was perfectly well aware who Monica was but that her assistant did not have her details on her Rolodex file. Interestingly, in her Grand Jury testimony Scott denied that the President had asked her to find a job for Monica. She confirmed only that, the day before her conversation with Monica, she had received a call from Betty Currie, who had asked if Scott could help a young friend who was unhappy in her job at the Pentagon.

A few days later, on June 16, Monica met Scott in her office. During this interview, Scott asked a lot of questions about Monica's relationship with the President, and about why she had left the White House. In answer, the younger woman offered what she called the "vanilla" story, explaining that she and the President had been friendly, and that senior White House staff, in particular Evelyn Lieberman, had felt that her behavior was "inappropriate." Scott was also curious about why Monica wanted so badly to return to the White House that she was prepared to accept less pay, less responsibility and fewer perks than she enjoyed at the Pentagon.

Monica was dismayed by being asked such personal questions, especially those concerning the President. "I was so upset," she told Catherine by e-mail on June 17. "i really did not feel it was her place to question me about that . . ." She did not get the NSC job, though she was interviewed twice, reaching the shortlist. She telephoned Scott about it and, according to Scott, became indignant and upset. Scott later called this the "triple whammy" conversation. During it she informed Monica not only that the NSC position had been filled, but that two other potential avenues of employment at the White House, including working as a "detailee"—that is, in a temporary capacity, with a view to being taken on permanently later—were also closed to her.

A despondent Monica seemed in her e-mail to Catherine Allday Davis as though she might throw in the towel: "i found out today that i didn't get the NSC job . . . i think I'm going to have to walk away from it all. i don't know yet. i know it's annoying—i'm always saying this and then i change my mind."

Catherine was all in favor of a fresh start. Two days later she e-mailed back, "[Y]our email made me sad, Monica. I'm sorry for all the s— that went down with that woman . . . In my opinion walking away sounds like the best thing because it sounds like you will just get the run around from those clowns and continue feeling bad . . . I hate that kind of stuff. I hope you can put it behind you."

Monica sent Scott a "gushy" note of thanks following their meeting, but in fact Scott had reawakened her deepest fear: that, for the last three months, the President had been lying to her about finding her a White House post. Andy Bleiler had lied to her and betrayed her. Could Bill Clinton now be doing the same?

Everywhere, doors seemed to be closing in Monica's face.

Monica wrote to Betty Currie on June 24, outlining her disappointment over her meeting with Scott and her pain at the President's refusal to see her. She rehearsed her concerns about Scott's probing questions, and her surprise that Scott should have taken issue with the President's judgment that Monica had got a "bum deal" in 1996 and should be given a good job in the West Wing, where the President works. Left unsaid, however, was Monica's belief that at one time in their lives Marsha Scott and Bill Clinton had been "an item," and that Scott was therefore the wrong person to be finding her a job at the White House. Near the end of the letter, she wrote, "Betty, I am very frustrated and sad. I especially don't understand this deafening silence, lack of response and complete distancing evidenced by him. Why is he ignoring me? I have done nothing wrong . . . I would *never* do anything to hurt him . . . I'm at a loss, and I don't know what to do."

On June 29, encouraged by Linda Tripp, she sent a handwritten note to the President himself, imploring him to see her so that she could discuss her job search with him.

> Dear Handsome,
>
> I really need to discuss my situation with you. We have not had any contact for over five weeks . . . <u>Please do not do this to me</u>. I feel disposable, used and insignificant. I understand your hands are tied but I want to talk to you and look at some options. I am begging you [she originally wrote here, "from the bottom of my heart," but then crossed it out] one last time to please let me visit briefly Tuesday evening.

It is interesting to note that the words "I feel disposable, used and insignificant" were added by Linda Tripp.

The following day she called Betty Currie, only to be told that the President was too busy to see her. At this point, she says, "I started to get really annoyed and by the end of June, I was beside myself. I was a huge pest to Betty." On one occasion Monica started crying on the phone to Betty, a woman of great calm and patience, who took the time to phone her back to soothe and reassure her. To add insult to injury, however, when Monica called on the day after she delivered her note to the President, he was, she found out later, actually standing beside his secretary. Betty told her that he would return her call in a day or two, but inevitably he did not.

Although she was thousands of miles away in Tokyo, Catherine caught Monica's mood, and on July 2 e-mailed her, anxiously urging her to think seriously about leaving Washington. "I'm worried about you, Monica. Again, I think your idea to leave the area or get out of gov't work is a good one. I think you are in the midst of a dangerous, psychological situation. It all sounds so painful for you . . . I cannot help being very concerned."

After sending her letter to the President, Monica stewed for a couple of days. Then she boiled over. She woke up on the morning of July 3 determined to write to him and tell him what she really thought. In a three-page handwritten note, opening "Dear Sir," she chastised him for breaking his word over helping her to find a job at the White House, and wrote angrily about her treatment at the hands of Marsha Scott. Then, although she never intended it as a serious threat, she reminded him that she had left the White House like a "good girl" in April 1996, and hinted that she might have to disclose the nature of their relationship to her parents, so that they would at least understand why she was not returning to the White House. "I only intended him to realize what not helping me meant," she explains.

She also raised for the first time the possibility that, if she could not work at the White House, the President could at least help her find a post with the United Nations in New York. "It was," she recalls, "a real stream-of-consciousness letter, saying how he reminded me of my mom because, like her, he was an ostrich, putting his head in the sand because he didn't like confrontation. I told him that if he wasn't going to bring me back, just tell me." She ended by saying that she had always followed her heart and that she was doing so in this matter, allowing him one last chance to atone for his earlier behavior.

She sealed the letter in an outsized envelope addressed to "Mr. P.," her usual sobriquet for him, and handed it over to Betty Currie at the North West gate of the White House. A few hours later Betty called and told her to be at the White House at nine-thirty the following morning, Independence Day. It was rather early in the day for fireworks, the traditional way of celebrating the Fourth of July, but they were not long in coming when the President and Monica met.

He came out of his office and coolly looked her up and down before beckoning her inside. As they went into the back study, Betty caught her eye and said, "Remember—no tears," before leaving them alone together. They took their usual places, the President in his rocking chair, and Monica in the black swivel chair at his desk. Then he told her reproachfully, "I have three things to say to you. First, it is illegal to threaten the President of the United States," at which Monica butted in angrily: "I didn't threaten you." "Second," he continued, ignoring the interruption, though Monica heard a hint of nervousness in his voice, "you sent me this letter." Before he could go on she asked him if he had read it, but he told her that he had read only the first paragraph before throwing it away. Then, his third point forgotten, he delivered a stern lecture in which he said that she should not talk to him in that manner, that he was trying to help her, that she should not commit sentiments like that to paper and that she was ungrateful. Monica retaliated by running through a litany of his shortcomings, in particular his failure to help her secure a job. Then, despite Betty's words of warning, she burst into tears.

At once Clinton went over to her and began hugging her and stroking her hair, saying, "Please don't cry." She nestled against him with her head on his shoulder, but then she noticed a gardener working outside and suggested that they move. They went near the bathroom, and as he leaned against the door hugging Monica's disconsolate figure he told her, "People like us, we have fire in our belly, and there are a lot of people who don't know how to react to people like us. We're bright and passionate about things but we can get so angry, and you have to learn to curb your temper and to control yourself because it scares people. I can handle you but Betty can't."

While they talked, he continued to hold and stroke her, in a way that was romantic, but also emotional and needy. Monica says: "I had never felt so complete as I did in his arms that day and it sustained me for the next few months. He was someone who complemented but completed me. That was how I felt." He complimented her on her beauty and spoke of the bright future that lay ahead for her, ruefully adding, "I wish I could spend more time with you. I wish I had more time for you." Monica replied, "Maybe you will in three years," meaning that when he was no longer President he would have more free time. His answer shocked her: "I don't know, I might be alone in three years." Then she jokingly spoke about them being together, saying, "I think we'll make a good team," to which he replied, "Yeah, but what are we gonna do when I'm seventy-five and I have to pee thirty times a day?" He smiled when she said, "We'll deal with it."

Monica went on to talk about his marriage, something they had rarely done. "I know it's not my business," she told him, "but I think that you and your wife connect at a level that most people can't understand. I don't doubt that you have a deep bond, but to me I think she has cold eyes. You seem to need so much nurturing and the only person you seem to have worth for is your daughter. You are a very loving person and you need that, and I think you deserve it."

Remembering that conversation today, Monica says, "That's how I always saw him, his guilt from childhood and from his religion, his feeling that he doesn't deserve to be happy. But he does, which is why he has these illicit relationships. It's getting what he needs but he doesn't think he deserves it. Dick Morris [Clinton's former political consultant] once said that he has a Saturday-night personality where he gives in to his desires and a Sunday-morning personality where he goes to church full of remorse. I agree with that."

It was an intense interlude, and one that left Monica in an emotional daze, still trying to come to terms with what he had said about the future.

Later that day she saw Ashley Raines and told her about the meeting, adding that, in her heart, she believed that the President was in love with her. She realizes now that she will never know what really lay behind his words. "No one will ever know what he meant except him. He's the only one who knows the truth—and he never tells the truth." Wiser heads than Monica Lewinsky's have noticed this characteristic in Bill Clinton. As Democratic Senator Bob Kerry once said, "Clinton is an unusually good liar. Unusually good."

Before she left, however, it was Monica's turn to be less than honest. The Kathleen Willey business had been bothering her, especially because Linda Tripp had told her Michael Isikoff was snooping around again. Monica felt that if she failed to alert the President, and a damaging story were to come out, she would have let him down. She had discussed her concerns with Tripp, who had encouraged her to tell the President. She therefore said that an unnamed Pentagon colleague had been approached by a *Newsweek* reporter about Kathleen Willey. Monica was concerned, she said, because she didn't want to see him landed with another Paula Jones case, and opined that, if Willey was given a job, the issue would go away.

The President considered all this, then confirmed that Willey had spoken to Nancy Hernreich, Director of Oval Office Operations, the previous week, claiming that Michael Isikoff was hounding her and asking Hernreich's advice on what to do. This seemed strange to Monica, who knew that as long ago as March Willey had given Isikoff an off-the-record briefing, plus the names of several corroborative witnesses, including Tripp. Monica told the President that Willey was trying to play both ends against the middle because of the intervention of her unnamed friend, who had already watered down the story when she met the *Newsweek* reporter. As to whether or not the President had indeed groped Willey, he merely said off-handedly that she wasn't his type, anyway—because she was flat-chested.

Unknown to the President, when Monica left the White House after this meeting, she reported their conversation to Tripp. The latter seemed anxious about whether the President knew her name, yet at the same time excited by the idea that he might. "It's very clear to me now that she really wanted to be a player," says Monica. "She secretly had a crush on him, and, while she enjoyed living through me, there was another part of her that was jealous of my relationship with the President." (Indeed, during her testimony to the Grand Jury, Linda Tripp boastfully claimed that she had been moved from the White House because the President had been attracted to her and the First Lady had become jealous.) There the matter rested for the time being.

Just a few days later—and three thousand miles away—Monica and the President saw each other again when they both attended a NATO conference in Madrid. Monica, who was part of the Pentagon delegation, made eye contact with the President at a reception in the US Ambassador's residence, and for a time it reminded her of the good old days of light-hearted flirtation. While she was in Spain, Linda Tripp called her and said that there was a story about Kathleen Willey on *The Drudge Report*, an Internet gossip site run by Matt Drudge. Clearly, the Willey scandal was beginning to heat up. After a whirlwind tour of other European countries, including Hungary, the Ukraine and Bulgaria, Monica arrived home weary and jetlagged. She got a call from Betty Currie summoning her to the White House to see the President.

On July 14, as Monica got ready for the meeting, she fondly imagined that a combination of the intensity of their meeting on Independence Day and the sexual tension in Madrid meant that the President's determination to end the affair was weakening. That illusion was quickly dispelled. Although, as usual, she had brought him a gift—a wooden letter B with a frog inside which she had bought in Budapest, he was cold and distant toward her; furthermore, he was in pain, complaining about his back. They went into Nancy Hernreich's office nearby, and Monica sat on the sofa. The President sat on a chair, and only came and sat next to her at her insistence.

Almost without preamble, he asked her point-blank if the "unnamed" woman in her office was Linda Tripp. Monica confirmed that she was. He then told her that Willey's lawyer had called Nancy Hernreich that week and complained that the White House was trashing his client to *Newsweek*'s Michael Isikoff, and that the journalist knew that Willey had previously spoken to Hernreich. Only four people—himself, Hernreich, Willey and Monica—knew that fact, yet Isikoff had found out. It followed, he said, that Monica must have told Tripp, who in turn had spoken to the journalist. Though Monica confirmed this, she also lied and said she had told Tripp that the source of the information was Betty Currie, not the President. He asked, "Do you trust this woman?" Monica replied that she did, adding that Tripp was a great admirer of his, even displaying his picture on her desk. At this he nodded, then asked Monica to try and convince Linda Tripp to contact Bruce Lindsey again, to discuss how she should handle the matter. She said she would try, but added that Tripp was a proud woman and had been angered by Lindsey's previous rebuff.

Looking back on this conversation, Monica reflects, "Everyone has tried to make a huge deal out of this meeting, as though the President was obstructing justice and trying to get me to suborn perjury. That's baloney. At this time Kathleen Willey hadn't even been pulled into the Paula Jones case. All we were trying to do was squash a negative *Newsweek* story."

From that moment on, though, Monica began to grow wary of Linda Tripp, because she was leaking information to Isikoff. When the two women next met, Tripp confirmed that she had spoken to Isikoff at that time, but denied that she had told him of Willey's call to the White House. Now on her guard, Monica did not mention her July 14 meeting with the President, but even so managed to persuade Tripp that she should contact Bruce Lindsey again.

When Tripp did so, Lindsey suggested that Tripp should meet with Clinton's attorney, Bob Bennett, who was handling the President's defense in the Paula Jones case, and a meeting was duly arranged for the end of July. Tripp was nervous about seeing Bennett, afraid that he was going to be unpleasant. She went for a hair appointment to calm herself down, and then met with her own attorney, Kirbe Behre. In the event, she did not keep her appointment with Bennett, explaining to Monica that her own lawyer had advised her to remain neutral and not to become involved.

Monica was baffled. Tripp was a political appointee, so she was by definition working for the President, and therefore not neutral. Nor could Monica understand why Tripp subsequently gave a named quote to Isikoff for his story on Kathleen Willey.

At *Newsweek*, meanwhile, the importance of the as yet unpublished story had come into sharp relief only after Kathleen Willey was subpoenaed in late July by Paula Jones's lawyers. This gave the magazine a legitimate public-interest peg upon which to hang Isikoff's tale of presidential peccadilloes, and in early August 1997 the story was duly run. In it, Linda Tripp was quoted as saying that when Willey emerged from the Oval Office she was "disheveled, her face was red and her lipstick was off. She was flustered, happy and joyful." This confirmed the meeting between the President and Willey, but it also contradicted Willey's claim that she had been sexually harassed, a claim she elaborated upon when she appeared on the TV show *60 Minutes* in March 1998.

President Clinton later emphatically denied any sexual impropriety, saying that Willey had come to him in an emotional state because of money worries. They had sat at the table in the dining room off the Oval Office, and, after they had discussed her request to him for a paid job, he embraced her, and might have kissed her on the forehead. Clinton's version rings true with Monica. Reviewing the whole sorry business, she says, "I now find a lot of things about the Willey story strange. I couldn't imagine the President letting her leave the office looking like that. Maybe her lipstick was off, but her shirt untucked? No way. No way. In fact, we were always concerned about appearances. I would always leave with a Diet Coke; it looked a little more friendly and less sexual."

When the *Newsweek* story appeared, Bob Bennett dismissed Tripp as a woman who was "not to be believed," a comment that enraged her. Equally damaging to her credibility were allegations that it was Tripp who, earlier that year, had anonymously tipped off Paula Jones's lawyers about Kathleen Willey.

Filled with self-righteous indignation, yet excited by the attention she was receiving, Linda Tripp now saw herself, according to Lucianne Goldberg's son, Jonah, as a major player—an echo of Monica's own words— in a drama she had been instrumental in constructing. "Linda tends to view her role in things as much more important than it is," he says. "She was both thrilled and terrified by the play Isikoff gave her in this piece. She thought the whole world was now watching her and she thought she also could come center stage with what she knew about Monica."

Despite her unease about Tripp, Monica was still loyal, and she worried that her friend might lose her job because of her indiscretions. Tripp already had a reputation for being disruptive, churlish and uncooperative, as Pentagon internal-management memos attest. Tripp's and Monica's boss, Ken Bacon, had been upset with Tripp when there was a media uproar involving her and the Whitewater affair and he had asked her to inform him in the future if her name was going to be taken up by the media. Monica therefore pushed Tripp to tell him that the *Newsweek* article was going to be published and, in this climate of suspicion and hostility, characteristically went all out to help her friend. She anonymously called Tripp's attorney, Kirbe Behre, and made it clear to him that his client had been misquoted in the *Newsweek* article. She urged him to make a more complete statement, which, after consulting Tripp, he duly did.

When Tripp got back to the Pentagon, she admitted to Monica that she was worried about losing her job. She therefore decided to write a letter to *Newsweek*, complaining that she had been misquoted, and showed a draft to Monica. Monica suggested several amendments and even found the fax number so that Tripp could dispatch her letter to the magazine's editor. Though it did not contradict any facts about the Willey scandal, it did make the point that "Whatever happened in the Oval Office, if anything, is known only to two people." (Ironically, it was not until the scandal involving Monica herself hit the headlines, that *Newsweek* published Tripp's letter.)

There was more to come, however. Tripp, still in high dudgeon about Bob Bennett's attack on her veracity, told Monica that if she was fired she was going to write a "tell-all" book. "That made my spine curl," says Monica, and she worriedly asked Tripp if she would ever reveal the story of her affair with Clinton. Tripp—the woman who had told Michael Isikoff about the "young intern" and the President—replied soothingly, "Of course not. I would never hurt you."

Anxiety about Tripp's behavior was an added strain on Monica, at a time when she was still on tenterhooks about securing her return to the White House. On July 16, two days after she had seen the President about

Kathleen Willey, and then met with Linda Tripp, she had met Marsha Scott for the second time. After an hour-long discussion, Monica had felt much more confident about her future. It was her understanding that Scott had offered her a post as a "detailee," in Scott's own office, starting on September 1. She recalls, "It wasn't a done deal but very close. I just thought, 'I'm going back.'"

Once again, Catherine Allday Davis sensed that a storm was brewing, and on August 4, she e-mailed her friend: "I hope things get straightened out and you don't get dragged into anything too sketchy. Please don't forget to look after yourself Monica, no matter how tantalizing it is to put someone else in front of your needs."

The warning was justified. As so often in Monica Lewinsky's story, her high hopes were soon dashed. In August, Marsha Scott told her that there were now doubts about the post of detailee, and that in any case Monica would have to wait until Jody Torkelson, another of her "Meanies," left the White House in December before she could return. Once again Monica's suspicion that she was simply getting the runaround seemed to be confirmed.

She raised the issue with the President when she saw him in his study on August 16 to give him her presents for his fifty-first birthday on the 19th. This was the first time she had seen him since a brief meeting on July 24, the day after her own birthday, when he had given her presents of an antique hat pin in a little wooden box and a porcelain objet d'art from Norway. She had taken considerable trouble to find out what he wanted for his birthday. Sometime previously she had seen a newspaper report saying that he had spent time browsing in a bookstore in Baltimore that dealt in rare and fine editions. So she had driven to the store and told the staff a fake story about how her uncle knew someone who knew the President, and how they wanted to buy him a book he liked from among the volumes he had examined. It emerged that the President had shown considerable interest in an 1802 biography of Peter the Great, Tsar of Russia from 1682 to 1725. The book was expensive—$125—but Monica had bought it.

When she arrived at the White House, she was shown into the Oval Office, although the President was not yet there. She went into the back study, lit a birthday candle in an apple square (she knew apple pie was one of his favorites), and set out her gifts; besides the book, she had brought a game, "Royalty," and one of her psychology texts from college, *Disease and Misrepresentation*.

Eventually the President arrived—in a foul temper. His knee was hurting and his schedule had gone haywire. Even so, Monica sang "Happy Birthday" and he opened his presents, although he was distracted and irritable. They then proceeded to get into a huge fight about Marsha Scott. Monica complained that Scott was actively hindering her return to the

White House, and argued so vehemently that at one point the President ordered her to lower her voice. Eventually they calmed down, although the President made it clear to her that he did not want any intimacy, telling her, "I'm trying not to do this, and I'm trying to be good." Monica could see that he was upset, and she hugged him close before they shared a birthday kiss. The President was about to go on vacation to Martha's Vineyard, and before he left Monica sent him a card wishing him a good vacation and a copy of the book *The Notebook*. The book, she felt was significant because in it, *Leaves of Grass* was mentioned and quoted. In return, she asked, in her card, if the President would bring her back a T-shirt from Martha's Vineyard.

A few days later Monica received another metaphorical kick in the teeth. In the first week of September she had what she calls a "pissy" phone conversation with Scott, who told her there was no opening at the White House for her. Monica voiced her bitter disappointment in a handwritten note to a family friend, Dale Young, whom she and her mother had met at a health spa in 1995. "Unfortunately," she wrote, "I came back to DC only to learn that the detailee slot in Marsha's office is no longer available. I had a long conversation with her and it is clear to me now that I won't be able to come back any time soon. I think the end of this whole trauma is over. I just wish my heart didn't have to be broken in all of this." As Dale Young says: "Despite constant disappointments, she always had faith that his word had meaning and she expected him to produce the results he promised. One way of looking at her blind faith in him was that she expected him to be as honest with her as she was with him."

After she received the bombshell news from Marsha Scott in early September 1997 that there was no job for her at the White House, nor even the hope of one, a blow only marginally softened when Betty Currie gave her a bagful of goodies, including a cotton dress, which the President had brought back for her from Martha's Vineyard

The roller coaster was now on a steep downward dive, and Monica plunged once more into unremitting depression. She constantly called Betty Currie, begging her to ask the President to speak to, call or see her about her job prospects. Every time, Betty put her off, saying that he was too busy, or in a meeting. Hurt and angered at being continually fobbed off, Monica was again vulnerable to Linda Tripp's insistence that she should not give up hope. Monica felt otherwise. In a sad note to the President which she drafted but did not send, she talked of throwing in the towel: "My conversation with Marsha left me disappointed, frustrated, sad and angry. I can't help but wonder if you knew she wouldn't be able to detail me over there when I last saw you. Maybe that would explain your coldness. The only explanation I can reason for your not bringing me back is that you just plain didn't want to enough or care about me enough."

On Friday, September 12, knowing that the First Lady was out of town, Monica called Currie and asked if she could see the President after he had recorded a radio address that day. She even went to the South West gate of the White House, from where she phoned Currie endlessly, begging her to tell him she was waiting for him. After Monica had waited for forty-five minutes, Currie spoke to her: the President, she said, had a date with Chelsea, and couldn't see her. "I was crying," Monica remembers, "I was angry, I was frustrated, I was out of my mind. I was such a moron—I should have walked away from it all much sooner."

Currie did, though, agree to let Monica come and talk to her, saying, "You really worry me when you are like this." When the two women sat down in her office, Currie, in her motherly way, gently explained that the President was doing all he could to get Monica a job, but that his hands were tied. She promised to talk to him and see if she could arrange a meeting between him and Monica that Sunday, promising that she would herself come to the White House specially on her way back from Chicago to aid their rendezvous.

That Sunday, September 14, Monica stayed in her bedroom all day and waited by the phone. She called Currie repeatedly and frantically, desperate to find out if it was possible to see the President. As the minutes lengthened into hours, she became increasingly hysterical, until her condition began to cause real concern to her mother, who was visiting from New York. "It was one of those moments," Monica remembers, "where I said, 'Forget it, I've had enough, I can't take this any more.' I cried so much it hurt. I was in so much pain and confusion. I didn't understand him, why he couldn't be straightforward and tell the truth."

It is one of the endearing things about Monica that, even in her darkest moments, her self-deprecating humor is never far away. In the midst of her "pain and confusion," she joked to Catherine that the job she would really like would be that of the President's dresser. When the phone did eventually ring that day, for a short while the clouds parted and sunshine poured into her life. Late in the evening Currie called to tell her she had spoken to the President, who had suggested that John Podesta, the Deputy Chief of Staff, be tasked with finding Monica a job. The involvement of a heavy hitter like Podesta was a major cause for optimism.

In a calmer mood, Monica also realized that every recent conversation and meeting with the President had been punctuated by an argument. Resolving to turn over a new leaf, she decided to send him a "cute" note and laid it out to resemble an official memo. Dated 30 September, it was addressed to "Dear Handsome" and signed with an "M", and the subject was given as "The New Deal." Monica promised that if he would let her visit him "sans a crisis" she would be on her "best behavior and not stressed out," and would not cause a scene. In a postscript, she added that

Franklin D. Roosevelt, President of the United States for a record four terms, would never have refused a visit from his long-standing mistress, Lucy Mercer.

But if Monica was for the moment on an upswing, her mother, who had lived for years with the dramatic oscillations in her daughter's moods, was at her wits' end as to how to resolve the emotional torture Monica was putting herself through. Feeling lost and helpless, Marcia called her friend Dale Young at her home in Westchester, New York, to ask her advice. The latter thought that a direct approach, mother to mother, to the President's secretary might work. If Currie agreed not to let Monica speak to the President again, that would effectively cut off her supply of hope—and it was hope that was fueling her dreams. Marcia thought long and hard about the suggestion, but in the end just couldn't summon up the courage to make the call.

Monica's friends were also alarmed about her. "Unlike the Andy Bleiler relationship, her affair with the President got totally out of control, so that she couldn't get back down to normal life," remembers Catherine. "It was scary, it was disturbing and it really bothered me because I knew it wouldn't end until she moved. So I was really an advocate for her to leave." Ashley Raines, the only true friend Monica had made in Washington, echoed these sentiments in an e-mail to her boyfriend: "I'm glad I didn't keep in close contact with her over the last month because she told me she was pretty messed. And when she says that, it's scary."

Even the President's unflappable personal secretary was startled by Monica's behavior. The girl she had once thought of as someone who had been "maligned improperly" was fast becoming a "pain in the neck" because of her tears, her tantrums and her endless phone calls. Yet when Currie reluctantly advised the President against bringing Monica back to the White House, he insisted that the matter be pursued and, according to Currie's Grand Jury testimony, instructed her and Marsha Scott to continue their efforts to find her a position. Indeed, when he called Monica soon after receiving the "New Deal" memo of 30 September, he promised to speak to Erskine Bowles, the Chief of Staff, about bringing her back.

By now, Monica's desire to return to the White House was fueled as much by the need to prove she could do it as by any career goal. And, of course, above all else there was her overwhelming longing simply to be close to the President. "I still had the hope that our relationship could get back to normal," she says, "and remember, he was always very affectionate and loving towards me. At the same time I had a level of desperation: I wanted a job at the White House, I felt entitled to a job after all I had been through."

Understandably, Monica had become extremely skeptical about supposed attempts to help her get a White House job. She heard nothing from John Podesta in spite of badgering Betty Currie about the matter, and had become convinced that there was a cabal of senior White House staff, particularly women who had once been close to the President, working against her return. She heard all the time of low-level jobs at the White House, for which she would have been eminently suitable, being filled. Monica's suspicion that the President was giving her the runaround flared up again—indeed, it seems still to haunt her: "If he wasn't going to bring me back," she says, "he should have said so and been up-front about it. He should have told me that he couldn't do it. Instead, he strung me along month after month."

In fact, she was doing him an injustice: Clinton had indeed ensured that the question of a White House job for her was raised with both Erskine Bowles and John Podesta. For discretion's sake, though, he had asked Betty Currie to contact them for him, and Bowles and Podesta, believing that the job was for a friend of Currie's, rather than for someone in whom the President took an interest, naturally did not give the matter the top priority.

At this desperate time, just when Monica needed all the support and comfort she could get, suddenly the behavior of her friend, guide and advisor, Linda Tripp, changed completely and inexplicably. From the beginning of October, she became hostile and argumentative, and, far from encouraging Monica to keep trying to return to the White House, argued forcefully that she should not. Monica, she now said, should move from Washington, and the President should find her a job elsewhere. Monica was bewildered and deeply hurt by this change in one whom she believed a close friend.

On the morning of October 6, Monica was at her desk at the Pentagon when Tripp, who was at home that day, called her with a piece of news that literally stunned her. Tripp said she had spoken the previous evening with her friend Kate Friedrich, Special Assistant to the National Security Advisor. During their chat, Friedrich had said that she had heard startling rumors about Monica Lewinsky. Apparently, there was a permanent black mark against her name, which meant that she was never going to be allowed to work at the White House again. Monica was now persona non grata, and the best advice Friedrich could offer her was "to get out of town."

Monica was devastated. She wept and began to hyperventilate, becoming so distressed that she had to leave work early. "It was one of the most painful days of my life," she remembers. Tripp's call finally tipped the balance: by turns miserable and angry, Monica decided once and for all to make a new start in New York.

During the course of that day, she had several conversations with Tripp, during which they chewed over the implications of Friedrich's information. In fact, though, Tripp's account of the fateful phone call was a lie.

Kate Friedrich did indeed speak to Tripp on the evening of October 5, but she had never, as she emphasized in her subsequent testimony to the Grand Jury, so much as heard of Monica Lewinsky in the context of the White House or of the NSC.

Linda Tripp's lie was yet another strand in the web of deceit she was spinning around Monica. In truth, Tripp was now involved in a conspiracy to snare the girl she had befriended and thereby, it was hoped, entrap the President. For on that day she secretly met with *Newsweek*'s Michael Isikoff and Lucianne and Jonah Goldberg at Jonah's Washington home. Her betrayal of Monica was about to take on a new and more explosive dimension as the unlikely quartet plotted and schemed.

Tripp's treachery began in earnest after she had warned Monica in August that she intended to write a "tell-all" book about Clinton and his women. In September, she had again contacted Lucianne Goldberg, and had expressed her concern that, because of her connection with Kathleen Willey, she might be forced to testify in the Paula Jones case; she was worried that, given hostility shown to her previously by Bob Bennett, the President's attorney, no one would believe her. They also discussed Isikoff's approaches to Tripp that summer regarding Willey, as well as the fact that he wanted to talk to her further about Monica Lewinsky, although at that time he apparently did not know the "young intern's" name.

Linda Tripp claimed she faced a serious dilemma. If she was subpoenaed in the Jones case, she feared she would be asked if she knew of other women who had had sexual relations with Clinton. She did not wish to perjure herself, but she was scared that if she told the truth—that she did indeed know of such a woman—she would lose her $80,000-a-year job and face another attack on her integrity from Bennett.

Hearing all this, Goldberg, according to her FBI deposition, suggested that Tripp record her conversations with Monica Lewinsky, so that she would have independent corroboration of her story (although Tripp denies receiving such advice from her). The secret, and probably illegal, recordings, made with a $100 tape recorder Tripp bought from Radio Shack, were to be her proof and her protection. In reality, however, Tripp was the architect of her own dilemma; the only protection she required was from herself and her actions.

This particular well had originally been poisoned in early 1997, thanks to a tip-off to Paula Jones's attorneys about Kathleen Willey and her allegations of sexual harassment by the President. Tripp, a longtime friend of Willey, was the suspected source. Whether or not she actually was, it was undoubtedly Tripp who had confirmed, on the record, *Newsweek*'s story about Willey, and it was also she who, in March 1997, had originally hinted to Isikoff about Monica's affair with Clinton. Tripp had deliberately avoided meeting Bob Bennett, even though she was a political appointee and could not therefore claim disinterest where the President was concerned. And, according to Jonah Goldberg, it was Tripp who, in October, anonymously alerted Paula Jones's lawyers to the existence of Monica Lewinsky.

On October 3, 1997, Tripp, began secretly to tape her friend's calls—an illegal act in the state of Maryland, where Tripp lives—so that she would have independent evidence of events, some of which she herself had helped to set in motion. Both she and Lucianne Goldberg insist that the recordings were made for Tripp's protection, and not as means of providing material for a "tell-all" book—in other words, she was not acting as an agent provocateur.

If her story is taken at face value, Tripp was taping Monica Lewinsky solely in order to provide corroborative evidence if she were asked to testify in the Paula Jones case. Even in that eventuality, the tapes would be used only if her testimony were challenged by Clinton's lawyers, and for no other reason. Until then, the recordings should have remained strictly confidential, their content not to be revealed except as a last resort, and then only in a courtroom.

As with her story about Kate Friedrich's phone call, however, Linda Tripp's reasons for taping her friend's calls were clearly bogus. If she had been sincere about not using the illicit tape recordings unless she had to testify in the Paula Jones case, she would have kept their contents confidential. Yet within hours of having started to record them, she was telling Lucianne Goldberg about her chats with Monica. On Sunday, October 5, for example, after she and Monica had joked briefly about the President's supposed drug-taking—which had no relevance to the Jones case—Tripp reported the conversation to an excited Goldberg. She also ascribed to Monica comments she herself had made about the President, trying to make it seem that he was indeed taking drugs. In fact, exaggeration and embellishment were to become the hallmarks of her modus operandi, not just with the Goldbergs and Isikoff, but also later with the FBI and the Office of the Independent Counsel.

Furthermore, although this did not become clear until much later, Linda Tripp did indeed intend to write a "tell-all" book and, despite the assurances she had given her friend, it would contain details of Monica's affair with the President. For her own reasons, Lucianne Goldberg secretly recorded conversations she had in September with Tripp, in which the latter talked about writing down "dates, times and phone calls" relating to an affair between the President and a "young friend of mine . . . This is so much more explosive, it makes the other little thing [the Kathleen Willey story], you know, pale." In answer, Goldberg, who had become increasingly interested as the conversation progressed, suggested that Tripp make a deal with Isikoff, the aim being for *Newsweek* to publish an article by him as advance publicity for Tripp's book. In her Grand Jury testimony, Tripp denied that she had had any intention of "putting Monica in a book," something to which the transcripts of Goldberg's secret tapes give the lie.

It is significant that there is no record of Tripp's conversation with Kate Friedrich, nor of her call to Monica during which she passed on Friedrich's "information." The skeptical may be forgiven for thinking that the reason there is no record of either call is because they would clearly demonstrate Tripp's duplicity. The omission of key conversations between Tripp and Lewinsky was to become more important in the coming months.

What Tripp reported from her conversations with Monica did not long remain at the level of idle tittle-tattle. Three days after she began taping, she, Isikoff, and the Goldbergs held their meeting at Jonah Goldberg's Washington apartment—it was on that very day that Tripp had told Monica the cock-and-bull story about her being blacklisted by the White House. Tripp brought with her to the meeting two tapes which she intended to play to Isikoff.

Undoubtedly there had been discussion before this summit meeting, a conference deemed important enough for Lucianne Goldberg to fly down from New York. Indeed, Isikoff—who used the code name "Harvey" in his dealings with Tripp—has admitted that he spoke to Tripp about Monica Lewinsky beforehand. This affirmation is critical, because it provides evidence that Tripp already had a sense of what Isikoff needed *before* she spun Monica the yarn about being banned from the White House.

In her previous discussions with Lucianne Goldberg, Tripp had rejected as too "sleazy" the agent's suggestion that she sell her story to the tabloid media. She wanted to retain her credibility by seeing the story published in *Newsweek*. But, as Isikoff had made clear time and again, his magazine would not print a mere sex story. It had to have an ingredient of public importance, an angle that would link it to matters of legal, political or constitutional consequence. The Paula Jones case was a perfect fit.

If, as seemed likely, Monica was not going to get a job—any job—at the White House, wouldn't it make a better story if the President got his girlfriend a government job in New York at a higher salary? That would dovetail nicely with the central charge in the Paula Jones case: that Clinton harassed women employees for sex in return for job benefits. Jones's lawyers would be able to argue that, just as Jones had allegedly suffered because she spurned his advances, Monica Lewinsky prospered by accepting them. This, of course, begs the question whether Jones's lawyers, who later claimed that during October they received three separate anonymous phone calls from a woman about Monica Lewinsky, were involved in discussions at an earlier stage than they have hitherto admitted.

Certainly that scenario explains much about Linda Tripp's behavior in the fall of 1997: her sudden and bewildering about-face with regard to Monica's job prospects at the White House, the false blacklist story, and her hostility towards Monica, something which Monica now sees as Tripp's way of coping with her guilt at her treachery.

At the meeting in Jonah Goldberg's apartment, Isikoff, fearing that he would become part of the process of entrapment if he listened to the tapes, apparently heard a verbal description of their contents. Before he dashed off to appear on a TV show, he again emphasized that the story must be linked to something official, and that it must have more sources. Even so, where Tripp and her three fellow schemers were concerned, everything was beginning to come together: once details of Monica's affair with Clinton came out, Paula Jones's lawyers would have their case, Isikoff his story, Goldberg a liberal President in the dock, and Tripp . . . what would Tripp have?

A book, certainly, although at the time of writing it has yet to materialize. It may be, also, that she was driven by something more—revenge for all those years of slights and insults at school and home, retribution against the White House, which had called her a liar and sidelined her career, and the satisfaction of chastening a girl who represented everything, deep down, she loathed.

For in Linda Tripp's eyes, hadn't Monica Lewinsky committed the greatest sin of all, that of being born on the right side of the tracks? She was young, pretty, well-educated, sexually liberated, and enjoyed the love of sophisticated and well-to-do parents, the support of caring friends, and the patronage of influential movers and shakers. They all needed to be shown who was really in control, and Monica perhaps most of all. During their September discussions about Tripp's book, Goldberg warned her client of the effect her publishing such a book would have on Monica. "This will destroy her," she said, later adding, "You have to be ready to lose her as a friend." Linda Tripp's reply was unequivocal: "Oh, I'm [ready for] that. I have already made this decision."

Whatever Tripp's true motivation, when she pressed the "record" button on her Radio Shack tape machine she began a process of entrapment that would lead to the humbling of a President, and the near-destruction of his lover.

CHAPTER NINE

● ●

"Everyone Gets a Job with a Little Help"

*T*ALL AND VERY IMPOSING, Vernon Jordan is every inch the urbane Washington insider, a lawyer who counts presidents—including Bill Clinton—and potentates among his friends. Everything from his custom-made shirts to his way of speaking exudes class and style. Even self-confessed style-cop Monica Lewinsky was impressed. Indeed, when, on November 5, 1997, she first met Jordan, to discuss her job prospects, she found him more intimidating than the President.

Jordan had first appeared on Monica's radar a month earlier, on that fateful day, October 6, when Linda Tripp had dropped her bombshell about the White House blacklisting her. When the two women subsequently discussed Monica's ambition to move to New York, Jordan's name came up as a Mr. Fix-It who, besides being a partner at the Washington law firm of Akin, Gump, Strauss, Hauer & Feld, sat on the board of numerous big-shot companies.

At that time, Monica was still confiding constantly in Tripp, and the latter was still playing the part of the concerned and supportive friend. "I want you with a life," she told Monica, urging her to leave Washington. She encouraged her to demand that the President find her a job that paid better than her Pentagon one, ridiculing her friend's aim of $60,000 a year as way too low. When, in a note to the President, Monica suggested that she would accept a government job with a G12 or G13 rating—junior level—Tripp told her that she could do much better.

Monica wanted two things from the President, an apology and a job. He ought to "acknowledge that he helped fuck up my life," she told Tripp during a phone conversation. "If I ever want to have an affair with a married man again, especially if he's the President, shoot me."

Besides confiding in Tripp, Monica's first instinct when she was told that she would never work at the White House was to call Betty Currie and demand to speak to the President. Unfortunately, he was hosting a dinner for the President of Israel and was unable to take her call. So, with Tripp's approval, she wrote him a note, one of a series she sent him that fall expressing her anger and unhappiness and the hopes she had had for their relationship, which had promised so much but delivered so little. In the note, she said it was now clear that there was no way she was coming back to the White House in the near future, and asked to see him to discuss her job options. Sadly, she said, "Handsome, you have been distant the past few months and shut me out. I don't know why. Is it that you don't like me any more or are you scared?"

She sent the letter by courier the next day, October 7, and then called Betty Currie to ask when she could see the President. When Currie told her she could offer only the prospect of a phone conversation with him, Monica flipped her lid. "I've had enough of you two," she said furiously. "I never want to speak to you again. You've strung me along for a year and now I'm giving you the easy way out." Currie listened calmly, and later in the afternoon called Monica back and said that he would call her that night. She stressed that if he wanted to see Monica in person Currie herself would come to the White House, however late, to clear the girl into the building.

"I didn't know if he was going to call," Monica remembers. "It was real do or die. Even before the relationship was over I would always go to sleep not knowing if he would call. I would wake up all the time and look at the clock and sometimes I would start to cry. It was so torturous. It wasn't his fault; he never had any idea how much pain I was in. I was such a glutton for punishment—it's scary not being clear-headed enough or having the strength to get out of an emotional situation."

For once the President did call, at two-thirty in the morning of October 10. Even at that time of night she wanted to dash over to the White House to see him, but he turned her down, saying it was just too late that evening. "You don't always get your own way, so don't go getting angry with me." That was the prelude to the fiercest and longest argument of their affair, a ninety-minute "huge screaming match," as Monica puts it. "He got so mad at me he must have turned purple."

She cried, he yelled at her, dismissing her complaints about her job and arguing that her time at the Pentagon had been a good experience for her. Worse still, during the shouting match he told her, "If I'd known what kind of person you are, I would never have gotten involved with you." For Monica, that was the most wounding thing he had ever said. "It really hurt," she recalls.

At one point she told him that when she found out that she was going to be transferred to the Pentagon in April 1996, she had desperately wanted him to intervene so that she could stay. But, she said, "I didn't want to put you in that position. I knew the election was more important.

If there was trouble I just needed to be patient so I never asked. I was a good girl and I believed your promise." Her remark cut little ice. The President snorted and again hit back hard: "If I'd known it was going to be this much trouble, I would have stopped it in the first place."

Then, speaking in a loud whisper, as he always did when he was angry, he continued, "All I think about is you and your job. I'm obsessed with you and finding you a job. I wake up in the morning and it makes me sick thinking about it. My life is empty except for you and this job search. All I have is my work and this obsession. I'm on your team." Monica took these surprising sentiments to mean that he was on her side in her quest for a job at the White House, and that it was not his fault that it had not come to fruition. In the usual rhythm of their conversations, once they had vented their frustrations they both calmed down. Moreover, before he hung up—at four in the morning—the President agreed that he would help her find a job in New York.

Since that day, Saturday, October 11, 1997, was the Clinton's twenty-second wedding anniversary, Monica was surprised to receive a call from Betty Currie asking her to go over to the White House. As it was still only about eight-thirty in the morning, she immediately postponed her plans to meet her brother in New York, and went to see the President, arriving a little after nine-thirty. She was shown into the Oval Office, to find that calm had returned after the storm: the President said rather sheepishly that when he got off the phone he had realized that he didn't know what she wanted to do.

Monica, who stood across from him at the dining-room table, told him that she wanted to move to New York, where her mother now lived, and, since the Watergate apartment was to be sold, she would have to move out of it before the end of October. This was not strictly true but, given her experience of his dilatoriness in finding her a job at the White House, she didn't want this to turn into a long-term project. She went on to mention that she would need a job reference from someone in the White House, and then outlined various employment possibilities—the United Nations, or else maybe his friend Vernon Jordan could help her find something in the private sector. "Good idea," replied the President to the latter suggestion (which had in fact arisen only a few days earlier from Monica's conversation with Tripp).

It was a light-hearted meeting, the President smiling affectionately at her as she talked about her career ambitions. When she finished her spiel she noticed that he was beaming at her, and asked, "What's so funny?" "Nothing," he replied, "I'm just happy to see you. Come over and let me give you a hug." As Monica remarks, somewhat ruefully, "This was part of the relationship that people never focus on. It was very tactile, very warm and very affectionate. He was always tender and loving and there was always a chemistry between us, even at the end." Before she left, the President, who was due to visit South America the following week, asked her to send over a "wish list" of jobs so that he could study it when he returned.

Monica left the White House wrapped in a warm glow of love and affection for her "Handsome," and when she eventually arrived in New York later that day she pottered around the flea markets looking for a Christmas present for him. Knowing that he collected White House memorabilia, she was delighted to find, for just $10, an antique glass paperweight with a painting of the building. Then her generosity overcame her budget, and she splashed out on an expensive antique cigar stand for him as well.

That weekend, as she considered her options, she realized that she did not want to work at the United Nations; it would be too much like the Pentagon. When she sent the President her wish list of jobs, therefore, she made it clear that she had changed her mind about the UN, instead emphasizing her interest in jobs in public relations, where she would feel "challenged, engaged and interested."

She was too late. For once, the President had already gone into action, telling Betty Currie that he could place Monica in the United Nations "like *that*." During the South American trip the Deputy Chief of Staff, John Podesta, who had previously been involved with Monica's request to return to the White House, spoke briefly to the US Ambassador to the UN, Bill Richardson, about possibly finding an "entry-level" job at the UN in New York for a friend of Betty Currie.

So Monica was alarmed to receive, one weekend in late October, a call from a woman who told her, "Please hold for Ambassador Richardson." Then, she recalls, this "jolly guy" came on the line. "Hi, Bill Richardson here," said a friendly voice. "I understand you want to come and work for me." After talking for some minutes they arranged to meet on October 31; then, puzzled and rather annoyed, Monica called Betty Currie and said that she needed to talk to the President about this latest twist in the job saga, worried that he would try to railroad her into working at the UN.

He did call her, and for once there were no harsh words or hysterics. According to Monica, they enjoyed a "sweet" conversation, during which she told him that she didn't want to work at the UN. "I want you to have options," he said in answer to this. "Bill Richardson's a great guy." Then, referring to his promise to talk to Jordan, he added, "Vernon's out of town but I'm gonna talk to him soon."

Then they started swapping dirty jokes—a Lewinsky specialty—mainly on a Jewish theme. One of Monica's ran, "Why do Jewish men like to watch porno films backwards? So that they can see the hooker give back the money." The President responded in kind: "What do you get when you cross a Jewish-American Princess with an Apple? A computer that won't go down on you." They also laughed about the latest batch of raunchy e-mail jokes she had sent him. As they were signing off, she said, "I love you." Then, realizing that this was too serious a comment in a light-hearted conversation, she added quickly, "Butthead!"

Monica did not speak to the President again until October 30, the night before her interview with Ambassador Richardson. As the big day approached, she became increasingly nervous, so asked Betty Currie if the President would call her to "prep her" on the correct approach for the interview. He responded to her appeal, telling her that she was going to be "just great," and soothing her fears that the White House staff who believed her to be a "stalker" would give the Ambassador a misleading impression of her worth.

As they finished their chat she asked if he was going to wear a Halloween pin she had sent him, and he promised her that he would. So she was delighted when next day, in a speech during a visit to a school, he made a point of saying that he had been relegated to just a tiny pin for his Halloween costume. One youngster asked if he could have it, but the President refused: "A friend of mine gave it to me."

Monica's pre-interview nerves had been aggravated, however, by a "bizarre" conversation with Linda Tripp, during which the latter became furious when Monica said she was due to meet the Ambassador at his suite in the Watergate complex. "Over my dead body will you go to that hotel room. They are trying to set you up," said Tripp, a paragon of protective concern. She repeatedly insisted that Monica should ask for the interview to be held in the hotel's dining room, in order to forestall a potentially compromising situation.

Monica thought her friend's insistence rather extreme, but did not question her motive. In fact, Tripp's insistence was part of an attempt, devised with Michael Isikoff, to compromise both Monica and the President. Isikoff had arranged for another *Newsweek* reporter to sit in the dining room, pretending to be just one more guest. The reporter would see Monica and Richardson together, thus verifying Tripp's contention that the President was misusing his position to secure a government job for his girlfriend.

It was around this time, too, that Paula Jones's lawyers received several anonymous phone calls from a woman, believed to be Linda Tripp, saying that they should subpoena both Monica and Tripp. The Jones legal team was in a much stronger position in October, having earlier that month won two crucial judgments under which they secured the right to ask the President for information about his "sexual relations" with other women, and to name any person with discoverable information.

Blithely ignorant both of these legal developments and of Tripp's Machiavellian scheming, Monica was worried that her only option at this point was a job at the United Nations. Her interview had gone well, and a few days after meeting the Ambassador she was offered a junior post with the US delegation to the UN.

Still concerned that she had not yet met with Vernon Jordan, she sent a "hurry-up" note to Betty Currie, expressing her misgivings about the UN job and her desire to meet Clinton's Mr. Fix-It. Currie called Monica and told her to phone Jordan's secretary and arrange a meeting. Monica did as she was asked, and an interview with Jordan was duly scheduled for November 5.

Before she met him, all Monica knew about the President's lawyer friend was that he played a lot of golf with Clinton, was prominent in the African-American community and, most importantly, had a reputation as a "can-do" individual. Much later, she discovered that one of his close friends was Peter Straus, Monica's future stepfather, whom he had known for over twenty years.

Monica was nervous, not to say a little scared, about meeting the attorney, and at first found his stern gaze and taciturn manner intimidating. He asked her why she was there to see him, and she launched into the "vanilla" story once more, telling him that she wanted to leave Washington, and explaining that she had wanted to get back to the White House, but that senior staffers, notably Evelyn Lieberman, were hostile to her. "Oh, she doesn't like me, either—don't worry about that," Jordan said with a smile. Then, after they had talked for some twenty minutes, he announced, "Well, we're in business. I'm going to help you get a job in New York," adding cryptically, "You come highly recommended." It was a comment that Monica interpreted as a reference to previous conversations he had had with the President. They agreed to meet again in two weeks.

The following day Monica wrote Jordan a thank-you note saying, "It made me happy to know that our friend has such a wonderful confidant in you." While Monica was much impressed by the charismatic Washington lawyer—she told Catherine Allday Davis that she had never met such a "real person in all her life"—Jordan was apparently less taken with her. Indeed, he later told the Grand Jury that he did not recall meeting her at that time, a memory lapse that Independent Counsel Kenneth Starr ascribed to the "low priority" Jordan attached to Monica's job search. This contention helped Starr's case against the President by suggesting that Jordan only became interested in helping Monica *after* she was served with an affidavit in the *Jones v. Clinton* case. Yet while Starr has focused exclusively on Vernon Jordan's role in obtaining Monica a job, in reality he was just one weapon in her armory, only becoming involved in the first place at her own suggestion.

There were many others riding out in the quest for a job for Monica. Most prominent among these was Marcia Lewis, who, since she had moved to New York in September, had constantly urged Monica to join her, extolling the virtues of the Big Apple. So there was understandable celebration at her mother's Fifth Avenue apartment when, in October, Monica made her momentous decision that enough was enough.

Once Monica had made her mind up, her mother needed no further bidding to take steps to ensure that there was no backsliding. She lobbied friends in the city to see if they knew of any possible openings, and contacted a career counselor, Marilyn Ullman, to help in the job search. Monica duly met with Ullman in early October (the same weekend she bought the President's White House paperweight). She had learned a harsh lesson over the last year. No longer was she going to rely on other people's goodwill, not even the President's. She discussed with her contacts in Washington and the Pentagon correspondent at NBC the possibility of working full-time in the media. She even applied for a job working with broadcaster Connie Chung, although she was unsuccessful because the post had been filled internally.

During this process her mother constantly encouraged her, realizing that every step that Monica took on her own was a stride away from Washington and the President. Remembering that time, Marcia reflects, "Her decision to willingly move away from Washington was, as far as I was concerned, a victory. It meant that she was letting go of this fascination for him, coming to terms that it was a self-destructive, going-nowhere relationship."

Besides putting Monica in touch with Marilyn Ullman, Marcia asked her fiancé, Peter Straus, if he would help. Later that fall, Straus spoke independently to his old friend Vernon Jordan, and also sounded out other people in his social circle, notably Edgar Bronfman, chairman of the liquor giant Seagram. "I called a bunch of people we know," Straus remembers, "to say, 'Have you got a place for a bright young intern who wants to get away from the White House?'" He stresses that each year his friend Vernon Jordan regularly places a couple of dozen ambitious young people into private-sector jobs, although Straus concedes that, where Monica was concerned, his own friendship with Jordan and the President's influence would have encouraged the attorney to go the extra mile.

Indeed, Monica's circle felt that presidential help on her behalf was no more than she deserved. Since she had lost her job at the White House because of her affair with the President, it was only just that, after a year of giving her the runaround, he should do the decent thing and help find her another position. "We all thought that it was fair and reasonable that the President would help her find a job," her Aunt Debra remarks. "So when he started putting in some effort to make things right for her we thought that was terrific." It is a view echoed time and time again by her friends. "I was so happy when she decided to get out of Washington away from that scene," says Catherine Allday Davis. "I didn't think it was a big deal that the President would help her find a job: everyone gets a job with a little help."

It was not only Monica's friends and family who favored her move to New York. Linda Tripp, too, argued strongly that she should leave Washington. Although the knowledge that Tripp was the source of the leak about Kathleen Willey, and the sudden change in Tripp's behavior, had made Monica uneasy, she still trusted her and confided in her. With hindsight, perhaps Monica should by now have begun to question the true nature of Tripp's friendship, but the loyalty that is one of Monica's key characteristics would not allow her to do so.

She took it as just another an act of friendship when Tripp suggested using a cheaper and more efficient courier service to deliver her packages for the President to Betty Currie at the White House. Once again, though, Tripp was concealing malevolence behind her smile. The recommended service was owned by the Goldberg family, who later supplied Michael Isikoff with receipts and other documentation as tangible evidence of Monica's closeness to the President.

However, there were other straws in the wind which did alarm Monica. She and Tripp had begun to have frequent fights, which the latter seemed to trigger deliberately, then flying into a towering rage. Monica was sometimes frightened of her and of what she might do. "I could see at this point that she was quite a vindictive person," she remembers, "so I started to kiss her ass because I was worried that she might go public about the relationship. What really concerned me was that if that happened, then the President would know I had told someone about our love affair."

As she mused on this thorny problem, she began to make "worst-case" contingency plans in her own mind. If Tripp did go public, Monica decided, she would call a press conference and categorically deny Tripp's allegations. If need be, she would even say that she herself had made up the whole story about an affair with Clinton, and would accept the resulting public ridicule and humiliation.

During the year Tripp, with Monica's encouragement, had gone on a long-term diet that had proved so successful that her weight was now at a point where she could fit into some of Monica's larger dresses. As a result, and by way of a congratulatory gesture, in September Monica had invited Tripp to her Watergate apartment to choose clothes from what she calls her "fat closet." As they went through her wardrobe, picking out suitable clothes, Monica had showed her friend the now notorious semen-stained blue dress.

Far from having kept the dress as a trophy—or as evidence—as has sometimes been suggested, she had not worn it since February because she could not. Monica's weight has always fluctuated widely, and when she next tried the dress on she found that it did not button up properly.

Being both a carelessly untidy young woman and one who has to keep a strict eye on her budget, she had seen no reason to have it cleaned immediately: doing so when she couldn't wear it would be a waste of money. By November, however, she had lost enough weight for the dress to fit her again, and she decided to wear it for a Thanksgiving dinner in San Francisco with her father's side of the family. Monica was—and is—always worried about what she should wear, particularly so in this case, as all her cousins are slim. The blue Gap dress was both slimming and attractive, and she therefore decided to send it to the cleaners.

She then made one of the biggest blunders of her life. On 16 November, she told Linda Tripp about her plans. The latter, knowing that one day the dress might be a vital piece of corroborating evidence, desperately tried to get her to change her mind. Their conversation, which Tripp recorded, reveals how she manipulated, even entrapped, Monica into incriminating the President. Tripp strongly, even vehemently, cautioned Monica to leave the dress alone, telling her, "Now, all I would say to you is, you have a very long life ahead of you and I don't know what's going to happen to you. Neither do you. I would rather you had that in your possession if you need it years from now."

She went on to say that she had a cousin with a background in genetic fingerprinting who had told her that DNA samples can be matched simply by removing a sample of dry semen using a wetted Q-Tip. Not surprisingly, this "cousin" was nothing of the sort. He was Mark Fuhrman, the detective stigmatized for racism in the O.J. Simpson trial in 1995, who was now a client of Lucianne Goldberg. Faced with the prospect of losing such valuable evidence, Tripp urgently advised Monica, for her own protection, to save the dress in a plastic bag and keep it with her "treasures". When the girl seemed baffled as to why she should do so, Tripp remarked ominously, "It's just this nagging, awful feeling I have in the back of my head."

Since Monica had no intention of keeping the dress as a souvenir—all she wanted to do was wear it—she was not wholly convinced. Tripp therefore changed tack. When the two women talked later at the office, she again derided Monica's plans to wear the dress, but this time argued that she thought Monica looked really fat in the dress, and suggested she wear something else. This tactic was more successful. Monica, ever anxious about her figure, decided to take her friend's advice and leave the dress in her closet.

The matter did not rest there, however. At around that time, Monica had one of her more bizarre conversations with Tripp. As they chatted in the office, the latter, complaining that she was short of money, said she had decided to sell some of her old clothes to raise cash. She claimed that a friend wanted to buy the very suit she was wearing that day, and asked if she could go to Monica's Watergate apartment to borrow a sweater and skirt to wear instead. Monica offered to go with her, but Tripp would have none of it, saying that she would go alone to save her friend any trouble. Monica demurred at this, but Tripp became ever more insistent, accusing her of a lack of trust when Monica said that she felt uncomfortable about letting anyone into her apartment without her being present. In the end, Tripp haughtily dropped her demands and Monica, rather bemused, resumed her work.

She only realized Tripp's ulterior motive after the scandal broke, when *Newsweek* reported that Tripp and Goldberg had "jokingly" planned to steal the semen-stained dress from her apartment, to use it as evidence of the affair. Monica, unsurprisingly, doesn't find the "joke" funny: "The episode with the dress is one of the most humiliating aspects of the whole scandal. It is just so embarrassing."

While Tripp's treachery is now obvious, one question remains unresolved and largely unexplored; namely, how far were Tripp's actions motivated by her relationship with the right-wing Goldberg and with *Newsweek* reporter Isikoff, as well as by their links to the Paula Jones people, funded by wealthy anti-Clinton organizations? Ostensibly she was taping Monica in case she herself were accused of lying by Bob Bennett if—and only if—she were called as a witness in the Jones case.

Yet she did more than illicitly tape her friend. Was the fuss over Monica's meeting with Ambassador Richardson, the courier receipts, and the attempts to purloin her stained dress part of a larger picture? Was it merely coincidental that this process independently tried to demonstrate the contention of Paula Jones's lawyers that Clinton was offering jobs for sex—and that it suited the "public importance" element required by Isikoff?

By chance, Tripp was staying overnight at Monica's apartment on November 12 when the President called. After the scandal broke she yet again gave a less than honest version of events. She implied that she had been sitting with Monica that night when the call came through, and so had heard her friend's side of the conversation. In fact, according to Monica, she was asleep in the next room and did not hear a word.

Earlier that week Monica, anxious about the outcome of her interview with Vernon Jordan and worried that this project, like her job at the White House, might take forever, had left the President a message and asked him to call. Her anxiety was heightened by the fact that, all the while, Linda Tripp was feeding her sense of anger and injustice, encouraging her to push for more and more. At this time, she veered wildly between her desire to leave Washington, and an aching sense of loss at the thought of not seeing the President again, compounded by her disappointment at being barred from working at the White House.

Two days before the President called, Monica had sent him a note in which she asked to see him on Veterans Day, November 11, and aired these wider concerns. She added a plea for his attention: "I asked you three weeks ago to please be sensitive to what I am going through right now and keep in contact with me, and yet I'm still left writing notes in vain. I am not a moron. I know that what is going on in the world takes precedence but I don't think what I have asked you for is unreasonable . . . This is so hard for me, I am trying to deal with so much emotionally, and I have nobody to talk to about it. I need you right now not as President, but as a man, PLEASE be my friend."

The President was, indeed, friendly during that late-night chat. He told her that Nancy Hernreich, Director of Oval Office Operations, was due to testify about campaign finances on Capitol Hill the following day. With her out of the way, Monica could visit him. He also asked if she could get him some herbal medicine, which Betty Currie had forgotten to buy.

The day of the hoped-for meeting was a classic example of a communications mix-up. As expected, Hernreich was away from the White House, leaving the way clear for Monica to visit without any eyebrows being raised. So she called Betty Currie, as requested, to arrange an appropriate time, since she also had to juggle her day at the Pentagon. Betty kept putting her off, saying that the President was playing golf and that she had not had time to talk to him.

Monica had got not only the medicine he had asked for, but some zinc lozenges. It was not the first time she had given him such sweets. On one occasion she had sent him some "memory pills" that were jelly beans. She wrote a prescription: "Take one pill to remember how happy you are when you see me. Take one pill to remember how adorable I am," and so on. In the afternoon she dropped off the herbal remedies at the White House, leaving them with Betty. As the day wore on, however, she became increasingly upset and resentful at the apparent prevarication.

At last, in the early evening a contrite Betty Currie called and, saying that the President was mad at her because she had failed to arrange Monica's visit, told her to come over to the White House immediately. Given the increasingly clandestine nature of these meetings, Monica's arrival at the White House was like a scene from a B movie. Betty had suggested that the girl should wait in her, Betty's, car in the White House parking lot, but when Monica got there the car was locked. She therefore waited by the car in the rain, her hat pulled down over her face, until Betty eventually appeared and sneaked her into the White House. Anxious not to be seen by anyone hostile to Monica, they raced through the corridors so fast that they were breathless when they arrived at the President's back study. Then, because Betty didn't want anyone to ask who was in the back study, Monica had to wait there with the lights off.

While she waited for the President she fumbled around in the gloom, idly trying to open desk drawers, which were locked. She did notice that a bag containing her gifts to him, which, on an earlier occasion, she had been distressed to see had just been casually left there, had now gone.

Since Betty had not informed the President that Monica was in the back study, he continued working in the Oval Office. As a result he saw her only for a brief chat before he had to leave to attend an official dinner for President Ernesto Zedillo of Mexico. She was able to give him the antique White House paperweight, and then joked about the beneficial effect of chewing Altoid mints before performing oral sex. They managed a brief kiss before he departed.

It was a disappointing end to a day that had combined delicious anticipation, furious disappointment, and a large measure of farce, and Monica was rather crestfallen. She felt that, now she had removed from the President the burden of finding her a job at the White House, he should spend a little more time with her as a friend and former lover. In one draft letter, typed on her computer at the Pentagon, she spoke of her depression. "I don't want you to think that I am not grateful for what you are doing for me now—I'd probably be in a mental institute without it—but I am consumed with this disappointment, frustration and anger." Then, reflecting on their all-too-brief meeting, she continued "All you . . . ever have to do to pacify me is to see me and hold me. Maybe that's asking too much."

Her experience had taught her that physical proximity was the key to maintaining their relationship, and to this end she decided that, rather than send yet another letter, she would speak onto a tape and send him the cassette. She wanted not only to express how she felt, but also to propose a plan as to how he could see her without attracting suspicion. She even suggested a night at the movies in the White House theater so that they could just "hang out and have some fun."

Monica recorded two versions, and on November 20 played both over the phone to Linda Tripp, who of course taped her lovestruck friend's every word. As she listened to the tape, Tripp remarked that Monica had a voice like a "little Marilyn Monroe vixen," so it was no wonder the President enjoyed phone sex with her. Like so many of Tripp's comments, this remark was not part of the ebb and flow of the conversation, but seemed to be introduced to prove to a third party the true nature of Monica's relationship with the President.

Early in the morning of the following day, Friday, November 21, Monica sent the package containing her taped message by courier to Betty Currie, eagerly anticipating the President's response. Remembering the mix-up of the previous week, she urged Betty to give it to him promptly. Throughout the day Monica called, each time becoming more and more frustrated and tearful because the President had not yet received her private message. Finally, at seven in the evening, he got her package, but told Betty to tell Monica that he had too much work to do and couldn't see her that evening.

In the meantime, however, Monica had found out from talking to the President's steward, Bayani Nelvis, that he was watching a movie with Erskine Bowles—exactly what she had suggested, albeit without the Chief of Staff present, in her taped message. Livid and almost hysterical with rage, Monica called Betty and told her not to let him open the package containing the tape. Between sobs, she told his secretary, "I can't take this anymore"; then she slammed down the phone. Later that evening, a concerned Betty called back to make sure Monica was calmer. But her concern did little to placate the furious girl, who told her, "I'm telling my parents tomorrow. I want nothing to do with you guys. I cannot deal with this anymore. Thanks for the times when you have been nice to me and for the times you haven't."

Her remarks were as untrue as they were mean, for Monica did not for a moment intend to speak to her parents; in any case, Marcia already knew, and had kept silent. Monica simply felt that the President had taken such advantage of her that she wanted to hurt him in return, to make him understand how their affair was affecting her life. She had made much the same point in a short conversation with Andy Bleiler the previous month, during which she had reminded him that she was still around and that she still hurt.

In between her calls to Betty, she phoned Linda Tripp for comfort and consolation. Tripp, naturally, taped every sobbing, sorry word. Monica observed later, "The fact that this conversation of me whimpering down the phone was broadcast for the world to gloat over was one of the most violating and humiliating experiences of this whole nightmare."

Later that night Monica phoned Tripp again to tell her that she was going to apologize to Betty for her earlier behavior. She was completely taken aback by the other woman's extraordinary response. Tripp told her that the White House would think she was crazy if she called and that she, Tripp, was sick of dealing with the situation. She then delivered an ultimatum: if Monica apologized to Betty Currie, Tripp would never speak to her again. With that she slammed the phone down.

Monica was now faced with a cruel dilemma, for whatever course she chose she would lose a friend. In the end, she decided to do the proper thing and make it up with Currie. Betty accepted her apology and promised that she would try to get the President, who would then be visiting Vancouver, to call her over Thanksgiving (he did not).

Having placated Betty, that Friday Monica tried to soothe Tripp, and once again they got into a fight. Significantly, this stream of bitter exchanges over the phone was not recorded or, if it was, the tapes were destroyed. Finally Tripp, deciding that she did not wish to speak to Monica anymore, left the answering machine to record the girl's frantic messages. Their fight continued the following Monday at work with a series of office e-mails, in which Monica told Tripp that if she wished to end their friendship that was up to her, but that she had no right to be angry because Monica chose not to do what Tripp wanted. They did not speak again until early December. Reflecting on her erstwhile friend's behavior, Monica says, "Even though she was taping me, I think the reason why she put the phone down was because she is very short-tempered and just flipped out when I would not do what she wanted. She wanted to pull the strings and when the puppet wouldn't dance she couldn't handle it."

When Monica left for the West Coast to celebrate Thanksgiving with her family, she had burned most of her bridges in Washington. Not only had she fallen out with Linda Tripp, but she had decided to turn down the job at the UN, and had handed in her notice at the Pentagon. She was scheduled to leave the city that had broken her heart on December 24. In New York her mother was already making plans to find her an apartment, even lining up a potential roommate, so Monica's most pressing worry was not somewhere to live, but the fact that she still hadn't found a job. During her visit to the West Coast, she managed to speak to Vernon Jordan, who was surprised that she was quitting her job. He suggested she call him the following week to arrange another meeting, and promised to put extra effort into finding her a position in New York.

Monica had heard that story too many times, though, and so, leaving nothing to chance, she wrote to the President saying that she wanted to discuss her job prospects as a matter of urgency. The note, which was written in late November just before she flew to Britain and Belgium on her final Pentagon assignment, also emphasized that she hoped to see the President on the first weekend in December. On her return from Europe, she discovered to her dismay that Betty Currie had not been able to give him the letter, and when eventually he did receive it—after much pestering by Monica—he sent back a message saying that he couldn't see her as he had meetings with his lawyers scheduled.

By coincidence, during the flight home from London on December 5, she chatted to Bob Tyrer, the Chief of Staff for the Secretary of Defense. When he told her that he was going to a White House Christmas party that evening, she asked, "Can I be your date?" So a very surprised President Clinton spotted Monica in the receiving line at the party, even, as she recalls, smoothing back his hair as though he was on a date before he greeted her. He gave her a hug and, turning to Tyrer, asked, "Are you taking good care of Monica at the Pentagon?" Yet although he was charming and affable, Monica was still annoyed with him because he could not make time to see her that weekend.

She had spoken in the meantime to Betty Currie, who said she was coming into the White House the next day, Saturday, December 6, to take some visitors on a tour of the building. Betty added that she would try to see if the President could meet Monica first thing in the morning, before his lawyers came in.

It was a forlorn and melancholy Monica who returned home that evening. Her mind was filled with thoughts of what might have been, her sorrow at the end of the affair and her fears about her lack of a job in New York. In addition, the thought of never being alone with the President again, and of never again speaking to him as a man rather than as the President, weighed heavily.

Once back in her apartment, she decided to tell him exactly how she felt, typing a letter on her computer. In a spirit of reflection as well as regret, she tried to express her feelings for him and to capture the essence of their love affair: "It was so sad seeing you tonight because I was so angry with you that you once again rejected me and yet, all I wanted was for everyone else in the room to disappear and for you to hold me."

She went on to say that she loved him with all her heart and wanted nothing more than to be with him all the time, remembering that when he had given her *Leaves of Grass*, it had signified to her that he was in her soul, that she, for her part, felt his pain; now she had to set beside that moment the dismal realization that he no longer wanted her in his life. Self-pityingly, she went on to refer to their 2.30 A.M. fight over the phone, and lamented, "i'm sure you're not the first person to have felt that way about me. i am sorry this has been such a bad experience." She ended the letter with one last dramatic flourish: "i knew it would hurt to say goodbye to you; i just never thought it would have to be on paper. take care."

Monica's mood of quiet melancholy was soon punctured. The next day she phoned Betty Currie and left a message to say that she would meet her at the South West Gate so that she could hand over the letter, further Christmas gifts for the President, and gifts for Currie, and possibly see the President for a time. When Monica arrived at the White House she spotted Marsha Scott, so she quickly tried to call Betty again. The uniformed Secret Service officer on duty there told her that she was giving a tour, and after some time also let slip that the President and his glamorous friend Eleanor Mondale, a high-profile CBS TV reporter, were inside.

So much for meeting with his lawyers. With an immense effort of self-control, Monica said, "OK, I'll just come back later." Then she turned around and walked away, filled with uncontrollable anger: not only had she been deceived, but he was seeing another woman whom she considered to be an arch-rival. She found a pay phone in a nearby bar and called

Betty Currie. When Currie answered, Monica launched into a vicious tirade, which she admits was very wrong of her: "I was out of line—what I said to Betty Currie was wholly inappropriate."

When she got back to her Watergate apartment, she received a plaintive pager message from the President's secretary, and grudgingly responded. Virtually in tears, Betty pleaded with her to calm down, adding that she herself would be fired if the President heard about this. In answer, Monica insisted that she talk to the President but Betty refused, saying that he was talking to the Attorney General, and that in any case Monica could not be allowed to speak to him in the state she was in.

Still shaking with anger and frustration, Monica decided to catch a plane to New York and visit her mother. She quickly packed a bag and took a taxi to the airport, but as soon as she got there she realized she had left her wallet behind. She therefore returned to her apartment, by now in a calmer and more receptive frame of mind. Once there, she decided to call Betty Currie yet again and ask to speak to the President. "I have calmed down now so I would like to speak to him," she said. Betty called her back and then put her through.

Now it was Monica's turn to get a tongue-lashing. In the fifty-six-minute call the President was as furious as she had been. "In my life no one has ever treated me as poorly as I have been treated by you," he said. "Outside of my family and my friends and my staff, I have spent more time with you than anyone else in the world. How dare you make such a scene? It's none of your business who I see."

Monica was having none of it, however. She accused him of having an affair with Eleanor Mondale, to which he retorted, "I am not having an affair with her—it's ridiculous. She is a friend of mine; in fact I set her up with her current boyfriend." Monica riposted by citing the time when, while he was on a trip to California, Mondale had been with him until three-thirty in the morning, and had then gone running with him the next day. "Do you think I would be stupid enough to go running with someone I was foolin' with?" he asked, earning the instant reply, "Do you want me to answer that?"

The President changed tack. "You should not have said those things to Betty," he told her. "You had no right to talk to anyone like that. You demand to see me and then you get angry when I am busy." Monica launched a counter-attack. "Demand to see you?" she spat. "I say I am going to New York to get out of your hair. All I want to do is see you and you don't give me an answer. I don't understand—why is it so hard?"

In bewildered tones, he echoed her question, complaining, "I don't understand—this has become your everything." Then he added, "You told me when this affair started that when it was over you would not give me any trouble." Monica, with extraordinary, if unintentional, prescience, replied, "Trouble? You think I have been trouble? You don't know trouble."

As in all their fights, they eventually turned the corner and calmed down, the President even agreeing that she could come and see him. Needing no second bidding, Monica returned to the White House, arriving at about 1 P.M. She took with her his Christmas gifts, which included the antique cigar holder she had bought in New York, a "Santa Monica" Starbucks coffee mug, and a tie she had found during her recent visit to London. She left her "Farewell, my lovely" letter at home.

When they met, the mood was very different from their fight on the phone. The President was affectionate and open, sitting in his rocking chair and stroking Monica's hair as she sat at his feet. Monica was adoring and winning, expressing many of the sentiments in her letter. They chatted about all manner of topics, including his attractiveness to women. He modestly demurred when Monica told him that millions of women find him good-looking, and went on to tell her about his own battle with weight. When he was a small boy, he said, he had been so heavy that in the annual Easter-egg race he couldn't run as fast as the others, so there had never been any chocolate eggs left when he finished. He added that his problems with weight had continued throughout high school. "It was so sad," recalls Monica. While he managed to resist discussing her ideas on education reform, which she had set out to him in an earlier memo, he did tell her that while he was in Vancouver he had bought her a present, which he would give her nearer Christmas Day, and promised to give her a Christmas kiss as, he said, kisses at Christmas were allowed.

For Monica, this was a breakthrough—the promise of a further meeting, when only the previous night she had thought she would never see him again. As she prepared to leave, the President told her solemnly, "I promise I won't jerk you around like I did before, and I won't abandon you. I will call you and you can come and get your Christmas present." It was an interesting choice of words, admitting his responsibility for her distress and implying that their relationship would continue.

Monica left the White House and, in a haze of mixed emotions, flew to New York to spend the rest of the weekend with her mother. Though still raw about what she felt was the President's deception over her job, she was intuitively aware that here was a man, who, if he would but admit it to himself, was her soul mate. As she wrote in one of her musings on the relationship at this time: "For the life of me I can't understand how you could be so kind and so cruel to me. When I think of all the times you filled my heart and soul with sunshine, and then think of all the times you made me cry for hours and want to die, I feel nauseous."

Later that afternoon, President Clinton learned from his lawyers that Monica's name was on the list of possible witnesses supplied by attorneys acting for Paula Jones in her long-running sexual harassment case against him. It remains a mystery why it took him nearly two weeks to tell her.

Innocently unaware of these developments, a couple of days later Monica sent him a funny card on which was printed: "Nothing would make me happier than seeing you again, except to see you naked with a lottery ticket in one hand and a can of whipped cream in the other." Inside, she added a note saying that she felt bad about their fight and that she wanted to be a source of pleasure rather than pain for him. She also pinpointed the cause of their conflicts—the miscommunication between herself, Betty Currie and the President. Then, as she says, "I threw my two cents in about something that was none of my business—the Paula Jones case."

Concerned as ever to protect her man, Monica suggested that, besides his attorney, Bob Bennett, the President should hire a female lawyer to ridicule Jones's arguments and evidence. She felt a woman's touch would play better than a man's with the American public. Little did she realize that all too soon she herself would be cast, albeit unwillingly, in a central role in this unfolding saga. Her personal emotional drama was about to reach a wide audience, wider even than that same American public.

CHAPTER TEN

●●●●●●●●●●●●●●●●●●●●●●●●●●●●●●●●●●●●●●

Enter Kenneth Starr

*W*ITH A LIGHTED CIGARETTE in her hand and tears brimming in her eyes, Linda Tripp stood with Monica in a back alley outside the Pentagon, braving the early December chill. As she puffed nervously on her Marlboro Light, she uttered the contrite words Monica had longed for weeks to hear: "I'm sorry." "Oh, I'm such a shitty friend," she wailed. "I'm such an awful person that I did that to you. I think of how mean I was. I'm so sorry—I'll never do it again." This meeting, on Monday, December 8, was the first time they had spoken since their late-night quarrel on November 21.

One of the most attractive things about Monica is that she is never mean-spirited. Despite that quarrel, before she had left for the Pentagon mission to Europe, she placed Tripp's birthday present on her chair at work. Inside the carefully wrapped package was an antique bookmark inscribed, ironically, with a sentimental Victorian poem about the virtues of friendship. The contrast between Tripp's "mean" behavior and Monica's generosity is notable.

Monica was due to leave the Pentagon shortly, and there were several matters, besides her personal life, that she wished to resolve before her departure. She was particularly anxious, and with good reason, that her search for a job should not end up in the usual Clinton black hole. During her meeting with the President the previous weekend, he had told her that Vernon Jordan was working on a job for her—a new player, but the same old, old story.

Just to make sure he did not forget her, Monica sent Jordan a baseball cap, a box of chocolates, a short note and a copy of her résumé, as a friendly reminder. It seemed to do the trick. On December 11, she met him at his office, where, over a working lunch of turkey sandwiches and Diet Coke, they discussed her job options. Jordan gave her contact names at three companies—MacAndrews & Forbes (the parent company of Revlon), Young & Rubicam and American Express—that he wanted her to write to, and promised to phone several other business contacts. They discussed the structure of the letter she should write and he asked her to send him a copy.

They talked, too, about their mutual friend—and the reason why Jordan was seeing her in the first place—the President of the United States. Monica said that she saw Bill Clinton more as a man than as a president, and that she treated him like a regular guy and got angry with him if he didn't call or see her enough. For once the urbane Mr. Jordan was taken aback: "Monica, you can't go yelling at the President when he's dealing with Tony Blair [the British Prime Minister] on issues of Iraq. He can't hang up the phone and then have you yelling at him. From now on, when you're mad at him I want you to call me and yell at me, and I'll deal with it." Then he teased her about her behavior, telling her, "Don't deny it: your problem is that you are in love." Monica blushed but said nothing, assuming that Jordan knew more about her relationship than he was saying.

They went on to talk about his friendship with Peter Straus, Jordan even trying to call him there and then to report on Monica's progress. Certainly, after this meeting the wheels rolled, for Jordan called all three of the contacts whose names he had given her. Before long, Monica had lined up interviews for the week before Christmas with New York-based companies, among them American Express and MacAndrews & Forbes.

Yet even as she tried to escape to a new life in New York, the city that had broken her heart was about to crush her spirit. Soon after her meeting with Jordan, she discovered that Linda Tripp had been subpoenaed in the Paula Jones case—in fact, the subpoena had been served on November 24, Tripp's birthday. Although she had discussed the possibility constantly that year, Tripp did not mention the subpoena during their kiss-and-make-up conversation in December; a sign of how much she was keeping from her friend. In fact Monica discovered it more than two weeks after it had been served.

Tripp had always said that she would never tell anybody about Monica's affair with the President, so at first Monica did not worry about that. Instead, her instinctive reaction was concern that Tripp might lose her job if she had to testify. At first, her fears seemed groundless. Tripp told Monica that she was seeing her attorney, Kirbe Behre, who advised her that she could take the Fifth Amendment—that is, decline to say anything in the matter. She even left a message on Monica's answering machine saying, "I talked to Kirbe and don't worry, everything's OK."

The reunited friends went to the concourse at the Pentagon later that week to buy a Christmas present for Behre. As they shopped, Tripp dropped her first bombshell. She told Monica that she had written down the details of her relationship with the President, placed them in a sealed envelope and given them to her attorney to be opened in the event of her death. Monica was horrified. "That was one of the most startling things that had ever come out of her mouth," she recalls. "That really frightened me, and I began to see that this woman was really, really dangerous."

Tripp's second missile soon followed. "You know," she told Monica, "if they ask about you, I'm going to have to tell." Stunned and now very scared, Monica reminded her that she had always promised to keep her friend's trust, even to protect her. Monica added that she thought it was "ludicrous" that anyone would even ask about her. Tripp stood firm, though, and said that if she was asked whether she knew of anyone else who had a relationship with the President, she would have to give that person's name. The reason, she said, was that if she denied, or failed to declare, that she knew of such a person, and Paula Jones's lawyers had independent proof that in fact she did know, she might be charged with perjury and could even face jail.

All this was worrying enough for Monica, but worse was to follow. At around 2.30 A.M. on December 17, she was awakened by the phone. Fumbling for the handset, she heard a familiar voice, her "Handsome." Although used to him calling at strange hours, this time she was startled, for she followed Hillary Clinton's daily movements on the news, and knew that the First Lady was in Washington; the President rarely called when she was around. This must be important; and he sounded concerned and upset.

Without preamble he announced, "I have two things to tell you. Betty's brother has been killed in a car accident." Shocked by this awful news—Mrs. Currie had already lost her sister that year, and her mother was then in the hospital—Monica burst into tears. They talked about Betty for a while, and the President suggested that Monica call her in the morning. Then he unveiled the second piece of bad news. "I saw the witness list today for the Paula Jones case and your name is on it. It broke my heart when I saw your name on the list." The President had originally learned that Monica's name was on the list almost two weeks earlier, on December 6, when it had been faxed to his lawyers but, inexplicably, did not tell Monica.

Although someone whose name is on a witness list is not automatically subpoenaed, Monica was seriously alarmed. But the President played down the risks, saying it was unlikely she would be subpoenaed. Monica asked what she should do if she was subpoenaed, and he told her she could maybe sign an affidavit to avoid testifying. In the unlikely event that she were subpoenaed, he said, she should contact Betty.

Ever ready with a suggestion, even though she knew nothing about the legal technicalities, and very little about the political implications, Monica told him she had read that as Paula Jones had reduced her claim to $500,000 he should end the case by making a statement that he was tired of spending the energy on the case and that it was taking a toll on his family. (In the event, although he admitted no guilt, he settled with Jones in January 1999, paying her $850,000)

At the end of their forty-minute conversation he said that if she wanted to come for her Christmas gift, he could arrange for Betty to come into the White House. However, Monica turned down the date with a mild reprimand: "Don't you dare bother Betty this weekend when she is grieving."

Feeling physically sick, Monica burst into tears the moment she hung up. "The President is not very good at giving bad news," she says. "It was straight from the shoulder and I was really freaked out. I was scared, I was nervous—I didn't know then, but this was the start of my waking nightmare."

Unable to get back to sleep, she badly needed to talk to someone. For once she hesitated before calling Linda Tripp, but in the end decided that, as they were both in the same boat, they should talk the problem over. So a tearful Monica phoned Tripp in the early hours of December 17 and told her that she too was on the witness list in the case of *Jones v. Clinton*.

Monica passed what was left of the night in restless anxiety. In the morning she went over to Betty Currie's house to offer her condolences. She spent a few hours there, comforting Betty, and helping with the arrangements for her brother's funeral. But, even as she tried to help, Monica could not help thinking of the latest turn of events, which weighed very heavily upon her. She simply couldn't understand how her name could have been obtained by Paula Jones's lawyers, and strongly suspected that her phone might have been tapped or her apartment bugged.

On the following day, December 18, she had two job interviews in New York. Before she flew out on the evening of the 17th, she rang her mother and begged her to meet her at the airport. She wanted to discuss the awful last twenty-four hours, but feared her mother's apartment might also have been bugged, and so decided that the only safe place for a confidential conversation was in Marcia's car. In the event, Marcia collected her in a taxi, and since neither of them knew or understood the legal jargon, Monica spoke in general terms about the fact that she might be called as a witness in the Jones case. Privately, she was deeply concerned about Linda Tripp's about-face, and her own growing suspicions about the latter's behavior.

The first of the interviews was with MacAndrews & Forbes, the second with Burson-Marsteller, a public relations company. She did especially well at the latter, and was invited to take a formal written test a few days later. Even this encouraging start could not make her happy, however. In the taxi on the way to the airport to return to Washington, she burst into tears. It truly hit home that her dream of working at the White House was over. She had lived with the idea for so long, had had her hopes of a return raised and then dashed, and had accepted at face value Tripp's claim that she had been blacklisted; but always, however deeply buried, a small ray of hope had persisted. Now, seeing another office in another city, and being considered for a post involving a wholly new line of work, that hope had finally been extinguished. "I realized then that no office atmosphere would ever compare to the White House," she says. "It was very painful to come to terms with that bitter disappointment."

If the President's early-morning call to Monica had been a bad dream, the true nightmare began two days later at 3.30 P.M. on December 19, 1997, when she received the message she had been dreading. The phone rang. "Monica Lewinsky?" said the voice on the other end. "I have a subpoena to deliver to you in the Jones versus Clinton case." She put on a show of surprise and indignation, but that did not delay the moment of truth.

She picked up the subpoena from the process-server at the Metro entrance of the Pentagon and walked away in a daze, tucking the papers into her bag. "I was just tense and hyperventilating and freaking out," she recalls. "I just burst into tears—I didn't know what to do." She had no way of contacting the President except through Betty Currie, whom she could not bother while she was mourning her brother Teddy. In desperation she went to a pay phone and called Vernon Jordan.

She sobbed so much over the phone, however, that in the end an exasperated Jordan, complaining that he couldn't understand a word she said, told her to come to his office at five that afternoon. Monica calmed herself down, washed her face and returned to the office, where she told her boss, Ken Bacon, that she had to leave early because of an emergency. He was so concerned at her demeanor that he told his wife, Darcy, who called her later to check that she was all right.

To make matters worse, when she arrived at Vernon Jordan's office he was brusque and unsympathetic. He said he thought the subpoena was not much of a problem, as it seemed to be a fairly standard document. Even so, they agreed that she needed a lawyer, and Jordan called Frank Carter, a top Washington attorney, and made her an appointment with him. Monica told Jordan that what made her really nervous about the subpoena was that it specifically mentioned the President's gift to her of a hat pin, something only a few people knew about.

At that point Monica had no idea what Jordan knew about the true nature of her relationship with the President. Every time she had spoken to Linda Tripp about the attorney, Tripp had blithely stated that he knew what had happened. Yet during their conversations he had given Monica no real clue that he did. So when, during their meeting, he asked her bluntly, "There are only two important questions. Did you have sex with the President? Or did he ask for it?" she gave him the "vanilla" answers. "No," she said, believing that if Jordan in fact did know about the relationship he was testing her to see how she would stand up as a witness.

Since Jordan was seeing the President that evening, Monica emphasized that the lawyer should tell him about the subpoena, as Clinton had asked, adding, "Will you give him a hug for me?" He replied, "I don't hug guys," then patted her on the backside in a gesture that meant "Get out of here, kiddo."

There was one positive side to being subpoenaed—it let Linda Tripp off the hook. That night, therefore, Monica called Tripp to reassure her that she would not be the only one who would have to take the witness stand. Worried that her phone was bugged, Monica talked in cryptic terms about the "flowers" being delivered, referring to her subpoena. When Tripp finally got her drift, they had such a guarded conversation that neither really understood what the other was saying.

What Monica really needed was to see her friend in person, and the opportunity arose at Tripp's Christmas party at her home the next night. It was a strange affair. When Monica arrived to help set up, she discovered that, even though only a few people were due to attend, the refrigerator was groaning with food and drink. For a woman who constantly complained that she barely had enough money for the bus ride to work, this seemed odd. Indeed, far from selling her clothes to raise cash, as she had said she was doing the previous month, Tripp had recently been splurging on new outfits. It seemed to a puzzled Monica that she had suddenly come into some money. "I thought, 'Gee, how can you afford a $500 party?'" she recalls.

It was only as she was leaving the party , however, that she got the chance to talk to Tripp. They sat outside in Monica's car and Tripp read the subpoena, which required that Monica produce every one the President's gifts to her, and specifically cited "hat pins." After expressing surprise and wondering just who could have put the Jones legal team onto Monica, Tripp seemed receptive when the girl argued that she, Tripp, would now no longer be alone in saying under oath that nothing had happened between Monica and the President. Before she left, Tripp insisted that Monica call her after her meeting with Frank Carter, scheduled for 11 A.M. on Monday, December 22, so that they could discuss their strategy.

Worried about the subpoena, anxious about Linda Tripp and concerned about finding a job, Monica took the sensible course that weekend and took Saturday off to drown her sorrows. She spent the next day recovering from a hangover and deciding which of her gifts from the President to take to Frank Carter's office.

Before meeting Carter, she saw Vernon Jordan, to whom she now admitted that she and the President had had phone sex. When Jordan asked what phone sex was, Monica had to explain. He then drove her to Carter's ofice. Like Jordan, he did not seem unduly concerned, and thought that Jones's lawyers were on a "fishing expedition." She told him that she had never had sex with the President, but had met him a few times, and had delivered documents to him at the weekend. She also made it clear that she was on the President's side in the Jones case.

Back at work later that day, she finally realized that she could no longer rely on the support of a certain fair-weather friend. During another conversation in the Pentagon alley, it became clear that she faced enormous difficulties and that Linda Tripp's promises were worthless. "Monica, don't ask me to lie. If I'm asked about you, I'm gonna tell," Tripp said.

As worried and alarmed as she was, Monica felt a brooding sense of outrage that Paula Jones's freedom to sue the President for money should take precedence over her right to privacy. As she says, "It was nobody's business what the President and I did. I was never harassed. I lost my job because I was his girlfriend and the bottom line is that my affair with the President hampered, rather than helped, my job prospects. In fact, my experience ruined Paula Jones's arguments about sexual harassment."

Such arguments cut little ice with Linda Tripp as she talked and taped her way through the gathering storm. In one conversation before Christmas she told Monica, "I am being a shitty friend and that's the last thing I want to do because I won't lie under oath. How do you think that makes me feel? I can make you stop crying and I could make your life so much easier if I could just fucking lie . . . I feel like I'm sticking a knife in your back, and I know at the end of this, if I have to go forward, you will never speak to me again and I will lose a dear friend."

Monica was frightened, more frightened than at any time in her life. In particular, she feared that the President would find out that she had in fact told someone about their affair. She was prepared to use almost any means to make Tripp agree to keep quiet.

Over the last few months, as their relationship deteriorated, Monica had realized she might be able to take advantage of Tripp's strange obsession with Monica's mother. Tripp was always asking what Marcia thought about any given situation, and often deferred to her judgment, even though they had never met. The perpetually broke Pentagon secretary was so keen to glean financial details about Marcia's wealthy fiancé, Peter Straus, that at one point Monica suspected that Tripp might try to blackmail her in return for her silence. In a moment of desperation, Monica, who had a half share with her brother in a condominium on the outskirts of Sydney, Australia, even offered Tripp, on the phone, her part of the $50,00 apartment if Tripp would stay silent. She recalls: "I would have done anything at that stage. I was desperate."

By invoking the name of Marcia Lewis—who most times knew nothing about these conversations—Monica was often able to smooth over an argument or resolve a problem. In their conversations Marcia acted as a kind of unseen referee, a talisman to be waved as a means of appeasing Tripp. Monica would say, for example, that her mother had told her that she had been wrong to get into a fight with Tripp, thereby making it easier for them to kiss and make up. When Tripp mentioned that she might go to

California for foot surgery to avoid testifying, Monica told her later that Marcia thought it was a great idea and had even offered to help pay for the operation. "All I wanted her to do was keep my secret," Monica reflects. "I would have given her my left arm for her silence. That's how my mom got into trouble, because I kept talking about her on Tripp's tapes."

The consequences of talking to Tripp were equally dire for Monica. In one now notorious chat, she confessed that she had got along in life by lying, and that she had perfected that dubious art after her parents' divorce. "I was brought up with lies all the time," she said. That exaggerated reference to her childhood was part of an overall argument designed to make Tripp feel comfortable about maintaining her silence to protect her friend. Taken at face value, the remark, like many of her comments on the tapes, was far more incriminating and damning than the context in which it was uttered should have allowed.

Because Tripp was all too well aware that their conversations were being taped, many of her own comments appear as sanctimonious as they are self-serving. When Monica reported the results of her first meeting with Frank Carter, as Tripp had requested, the latter's answer is consistent with her preparing the ground for the impression she wished to make upon a third party: "Look, Monica, we already know that you're going to lie under oath. We also know that I want out of this big time. If I have to testify—if I am forced to answer questions and answer truthfully—it's going to be the opposite of what you say, so therefore it's a conflict right there."

In context, therefore, the contents of the Tripp tapes—more than twenty hours' worth—take on an entirely different complexion. It is also significant that the tapes themselves are a partial and deeply misleading account of the events of October, November and December 1997. This became crucial when Tripp approached Special Prosecutor Kenneth Starr in January 1998.

In many respects the conversations which do not appear on the tapes are just as important as, if not more important than, those that did. Tripp evidently did not produce recordings of conversations with Monica in which they talked about important meetings or discussions; nor conversations—particularly about Vernon Jordan—which, by a strange coincidence, would have considerably diluted any case Starr might have had for "hotwiring" his Whitewater investigation to Monica's affair with the President, by way of the Paula Jones case.

Just as the tapes take on a different complexion when considered in context, so too does a photograph of Monica and Linda Tripp taken on December 23 at Monica's farewell party at the Pentagon. The distraught girl had spent much of the previous night on the phone, attempting to persuade Tripp to stand by her, though with little success. She had been crying before the party began, and felt wretched, but in typical Monica fashion she put on her happiest face and thanked her colleagues for their gifts and good wishes.

During the party, Tripp insisted that a picture be taken of her with Monica, a photograph that was duly published within days of the scandal breaking. With hindsight, it is entirely possible that her motive was to have a photograph that would enable her to prove to others that they were friends. In fact, she had spent most of Monica's last day at work dodging her, so as to avoid having to resume their anguished conversation of the night before. From then on, Tripp stopped returning Monica's increasingly frantic phone calls.

The only bright spot in a cheerless Christmas was a date with Washington journalist Jake Tapper, who recalled her as a young woman "looking for a decent, challenging job, and a happy life to go with it." She spent a lonely Christmas Day at the Watergate apartment, pondering her problems. At this point in time she had no job—a couple of days earlier, she had been turned down by American Express—and no boyfriend, and was entangled in a legal and personal dilemma of hideous proportions. "I remember feeling really sad, nervous and alone," she says. She found consolation only in a TV re-run of her favorite childhood movie, *Willy Wonka and the Chocolate Factory.*

Uppermost in her thoughts was the President. She debated endlessly whether or not to tell him that she had betrayed the secret of their affair to Linda Tripp. In the end she decided not to, a decision made more difficult because she was due to see him shortly. Remembering that he had said, during his early-morning call to her on December 17, that she could come to the White House to collect his Christmas presents to her, Monica rang Betty Currie after Christmas, and they arranged for her to go there at 8.30 on the morning of Sunday, December 28. Despite her decision not to confess to him, she spent the night before she went to the White House in an anxious and agitated state.

When she arrived at the White House, she was shown into the Oval Office, where she, Betty and the President played with the President's dog, Buddy, who kept scampering around the carpet as though it were a racetrack. Later, when she and the President were alone in the back study, Buddy insisted on putting his head between her legs and Monica joked: "You are better at this than your dad.".

Meanwhile, Clinton produced a large canvas bag from the Black Dog shop in Martha's Vineyard. Inside it were her presents, an odd but endearing assortment—a Black Dog stuffed animal, a Rockettes blanket from New York and a small box of chocolates, plus a joke pair of sunglasses (which they both laughed about and modeled) and a stone bear's head which he had bought in Vancouver. The fact that he was giving her presents after she had been served with a subpoena that mentioned his gifts to her displayed a certain insouciance in the face of legal adversity, as well as an unspoken trust in Monica.

His choice of gifts reflected something of the history of their two-year relationship. The silly plastic sunglasses referred to a long-running private battle between them over his own sunglasses. Monica always complained he looked "dorky" in them, for which he offered the explanation that he borrowed them from Secret Service agents. Typically, she bought him a pair of trendy designer glasses from the Barney's outlet store and then pestered him to wear them; later she sent him a note to remind him, followed by a picture of him wearing "dorky" glasses which had appeared in the *New York Times*. When she sent the picture, she said that she would continue harassing him with these pictures of him "looking like a geek" until he wore the cool sunglasses. "If you don't think they're cool, ask Chelsea," she said in a note after she had given them to him. From then on he kept them in his briefcase, and they went everywhere with him. It therefore gave her a certain grim satisfaction to see, a few days after the scandal broke in January 1998, a picture of the President in her sunglasses on a magazine cover; the caption was "Presidential Style."

Perhaps the most meaningful gift was the stone bear carving, which he gave her with the comment, "When you need to be strong hold onto the bear." The Special Prosecutor interpreted the President's meaning as being that she needed to be strong in relation to the Paula Jones case, but to Monica it was a reminder of their conversation on Independence Day, when "Handsome" had lectured her about controling her temper.

After handing over her presents, the President gave her what she really wanted—a kiss. Their not quite final embrace, which took place in the back study hallway, epitomized the passion and guilt of their two-year affair. As they embraced, Monica opened her eyes slightly and noticed that his eyes were wide open and that he was looking out of the window. Angrily pushing him away, she said, "Don't kiss me if you don't want to." The President soothed her, replying, "No, I'm just worried, I want to make sure no one sees. It's hard to go from being good and telling myself I can't do this and change that pattern and kiss you."

For once, Monica took control. "Come here," she said, and led him into the bathroom, where she ordered him to close his eyes. As she recalls, "We then shared a fabulous, emotional and passionate kiss that reminded me of how good it was between us." This moment of yearning, passion, regret, and a host of other emotions, is reduced in the Starr report to one of sleazy banality.

During their hour-long meeting they did briefly discuss the issue that was so troubling Monica, her subpoena in the Paula Jones case. "We didn't spend very much time talking about it," she says. "I was resigned to the fact that I was going to deny it, I assumed that he was, and so I thought, 'Whatever happens, happens. You can't control everything.'"

They also talked about how her name could have got on the witness list in the first place, and discussed the specific reference to the hat pin which, he said, "sort of bothered" him as well. When he asked Monica if she had told "that woman from last summer," meaning Linda Tripp, she denied it, and then went on to ask if she should put away the other gifts he had given her, or perhaps get Betty Currie to hold them. He replied with something on the lines of "I don't know," or "I'll think about that."

He was more definite when they talked about her move to New York, and asked how he would be able to contact her. Monica told him that Betty had her phone and pager numbers, adding hopefully that they would therefore be able to talk soon. Then, as they walked back into the Oval Office, he put his arm around her, kissed her on the forehead, and said, "OK, Kiddo—good luck in New York and be good." She has never seen him in person again.

That afternoon Betty Currie called and said, "I understand that you have something for me," a reference, Monica thought, to the gifts to be handed over for safekeeping. She packed some items, including the hat pin, in a box which she marked "Do not throw away" (later, Betty picked this up and put it under her bed at home). But she could not bear to part with her treasured copy of *Leaves of Grass*, and so hid it in her closet. It was a decision that epitomized her state of mind: she longed to get away from Washington, but could not bring herself to let the President go.

When, early in the New Year, she and her friend Ashley Raines went to watch the blockbuster movie *Titanic*, Monica cried her eyes out. The story of the doomed love affair between two passengers from different social classes and backgrounds touched a deep chord within her. It seemed to parallel her own unfulfilled relationship with "Handsome," reminding her of the angst and anger she had endured during their bittersweet affair.

She wrote him a "mushy" note in which she lamented the fact that they had never truly become lovers; she would always wonder about what might have been. It was part of the romantic tragedy of their love, she said, that they had never been together for so much as a single night of passion. That this was but a sentimental pipe dream was forcibly brought home to her a few days later, when she saw TV pictures of the President and First Lady dancing romantically together in their swimsuits during a beach vacation. As in her affair with Andy Bleiler, she had to face up to the bitter reality that she loved a man who was not free.

On Sunday, January 4, 1998, Monica called Betty Currie and said she had something for the President. They agreed to meet at Currie's home later that day, and when they did so Monica handed over a parcel containing the "mushy" note and a book, *The Presidents of the United States*, which she had picked up in an antiquarian bookstore.

Because she still felt angry, jealous and sad, she did little to hide her feelings when the President called her in the evening of January 5, responding to a request she had made, via Betty Currie, that afternoon. Monica was spoiling for a fight. Still smarting over the TV images of the Clintons cavorting on the beach, she grudgingly apologized for sending the "embarrassing" note—he had told her not to write down such thoughts—but was pleased that he liked the book.

Earlier that afternoon Monica had had a meeting with her attorney, Frank Carter, at his office. She agreed to sign an affidavit, which he would draft, hoping thereby to avoid being called as a witness in the Paula Jones case. Since she was due to pick up the draft affidavit the following day, she went over with the President a couple of points that bothered her, particularly the reasons behind her transfer to the Pentagon. They also discussed what might occur in a deposition. She was especially concerned about White House staff getting her into trouble by saying that she had acted "inappropriately" around the President. Clinton simply suggested that it was colleagues in Legislative Affairs who got her the job, an answer that was true if evasive. Then, still annoyed with him, she abruptly ended the conversation after about fifteen minutes. She did not think for a moment that she would never speak to him again, and it remains a source of sadness to her that their relationship, which had lasted so long and survived so much, should have ended so brusquely.

The truth was that by now Monica felt utterly lost and, more than ever, alone. The combined and juxtaposed effects of the TV pictures of Bill and Hillary Clinton, the *Titanic* story and an unexpected conversation with Vernon Jordan had merely added to her emotional turmoil.

On December 31, she had gone to see Vernon Jordan to explain, in a roundabout way, that she suspected Linda Tripp of being the source of the leak. Rather than tell him the truth, however—that she had confided in Tripp for many months—she said that Tripp had stayed at her apartment and could have seen notes she had drafted to send to the President. Jordan's response was emphatic: "Well, go home and make sure they are not there," which Monica took to mean that she should throw away or destroy the letters.

As they were chatting, she rather cheekily asked the attorney if he thought the President would stay married to the First Lady. He replied, "Yes, as he should be," and quoted a line from the Bible to her. After a minute or so he added, "Well, maybe you two will have an affair when he's out of office." Monica was taken aback by Vernon Jordan's comment. Once again the mirage of marriage to the President seemed to shimmer in the not too far distance, but she then let him know that they had indeed had an affair, but that it had stopped just short of full sex.

It was a perplexing exchange in a perplexing week. She didn't know what to think anymore, about either her erstwhile lover or her fair-weather friend Linda Tripp. Her difficulty with Tripp was more pressing. The woman who had called her constantly for months was now avoiding her. Her silence was deeply worrying and Monica did not know what to do, or whom to ask for advice. When, earlier in December, she had spoken to her mother about her dilemma, Marcia had seen the issue not in legal but in human terms, and had suggested the name of a Christian Science counselor in New York who might be able to give her daughter some confidential advice.

Because, at that time, Monica had had in any case to fly to New York again for her interviews with MacAndrews & Forbes and Burson-Marsteller, she had decided to give it a try. After all, she reasoned, she had nothing to lose. She had met with the Christian Scientist and outlined her problem in general terms: there was a woman at her office who was about to betray a confidence, and if she did it would endanger her and several other people. The counselor suggested that Monica should look at her colleague's positive virtues, and that focusing on her good qualities might well induce her to change her mind. She had also suggested that Monica meditate on the Ninety-First Psalm, which says that trust in God is rewarded with personal protection.

With this advice in mind, and despite her rising sense of panic, on New Year's Day Monica left Linda Tripp a friendly message on her answering machine, wishing her a Happy New Year and hoping that all was well with her and her family. It seemed to work; Tripp called back and left a message a few days later, and the two then played phone tag until Monica, who had become wary of phoning the older woman at home, called her at the Pentagon. Her trust in Tripp, once so absolute, had by now evaporated.

Whatever Linda Tripp may have been thinking, at the end of the first week in January 1998 Monica faced her own moment of truth. On January 6 she collected the draft of her affidavit in the Paula Jones from Frank Carter's office, and arranged to return on the following day to sign it. She made a number of amendments—some of them after calling Vernon Jordan—to the draft, according to her version of events, and at ten o'clock on January 7, 1998, duly presented herself at her attorney's office. "I took a deep breath and walked down the hall to his office," she recalls. "I was prepared to deny the affair because of my love for and loyalty to the President. When I saw that the document said that I did not have sexual relations I thought that I could buy that, as we had never had sexual intercourse. That made made me feel much more comfortable. By signing the affidavit I was in effect putting on my team jersey, to be on the President's side."

Whatever gloss she may put on it, however, the affidavit she filed was false. In it Monica, who was referred to as Jane Doe 6 to preserve her anonymity, said she could not "fathom any reason why the plaintiff [Jones] would seek information from me for her case," outlined her work at the

White House, and stated that she had met the President several times in the course of her employment. The document continued:

7. I have the utmost respect for the President who has always behaved appropriately in my presence.

8. I have never had a sexual relationship with the President, he did not propose that we have a sexual relationship, he did not offer me employment or other benefits in exchange for a sexual relationship, he did not deny me employment or other benefits for rejecting a sexual relationship. I do not know of any other person who had a sexual relationship with the President, was offered employment or other benefits in exchange for a sexual relationship, or was denied employment or other benefits for rejecting a sexual relationship. The occasions that I saw the President after I left employment at the White House in April, 1996, were official receptions, formal functions or events related to the U.S. Department of Defense, where I was working at the time. There were other people present on those occasions.

I declare under the penalty of perjury that the foregoing is true and correct.

(signed) Monica S. Lewinsky

It was paragraph 8 that fatally compromised her, and which was eventually to force her to accept an immunity deal from Independent Counsel Kenneth Starr to escape being charged with perjury, for which the penalty on conviction is a jail sentence.

Though she had signed her affidavit, it was not filed in court until nine days later. At this point, therefore, Monica still had an escape route. Though filing a false affidavit is a federal offense, merely swearing one is a minor offense and rarely prosecuted. This important distinction became crucial on the day she was betrayed by Linda Tripp to the FBI.

Once she had signed the document, she felt a sense of relief, believing that she was one step closer to getting the whole matter out of the way, something that would allow her to get on with her own life. It is important to understand that there was no intention that her affidavit would not be filed until she had got a job; in no sense was she blackmailing the President and his advisors by offering the false affidavit in return for his influence in finding her a position. So far as Monica was concerned, that issue did not even arise, and it became important later only because of Linda Tripp, and then the Special Prosecutor.

On January 8, the day after she signed the affidavit, she had her second interview at MacAndrews & Forbes in New York. Monica, whose natural pessimism tends to cloud her judgment, felt that the interview had not gone well and phoned Vernon Jordan—who was a member of the board of directors of the MacAndrews & Forbes subsidiary, Revlon—to express her disappointment. He then called the company's chairman and chief executive officer, Ronald Perelman, and recommended Monica as a "bright young girl, who I think is terrific." Perelman duly conveyed those thoughts to Jaymie Durnan, the executive who had interviewed Monica, and said, "Let's see if we can be helpful."

In fact Jordan's intervention was not necessary, and merely muddied the waters once Judge Starr waded in. For Durnan had been impressed by Monica and, before Perelman spoke to him, had already been in discussion with colleagues at Revlon to see about an opening in their Communications Department. Monica was interviewed the following morning by a senior officer of MacAndrews & Forbes and two Revlon executives, and immediately clicked. She loved them and they loved her, and later that day they informally offered her a job in the Public Relations Department at $40,000 a year (less than she was making at the Pentagon). A "thrilled, very excited," Monica informally accepted their offer.

The same day, she called Jordan with the news, and that afternoon he called Betty Currie and told her, "Mission accomplished." He also passed on the news to his friend the President, who said simply, "Thank you very much."

Once back in Washington, Monica had a longer and more emotional encounter with Jordan, and gave him a snappy tie and pocket handkerchief as a small thank you for all his help. "You are the only person who did what they said they were going to do for me," she told him. "You were the only one who came through." When Jordan snapped his fingers, things happened; comparison with the President's efforts was inescapable.

It seemed that the girl who had been an unhappy Cinderella, both in love and at work, was at last about to go to the ball. Though she left her heart at the White House, she had packed her bags for New York and reconciled herself to life without "Handsome." But this fairy tale had no happy ending. The two Ugly Sisters, Linda Tripp and Lucianne Goldberg, ensured that Monica never made it to the ball.

Wary and cautious, Monica finally spoke to Linda Tripp on Friday, January 9. As they talked, to Monica it seemed that the Christian Science counselor's advice had worked; inexplicably, Tripp had changed tack. She now said she had decided to be vague about Kathleen Willey, and implied that she wasn't even going to mention Monica in her testimony. At last it looked as though Monica was safe. In fact, precisely the opposite was true. She was being led into a trap.

Tripp, who herself used to boast of her "witchy feelings," attributed her personal epiphany to a psychic, who had told her that a friend of hers was in danger because of the words she, Tripp, would say. The truth, however, was that she had fired her lawyer, Kirbe Behre, because he had threatened to go to Bob Bennett, the President's attorney, and tell him to settle the Jones case. What Tripp and Goldberg wanted was not a settlement but a story. By the time Monica spoke with her, Tripp had, through the offices of Lucianne Goldberg, engaged a new attorney, James Moody, and they were preparing to contact Special Prosecutor Kenneth Starr.

When they spoke, Monica was anxious not to arouse Tripp's jealousy, and so played down her success in New York, saying only that she might have secured some temporary work. Tripp at once bragged that she too had been advised to move to New York and get a job in public relations because she was so "savvy." This worried Monica somewhat, as she had always had the suspicion that Tripp might be copying her lifestyle.

In order to maintain the fiction that Tripp held the whip hand in their relationship, Monica said she had not yet signed her affidavit. "Monica, promise me you won't sign the affidavit until you get the job," Tripp demanded. "Tell Vernon you won't sign the affidavit until you get the job." To keep her sweet, Monica agreed.

Tripp's insistence on this point became critical, for only by showing that Monica was being given a job in return for her silence, and that Jordan and the President were involved in a cover-up in order to obstruct justice, that the Starr inquiry was able to expand its jurisdiction and, ultimately, to make a case for impeaching the President. It is therefore curious indeed that Tripp should have invoked precisely the scenario needed to bring in Special Prosecutor Starr, even before the date at which, it is claimed, Starr did actually become involved.

Over the phone, the two women agreed to meet later that week. The suggestion was Monica's; she now thoroughly distrusted Tripp, and thought a face-to-face meeting would give her greater control over the course of the conversation. By this time she had also come to think that Tripp might even be so underhanded as to try to tape their confidential exchanges. She therefore had it in mind to look in the latter's handbag when she went to the bathroom and, if she found a tape recorder, remove it. She could not, however, in her wildest dreams, have realized the extent of her "friend's" treachery.

Whatever she might or might not have known or suspected, Monica was right to be skeptical of Tripp's curious about-face, a change of heart which, given the imminent involvement of the Independent Counsel, seems with hindsight suspiciously like conspiracy to entrap. For Tripp had realized, way back in November, that it was against the state law in Maryland to tape someone without their knowledge and consent. Far from protecting her, therefore, the "insurance policy" of the tapes—this evidence of her integrity and honesty—could instead land her in jail.

According to Lucianne Goldberg, when Tripp's former attorney, Kirbe Behre, had found out about the illicit recordings, he went "ballistic" and told her to stop. Instead, she fired him and hired James Moody in his place.

Tripp apparently felt so worried about being prosecuted—though this did not stop her taping her conversations with Monica—that she asked Lucianne Goldberg to find a way of contacting the Office of the Independent Counsel, hoping thereby to obtain immunity from prosecution for her illegal actions in exchange for her cooperation in their investigation.

So on January 12, 1998, according both to Tripp and the Office of the Independent Counsel, she called that office and told investigators that the President was having an affair with a government employee who had been subpoenaed in the Paula Jones case, and that the President and Vernon Jordan had told this employee to lie about the affair. She had, Tripp added, twenty hours of taped conversations to back her story. Over the phone she said that the employee had already signed a false affidavit— although she continued to stress to Monica, in their subsequent meetings, that she should not sign until Vernon Jordan had got her a job.

For once in her life, Linda Tripp was the center of attention. Within an hour of her call to the OIC, six federal prosecutors and an FBI agent had descended on her home in Columbia, Maryland, to hear her story. It transpired later that the reason for their enthusiasm was that Starr's office had already heard, apparently from Paula Jones's lawyers, about Monica and the President. Tripp was debriefed that night, and told them all she knew. Seemingly, however, a verbal betrayal, backed by her tapes, was not enough—Tripp agreed to the investigators' request that she wear a body wire when she and Monica met, so that the OIC could overhear and record their conversation.

The arrival of the Special Prosecutor took Tripp's story onto a different plane. No longer was this about personal betrayal in order to make money out of a "tell-all" book. It had become a plot to trap the President.

For the previous four years, the Independent Counsel to the Whitewater investigation, Special Prosecutor Kenneth Starr, a right-wing Southern Baptist, had zealously tried to find evidence of presidential wrongdoing. (The office of Special Prosecutor had been established in 1978 after the Watergate scandal, specifically to investigate the executive branch of government—that is, the presidency.) Starr had originally been appointed to look into the Whitewater land deal scandal, in which both Bill and Hillary Clinton were caught up, and to gather evidence of any wrongdoing, especially on the part of the President.

By January 1998, after four years and $40 million of taxpayers' money, his investigation had got nowhere, so Tripp's call was manna from heaven.

If her allegations and evidence held up, Starr would at last have evidence of wrongdoing by the President, albeit in a matter far removed from Whitewater. His prosecutors were particularly interested to hear Tripp's tale of Vernon Jordan finding Monica a job, for Jordan's name had cropped up in the Whitewater investigation in relation to alleged hush money paid to former Associate Attorney General Webster Hubbell.

Starr needed legal approval each time he wished to expand his inquiry, so he had to have some form of evidence linking Whitewater to Monica Lewinsky. Vernon Jordan was the link that enabled Starr to connect his existing investigation, into a dubious land deal, to an allegedly corrupt presidential love affair.

Essentially, if the President could be proved to have found, through Jordan, a job for Monica in return for her silence, he would be guilty of abuse of his position—in Starr's view an impeachable offense. Hence the importance of Tripp's tapes and her testimony in demonstrating Jordan's involvement with Monica's job search. Yet, just as the contents of the conversations between Monica and Tripp were prejudiced by their context, so too the tapes gave a highly misleading picture of Monica's life in the fall of 1997, a deceptive impression upon which Tripp dramatically embellished, misrepresenting to Kenneth Starr the true nature of events.

Whether by accident or design, Tripp either did not record or held back the recordings of numerous significant conversations which would have seriously diluted Starr's case for including Monica Lewinsky in his investigation. They would have shown that Jordan's involvement with Monica had been at her own suggestion, and well before any notion of her being connected with the Paula Jones case had become apparent to her, to the President or to Jordan. Conspicuously absent, too, was a record of Tripp's October 6, 1997, conversation with her friend Kate Friedrich, during which Friedrich had allegedly said that Monica was blacklisted by the White House. This was a lie, as Friedrich later testified, and Tripp's demonstrable perfidy would therefore have undercut her credibility as a witness. According to the Starr Report, subsequent investigation by the FBI has also uncovered evidence that the tapes themselves may have been tampered with or duplicated; if that is true, it means that Tripp lied under oath before the Grand Jury and in her FBI deposition.

As one commentator, Elise Ackerman, noted, "The picture that emerges [from the tapes] is not one of illicit sex or obstruction of justice, but of girl talk raised in a frothing boil by a devious, knowing Tripp in an attempt to provide material for the Independent Counsel, the attorneys for Paula Jones, and—most lucrative of all—a book about how Tripp 'uncovered' a vast conspiracy to obstruct justice and cover up illicit sex."

As for Kenneth Starr, at this early stage he took a gamble. In essence, he bent the rules in order to catch the man he suspected of breaking the law. Technically, the Independent Counsel only had authority to investigate Whitewater. So when, at Starr's behest, Linda Tripp wore a body wire to record their conversation at her meeting with Monica, he was acting beyond his mandate. Many have argued that he acted beyond his remit in order to uncover possible evidence that would convince Attorney General Janet Reno that he should be allowed to bring Monica Lewinsky into his existing investigation.

Wearing a secret listening device beneath her clothing, Linda Tripp met Monica for lunch at the Ritz-Carlton in Pentagon City on Tuesday, January 13, 1998. She greeted her young friend with a kiss, knowing all the while that, in an upstairs room of the hotel, agents from the Office of the Independent Counsel were listening to all they said.

It was a long—an interminable three hours—and brittle meeting, during which Linda Tripp took Monica through her affair with the President. Monica, as she had planned, took the opportunity to check Tripp's bag for a hidden tape recorder when she went to the bathroom, but of course found nothing, for both microphone and transmitter were concealed on Tripp's person. Once again Monica said what she thought Tripp wanted to hear, soft-pedaling her new job, bemusedly answering endless questions about Vernon Jordan and the President. At one stage she resorted to emotional blackmail, saying that her mother had taken her to the hospital for sedatives because she was so overwrought.

It was in the course of this lunch, during which her conversation was largely a mixture of lies and exaggeration, that Monica unwittingly incriminated herself. Upstairs, the listening prosecutors realized at once that they had a good case to ask for permission to extend their investigation. Crucially, she repeated to Tripp her lie that she was not going to sign her affidavit until Vernon Jordan (whom she had seen that morning when she dropped off her "thank-you" gifts) got her a job. This, to the listening prosecutors, was evidence that the President had abused his position by involving Jordan on behalf of the woman with whom he was having an affair.

Monica's lie raises some vital questions. She told Tripp—and thus, albeit unwittingly, the OIC—that she had not yet signed her affidavit. How, therefore, could Starr's team have known that it had, in fact, already been signed unless they had been told by a third party? Who was that third party? Was it Paula Jones's legal team? By then, the Jones camp had certainly received by fax from Monica's lawyer a copy of Monica's false affidavit, which she had signed six days earlier (on January 7). Just how far the Jones legal team, whose fees were paid by the right-wing—and almost rabidly anti-Clinton—Rutherford Institute, collaborated with the Office of the Independent Council is a murky issue, raising the question of how "independent" the Independent Counsel really was.

Monica found her lunch with Tripp as irritating as it was confusing. Far from being on her side, Tripp seemed to be backtracking, dancing around the subject of what Monica was going to say in her affidavit. For three hours she was friendly, conspiratorial and sympathetic; she must have known all along that she was steering Monica down a path that might lead to a prison cell.

Unlike Lucianne Goldberg or Michael Isikoff, Linda Tripp had come to know Monica well and to enjoy her friendship. Yet she was prepared to throw this vulnerable, naive and trusting young woman to the legal wolves. Monica finds it hard to look back at this devastating period of her life without anger. She cannot understand, let alone forgive, Tripp's betrayal—or the manner of it. She says, "I had been good to her as a person. She knew my weaknesses as a person and I had trusted her absolutely. Yet she betrayed me for no other reason than malice and spite. I don't know how she sleeps at nights or looks at herself in the mirror. She is just a disgusting, despicable, venomous and evil human being."

Early on Wednesday, January 14, the day after that fateful lunch, the two women spoke again, and Monica told Tripp that she planned to sign her affidavit. For her part, Tripp said that she was thinking about getting a new lawyer, as her present attorney was too "neutral." Neither was being truthful.

They spoke several more times that morning, Monica maintaining the fiction that she was getting ready to sign her affidavit. Tripp then asked if Monica would drive her to her lawyer's office for moral support, and, good-hearted as ever, the girl agreed. Before she did so, however, Monica suggested that it would be a good idea if she drafted a few notes—based on their previous conversations and on what she herself had learned in the process of writing her own affidavit—about what Tripp could say in her own testimony. It took her a couple of hours to sketch out the areas that she felt Tripp should cover, arguments that later became famous as the "Talking Points." Moreover, she wrote two versions, one for Tripp to read in the car, the other for her to give to her lawyer as though she herself had written it.

The document focused almost entirely on the issue of Kathleen Willey, as Monica had been arguing for the last month that it should. There was only a passing reference to another woman, someone who, at one time, Tripp had thought was significant, but who turned out to be a "huge liar" who stalked the President. In essence, the three-page brief reflected what Monica had understood Tripp to have been saying about Willey over the last few months, both in relation to her comments in the original *Newsweek* article and in her private conversations. At the same time, by concentrating on Willey, it took Monica out of the firing line.

When the scandal broke, Tripp publicly doubted that Monica herself had written this brief, reasoning—insultingly—that the thinking behind it was too subtle and organized. All kinds of authors were mooted, from the President's lawyer, Bob Bennett, to Deputy White House Counsel Bruce Lindsey, to Vernon Jordan and even to the President himself. "If Monica Lewinsky wrote it, she is one sharp lawyer!" one commentator remarked.

Yet even a cursory glance through the transcripts of the Tripp tapes, a reading of the *Newsweek* article, and a knowledge of the structure of Monica's recently signed affidavit, show that only Monica could have been the author. Indeed, the fact that there were only a couple of hours between her suggestion and the finished document proves her authorship, for there was no one else with the background knowledge to have even attempted so comprehensive a document in such a very short time. This was yet another canard aimed at Monica, and one which it took months to disprove.

When Tripp saw the "Talking Points," she told Monica that she thought the document was "brilliant." She read through each point, murmuring, "True, true." Then she told Monica that she had fired her attorney, Kirbe Behre, and had engaged another who was a family friend. In fact, as we have seen, her new lawyer, Jim Moody, came courtesy of Lucianne Goldberg's contacts.

Later that day Tripp and Monica spoke again, Tripp, now under the umbrella of the OIC, once more trying to get her friend to incriminate herself. She made comments which, given what she knew, seemed ludicrous to Monica. For example, she suggested that Monica had full sex with the President, a bizarre assertion from someone who knew every wrinkle of their relationship.

Exasperated and tired by Tripp's behavior, Monica had at last decided how she would deal with her erratic friend. If Tripp's testimony incriminated her, she would either deny that she had ever made any remarks about her relationship with the President, or else say that she had made them up—and take the rap.

It was too late. On the following day, January 15, it emerged that Paula Jones's lawyers had subpoenaed records from the courier company owned by the Goldberg family, the very company that Tripp had recommended to Monica. The legal document referred to the packages Monica had sent to the White House. At the same time, Michael Isikoff called Betty Currie and pestered her for information about the contents of these mystery packages.

Over the last few months Linda Tripp and her fellow conspirators had braided the rope, and in the last weeks Tripp had fashioned the knot. In just a matter of hours, on Friday, January 16, 1998, in Room 1012 of the Ritz-Carlton Hotel in Pentagon City, she would see officers of the FBI and the Office of the Independent Counsel place the noose around Monica's neck.

• •

CHAPTER ELEVEN

Terror in Room 1012

LTHOUGH SHE WAS DRESSED FOR ACTION—she was still in her gym gear after her morning workout—Monica Lewinsky, at five foot six inches, looked small and frail compared to the two armed FBI agents and the cold-eyed prosecutor facing her. She was fierce in her demands, however. "Make her stay and watch," she hissed. "I want that treacherous bitch to see what she has done to me."

So for the next forty-five minutes Linda Tripp sat silently in Room 1012 of the Ritz-Carlton Hotel in Pentagon City, Arlington, Virginia, and watched as Monica's world collapsed around her. As the time passed Tripp remained motionless, her hands clasped across the pants of her brown suit, a look of cold indifference on her face, as though she were quietly congratulating herself on her own fortitude, courage and wisdom. A good citizen doing her duty in painful but necessary circumstances.

Just how painful was quickly apparent to everyone in the room. Monica was by turns bewildered and angry about how she came to be in this tenth-floor room of the Ritz-Carlton. The hostility she felt towards the two stony-faced FBI agents who had approached her in the food court at Pentagon City Mall a few minutes earlier was exceeded only by the loathing she felt for Linda Tripp.

It was Tripp who had enticed her to the meeting, as part of an elaborate "sting" operation to trap her friend. The consequences of her treachery were made clear to Monica the moment Mike Emmick, one of Kenneth Starr's legal deputies, walked into the room. Although he was a dark-haired, blue-eyed six-footer with a soft, even voice, she came to view him as a revolting specimen of humanity.

There was, she noticed through her rage and distress, a trace of nervousness in his voice as he talked to her, outlining what had happened over the last few weeks and days. Most of it was mumbo jumbo: "Attorney General Janet Reno . . . Independent Counsel . . . federal crimes . . . detailed investigation . . . Kenneth Starr." At that last name she mentally shook herself. "What on earth has he got to do with me?" she thought.

"All I'm trying to do is cover up my affair with the President—what's my little relationship got to do with him?"

She soon found out. Emmick told her they had evidence that she had committed a number of crimes. "We are prepared to charge you with perjury, obstruction of justice, subornation of perjury, witness tampering and conspiracy," he said bleakly. "You could spend up to twenty-seven years in jail."

He went on say that they were prepared to prosecute her unless she agreed to cooperate with the OIC's investigation then and there. Monica collapsed into hysterical tears not even knowing what most of these crimes were. The pain and terror of that day haunt her to this day: "I find it difficult to describe the raw openness, the fear I felt. It was as if my stomach had been cut open and someone had poured acid onto my wound. I just felt an intense stinging pain and overriding terror. It was surreal. I couldn't understand how all this was happening."

The chain of events that had led Monica to Room 1012 had begun with Tripp handing over her illegal tapes of their conversations to Starr's deputies earlier that week, had continued with the lunchtime meeting with Monica when she had worn a body wire, so that OIC prosecutors could listen in to their chatter, and had culminated on the afternoon of Friday, January 16, 1998, when a panel of three judges approved Attorney General Janet Reno's request to extend Starr's investigation from the Whitewater land scandal to cover the President's secret relationship with Monica Lewinsky.

The link between Whitewater and Monica was the presence of the President's friend Vernon Jordan in both affairs. Starr argued that Jordan and the President had conspired to pervert the course of justice by offering Monica a job in return for her false affidavit in the Jones case (in fact, Jordan had begun helping Monica before either of them had the faintest idea that she might become involved in the Paula Jones case). As far as Starr was concerned, here were the ingredients of a case against the President, and Monica's agreement to cooperate, like Tripp's, was a key constituent in amassing evidence of wrongdoing by Clinton.

In Room 1012, as the harsh reality of her predicament began to sink in, Monica's moods swung from hostility to an indignant acceptance of her fate, interspersed with long periods when she just cried and hugged herself. "If I have to go to jail I will do so to protect the President," she thought. "I can't do this to him. I can't turn him in." She felt overwhelmed by guilt, knowing that she might ruin the life of the man she adored.

At first, the only means she could think of that would both prevent her going to jail and protect her "Handsome" was suicide. "I couldn't bear to go to jail," she says. "I would come out an old lady and no one would ever want to marry me. I would never have the joy of getting married and starting a family. My life would be over. So I thought there is no way out other

[176]

than killing myself. If I killed myself, then there would be no information and I wouldn't have to deal with the hurt and trouble I had caused the President."

The room had sliding windows, and she considered throwing herself out, to crash to her death through the glass canopy below. In her overwrought and terrified state, she thought that the FBI had a sniper on the opposite building, ready to shoot her if she made any threatening or otherwise untoward movement. Even so, at one point she mused out loud, "If I kill myself, what happens to everyone else in this investigation? Does it all go away?"

She repeated what she had said when the agents had first approached her in the mall—she wanted to speak to her lawyer, Frank Carter. The prosecutor and FBI men facing her across the room looked at each other, then said that they really didn't want her to tell anyone about this matter as it was "time sensitive." The only reason she could think of for this was that the President, she knew, was filing his deposition in the Paula Jones case the next day; their insistence on her cooperating immediately might have something to do with that. Equally important for Starr, however, was the fact that *Newsweek* magazine was on the brink of publishing the story, which would have ended Monica's possible usefulness, as once her name had become public Clinton and his legal team would have been more cautious.

After a while, Emmick explained to her that if she agreed to cooperate she had to go to the room next door, where his colleagues would debrief her about her relationship with the President. He emphasized that she had to tell them the whole truth. Then he explained that she would have to make some phone calls, which they would monitor, or perhaps put on a body wire and go and talk to Betty Currie, Vernon Jordan, and possibly even the President.

It was not just the preposterous notion that these men were actually considering bugging the conversations of the President of the United States in the Oval Office of the White House that set her head spinning, but the idea that she should betray Betty Currie, a kind, gentle, church-going woman who had had more than enough misery in her life in the last few months. "The first thing I thought of," says Monica, "was what it would be like calling Betty and talking to her on the phone and trapping her like that. I couldn't do that. It was despicable, it was inhuman. She was a good person and I couldn't live with myself if I did that."

As the slow minutes ticked by, the room would be quiet for a while and then the pressure from Starr's deputies would start up again, becoming increasingly aggressive. They set up a tape recorder and offered to play her tapes of her lunchtime conversation with Linda Tripp earlier that week. It was then that she realized that Tripp had worn a wire throughout their meeting and that FBI agents had been listening to their conversation.

[177]

Worse still, they showed her black-and-white pictures of the two of them leaving the mall together after their lunch. Starr's men had her cold, Monica realized. She couldn't wriggle out of this one.

Then they talked about cooperation again. They told her that, if she did as they asked, they would speak to the judge and have him reduce her sentence from twenty-seven years in jail to, say, five—but only if she agreed to cooperate immediately.

All the while, Linda Tripp watched impassively as her young friend disintegrated before her eyes. For Monica, the very sight of her was enraging: "I wanted to hurt her. I felt like an animal wanting to claw at her skin." Finally Tripp was taken from the room, and a female FBI agent took her place. She had said not a single word in all the time she had been there. It is worth noting that after the scandal broke, Tripp said in an interview where she portrayed herself as a victim: "If I were an innocent bystander, I would believe that I was at best treacherous, at worst a fiend."

Once more Monica asked to speak to Frank Carter—maybe she could take a cab to his office if she was not allowed to call him? Again they said that they really did not want her to speak to him, this time adding that it was because of the way she had been put in touch with him. They were worried that he would tip off Vernon Jordan. Her mood shifting from belligerence to one of trying to appease them, Monica told them that she understood.

Throughout the afternoon, in moments of lucidity Monica asked again and again to be allowed to contact her attorney. On one occasion it was explained to her that, as Frank Carter was a civil, rather than a criminal, attorney, he would be of little use to her in this instance. They were being disingenuous: Carter had headed Washington's public defender service for six years. She then said that she would like to call him and ask him to recommend a criminal attorney, but they told her that she couldn't do that either, because it would make Carter suspicious. In desperation, she asked if she could phone Carter's partner and see if he could give her the name of a criminal attorney. This time they reverted to their original response: the whole matter had to be kept under wraps.

Finally, she asked what she was supposed to do without a lawyer. They offered to give her the telephone number of a criminal attorney but she refused, believing that any attorney they recommended would be acting on their behalf. As various commentators have pointed out, their behavior was in clear violation of Monica's rights as a US citizen; furthermore, these men, particularly the FBI agents, who more usually deal with mass murderers and mobsters, were taking advantage of an impressionable, frightened young woman who was largely ignorant both of legal processes and of her rights. Even the President, when he gave video testimony before the grand jury, castigated the prosecutors for treating Monica like a "serious felon" during their sting operation.

Having exhausted the subject of contacting her lawyer, Monica changed tack and asked if she could call her mother. Again they emphasized that they would rather she did not call anybody. All the time they watched her, monitoring her every move. When she asked to go to the bathroom, they made her empty her pockets. Then an FBI agent went into the bathroom and removed the phone before she was allowed to enter.

Next, the pressure started again as another of Starr's lieutenants, Bruce Udolf, walked into the room and went through his routine. Once again she was faced with the choice: twenty-seven years in jail, or immediate cooperation. The thought of being in prison for that length of time was simply overwhelming. At one point, she said plaintively to Mike Emmick, "My life is over. If I go to jail for twenty-seven years who is ever going to marry me? How will I be able to have children?" The prosecutor replied, "That's why we want to give you this chance to cooperate. It's the best thing for you to do. The right thing."

Then all of a sudden the air seemed to grow thicker, the room became hotter and more crowded as the imposing figure of Jackie Bennett, Jr., entered. One of Starr's top deputies, and a man more used to tough mobsters than to sobbing young women, Bennett, like a pit-bull terrier with a kitten, made short work of his reluctant witness. "Look, Monica, you've got to make a decision. You have had two hours." When she pleaded to be allowed to call her mother, he replied gruffly, "Monica, we know you're smart, you are twenty-four years old—you don't need to call your mommy."

As it happened, Marcia Lewis, who usually speaks to her daughter once a day, had by then paged her for the third time. Monica told them that if they didn't let her call, to reassure her mother that everything was OK, Marcia would have the police looking for her. Reluctantly they agreed to allow her to make a short call, but only on the condition that she limited the conversation to telling her mother not to worry. It was now three-twenty in the afternoon. Monica had been with the FBI for only two hours, but it felt like a lifetime.

As she had agreed, Monica told her mother that she was all right and would call her soon. During their brief conversation FBI Agent Fallon sat by her, his finger over the phone ready to cut her off if she tried to tell Marcia what was happening. Then the remorseless pressure to cooperate started again, Bennett's deep, rough voice cutting through the fuggy atmosphere in the room, warning her that she was running out of time, that if she didn't soon decide to cooperate they would not be able to help her with the legal consequences.

At one point Agent Fallon asked her, with a smirk on his face, "Does it bother you that I have a gun on? Because I can put it in the other room." Later, when they had again told Monica that she was facing twenty-seven years in jail, he nonchalantly flipped back his jacket to show her his handcuffs. Monica was being subjected to intimidating and remorseless psychological pressure, her inquisitors telling her, for the record, that she could leave when she liked, while making it very, very clear what the consequences would be if she did. Understandably, Monica disagrees with the assertion made by Kenneth Starr—who was never present—that she was not held against her will by the assorted law officers crowded into room 1012. "I still have nightmares about it," she says, "the sense of being trapped and drowning."

For ten hours Monica was alone with as many as nine armed FBI agents and Starr's deputies, hard-boiled characters who normally hunt or prosecute those responsible for the most serious and brutal federal offenses. It is worth noting, too, that Udolf had previously been found by a jury to have "maliciously and arbitrarily" violated a defendant's civil rights when he was Georgia's State Prosecutor; the jury awarded the plaintiff $50,000 in damages.

Yet, in spite of all the bullying and occasional blandishments, Monica stoutly resisted their demands that she betray her lover and her friends by wearing a body wire or by allowing their investigators to listen to her phone calls. She was sustained by thoughts of Hannah Senesh, the Hungarian-Jewish poet whose heroism and love for her mother had figured in one of Monica's school essays.

These thoughts gave Monica strength. She defiantly told Bennett that, since they were not going to allow her to make any phone calls or to speak freely to her mother, she was leaning towards not cooperating. Bennett, who is known in legal circles as "The Thug," played his ace: "You should know that we are going to prosecute your mother too, because of the things you have said she has done. We have it all on tape."

For Monica, this whole terrifying experience had now come down to the cruelest of dilemmas: did she save the man she loved, or her mother? She broke down in tears again, sobbing to the roomful of prosecutors and agents that, while she could choose her own fate, she could not make a decision that would hurt her mother. In her heart, Monica conceded that she was no Hannah Senesh.

She pleaded with them to let her call her mother once again. They remained very reluctant to grant her request, fearful that Marcia would speak to a lawyer. Monica was made to promise that, if she was permitted to speak to her mother, she would make sure that Marcia did not tell a soul about what was going on.

At last, they agreed. Prosecutor Emmick said that Marcia could call him, so that he could explain the situation. Monica insisted that she speak to her mother alone, away from Room 1012. Even though they assured her that they would not listen in, she was adamant that she wanted to call from somewhere where she could be reasonably certain the phones were not bugged. They laughed in her face as though she were insane when she said that all the phones in the mall were probably bugged as well. Monica remembers thinking, "They have taken my picture, listened to my conversations, Ken Starr is prosecuting me—and I'm supposed to be paranoid?"

They allowed her to leave the room on the conditions they had discussed, and promised they would not follow her. Within moments of walking out, though, she was being monitored by an FBI agent. As in a movie, she lost him by changing elevators, and eventually reached the mall without a tail. Then, to her amazement, as she passed the Museum of Art store she saw Linda Tripp, carrying several bags. The woman who had plunged her into this nightmare was calmly shopping, seemingly without a care in the world. As Monica passed her she snarled, "Thanks a lot!" Clearly startled, Tripp simply recited, like a mantra, "They did the same thing to me, they did the same to me." Monica walked on. Had she then known the full extent of Tripp's treachery, she says, her response would have been very different. "I would have tried to kill her," she says simply—and means it.

From the mall Linda Tripp went home to another reception committee—Paula Jones's lawyers, who were scheduled to question President Clinton the following morning, after he had made his deposition regarding the case. Tripp gave them a full briefing about Monica Lewinsky.

As media commentator Steven Brill noted, "Thus the President's criminal inquisitors [the OIC], having just finished with Tripp, had now made it possible for his civil case opponents [the Jones legal team] to be given ammunition with which to question the President in his sworn testimony—from which Starr, in turn, might then be able to extract evidence of criminal perjury." When, on January 17, the President came to make his deposition, he was ambushed by Jones's lawyers with information about Monica supplied the previous day by Linda Tripp.

It proved deadly. Cross-examined by Jones's attorney, the President denied under oath having had an affair with Monica. Then the attorney asked, "Have you ever had sexual relations with Monica Lewinsky?" Clinton's answer may have sealed his political fate. He said, "I have never had sexual relations with Monica Lewinsky. I've never had an affair with her." As the saga unfolded, much would depend on the strict definition of "sexual relations" and on whether oral, as opposed to penetrative, sex came under that definition.

As for Monica, though she was acutely aware of the danger facing the President, her first concern as she wandered through the Pentagon City mall was to speak to her mother. Eventually she found a phone, called Marcia and, between gusts of tears—she managed to keep her voice fairly calm—told her what was going on. Her fragile self-control shattered when an overweight bag lady sidled up to her: still disoriented by shock and fear, Monica at once suspected that the woman was an undercover FBI agent. Lowering her voice to the barest whisper, she begged her mother over and over again, "Please don't make me cooperate, please don't make me cooperate."

Monica kept the bargain she had made in Room 1012: she made her mother promise not to speak to anyone else, but to call Prosecutor Mike Emmick at the Ritz-Carlton. Then, having ended the call, she returned to the room to let them know that her mother wanted to talk to them. One of them called Marcia and, after a short conversation, agreed that she could come on the train from New York to join her daughter.

In Marcia's Fifth Avenue apartment, Debra Finerman was sitting with her sister and mother when Monica called. The scene is burned into Debra's memory. "We were just sitting chatting when the phone rings. Marcia answered it and started to shake. She said, 'Where are you? Where are you?' and started screaming over the phone. I thought, 'Oh no, something's happened, Monica's had an accident.' Then she hung up the phone and Marcia was drip white. She said, 'The FBI have Monica. I don't know why exactly but Linda Tripp has trapped her at the Ritz-Carlton at the Pentagon. The FBI have her in a hotel room and they won't let her call a lawyer. She was crying and we have to go right away.'"

Appalled, the three woman grabbed their coats and headed for Penn Station to catch the 5 P.M. Washington train. During that interminable journey, they tried to absorb the enormity of the situation. They simply could not understand why Monica was in danger of going to jail because of the Paula Jones case. They could not believe it might be true. "We were frightened and bewildered. We didn't know what terrible danger she was in. It was scary enough that she was in a room full of FBI agents," says Debra.

As the train rumbled on, Marcia desperately jabbed at the buttons on her mobile phone, trying to contact her ex-husband, Bernie, in Los Angeles to tell him of their daughter's awful predicament. It was beyond frustrating. First she couldn't get hold of him, then the connection kept breaking and, since the train was delayed, she had to stand in line because everyone wanted to use the train's phone.

Bernie Lewinsky was chairing a meeting of the Los Angeles County Radiation Oncology group when he was beeped. When told that Marcia was on the phone, he thought her call would be to say that Monica, because she was moving to New York, needed some assistance until she was settled. Marcia swiftly shattered that illusion, explaining that Monica was in the hands of the FBI and in deep trouble because of something to do with Whitewater and a relationship with the President.

Though he was in the dark about the entire business—Monica had confided in her mother a little about her affair, but had told Bernie nothing—his instinctive response, when he heard that the FBI had threatened his daughter with jail if she didn't cooperate, was that she must do what the G-men told her. Bernie, a man who won't even jaywalk, has a deep respect, amounting almost to fear, for the Federal Bureau of Investigation. As he says, "You just don't mess with those guys."

Over the phone, he and Marcia agreed that they urgently needed to find a lawyer. Neither of them knew of anyone in Washington, but Bernie's medical-malpractice lawyer, Bill Ginsburg, had an office there. Bernie told Marcia he would contact Ginsburg and get him on the case. From that moment on, Bernie worked tirelessly for his daughter, and the decade of bitterness between Bernie and Marcia since their divorce was forgotten. Marcia has said, "Bernie was truly wonderful, because he went through hell. He stepped up to the plate for Monica. I wrote to him to say that he was a father for the whole country." Even Debra Finerman, who had not spoken to Bernie since the divorce, was impressed. "He was everything a father should be. It really was his shining hour."

Back in Room 1012, meanwhile, Monica was feeling calmer, knowing that her mother was on the way. She had had plans to go out that night with her friend Ashley Raines, but knew that there was no chance she would make it now. Still thinking that the phones in the room were bugged, she insisted on going to a pay phone in the hotel lobby to call Ashley and cancel their date. Again as in a movie, an FBI agent lurked nearby. When she made the call, leaving a message on Ashley's machine, Monica hoped that she might by the tone of her voice alert her friend to the danger the President was facing, and thereby get a warning to him. It was, of course, a vain hope.

By now it was early evening and Frank Carter's office was closed. She asked how, the following day being a Saturday, she could contact her attorney over the weekend if she decided not to cooperate. Knowing that the immediate danger to their inquiry—that Monica should consult with her lawyer—was now past, Agent Fallon offered to phone Carter's office to establish his whereabouts that weekend. When he returned, he told her that Carter could only be contacted through the office answering service.

As it turned out, Fallon's call to Carter, whether by accident or design, later enabled Kenneth Starr to argue publicly that his men had not violated Monica's rights; the phone records showed that a call had been placed to her attorney's office, which proved that they had given her the opportunity to speak with him. As so often in this case, the facts may be accurate, but the truth lies somewhere else.

In the Ritz-Carlton, Monica was consumed by two thoughts: worry about her family, especially her mother; and a frantic, despairing determination that, somehow, the President had to be warned and protected. She felt she was going crazy in that crowded, airless room, and so suggested that she might kill time until her mother arrived by walking around the mall. The investigators agreed.

Accompanied by Fallon and Emmick, she strolled around the mall, pottering about in the Crate and Barrel household store and window shopping in others. Monica put on her bright and cheerful face, and was friendly and chatty, cracking jokes and trying, in her usual way, to make her wardens like her. If, she reasoned, she could show that she was just an ordinary, nice person, they might decide not to prosecute her.

Uppermost in her mind was the need to save the President. While they were mooching around Macy's store, she excused herself and went to the restroom on the third floor. There she saw a pay phone, and she tried to call Betty Currie to warn her, but there was no answer and Monica slammed down the handset in frustration. Stifling her rising panic, she spotted a mother changing her baby's diaper and thought if she gave her Betty's number, maybe she could call her. Then she was struck by the contrary thought that, if the FBI found out, the baby's mother would end up in jail as well. Paralyzed with fear, she did nothing. "It is exhausting just to think about it," she remembers. "I was so panicked I could hear my heartbeat going 'Boom, boom, boom,' and feel myself breathing."

When she emerged from the restroom, she discovered that Agent Fallon, anxious because she had been gone for so long, had left to search for her. When he returned she suggested that, to kill more time, they have supper. So at six-thirty in the evening Monica found herself sitting in a booth of Mozzarella's American Grill with an FBI agent and one of Starr's deputies. "It was just surreal. Everyone around us was laughing and enjoying themselves and here was I, my life in ruins. I thought of the President and his face when he heard what had happened. It was like imagining how angry your parents are going to be when you do something wrong as a kid.

"Emotionally I was shut down now, like a rape victim who screams for the first five minutes and then just stops. I had just closed down."

Even their dinnertime conversation was bizarre. Monica asked Emmick to explain why she would go to jail for twenty-seven years, whereupon he rapidly ticked off the number of years for each charge, using his fingers to emphasize each point. What he did not say, of course, was that these were the *maximum* sentences for each offense. In fact, as Monica had never been convicted of a felony, she would most likely have escaped with probation or a minimal custodial sentence.

Even Emmick's assertion that she had committed a crime was dubious, for the simple reason that when she was picked up and held, her attorney, Frank Carter, had not yet filed her false affidavit. Until it was filed it could have been changed, without serious legal consequences. This may explain why, throughout that long afternoon, the men from the OIC and the FBI worked so hard to stop Monica from contacting her lawyer. Carter has confirmed that, had he spoken to her, her sworn affidavit would not have been filed. As it was, he sent it to the court in Little Rock, Arkansas, where the Jones case was to be heard, by Federal Express at the end of that day's business.

Were Kenneth Starr and his deputies acting as agents provocateurs, wanting a crime to be committed and waiting for that to happen? They could easily have prevented the crime, had they so wished, but they knew that if Monica committed perjury they would have leverage not only over her but over the President, their real target. Again, if the President had known of Starr's interest in Monica Lewinsky that day, he would almost certainly have changed the nature of his deposition in the Paula Jones case, thus altering the course of history. This was not the first time Starr's investigation had sought progress by, at best, questionable means, nor would it be the last. As one hard-bitten American attorney has said of the OIC's methods, "What they did was par for the course, SOP, Standard Operating Procedure." It is worth noting, too, that in the United States in 1998 there were fewer than a handful of prosecutions in "victimless" civil cases for any of the charges Monica faced. "At the time they seized her they did not have a solid case," observes Billy Martin, who later became Marcia's attorney, agreeing with the view, expressed by the *New York Times*, among others, that this whole episode has been manipulated by the Paula Jones lawyers and other right-wing attorneys with the purpose of snaring the President.

Just as Starr's men had played fast and loose with the rules in order to link the Whitewater inquiry to Lewinsky, so in the twelve hours during which they held Monica they ruthlessly exploited her ignorance of the law and of her rights. Yet throughout her ordeal she resisted their threats and their browbeating.

Bernie Lewinsky has the greatest admiration for her: "The more they attempted to squeeze and intimidate her the stronger she became. I admire her tremendous strength—I don't know how many kids could go through what she went through. It was incredible that she was able to stand up to these bullies carrying a silver shield."

Their dinner over, Monica and her shadows returned to Room 1012 to wait for her mother. The FBI agents morosely flicked through the TV channels, carefully going past any news stations, before hitting on the 1954 musical *There's No Business Like Show Business*, with Ethel Merman, Donald O'Connor and, in a minor role, Marilyn Monroe. For a while Monica talked brightly about how she had been in school musicals, then she lapsed into agitated silence, taking up the room's Bible to read over and over again the Ninety-First Psalm, the psalm for divine protection that the Christian Science counselor had recommended. She found some small comfort in the lines: "I will say of the Lord, He is my refuge and my fortress: my God; in him will I trust."

Finally, at sixteen minutes past ten, the doorbell rang. An agent went to answer it, and suddenly Marcia appeared, like a guardian angel. "I have never been so happy to see her in my entire life," says Monica. "It was like being a little girl again and your mom was going to make everything all right. She was my lifeboat because for the last few hours I felt I had been swimming alone in the the vast ocean. I was alone in this dark, scary place and she rescued me."

Marcia, who had told her sister and mother to go to Debra's apartment in the Watergate complex when they got off the train, had steeled herself to be calm and composed for her daughter's sake. Even so, she quailed when she saw the state her daughter was in: "Monica was standing by the window, her eyes swollen from crying and her face was so full of pain and fear. She was holding a Bible in her hand and her whole body was shaking. Who did this to my daughter?"

Running to her, Marcia flung her arms around her and murmured the words all mothers comfort their children with—"Everything will be all right." Then, with all the calm and dignity she could muster, she introduced herself to the assembled agents and deputies sprawled around the room.

Starr's prosecutors had already agreed to give mother and daughter a few minutes together before speaking to Marcia Lewis on her own. Monica, who was convinced the room was bugged, insisted that she and Marcia be allowed to talk in the hallway. Once they were alone, Monica urgently told her mother, "I can't do this. I can't wear a wire, I can't tape record phone calls, I can't do this to the President." She insisted that they leave and try to contact Betty Currie so that the President could be warned. She wanted to explain to him the mess she was in, and to let him know that she would tell everyone she had made up the whole story of their affair. By this time she was so agitated that her mother had great difficulty calming her down.

After a few minutes, the two women were interrupted and told that they had had long enough alone. Marcia Lewis was whisked off to another room, where Starr's deputies explained Monica's predicament. "They told me that she faced twenty-seven years in jail for lying, and they were using all these words—'suborning perjury' and so on—phrases ordinary people never hear. I thought they were pretty fancy words just for telling a lie, for wanting to protect the man she was in love with.

"Part of me didn't believe what was happening, and I wanted to explain to these people that they had made a terrible mistake and that there was no way she should spend twenty-seven minutes in jail, much less twenty-seven years."

Faced with the prosecutors' hostility, Marcia began to tell them anything that came into her head which, she felt, might persuade them to let Monica go: she was young for her age; she had been suicidal six years before (which was an exaggeration, if a pardonable one in the circumstances); she was highly emotional. They listened to her, but insisted that Monica should decide whether or not to cooperate quickly, as the whole issue was—that term again—"time sensitive."

Marcia remembers looking at the clock, which by then showed eleven o'clock, and wondering what office could possibly be open at that time of night whose work or requirements would make the issue of Monica's co-operation "time sensitive." She even tried to compromise by pleading with them to let her hire a nearby room so that she and her daughter could both rest; they could, she said, station armed guards outside so they couldn't escape. The suggestion cut no ice with her daughter's accusers. Looking back now, Marcia vividly recalls the desperation with which she tried to resolve matters. "I didn't think that we would ever leave and I thought that the next stage would be arrest. There was no option. They said criminal charges would be filed unless Monica cooperated, and she refused to co-operate. It wasn't a case of 'You can go home and live happily ever after.'

"I said anything because I was desperate for them to let her go. In my naïveté I thought these men might go into conference and say perhaps we shouldn't do this to this girl, 'Perhaps it isn't right.' At this point I wanted them to pause, to say, 'Wait a minute, this is not Linda Tripp, this is not some middle-aged, hard-bitten woman who we're going to push around. This is a baby.'

"Were there no mothers working at the FBI? Was there no compassion? Who heard Monica's voice on Linda Tripp's tape, this young, innocent creature, and said it would be a good thing to get her? Who said, 'Let's sting her, put her in a hotel room, threaten her with jail and she will cooperate with our quest?'"

Cooperation was the key. Time and again they emphasized that, if Monica did as they asked, they would not file criminal charges against her. During her conversations with Starr's deputies that night, Marcia, who still did not understand what the whole thing was about, asked what would happen if Monica just told them what she knew, or if the Paula Jones case were to be settled, or if her daughter had lied in her conversations with Linda Tripp? For of one thing she was certain: "I know my daughter, and there was no way in the world that she would wear a wire to betray some-one. That was simply a waste of breath arguing about it."

Marcia had sufficient wit not to be gulled into trusting these men. She had followed the case of the Unabomber, Ted Kaczynski, who was arrested by the FBI after a tip-off from his brother David. The latter had turned him in only on condition that the FBI promised not to seek the death penalty. They agreed, and David Kaczynski, who had agonized over the decision, led them to his brother. Once in custody, the terrorist was charged with a crime for which the penalty on conviction was death; the FBI claimed that they had never promised anything.

In the light of this, and deeply mistrusting the motives of the men who were pressuring her daughter, Marcia told Mike Emmick that she would like to have one other person, her former husband, hear them repeat their promise that no charges would be filed if Monica cooperated. Emmick replied that they could not possibly call Bernie. Marcia, staying calm for her daughter's sake, explained that she wanted them to make that call so that there would be independent proof of the OIC's offer to Monica. Rather sarcastically the prosecutor responded, "You want it in writing?" After a moment's thought, Marcia accepted his unguarded offer. Flustered, Emmick left her, and went to confer with his colleagues. When he returned he told her that he could not give her a note as he did not have a typewriter. "At that point warning bells went off in my head," Marcia remembers. "Nobody uses a typewriter anymore. He could have scribbled something on a piece of paper. It was then that I realized that this was much scarier and more dangerous than I could ever have imagined." So now, well after eleven at night, she began firmly to insist that she call Monica's father.

Since receiving the emergency call from Marcia during her train journey, Bernie Lewinsky had been busy. He had managed to track down Bill Ginsburg, who was in court, presenting a case. When he was told that Bernie wanted to speak to him, Ginsburg announced, with a theatrical flourish that was to become his trademark, that a radiation oncologist had an urgent call for him, and asked for the hearing to be suspended.

Once Ginsburg had heard from Bernie what little he knew, he told him gravely, "Don't say anything more on the telephone. I'll see you as soon as possible." "After that," Bernie remembers, "I started shaking." He respected Ginsburg's judgment, knowing that his reputation as a trial lawyer, particularly for his cross-examinations in complicated medical cases, was second to none. He had been the malpractice lawyer for Bernie's practice—Western Tumor Medical Group—for some years, and the two of them got along fine, not least because they were the same age and had attended Berkeley in San Francisco at the same time, although they had only become friends during the mid-1990s when Bernie remarried. He and his second wife, Barbara, made up regular foursomes with Bill and Laura Ginsburg, going on wine-tasting weekends and for short holidays out of state. Most Friday nights they got together to watch a movie and eat sushi. With his trademark bow ties, avuncular manner and voice like a sober W.C. Fields, Ginsburg was to become an instant national celebrity.

That night, however, as far as Bernie Lewinsky was concerned, Bill Ginsburg was the man riding to the rescue of his daughter. The two men met in a club in downtown Los Angeles where, after what seemed like an eternity, Bernie at last received a call on his mobile phone from Marcia, who told him where she was and who she was with. As the reception in the bar was poor, he went outside and stood in the street trying to make sense of what was going on. Amid the traffic noise, he spoke briefly to Monica and, in between her hysterical sobs, told her, "Monica, don't say another word. We've got Bill Ginsburg here—don't say another word." Since the signal on his mobile kept breaking up, he found a pay phone on the street corner so that he could talk to Mike Emmick without the static interference. Emmick told Bernie, who had Ginsburg standing silently at his side, that anything he said was totally confidential and should not be communicated to anyone under any circumstances. "I was shaking in my shoes," Bernie admits. "I had never spoken to an FBI agent before and I was scared stiff."

Once again Emmick explained that Monica was in very serious trouble. As far as the investigators were concerned, she was involved in perjury, a conspiracy and a cover-up involving the President, and unless she cooperated she faced twenty-seven years in jail. Still baffled, her father asked, "What do you mean by cooperate?" So Emmick told him that Monica had to agree to wear a wire and record conversations with Vernon Jordan, Betty Currie, and possibly the President.

Despite his shock and alarm, Bernie had the presence of mind to ask, "Isn't she entitled to an attorney?" When Emmick asked whether she had an attorney—though he had known all day that she was represented by Frank Carter—Bernie said that she had, and that his name was William Ginsburg. Monica, who had met Ginsburg briefly a couple of years before, confirmed to the prosecutor that he was her attorney in Los Angeles. Emmick was wary, and advised Monica that she did not have to accept an attorney she had not selected. Bernie, of course, knowing nothing of his daughter's affair, or her putative link to the Paula Jones case, did not know that she had already engaged a lawyer. "At that point we knew nothing about Frank Carter," he says. "I was just trying to help my daughter in a difficult spot."

Bill Ginsburg, having spoken to Monica to establish a formal attorney–client relationship, then discussed his new client's legal options with Emmick, in particular the possibility of securing "transactional immunity" for her, which prevents any prosecution relating to any matter surrounding the testimony. Just as Marcia's instincts had shouted caution, so Ginsburg's legal antennae now began to twitch when Emmick told him that they might perhaps be able to offer Monica immunity.

That answer, Ginsburg believed, meant they were trying to pull a fast one. He covered the mouthpiece and whispered to Bernie that they were not allowed to offer transactional immunity without authority. He therefore decided to call their bluff: he asked them to put the agreement on paper and fax it to him. Once again Emmick demurred, this time saying that he didn't have access to a computer on which to type it, whereupon the attorney asked him to write it out longhand, sign it, and then fax it. Emmick kept asking Ginsburg to trust him, to which he received the dry answer, "I put my trust in God, not US attorneys." Finally, Emmick admitted that he was not empowered to offer anything in writing. His bluff had been comprehensively called. Furthermore, the OIC's questionable methods had been exposed. As Ginsburg says, "One of the persistent themes throughout this investigation has been high-handed, tough tactics to get people to say what they want."

Monica remembers that, during the exchange between Emmick and Ginsburg, the former offered to fax her new attorney a copy of her false affidavit. The two FBI agents, however, pulled him roughly away from the telephone. They realized Ginsburg would instantly understand that the OIC had seen a copy of her affidavit *before* it had been filed, which meant that in all probability it had come from Paula Jones's lawyers, to whom Frank Carter had sent a copy. The OIC knew, when they picked her up, that technically Monica had not committed any serious offense. Furthermore, by preventing her from contacting Carter, they effectively ensured that the serious offense—filing a false affidavit—was committed later in the day. Understandably, Starr's strong-arm tactics have been a matter for grave public concern.

The whole exchange about immunity was a waste of time, except in so far as it exposed the dubious methods employed by Starr's investigators, for Monica had absolutely no intention of wearing a wire and thereby betraying the man she loved. Her behavior moved her father to comment, "She showed tremendous presence of mind not to cooperate, and it certainly rankles that so few people have acknowledged that if she hadn't been so strong, if she had worn a wire tap, she would have done to the President what Linda Tripp did to her. No matter what it meant to her own safety, she was never going to betray anyone like she had been betrayed.

"Whatever faults she may have—a lack of appropriateness and discretion, perhaps—when the chips are down she sure comes through. People don't give her enough credit for that. They treat her like a bimbo, when the last thing she is is a bimbo. Many women would be taken in by the most powerful man on earth, and while I don't approve of what she did, she is not a bad person for having done what she did." It is a quality of steadfastness recognized by family friends. Dale Young observes: "She refused to benefit by betraying others. At that moment, knowing she would go to jail, she showed her true character. I will always be proud of Monica for that."

Once Emmick's bluff had been called, Ginsburg spoke to Monica again, and told her that he was flying to Washington the next day to see her. He told her and Marcia not to say another word, and to leave the hotel. "Just trust me," he said. "Everything will work out fine." After the two women informed Starr's deputies of their decision, they were each served with a subpoena prior to leaving the hotel complex.

Before they parted that night, Bernie Lewinsky asked Bill Ginsburg if he was qualified to take on such a daunting legal task; after all, he was primarily a medical attorney. The other man assured him that he had experience in civil litigation, and that he would have no difficulty in putting together a team of suitable Washington lawyers. Then Bernie asked what the bottom line was. "If it's an easy case, $150,000. If it goes to trial, it will be $1 million," Ginsburg told him. Furthermore, he wanted $25,000 for starters, before he even caught his plane to Washington and his meeting with Monica. That night Bernie and Barbara barely slept, their thoughts constantly turning to Monica, three thousand miles away and facing the threat of jail. "We held each other," Barbara remembers, "crying and shaking with fear and thinking that she is going to jail. It was just awful."

It was after one in the morning by the time Monica and Marcia reached their Watergate apartment. Wide awake from the adrenaline rush, yet fearing that the apartment was bugged, they barely dared to say a word to one another. Monica's mind raced with the awful dangers facing the President. Somehow he must be warned. Careless, as ever, of the consequences to herself, she allowed all manner of wild plans to form and re-form in her head. She considered taking a taxi to wake Betty Currie and warn her, or calling the President's attorney, Bruce Lindsey, even though she had never spoken to him. Even as Monica talked about warning the White House, her mother made her swear to stay silent, fearing that any such action would jeopardize whatever chance her daughter might have of securing immunity in the future.

At two in the morning, they drove to the Four Seasons hotel to phone Bill Ginsburg. They talked of leaving the country, of fleeing across the border to Canada, but that idea was discarded as soon as it was mentioned, because they believed that the FBI would have every airport and border post staked out. An indication of just how terrified they were came at the hotel when a young couple entered the lobby. The two women were instantly convinced that they were FBI agents sent to spy on them. "This absolute fear of being followed began immediately," Monica says.

By now Monica, who was veering between manic activity and an unnerving silence, had closed down again. When they returned to the apartment, Marcia had become so terrified that her daughter would commit suicide that she made her leave the door open when she took a shower, so as to be sure that she did nothing untoward. For what remained of that night, Monica lay on her bed, drifting in and out of consciousness, while her mother watched over her to see that she did not take her own life.

The horror had begun.

CHAPTER TWELVE

● ●

"*I Didn't Matter Anymore*"

*T*HE IMAGE of President Clinton's friend Susan McDougal, hand-cuffed and fettered, leaving a courthouse in Little Rock, Arkansas, in 1996 has come to symbolize the iniquities of Kenneth Starr's ruthless pursuit of the President and First Lady. McDougal's refusal to testify before a Whitewater grand jury in Little Rock because, she claims, Starr was seeking to ruin the lives of Bill and Hillary Clinton, rather than impartially investigating Whitewater, earned her an eighteen-month jail sentence for contempt of court, much of it spent in solitary confinement, and a place in the pantheon of all-American heroines: she became known wryly as "Joan of Arkansas."

The image of a shackled Susan McDougal was firmly fixed in Marcia Lewis's mind from the moment she and Monica escaped the clutches of Starr's deputies. "All I knew was that these were the same people who had put Susan McDougal in jail without a trial because she had not done what they wanted her to."

Ironically, Susan McDougal had featured in the last conversation Monica had with Catherine Allday Davis, just after the New Year. Catherine, sensing that events were closing in upon her friend, cautioned her not to go down the same path as McDougal because, she remembers, "I didn't want her to lie to protect the President if it meant that she would get into trouble."

When at last they left the Ritz-Carlton in Pentagon City, very early in the morning of Saturday, January 17, Marcia was confused about the nature of the charges her daughter faced, and simply could not understand why she herself was at risk, not knowing then that Monica had mentioned her name frequently during her taped conversations with Linda Tripp. After all, the only "crime" she had committed was to have listened to her daughter's romantic woes and then encouraged her to leave Washington. The memory of that time is etched on Marcia's mind. "When we went home we knew absolutely that Starr's deputies were just going to come later. That's how we lived in that apartment, in the darkness, all alone and completely isolated from everyone, with the door locked, thinking that they were coming at any minute.

Left: Monica with Andy Bleiler, the first man she fell in love with. They met when Monica was a high-school student and he was a drama technician at the school.

Below: Monica and Andy at her 21st birthday party during the summer of 1994, which he spent in Portland, Oregon.

Left: Hanging out with Lewis and Clark college friends.

Below: With Linda Estergard, who became a close friend and the "mother" of Monica's college group.

Facing page: Graduation Day in May 1995.

Monica with her close girl-friends: Neysa DeMann Erbland *(above)*, and Catherine Allday Davis *(below left)*. Both of these young women were called to testify before the Grand Jury. In spite of this their friendships with Monica have flourished.

Facing page: Catherine visited Monica during her internship at the White House. Pictured in front of the East Room on the North Portico.

Above: Monica's supervisor during her internship, Tracey Beckett, kindly gave her family a tour of the White House. As is customary, they all took pictures behind the podium in the press briefing room.

Below: Left to right, Monica's aunt, Debra, her grandmother, Marcia Lewis, her cousin Alex, Monica and her brother Michael.

Above: The very first photograph of the President and Monica together. It was taken at his 49th birthday party on the South Lawn of the White House on August 10, 1995. Even before the relationship started, it was clear that there was a mutual attraction.

Below: The President and Monica in the Chief of Staff's office during the furlough on Friday, November 17, 1995. Unbeknown to everyone else present, they had already met privately twice earlier that evening.

Right: Monica at an arrival ceremony for the President of the Republic of Ireland on June 13, 1996. She attended this event with her father and brother Michael. When President Clinton passed by he said: "I like your hat, Monica." Her father was amazed that Bill Clinton recognized her.

Below: Family outing to the White House to listen to the radio address on June 14, 1996. Left to right, stepmother Barbara, Bernard Lewinsky, President Clinton, Michael and Monica. Michael had just turned 18 and he was eager to let the President know that he would be casting his first vote for Bill Clinton.

Above: Monica shakes hands with the President at a White House holiday party in December 1996. The next night the President called to compliment her on her appearance. He also told her that he had Christmas presents for her – a hand-made hat pin from New Mexico and a beautifully bound edition of *Leaves of Grass* by the poet Walt Whitman.

Below: Monica's favorite picture of herself with Bill Clinton. It was taken in the Oval Office on February 28, 1997 and signed for her birthday in July that year.

To Monica – Happy Birthday! Bill Clinton
7-23-97

Above: Leaving for Bosnia on a C-17 cargo plane. This was Monica's first trip to Bosnia. Pictured with her boss, Pentagon spokesman Ken Bacon (left) and Colonel P.J. Crowley.

Below: Receiving an award for outstanding achievement from Ken Bacon on behalf of the Secretary of Defense in 1997. On the lapel of her "lucky suit" she is wearing the pin given to her as a 24th birthday gift by the President.

Above: Monica with her mother and her Aunt Debra
in Washington, D.C., in 1998.

Above: Monica's one-time friend and, later, betrayer, Linda Tripp, who secretly taped their private conversations, outside her home in Maryland in January 1998.

Below: Days after the scandal became public in January 1998, former lover Andy Bleiler called a press conference outside his home in Portland, Oregon, to make public his version of their time together.

Above: An emotional reunion with her father outside his home in Los Angeles in February 1998. It was the first time Monica had seen him since the story broke. He was her "Rock of Gibraltar" during the darkest days of her life.

Below: Stepmother Barbara holds off frenzied paparazzi as she and Monica emerge from a restaurant in Santa Monica later that week.

Left: Monica was sickened to see this picture of her mother emerging from her second day of Grand Jury testimony in February 1998. It made Monica more than ever resolved to stand up to the Office of the Independent Counsel.

Above right: The man behind the four-year investigation of President Clinton, Independent Counsel Kenneth Starr.

Below: Leaving the Federal Building in Los Angeles on May 28, 1998, after spending three hours giving fingerprints and handwriting samples to the FBI. Left to right, Todd Theodora, Monica and attorney Bill Ginsburg.

Above: Monica with her closest friend in DC and White House colleague, Ashley Raines, at Michael Lewinsky's graduation in June 1996. She was the first of Monica's friends to be called to testify against her before the Grand Jury.

Below: Attorney Jacob Stein (right) joins the legal team in June 1998 to try and secure Monica immunity from prosecution. He and fellow veteran Washington lawyer Plato Cacheris replaced Bill Ginsburg. Lawyer Nathaniel Speights (left) stayed on.

Above: Monica's family all gathered together for her 25th birthday celebration - the best birthday present she could have imagined. She had learned that day that it was likely that she would receive immunity. Left to right: stepmother Barbara, Bernard Lewinsky, Monica, Marcia Lewis, Michael and stepfather Peter Straus.

Right: The first day of Monica's testimony before the Grand Jury on August 6, 1998. By the end she had built up an affectionate rapport with the jurors, who offered her a "bouquet of good wishes" for the future. This meant the world to Monica.

"I can't help it if that sounds overly neurotic, but I cannot tell you just how frightened I was. How absolutely certain I was that these people were going to put us in jail and that Monica, who would not cooperate with them, was going to jail for twenty-seven years."

They were convinced that the FBI were tapping their telephones, that their Watergate apartment was bugged and their every move watched by unseen but accusing eyes. For most of the time before the scandal became public—and all the time afterwards—they stayed in the apartment with the curtains tightly closed, pacing the floor, afraid to speak except in whispers, and expecting at any moment the knock on the door that would be the dreaded prelude to a prison cell.

They hardly ate—their mouths were almost too dry to talk, let alone swallow food—and all the time they felt either very hot or freezing cold, as if their bodies were shutting down. Both women were in severe shock, shaking continually. Marcia says, "If I had been alone I would have thought I was dying, but as we both had the same symptoms I realized that it was a result of the fear and shock." Such was their terror that they dared not even throw out the trash, afraid that those they suspected were watching them would subsequently accuse them of destroying vital evidence. Each day Marcia bundled up the garbage in a bag and left it neatly in the kitchen, so that when the FBI came to take them away they would be able to show that they had acted correctly.

Marcia says, "You do crazy things because you are so full of fear. We were literally terrorized. For days we stayed there, frightened, isolated, afraid to speak to anyone. All I could think of was, if we both went to jail, who would be there to visit Monica? The other thing in my mind was my son, Michael—what happened when he married and had children? I couldn't stand the thought of my grandchildren visiting me in jail."

Naturally, Marcia's first thought was for her family. She dared not let Monica out of her sight, afraid that she would harm herself. As the days passed and they began to realize that the scandal was going to become public, her fear for her daughter's safety intensified. At the same time as seeking to protect Monica, she wanted those others she loved to escape this "ugly, horrifying mess." Shortly before the story broke on Wednesday, January 21, 1998, she spoke urgently to Debra, who still maintained her pied à terre in the Watergate, telling her to pack her bags and leave Washington. Afraid that the FBI would be watching the train station and airport, Marcia urged her to drive as far away as possible. Debra collected a few things from her home in Virginia and then drove for eight hours to be with her son, Alex, in Boston, Massachusetts. "I was really scared, I felt like a fugitive in my own country," Debra recalls.

Also before the scandal became public, Marcia briefly called her fiancé, Peter Straus, who was due to have eye surgery and was expecting her imminent return to New York, to say that Monica had had an accident and that she, Marcia, would have to stay in Washington for a while to be with her. "I felt awful," Marcia remembers, "because I didn't want Peter to know about it. At that time I really never expected to see anyone I either knew or loved again. It sounds melodramatic but there was a darkness, a strange nightmarish quality to this affair. While it is easy, now that the pieces are in place, to say, 'Why didn't I do this or that?' for an ordinary person who has never been in a criminal situation to be swept up by the FBI, Starr and the government . . . it was truly terrifying." Several days later she called Peter to see how he was, and explained that something terrible had happened but that she could not say what it was. She told him that if he never wanted to speak to her again when he found out about the scandal she would quite understand, and thanked him for the great times they had had. Peter recalls: "She was trying to protect me and I have never, ever been so touched."

One of the most difficult aspects of this awful affair for Marcia was having to lie to her son. Again, just before the scandal broke Michael phoned from Pittsburgh, where he was attending Carnegie Mellon University, to say that there was something about his sister on the Internet, and he asked what was going on. Still thinking that the affair would never become public, she told him that the rumors were nonsense. "I felt very bad about that because he trusted me, he took my word that it wasn't true. But a parent wants to soothe a child," she says. After the scandal broke, she found she could not even explain the situation to him on the phone; instead, she had to speak to him through the family's attorney, Bill Ginsburg.

For Marcia, as for her daughter, "There was just a paralyzing fear. I thought I would never go to New York again, never walk down the street, never breathe fresh air, never see my son again. I thought we were going to jail. Period."

A sign of just how scared they were came when they were watching television, for Marcia discovered for the first time the truth about the now infamous stained blue dress. Having watched a story about the fabled garment, she turned to her daughter and said, "Where is the dress now?" to which Monica replied, "Mom, it's in the closet in the New York apartment with all my other things."

With hindsight, it seems ridiculous that Marcia, Monica or someone with access to her apartment in New York did not simply remove the dress and destroy it. The reason was simple: at that time both women were too terrified to travel, to leave the apartment or even to make a phone call, fearful that they were being watched or followed by G-men. They were certain that at any moment they were about to be arrested. Paralyzed with dread, they left that most incriminating piece of evidence in a closet, waiting for its place in history.

As her mother declares emphatically, "Did Monica send the dress to her mother to hide? No. Did her mother spirit the dress away and hide it? No. Did her mother know where the damn dress was? Only when she found out about it on television."

They were not alone in feeling scared. From the moment he became involved, even as experienced an attorney as Bill Ginsburg was sufficiently anxious about the FBI following him to book six separate flights on different routes to get from Los Angeles to Washington. In fact, he flew via Pittsburgh, and from there caught the shuttle to the capital, arriving on the evening of Saturday, January 17, the day after the sting operation.

Monica went to the airport to pick him up, still fearing that any gaggle of men might be FBI agents waiting to arrest her. That night, in a charade of normalcy and with appropriate irony, she, her mother and Ginsburg went out for dinner to The Oval Room, which is only a short distance from the White House. Since neither Marcia nor Monica knew Ginsburg at all well, this was a "get-to-know-you" meeting, before which the lawyer questioned Monica and discussed his plan of attack.

At one stage she used a pay phone in the restaurant to speak to her father in Los Angeles. It was a tearful, traumatic exchange. Bernie made her promise that she would not harm herself, saying that "that bastard"— the President—was not worth it. Then, when this draining, difficult conversation had ended, Bill Ginsburg came on the line and immediately dropped a bombshell: because of Monica's emotional state, he said, he could not allow her to talk to her father again. He was afraid that, during such a call, she might blurt out something that would incriminate her, with disastrous consequences if the phone she were using happened to be bugged.

There was more. Bernie and Barbara had booked a holiday in Hawaii, but had decided to cancel it and fly to Washington so that they could be with Monica. Ginsburg, however, would not hear of it, arguing firmly that their presence would only complicate matters. He insisted that they go on vacation, and added that he would give them a daily update on developments. Bernie says, not without bitterness, "Unbeknownst to us, Bill Ginsburg never told Monica that we had wanted to come to Washington. She felt very hurt when we didn't. It wasn't until May that she discovered the true story."

The following day, Sunday, January 18, Monica waited anxiously in the apartment while Ginsburg went to meet prosecutors at Starr's office to assess their thinking. Her fate was now out of her hands—more even than she thought, because on the Internet *The Drudge Report*, the gossip column which had run the Kathleen Willey story, was reporting a rumor that *Newsweek* had spiked a story by Michael Isikoff about the President and an intern. As yet, however, Monica's name had not been mentioned.

Monica and Marcia picked up Ginsburg from the OIC to take him to the Ritz-Carlton Hotel, where he was staying. In the car, he announced that he was going to state publicly that the President had sexually harassed Monica, and that he was nothing more than a child molester. For the distraught girl, this was her first intimation of how Ginsburg's statements could hinder rather than help her case. The effect on her was instantaneous: "I just flipped out. I screamed at him that he [Clinton] hadn't molested me, that we had an adult relationship."

At that point, too, she said that she wanted to be committed to a psychiatric hospital. "It was all too much for one person to handle. I just felt I was having a nervous breakdown," she says. Instead of being sympathetic, Ginsburg told her brusquely to calm down, and then yelled at her that she would have to learn to get tough so that she could deal with this situation. It was an approach he followed for the next few months.

At the Ritz-Carlton, once they had composed themselves, the trio hired a conference room so that they could discuss the results of Ginsburg's meeting with Starr's deputies. There were, he said, two options, both equally bleak. The first was that Monica would agree to wear a wire and to place phone calls, something that she had already made crystal clear she would never do. The second option was that she face trial, in which eventuality, Ginsburg said, her defense would cost at least $500,000, which would, he pointed out, ruin her father's medical practice. Marcia burst into tears. This set off Monica, which provoked Ginsburg's anger. "It was a ludicrous meeting," Monica remembers.

In the meantime, Monica had been receiving increasingly frantic messages on her pager from Betty Currie. "This was breaking my heart," she admits now, for though she was longing to warn Betty and the President, she knew that if she did so she would lose her last slim chance of immunity, something which would imperil not just her but her mother as well. At that point Marcia faced the prospect of criminal charges relating to the issue of conspiracy. In any case, at that time the OIC prosecutors were offering not immunity from prosecution, but merely an agreement that they would inform the judge, if Monica was convicted, that she had cooperated with them. It was a type of plea bargain which Ginsburg had no hesitation in rejecting.

The following day—Martin Luther King Day, as it happened—Starr's deputies arranged to search Monica's apartment. In the event, they did not show up. Meanwhile Betty kept paging her—"Family emergency, please call," "Good news, please call," and so on. Then Vernon Jordan paged her, and so too did her former attorney, Frank Carter, but Monica was too scared to call them. Eventually, Monica, desperate to make Betty realize that she had not turned on the President and thus on Betty too, went to a pay phone to call her. Once again, thinking that she would be overheard by unseen enemies, she tried to think of some secret way of conveying to the President's secretary what had happened. So when Betty answered, Monica just said "Hoover" (referring to J. Edgar Hoover, the Director of the FBI from 1924 until his death in 1972), and then hung up. After that brief call she became so afraid of using the phones that she wrote Betty a note, in which she thanked her for letting "her daughter Kay [their codeword] visit the White House and the FBI building." She never sent it, nor would it have resolved the dilemma to which, in her misery, her thoughts returned again and again: immunity would betray the man she loved; the alternative, she believed, would see her mother prosecuted. "What was constantly going through my head was my mom and family and everyone on the President's side," she says. "I didn't care about myself. I didn't matter anymore."

As Monica wrestled with her conscience, Bill Ginsburg and the Washington criminal attorney he had brought on board, Nathaniel Speights, battled with Starr's deputies. For hours she waited in an office in the OIC building, being "babysat" by various prosecutors. Meanwhile her two lawyers, who had emphasized to her that their job was to make sure that she was OK, no matter what happened to anyone else, tried to strike a deal. The prospects did not look good. At one point Ginsburg outlined a scenario in which Monica, like Susan McDougal, might be jailed for contempt of court and sent to an all-women's prison if she didn't cooperate with the OIC. Even the possibility of winning at trial now seemed slim.

She was rapidly running out of road. Washington was buzzing with rumors of a presidential affair; *The Drudge Report* fueled the gossip that day, January 19, by mentioning Monica by name. She was now "radioactive." Starr's deputies said it was doubtful that they could offer transactional immunity—which prevents a person being prosecuted for matters arising from their testimony—anymore, as the White House could now be alert to her involvement in the case.

After hours of fruitless negotiation, Monica and her legal team went across the street to the Hard Rock Café for supper, hoping that Starr would make a firm offer of immunity, in exchange for which she would tell them what she knew, rather than wearing a wire and having her phone calls tapped, as Starr had originally wanted.

When they returned to the OIC about ten-thirty, Monica, anxiously waiting in the office, was stunned to hear Ginsburg's deep voice boom out, "You motherfuckers! You're going to subpoena the father?" He opened the door, grabbed Monica and said, "Come on. We're leaving." As they walked down the hallway he told her that they had tried to serve him with a subpoena for Dr. Lewinsky. At this point, Monica says, "I lost it. I fell to the floor in a delirium of despair. It was this feeling of never-ending torture. What were they doing to my family? I couldn't handle it anymore."

Brusquely, Ginsburg told her to get up and calm herself: "You can't let them see you're upset." While he and Monica left the OIC building, Nate Speights stayed behind and eventually persuaded Starr's deputies to drop the idea of serving Bernie with a subpoena.

Meanwhile, Marcia had by now appointed an attorney, Billy Martin. When they first met on January 18, after she had been served with a subpoena, he was deeply troubled. As a prosecutor with fifteen years' experience, practiced in everything from homicides to rapes, he knew that he was dealing with a woman who exhibited all the signs of being a victim of a very serious crime. "She was very, very frightened," he says, "and my initial impression was that she was overreacting. It didn't take me long to realize that her reactions were entirely appropriate."

There was a level of zealous malevolence behind the decision to force Marcia to testify against her daughter that alarmed many seasoned attorneys. As Billy Martin says, "Inside the Office of the Independent Counsel there seems to have been a decision to investigate this matter with the expectation of prosecuting the President, a view that has never varied. They wanted to prosecute Clinton come hell or high water."

Indeed, their decision to force Marcia to appear before the Grand Jury was part of that tactic. "It was to provoke Monica to agree to cooperate with the OIC as it was obvious that of all those who testified about the affair, Monica's mother knew the least," says Martin

Monica and Marcia, by now convinced that their phones were tapped and the apartment bugged, decided to pack their bags and move upstairs to Marcia's mother's sixth-floor apartment. As they had both been subpoenaed, and, further, warned not to talk about the case even to each other, they would go into the bathroom late at night, turn on the faucet and whisper to each other. "This was not how we should be living in America in this century. It reminded me of *The Diary of Anne Frank*. We were living in constant fear," says Monica, remembering how they would rarely sleep for more than a few hours each night before waking in a paroxysm of anxiety.

On her last day of anonymity, Tuesday, January 20, 1998, Monica left her mother's apartment as Starr's deputies finally arrived to search her rooms. She walked around aimlessly, killing time while they went through her personal possessions: "It was so violating, these men going through my things." By now Starr had also served a subpoena on the White House, requiring that anything linked to Monica Lewinsky be produced.

At five the following morning, unable to sleep, Monica went out into the hallway and picked up the early edition of the *Washington Post*. The story had broken. A front-page piece by Susan Schmidt cited "sources," who said that on Linda Tripp's tapes Monica could be heard describing "Clinton and Vernon Jordan directing her to testify falsely." This was emphatically not the case, as Monica has sworn on oath, and yet this assertion was the linchpin of Starr's expanded jurisdiction, and the premise behind every front-page news story and TV broadcast about the scandal for the next few weeks.

As she read the *Washington Post* story, time seemed to stand still, a feeling that was strengthened in the next few days by the endless waking nightmare. The mass media went into a feeding frenzy of a kind not seen since the O.J. Simpson murder trial in 1995. Senior TV news anchors covering the Pope's historic visit to Cuba were sidelined as details emerged of secret tape recordings, a mystery stained dress, the President's voice on Monica's answering machine, her secret visits to the White House, and every shade of rumor, supposition and invention in between. Ironically, she had even chosen that year's Valentine's message for him, some lines from a verse by Emily Dickinson which she had planned to put in the *Washington Post*:

> Wild nights! Wild nights!
> Were I with thee,
> Wild nights should be
> Our luxury!

Not for the last time, Bill Ginsburg upped the emotional temperature by accusing the President of being a misogynist, and Starr of having ravaged Monica's life. "Once the story broke," she remembers, "we stayed inside and this whirlwind roared around our heads. Everyone was talking about him having to resign. I couldn't believe that. I was still very much in love with the President, very protective of him and I did not appreciate Bill Ginsburg saying that he was a misogynist. At the same time, there was a sense of frustration because these charges were simply not true. He never told me to lie." She was very much behind the President, approving when he said of her in a TV interview that "there is no sexual relationship."

Just as she wanted to protect him, so she was consumed with worry about how her family and friends—none of whom she dared call—were coping with the news. Her Aunt Debra, who was by now in Boston, found the experience "scary," while her brother ascribes the fact that he was able to get through the first few traumatic days to the comradeship of fellow students in his fraternity house at Carnegie Mellon University. Michael was unable to speak to his family except in very short, cryptic phone calls, and it was a month before he heard his sister's voice. "For the two days before the story broke I was a wreck just worrying about what was going to happen," he recalls. "I felt very alone and when the story broke it just went crazy. I was in denial; to my mind the girl featured on every TV channel was not my sister. It was very, very ugly and I only came through thanks to my buddies and teachers in college."

The effects were just as distressing for Monica's friends. The problem she faced in dealing with her confidantes was encapsulated in two words: legal jeopardy. If she called her friends or they her, a phone record would be created, which meant they would come under suspicion from Starr. As a result, legal quarantine was established around Monica and her mother, shutting them off from those close to them and increasing their sense of isolation and fear. At that stage, while she knew that Tripp had taped her at their lunch in Pentagon City, she still did not know that Tripp had taped her private conversations; her closest friends were already implicated because Monica had told Tripp what she had said to them and how they had responded—all of which was recorded.

Monica was particularly concerned about Neysa DeMann Erbland, whom she had called, leaving a message, on the day before the sting. When Neysa returned her call, Monica had been abrupt, saying only that she would get back to her. Like all Monica's friends, the first Neysa knew of what was happening was when, while driving though Marina Del Rey in California, she heard a radio news broadcast that mentioned Monica's name. "I just flipped out," she says. For more than six months she was unable to speak to Monica again and offer her comfort; her only contact was through Bill Ginsburg.

For Monica's friends in Portland the news was just as traumatic, but with the added difficulty that within days they found themselves besieged by the media. Just as she had been at college, Linda Estergard, then heavily pregnant, acted as the "mother" to former students who phoned her Portland home from around the world to ask for advice. She told them to say nothing, and herself repeated that message each day to the hundreds of journalists who called her or hung around outside her house.

Like Linda and all Monica's former fellow students, Carly Henderson was shocked and fearful of the impact on Monica. Carly, who was studying for a psychology Ph.D., remembers that " Everyone was freaking out, we were so scared for Monica. I was crying and cussing at the TV screen. I thought that she would consider killing herself because I couldn't imagine her being able to deal with it. She was on the TV news before the Pope's visit to Cuba, for Christ's sake."

The reason why her friends had to rely on the television to find out about Monica was simple, if distressing. She and her mother existed in a twilight world, the curtains drawn, the Watergate building under siege from the world's media, and every phone call bringing tidings of hope or despair. They dared not go outside at all, for they had been warned by the apartment manager that film crews had taken over the apartments that overlooked their balcony. It was a life that was sharply brought home to Debra Finerman when she called one morning to see how they were. A storm had just passed, leaving a beautiful clear day in its wake, but Marcia didn't even know it had stopped raining because the curtains were drawn. For Debra, "This was a metaphor for this whole thing—they were living like caged animals. My sister, who had done nothing, was having to hide in the shadows like a criminal."

There was no respite. A few days into the scandal, the two women crawled unseen onto the balcony at two in the morning for a breath of fresh air. "I felt like I was dying, like I was being slowly tortured to death by this whole business. It was frightening," says Monica.

Inside the apartment the television played all day long. Marcia says of its harsh intrusiveness and apparent reality, "It was quite unreal, because the story was about us. They showed her picture all the time and Monica was sitting next to me and we were so frightened and overwhelmed by the enormity of it. It's very hard when you are watching your life being destroyed on primetime television."

Like piranhas with a fresh victim, the mass media quickly picked clean the lives of Monica, her mother and her family. Perhaps one of the least edifying moments was the scene outside a Los Angeles courthouse where scores of journalists eagerly grabbed details of the Lewinskys' divorce. Ironically, a few weeks before the scandal broke, Marcia had explored the possibility of having the papers legally "sealed" because of her impending marriage to Peter Sraus.

Her feeling of utter impotence and anguish was shared by Bernie, unhappily and unwillingly on vacation in Hawaii. Even though he and Barbara lived just a couple of blocks away from the O.J. Simpson murder scene in Brentwood, Los Angeles, nothing could have prepared them for their unwelcome role as the latest act in this prurient media circus. Bernie, an unassuming, phlegmatic man, was appalled as he saw his life dissected by total strangers, a media vivisection that drove him to the edge of despair. "Each time Bill Ginsburg called on the phone, it was more dire news," he says. "The worst was when the divorce papers came out." Barbara remembers him calling out, "Oh my God, the Lewinsky name is over the entire world. People in Mozambique will know about my divorce. I can only thank God that my father is dead."

As Barbara walked in manic circles around their eighth-floor room in their Honolulu hotel, her husband crouched on the bed constantly saying Kaddish, the Jewish prayer used for, among other offices, mourning. He still finds it very difficult to talk about that time, the darkest days of his life. "We were just so shocked," he says. "We knew nothing about any of this. There was a point during those awful days where I looked over the edge of the balcony and considered jumping. But I didn't think it was high enough."

But it was when they returned at the end of January that the nightmare really began. On Ginsburg's advice they had arranged for special security at Honolulu and Los Angeles airports, although these measures proved unnecessary. What relief they might have felt was short-lived, however, for their modern wood-and-steel home in Brentwood was under siege, TV trucks and banks of photographers and reporters crowding the road. Even now, their house is on the "Star Tour" which shows sightseers famous homes in Los Angeles.

Almost immediately on getting home, Bernie took the White House tea towels, aprons and other gifts Monica had bought for them in Washington and burned them on their barbecue. Then, on the advice of the Los Angeles police, he installed a paper shredder so that the media, who scavenged through their trash sacks, would find nothing they could use. Indeed, one of the first things he threw out was the card Monica had sent him for his fifty-fifth birthday a few days before the scandal broke. It read, with unintentional irony, "I know over the years I've caused you a few gray hairs, but I didn't mean for the rest of them to fall out."

They were told, too, that a well-known private investigator, who specializes in bugging houses, was in the neighborhood, which made them specially cautious about even routine conversations. Even when Bernie returned to work to tend to his patients at West Hills Hospital, he found himself pursued through medical wards by TV camera crews. "I was very nervous to meet my colleagues after all that had been said," he remembers. "In the canteen someone came up and gave me a hug. It was very emotional and difficult."

He was right to be concerned, especially about his daughter. By the time he and Barbara returned from Hawaii, a distinctly unjust and unflattering image of Monica Lewinsky was solidifying in the public mind. She was caught in a withering crossfire of competing political creeds, vested interests and self-interests, with no one venturing out into this dangerous terrain to defend her, not because her friends did not want to, but for fear of being subpoenaed.

Republicans condemned her as an adulteress, while Democrats lambasted her as a threat to the President. For enjoying and being at ease with her sexuality, she alienated moral America, while liberal feminists, who respect Hillary Clinton's work, dismissed her as a classic product of exploited femininity. At the same time, the wide streak of misogyny in the American psyche, and particularly in the media, remorsely and sneeringly lampooned her weight, her taste, her styles, and her Beverly Hills background. The mechanics of her sexual relationship with Bill Clinton were manna from heaven for talk-show hosts, stand-up comedians and dozens of sites on the Internet dedicated to the scandal. The very name "Monica" has become a byword for loose moral standards.

As well as foundering in the political and cultural cross-currents of American society, she was overwhelmed by several rivers of personal self-interest that converged on her, notably the White House, the Tripp–Goldberg axis, the Starr team, her former lover Andy Bleiler, and a walk-on cast of characters from her past.

A man-to-man conversation between the President and Dick Morris, a former Democratic campaign strategist and media "attack dog," on January 22, the day after the scandal broke, demonstrated just what she was up against. Morris, who had resigned from the administration—he had been one of Clinton's political advisors—six months earlier after being found to have had an affair with a prostitute, told the President that he was prepared to issue a statement attacking the Lewinsky story as the "fevered fantasy of a teenage mind," and going on to say that Monica owed the nation a "massive apology." He intended to call a press conference to elaborate on the theme of her "make-believe."

Before letting him off the leash, the President cautioned Morris to be careful, since, if that were the case, there was a slight chance that Monica might not be cooperating with Starr, and he did not want to alienate her. It was a revealing exchange. The man Monica loved for his vulnerability and humanity was now a creature of the past. Here was the President as lawyer and politician, fighting for survival.

Truth and Monica Lewinsky were the first casualties in this war. As Dick Morris, now a TV talking head, says, when the story broke the White House immediately adopted a strategy of "deceit, denial and delay." Clinton's denial of the charge that he had had an affair, made to his wife, his cabinet and leading Democrats, set the tone for the White House counter-attack.

Early on, the President told one of his senior advisors, Sidney Blumenthal, who was later to testify to the Senate, that Monica was a stalker who had tried to blackmail him into having sex. This was soon translated into public whispers that Monica was flirtatious, obsessed with the President and emotionally unstable. From there it was but a small step for the "stalker" notion to become fixed in people's minds.

The first stage of this campaign culminated in the Roosevelt Room of the White House on January 26, five days after the scandal was first reported in the mainstream press. President Clinton stood before the cameras and the American people and declared with a jab of his finger: "I did not have sexual relations with *that woman*—Miss Lewinsky. I never told anybody to lie, not a single time . . . never. These allegations are false. And I need to go back to work for the American people." It was a sound-bite that came to haunt him.

Almost all those who knew the truth watched in angry disbelief as he lied to the nation. Monica herself had mixed emotions. "I was pleased that he had denied it, because everyone was saying that he was going to have to resign if this was true. I didn't want him to resign. But I was very hurt when he said, 'that woman.' His distance and coldness were a very direct message to me of how angry he was.

"At the same time, if the President had come out and acknowledged the improper relationship, that would have taken a lot of pressure and attention from me. But he didn't do that and the consequences are plain to see."

Others were less charitable. When they saw Clinton's performance, both Neysa DeMann Erbland and Catherine Allday Davis yelled expletives at the TV screen. Bernie Lewinsky was more hurt than angry: "It was very painful when I heard him call her 'that woman.' When he denied an affair I knew he was lying—not from anything I knew but because it was clear that he had that liar's look in his eyes. He was acting and he did a lousy job of it."

After the President had spoken to the nation, the First Lady went on the attack. On the day, January 27, that a grand jury was convened in Washington to hear evidence about the Lewinsky affair, Hillary Clinton declared on the *Today* morning TV show that Starr was a "politically motivated prosecutor," part of a "vast right-wing conspiracy" of "malicious" and "evil-minded" people. These are sentiments with which Monica, in the front line of the war, entirely agrees.

While the White House was trashing her reputation, the Starr team were squeezing Monica, the President and Vernon Jordan, with a series of leaks to the media designed not only to up the ante in any negotiation, but to make Monica's legal team bow under the remorseless pressure.

Meanwhile, Lucianne Goldberg was feeding the media with Tripp's distorted account of Monica's relationship, portraying Tripp as the "truth-teller." Indeed the latter, in a statement made through her lawyer on January 29, declared nobly that she had "chosen the path of truth." She evinced an Olympian pity for Monica's plight: "She is a bright, caring, generous soul, but one who has made poor choices," although, she added darkly, "Monica's moral compass is her own."

Thus fact and embroidery were woven into a single tapestry that depicted Monica in the worst light possible. For example, Tripp ascribed the authorship of the "Talking Points" memo to others, notably the President, because, she said, she did not believe Monica capable of such subtle thought. Jake Tapper, a Washington journalist who dated Monica just before the story broke, has remarked, "The overriding characteristic that has unfortunately allowed her to become used as a pawn by every single player in this tragedy—Clinton, Starr, Linda Tripp, the media—is that she is too trusting."

Just as the White House were now singing to the tune of Presidential denial with orchestrated leaks saying that Monica was a besotted fantasist, so, by uncanny coincidence, a duet from Monica's past took up this chorus. A hurriedly called press conference on the front lawn of Andy Bleiler's Portland home on the evening of the President's State of the Union address on January 27, 1998, drowned any voices speaking for Monica.

Andy and Kate Bleiler, who have since separated, had tried to sell their story to the press, but when their negotiations leaked they decided to speak to everybody about Monica, saying that they intended to tell Starr's deputies what they knew. As Monica, her family and her friends watched in horror, the Bleilers painted a picture very different from the one that everyone else in Portland and Los Angeles had observed. Their tale finally fixed her image in the public mind as a sex-mad stalker with a penchant for married men who had "infiltrated" the Bleiler family. They claimed that Monica, having followed the couple to Portland, had threatened to tell Kate of her relationship with Bleiler, and had thereby forced her lover to continue their affair.

She was described as a "manipulative" young woman who had left Portland for Washington with an agenda—to earn her presidential "kneepads." They even claimed that soon afterwards Monica, who they said had a tendency to twist facts, had boasted about having oral sex with a "high-ranking person" in the White House, never using the President's name but always referring to him as "the Creep." She had even had an abortion while in Washington, they said, implying that the child might have been the President's. What was more, they added that, during her days at the White House, she had sent them documents, some "extremely important," which the public-spirited Bleilers had kept in a safety deposit box. In fact, as has already been noted, with the exception of the joke memo to "Andy", the "documents" were from the White House gift shop, while Monica's crack about "kneepads" was a reference to the nickname for one of the White House staffers.

While the couple looked on, their attorney, Terry Giles, told astonished journalists, "When this story first broke, like many Americans I assumed that this was a twenty-one-year-old intern that was taken advantage of by a very powerful man. I also assumed, by virtue of the way her story came out—she's confiding in a friend who tape recorded it—it didn't seem that she had an agenda. I took it from there her story was probably true. After having a chance to talk to Andy and Kathy, I have to say that I am less certain about that."

When Monica learned that the Bleilers planned to hold a press conference, she had hoped against hope that they would at least tell the truth, even if Andy did have to reveal that they had a relationship. She was wholly unprepared for the way they twisted the truth. "I was devastated. I was so angry, hurt and embarrassed. I felt helpless." In many ways, she found the lies to which Andy Bleiler put his name harder to bear than

Linda Tripp's treachery. "I gave Andy my soul, my body, my heart and my virginity," she says. "I just gave Linda Tripp my confidences. In a way my relationship with Andy was more real than the one with Linda, as I wasn't my normal self when I confided in her." Nor could her other "relationship" escape the taint of the Bleilers' self-serving falsification. Still in love with the President, Monica was both upset and deeply worried that the couple's abortion slur would reflect badly on him. "I felt so horribly guilty, I was just suicidal. I was hysterical, I was screaming and crying. I couldn't go outside, stuck in this small apartment with my mom."

Marcia's reaction to Bleiler's lies was to fight fire with fire. She wanted to contact the mothers of the other schoolgirls whom they believed he had romanced, and ask them to come forward to set the record straight. Monica, however, would not hear of it. She could not bear to see two other young women being put through the sort of media attention that she was then facing. For Marcia, "that showed remarkable moral strength—she wouldn't use another human being to save herself." Yet the incident also reveals Monica's chronic lack of self-esteem, consistently thinking herself unworthy of her friends' help, a mindset that merely exacerbated her feelings of despair and isolation.

Other friends were just as horrified as Monica. Former Lewis and Clark student Lenore Reese—another who screamed abuse at Bleiler's image on the TV—got together with other friends, including Linda Estergard, and sent a letter to ABC Television outlining the real story. Unsurprisingly, it was never aired. Linda Estergard says of the Bleilers' media performances: "There were so many times when they went on TV and lied. It wasn't true, for example, that she followed him to Portland—she was here a year before he arrived. In fact, he was having an affair with a student younger than Monica when she left California." Catherine Allday Davis, who now lives in Portland, highlights the moral bankruptcy of the couple's betrayal: "They just decided that she was fair game, even though they knew her. The country was having a field day destroying her and they just helped that process. It reached the stage where she was treated as though she wasn't human."

Carly Henderson, another friend who knew the truth, says, "It was untrue that Monica forced Andy to continue the relationship because she threatened to tell Kate. In fact, it was another of his string of lovers who exposed the whole thing."

In an atmosphere in which conspiracy theories multiplied by the minute, Monica's father saw the White House behind the timing of the revelations. "It is very likely," he believes, "that the White House forced Bleiler to come out at that time. It was a tactic to make Monica look like a slut. Bleiler took advantage of her for his own financial gain, saying things that were untrue but salacious." Allegedly, the Bleilers earned enough from their round of TV interviews to make a down payment on their house.

They were not the only ones cashing in on Monica's misfortunes. Her first boyfriend, Adam Dave, was for a time the toast of tabloid TV, his stories about her becoming more lurid with each media appearance. In one interview he claimed that Monica enjoyed being handcuffed to the bed during sex—even though they had never been lovers. Astonishingly, his mother, Larraine Dave, wrote to Monica boasting that Adam had paid for a trip to Brazil on the proceeds of his TV fame, as though she should be glad for him. "That, to me," Marcia scathingly remarks, "symbolizes Beverly Hills values."

It seems that such values command a high price. The Lewinskys' former neighbor Robin Wyshack, who said that she was able to buy a pair of boots from Saks Fifth Avenue with the money she received for media interviews, commented unfavorably on Monica's parents, particularly Marcia. She cited an incident when Marcia had allowed Wyshack's children to pick only one lemon from the Lewinskys' tree, apparently laden with fruit. What Wyshack did not mention was that she had sued another neighbor after allegedly falling while cutting across their lawn, and the Lewinskys didn't want a lawsuit from their awkward neighbor if one of her children was injured while picking lemons. Michael Lewinsky says of the former "friends" who now began to crawl out of the woodwork, "I thought it was disgusting that Adam Dave was trying to get a dollar for every word he could spit out. Former neighbors, who we didn't like then, were trying to make a buck on the back of Monica's misery."

Some of the offers from the media were very tempting. Neysa DeMann Erbland was offered $100,000 by the tabloid *The National Enquirer* for a picture of Monica in a bikini, but turned it down. Others were not so scrupulous. One former student allegedly paid for her wedding with photographs of Monica that she sold to the press. As that disastrous January of 1998 drew to a close, it seemed that there was no one to speak out for Monica and her family, no one to set the record straight, no one to insist that the media ignore the lurid and concentrate on the truth. As has already been said, however, there was reason for this, and it lay within the concept of legal jeopardy.

The problem was that, on Bill Ginsburg's advice—indeed, insistence—neither Monica nor her mother could allow their true friends to speak out on their behalf. Anyone who had spoken would themselves have come under Starr's inquisition, facing the real possibility of a subpoena to find out what they knew—and the attendant legal bills.

Though protecting their friends meant that Marcia and Monica were painfully isolated, they were prepared to pay that price, telling their friends to hold their tongues for their own good. "When good friends called," says Marcia, "we would make the conversation as quick as possible. We would say the same thing: don't call us, don't talk to anyone, be careful. So this left a void, and those people who hardly knew you then spoke, mainly for money. You can't defend yourself as you are in legal jeopardy."

Almost engulfed by the tidal wave of accusation, vicious speculation and pure falsehood, the captain of Monica's craft, Bill Ginsburg, steered the vessel skillfully at first, making a considerable impression on television. As the weeks passed, Monica began to feel that he should spend less time on TV and more on the case.

There were occasional moments of decency in the ferocious rush to denigrate Monica and her family. One was particularly heartening. Before the scandal broke Peter Straus, then seventy-six, had discussed the prospect of marriage with Marcia, although no formal announcement had been made. Fearing the worst, she believed that once the story became public he would want nothing more to do with her or her family. Indeed, she didn't even give him the telephone number of her mother's apartment in the Watergate, so convinced was she that the scandal would end her chance of happiness.

She was wrong. Peter Straus announced their engagement in the newspaper without telling her. A gallant gentleman of the old school, he observes, "If you love somebody and they have a problem you don't walk away. That's not how civilized human beings behave." Coincidentally, though equally happily, a quotation from a Walt Whitman poem that Monica discovered in a book at Peter's house helped sustain her during the scandal:

> All these—all the meanness and agony without end, I sitting look out
>   upon,
> See, hear, and am silent.

She had to remain silent when, at the end of January, she left the apartment for the first time. That initial encounter with the press was a frenzied cacophony of a thousand lens shutters and motor drives, and the shouted questions of sweating reporters. Amidst this surreal circus, Bill Ginsburg arrived in a limousine to take her to the downtown office of Nate Speights, where she was due to answer more questions from the Office of the Independent Counsel through her attorneys. Only the day before, she had thought she was out of their clutches because Judge Susan Webber Wright, the US District Judge presiding over the *Jones v. Clinton* hearings, ruled that Monica was not central to the Paula Jones case, and had therefore excluded all her evidence. Monica's euphoria was shortlived, however. The fact that she was no longer "material" to one case, her lawyers explained, didn't preclude her from being central to Starr's investigation.

As they left for the question-and-answer session with Starr's deputies, Ginsburg advised her to smile, adding that she should not let the photographers intimidate her. "It was this blitz of lights and everyone crowded the car," Monica remembers. "It was crazy, paparazzi on their motorbikes taking pictures and then falling off. I had to bite my lip to stop myself from laughing because I was so nervous."

Although she resented doing so, she took Ginsburg's advice and invariably smiled for the cameras, the theory being that Starr would see that he was not going to browbeat her into submission. Unhappily, this tactic backfired, for it led to media pundits sneering that her smiles meant that she was enjoying all the publicity.

Starr's deputies were not laughing, though. That day they posed questions to her attorneys about the contents of files of her home computer, suspicious also that pictures had been removed from the walls of her apartment as though in an attempt to conceal evidence. They seemed to have forgotten that she was in the process of packing up to go to New York. Nor, during their search of her apartment, had they found the most treasured of all the President's gifts to her, the copy of Whitman's *Leaves of Grass*.

As animosity and antagonism developed between Monica's legal team and Starr's deputies, the distrust the latter had shown became mutual. Ginsburg and Speights felt that they were constantly given the runaround by the OIC, which kept changing the rules of engagement. They offered Monica a deal they christened "queen for a day," under which she would tell them everything, letting Starr decide whether to grant her immunity. This was changed to "queen for a month," essentially the same deal except that Monica would have to take a lie-detector test as well. On one occasion the investigators said they wanted Monica to meet Kenneth Starr in person, so that he could give her the once-over. After Ginsburg and Speights agreed, the OIC changed their minds. After days of toing and froing, during which Starr formally notified Monica that she was a target for investigation as prelude to indictment, Ginsburg delivered an ultimatum: transactional immunity, or go to trial.

After much discussion and head scratching, the OIC agreed to his demand—albeit grudgingly. In late January two FBI agents appeared at the Cosmos Club, where Ginsburg was now staying. Because they feared that the document setting out the immunity deal might be leaked, instead of handing it over they read it out while Ginsburg and Speights wrote it down in longhand. Known legally as a proffer, it boiled down to a half-page statement, containing four main points. Monica, however, felt that the document was too vague, and therefore handwrote a comprehensive alternative, representing what she was prepared to say under oath in exchange for immunity from prosecution. As she later testified, she thought it would be a road map, not a perfect document.

In her ten-page proffer, she admitted that she and the President had indeed had an "intimate and emotional relationship" which included oral sex but excluded intercourse. She then detailed the history of the previous two years, outlining the reasons why she left the White House, her attempts to return there to work and her subsequent search for a job in New York. After they had gone through several drafts of the immunity agreement, the two sides verbally agreed to a deal. On Monday, February 2, Starr's office sent an FBI agent with a letter confirming the agreement, which was duly signed by Monica and her attorneys. Starr's deputies, once they had read Monica's version, agreed that it was acceptable—except in one crucial point. Ginsburg, they claimed, had said that the President had told Monica, "Deny, deny, deny," in relation to her affidavit in the Paula Jones case. Naturally, the investigators wanted this added to Monica's proffer. Sparks flew between Ginsburg and his client as she told him in no uncertain terms that she had never said that the President had spoken those words.

As Monica has said all along, during their affair the President and she had agreed, *at an early stage*, that they would deny their relationship if they were ever to be questioned about it. This became point Number 11 in Monica's proffer. It read: "At some point in the relationship between Miss Lewinsky and the President, the President told Miss Lewinsky to deny a relationship if ever asked about it. He also said something to the effect that if the two people who are involved say it didn't happen, it didn't happen. Miss Lewinsky knows that this was said sometime prior to the subpoena in the Paula Jones case." Thus the agreement to deny their affair was made only in general terms, and predated Monica's affidavit—hence her fury with Ginsburg.

She had mixed feelings, knowing that, though the agreement ensured that she and her family would not be prosecuted, it also meant that she would be alienated from the man she still loved, the man who had denied to the world that he had a relationship with her. She remembers that ambivalence with a tinge of bitterness: "I didn't feel good about it. I felt like Hitler's whore. I felt what Starr was doing was so wrong. They were trying to hurt people I loved. It wasn't just the President and my mother, it was those I felt a fondness and affinity for like Betty Currie and Vernon Jordan."

If the legal heat seemed to be diminishing, so too was the emotional temperature. After two weeks of pleading to be allowed to see a psychiatrist—her lawyers were worried that if she was seeing a doctor, their bargaining power with Starr would be weakened—Monica was finally permitted to see the woman who, she says, "saved my life." She spent six hours in consultation with Dr. Susan, who not only encouraged her to talk through the trauma of the scandal, but also gave her medication (two prescription antidepressants) to help her cope.

The best tonic of all, however, came when Ginsburg allowed her to speak to her father, now that immunity seemed imminent. Over the past few weeks, Monica had gained the impression that, because Bernie and Barbara—on Ginsburg's advice—had not come to Washington to support her, they were so angry with her that they had disowned her. Her phone call instantly calmed her fears: her father was obviously excited that at last he would be able to see his daughter. Until then, Bernie admits, "We had been living in a vacuum, as Bill Ginsburg was worried that I would be sub-poenaed if I spoke to my daughter."

In early February, as she boarded a plane to Los Angeles, Monica believed that, at long last, the nightmare prospect of going to jail was over. She was very wrong.

CHAPTER THIRTEEN

●●●

The Starr Chamber

*I*T WAS A SPECTACLE with which the residents of the affluent suburb of Brentwood in Los Angeles had become wearily familiar: the wailing cavalcade of police cars, the relentless camera crews, the reluctant celebrity emerging from the rented limo into the pitiless flak of flashlights. In 1994 Brentwood had gained instant notoriety as scene of the murder of O.J. Simpson's ex-wife and a male acquaintance, and for more than a year the media had prowled the quiet streets while the "Trial of the Century" took place in a courthouse downtown. Now, scenting a second such trial, they were at it again, TV crews and photographers commandeering the front lawns of Bernie Lewinsky's neighbors as they waited for Monica to come home.

For her, the trip was a "nightmare" from the moment she left her Watergate apartment that day in early February. In an attempt to escape attention, she flew, for the first time in her life, first class, with Bill Ginsburg in tow and with cameramen and reporters watching her every move, noting each morsel of food she ate. Rarely can the gap between reality and journalism have been wider, as was epitomized by a headline in the *New York Post* which, with that subtle understatement for which the paper is justly famous, yelled, "Stir-crazy Sex Siren Goes Home."

Arriving at Los Angeles, she and Bill Ginsburg were whisked through the airport by waiting police and then escorted in motorized procession, all flashing lights and sirens, to Bernie's home. Even the homecoming turned into a photo opportunity, a chance for the world to see that Monica had a family and was a real person with real emotions, not some bimbo brunette from Beverly Hills who had stalked the President.

As ever, Ginsburg was master of these ceremonies, attempting to whip his reluctant charges into the media circus ring. Even though they later recognized the public-relations value of the occasion, father and daughter did not want to perform. Bernie says, "We had Bill on his cell-phone telling us that when the car stops Monica will get out and greet you outside on the lawn. We felt like movie actors, and it wasn't what we wanted." Monica was equally unhappy about it, when Ginsburg ordered her out of the car and into a fatherly clinch with Bernie. "This was private," she says. "I didn't want to feel like I had to show my emotions so that the rest of the world could see. None of us liked that. However, when I look at it objectively, it was an image that brought sympathy, father and daughter together."

Even so, Ginsburg spoiled the show somewhat by saying to reporters that she had come home to her father just as Chelsea Clinton had returned to see the President after her first term at college. It was a comment that "really irked" Monica, who states emphatically, "I know how precious Chelsea is to the President and how valuable her privacy is. I've never wanted to be associated in that way with her." Indeed, the attorney's stream of remarks that Monica considered inappropriate, combined with his love of the limelight, gradually drove a wedge between the "avuncular Mr. Ginsburg" and his young client.

For the moment, however, all was hugs, tears and smiles as Bernie, Barbara and Monica shared their first hours together since the scandal had hit the press. For Monica, "Seeing my father was like having been lost at sea and suddenly seeing the lighthouse in the distance. We were all crying together. It was very grounding to see him. I needed him." Then, while the massed ranks of the media waited outside, they sat down to one of Bernie's famous meals (he is an excellent self-taught cook) and tried to make sense of the last few weeks.

They did not dwell on the legal issues, as they assumed that the house had been bugged by the FBI; if they had, Bernie would have been left open to a subpoena from Starr. "It was very emotional. We all cried and gave each other support," remembers Bernie, echoing his daughter. "It was a tremendously charged meeting because we all felt such an awful amount of pain at the way our family life had been so viciously torn apart. Monica had a true need to commune with her father."

Monica spent most of her time in LA cooped up in the house, although each day she managed to crawl onto the upstairs deck without being spotted and enjoy the fresh air and sunshine on her face. Barbara found that "it was very invasive and threatening to have these people standing outside the house," and the family experienced the full force of the media mob when they went out to a nearby restaurant, L.A. Farms, for dinner one night. As they finished their meal, they saw dozens of photographers and camera crews waiting outside.

While Bernie went for the car, Monica and Barbara tried to walk through the press of photographers, assuming naively that they would part and let them through. Instead, they were engulfed by a sea of snappers, one cameraman holding Monica in a vise-like grip and refusing to let her go. Finally Bernie, using all his strength honed from years of fitness training, managed to shove open his car door so that they could escape. "It was," says Monica, "very, very frightening."

Even that was not their worst experience. Next day, they were traveling along the freeway through rush-hour traffic when a trailing car full of photographers rammed them, flinging Barbara forward and causing her whiplash injuries. While a local KNBC TV news helicopter hovered overhead recording the scene, they called the Los Angeles police. The police told them that they must stay in the car at all costs, because ramming was a tactic used by cameramen to force their prey out of their cars so that they could take pictures. To their credit, even local media commentators were horrified by their colleagues' behavior; one noted that Monica was now hounded more brutally than the late Princess of Wales had been. Charlie Peters, editor of *Washington Monthly*, says of the media feeding frenzy, "For months they were insane. It was the most disproportionate coverage I've ever seen in my life."

It was not just members of the media circus who scented blood. Kenneth Starr was now circling his quarry, preparing for the kill. Before Monica left for Los Angeles, she and her legal team had agreed that she would be interviewed there for four hours a day by Starr's deputies as part of the immunity agreement.

The ink was hardly dry on the document, however, before Starr changed his mind. On Wednesday, February 4 he withdrew his offer of immunity, ostensibly because Monica refused to accuse the President of proposing or assisting in a cover-up. He also wanted to meet his star witness face to face. "There is no substitute for a looking a witness in the eye," he told reporters, "asking detailed questions, matching the answers against verifiable facts and, if appropriate, a polygraph [lie-detector] test."

Ginsburg huffed and puffed, filing a motion in court to enforce the written agreement. He recognized that Starr's decision marked a change of tactics: Starr was now trying independently to corroborate Monica's story, as recorded by Linda Tripp, by calling her family and friends and White House staff before the Grand Jury. Not only would this test the credibility of his key witness—which was then still in doubt—but it would also reduce her bargaining power with regard to any future immunity agreement.

Starr's enthusiastic employment of these "squeeze tactics" drove Monica to the brink of despair, but she refused to submit to his slow legal torture. She did not realize that, for the Special Prosecutor, this treatment was more than just a matter of the law: this was personal. As commentator Peter Maas noted, "There was a palpable air of almost puritanical frustration and anger emanating from Starr's office, as if Lewinsky must be punished for her obstinacy, dating back to her refusal to wear a wire."

While Monica was penalized for her sexual morality, her loyalty and her principles, the woman who betrayed her, Linda Tripp, was cosseted by Starr's deputies and given a safe house, as well as being allowed to retain her $80,000 a year government salary. In one exchange with Monica, Starr deputy Bob Bittman told her that when investigators went to Tripp's house she made them wonderful cookies and handed out platefuls of delicious sweets. If he meant his words to wound, he certainly succeeded.

The first indication that Starr was really playing hardball had come in late January, when two FBI agents arrived unannounced at Michael Lewinsky's university. A few days before the scandal had broken, Monica had sent her brother a sweater by Federal Express. The agents were suspicious that the innocent parcel might have contained presidential gifts to Monica which she had sent to her brother for safekeeping. Even though they knew by then that Bill Ginsburg was acting for the family, the two FBI men questioned Michael, then just twenty, in his room at Carnegie Mellon, asking him what he knew about Monica's movements, and the substance of their discussions when he had stayed with her in Washington. When they left, he had phoned Ginsburg and told him about his unwelcome visitors. The attorney became very angry, emphasizing that Michael should not speak to anyone without his authority. "I felt horrible," Michael says. "I thought I had messed up, but when you have the FBI on your doorstep waving badges and so on, your first instinct is to tell them what they ask."

Starr's gimlet gaze seemed focused on every smallest part of Monica's life. Not content with serving her with a subpoena to give up her computer and disks for investigation, the OIC subpoenaed a Washington bookstore, Kramerbooks & afterwords, for receipts of all her book purchases since 1995. "It was such a violation," she complains. "It seemed that everyone in America had rights except for Monica Lewinsky. I felt like I wasn't a citizen of this country anymore." Flexing their muscles further, the FBI, acting on the instructions of Starr's office, started putting pressure on Dr. Lewinsky. Ginsburg told Bernie that Starr's office or the FBI were either threatening, or were going, to investigate his personal tax returns, a tactic usually employed when searching for laundered drug money. When that failed to bear fruit, they moved on to the tax records of his medical practice, saying that they wanted to do a detailed audit of all Medicare billings. Bernie believes that "the harassment and threats against our family were made in order to force Monica to give them what they wanted. . . . At that time she had no immunity and the threat of prison was constant. Bill Ginsburg was always preparing us for that eventuality."

Harassing her father and brother was bad enough, but harassing Marcia was quite another. Indeed, the first time Marcia realized that she was facing the prospect of criminal charges was a few days after their ordeal in the Ritz-Carlton. Monica's lawyer Bill Ginsburg told her that Starr's deputies had decided, in their words, "to give mom a pass"—that is to say they had decided not to file criminal charges against her. "It must have been some kind of joke or game to them," says Marcia. "Remember, I did not know what was on those tapes or even that they existed." She was the most vulnerable point in Monica's defenses, and from the moment she was served with her subpoena as she left Room 1012 in the Ritz-Carlton Hotel, Marcia realized that she was being used against her daughter by Kenneth Starr. "They had found her Achilles' heel and that was me," Marcia says simply. "What better way to force someone to do what they don't want than to threaten those they love? My own family saw that technique used very effectively by Josef Stalin, which is why they left Russia."

On February 10, as she sat watching TV in the den of her father's house in Brentwood, a horrified Monica saw her mother walking in to testify before the Grand Jury in Washington. It came as a total shock because, before she had left for Los Angeles, Marcia's lawyer, Billy Martin, had assured Monica that her mother's appearance would be postponed. Marcia seemed to have coped well her first day's testimony, but after the second day she emerged distraught and clearly upset. In fact, she had broken down on the witness stand and a nurse and a wheelchair had been brought for her, although in the end she had managed to walk out unaided.

Monica, feeling both guilty and distressed, decided there and then to fly home to comfort her mother. Before she left, she and her father talked quietly outside the bathroom—the only place in the house, or so they had been advised, where they could talk without being overheard by outsiders. With tears in his eyes, Bernie made an emotional speech in which he told her how proud he was of her, and urged her to be strong through the trials and tribulations that lay ahead. As tears streamed down her own cheeks, Monica answered, "Dad, you are my Rock of Gibraltar."

It is worth noting in passing that, if the scandal has achieved anything worthwhile, it has brought father and daughter together again, the misunderstandings and bitterness of the last few years seemingly behind them. Monica acknowledges that "my dad was just so incredible, really supportive and there for me. It was really wonderful." Both recognize, however, that there is still much work to be done before their relationship can be fully repaired.

For Marcia Lewis, some things will never be the same again. The experience in Grand Jury Room Number Four, where she testified in early February, knowing that a single word out of place might send her daughter to jail, is seared into her memory. When she talks about those days, it is as if she were being forced to return to a dark and terrifying place in her soul. She speaks of her Grand Jury testimony with difficulty, taking deep gulps of air as though she were diving into a treacherous undersea cave.

Marcia, who had lost her fight to avoid testifying altogether, felt as if she were walking through a verbal minefield; she was desperate not to hurt her daughter but knew that she had to tell the truth. If, for instance, the prosecutors were to ask her where the stained blue dress was kept, she would have to answer. At the same time she knew that, far away in California, Monica would be watching and, just as she had tried to bolster her daughter's morale in Room 1012 of the Ritz-Carlton Hotel, she wanted to show her that it was possible to testify before the Federal Grand Jury and survive.

She negotiated the first day, but on the second, February 11, she arrived at the courthouse already upset. That morning she had read a vicious commentary which suggested that she was nothing more than a pushy Beverly Hills social climber who had in some way encouraged her daughter's romance with the President. The reality, of course, was that she had spent two painful years trying to wean Monica off this unfulfilling relationship.

On the second day of her cross-examination, she was asked about the family nickname for her grandmother, Babushka, which corresponded to the name Monica used for Hillary Clinton, Baba. At this point Marcia broke down. Explaining her reaction, she says, "These people had attacked my whole family, and for me my family is the most important thing in the world. They were going after my sister, my daughter, my son and me. Now this prosecutor was bringing up my grandmother, who had been dead for twenty-six years and who helped raise me when my father died and my mother had to go to work.

"So he dared to bring my grandmother's name into this evil place and it was just too much for me. I thought to myself that he could not subpoena my grandmother as she was dead—what are they going to do instead, dig up her grave? I was afraid they would arrest me if I left the courtroom so I just put my head down and started to cry. You are telling things to twenty-three strangers on the jury; they are listening to the most intimate things about you and your family. There is nothing in your family that isn't fodder for these prosecutors to throw in front of these strangers."

As the hearing staggered to a halt, Marcia refused to allow the people she considered to be her family's tormentors, Starr's prosecutors, to touch her, only responding when her attorney, Billy Martin, came into the courtroom. Gently, he led her to the bathroom, where she collapsed on the floor in hysterics.

When she had sufficiently recovered her composure, she left the courthouse. Billy Martin told the assembled media that "no mother should ever be compelled by a Federal prosecutor to incriminate her daughter." Then Marcia traveled to Baltimore to see a psychiatrist, Neil Blumberg. It was only thanks to the concern shown by Billy Martin, however, who cared about her as a person rather than as simply a client, that Marcia was able to pick herself up after this traumatic experience. He managed to convince the authorities to allow her to give a deposition instead of having to face the Grand Jury again.

When Monica returned to Washington to be with her mother, it was as if she were meeting a stranger. Marcia spoke about what had happened as though she were a rape victim, crying endlessly while her daughter tried in vain to comfort her. "It was this dark, violating experience for her," says Monica. "This was my mother . . . and I hated those bastards for what they had done to her. I hated them."

The image of the wan, disconsolate figure of Marcia Lewis emerging from the courthouse troubled many, and so, particularly, did Starr's tactic of pitting mother against daughter. His strategy was dubbed by the White House, "Throw momma in front of the train," while Bill Ginsburg attacked the "torture" of Marcia Lewis which, he said, "was intended to be a clear signal to others, including Monica, that he's [Starr's] going to be rough." As Margaret Carlson noted in a magazine article, "We are now on notice that the conversations we have with our children are not safe from the government . . . in Ken Starr's America, moms do tell—or else."

The sight of his ex-wife emerging in dazed misery from the courthouse reinforced a growing feeling in Bernie Lewinsky that it was time for him to speak up for the family. He therefore spoke to Ginsburg who, after some initial hesitation, agreed that Bernie should appear with Barbara Walters on ABC TV for his first television interview. He immediately warmed to her: she took his hand when they first met and told him, "This must be every parent's nightmare." During the twenty-minute interview, which was broadcast on February 20, he spoke with barely controlled anger about the way Marcia had been treated. "To pit a mother against a daughter, to coerce her to talk, to me it's reminiscent of the McCarthy era, of the Inquisition and even, you know, you could stretch to the Hitler era."

After the interview was broadcast, Monica called her father to congratulate him. She was at her Aunt Debra's apartment in the Watergate building, and as she and Bernie talked, she noticed that her mother was out on the balcony, moaning, wailing and gesticulating to herself. She was seized by fear that Marcia was going to throw herself over the edge, such was the utter despair in her every gesture. She rushed to embrace her, to comfort her, but the older woman, racked with sobs, pushed her away, saying that she did not want to talk to her. Then Marcia went inside and curled up in a ball on the kitchen floor, crying her eyes out. Monica felt helpless: "I had never seen my mother like this. This is the mom who makes everything OK, who always has hugs, kisses and solutions. Here she was breaking down in front of me."

She phoned her Aunt Debra and then Bill Ginsburg, who advised her not to call an ambulance, since then the media would claim that her mother had had a breakdown. Finally Marcia calmed down, and mother and daughter had a long heart-to-heart about what was troubling her. It was not, Marcia said, just the ordeal of testifying before the Federal Grand

Jury, but the vicious media comments afterwards, which had suggested, among much else, that she had faked her breakdown in court. To all this was added the constant worry that she and Debra might be instrumental in sending Monica to jail. Indeed, this emotional aspect, the torment felt by her mother and aunt at the thought that they might be responsible for Monica's fate, suffused their every waking moment. "The dread that they may have to testify against me at trial hung like an unspoken cloud over us all," Monica remembers.

That night, Monica was so worried about her mother's state of mind, and so afraid that Marcia was going to take her own life, that she couldn't sleep. She finally dozed off at four in the morning, only to be awakened by a sound like that of an animal being tortured coming from her mother's room next door. "I went in and she was crying and saying that she didn't want to go to jail and was afraid to the point of paranoia about what was going to happen. Finally she let me cuddle her. She was just crying and crying." On the following day the psychiatrist who had seen Marcia after her courtroom breakdown visited her in the apartment, and insisted that she take the medication he had already prescribed. In any other circumstances she would have spent some time recovering in hospital—although it has to be said that in normal circumstances she would never have been subjected to such intolerable stress.

Within a month of Monica having become front-page news, the fabric of the Lewinsky family had been torn to shreds. Both her parents had seriously contemplated taking their own lives, while Michael had internalized his problems. "I have a big pack on my back and everything I run into I throw into my backpack," he says simply.

Besides having been forced to stand idly by while Starr's investigators intimidated her brother, harassed her father and drove her mother to the point of collapse, Monica watched helplessly as her friends were subpoenaed by the OIC to appear before the Grand Jury. It was a terrible time for her. They had taken away her gifts from the President, read her private e-mails, listened to her intimate, unguarded conversations, subpoenaed her reading lists and searched her apartment. Now, not content with exploiting the bond between mother and daughter, they wanted to test the limits of friendship.

Every day, she and her mother sat before the television, transfixed with dread as they watched close friends and others, like Betty Currie, for whom Monica cared, make their way to the courthouse. She had no way of knowing who had been called, what they would say or how they thought of her in the light of the scandal. As one of nature's pessimists, she assumed that they would all despise her, perhaps for having had the affair and been caught, or for having driven the presidency to the brink of chaos, but certainly for having plunged them into this mess.

Her mother describes the scene as they waited for the television to bring the bad tidings: "Monica would put on the news and sit there staring at the screen. A car would drive up and at first you could not see who it was. Out would come maybe a blonde head and the camera would catch them as they emerged. Then Monica would cry, 'Oh my God, it's Ashley,' or whoever, and break down in tears. It was enough that they were coming after her, but to watch these friends whose only crime was that she had confided in them being marched in was unbearable for my daughter."

The irony was that, just as Monica felt terrible about Neysa, Catherine, Ashley and the others, they felt equally wretched at being forced to betray their friend's most intimate secrets, while also realizing that their testimony could send her to jail. After they had given their evidence, several sent her messages of love and support through their attorneys. It was at least a small consolation in a sea of woes.

Her friend Neysa was the first of her confidantes to tell the world of the use to which Monica had put one of the President's cigars. Neysa remembers that "at a certain point in my testimony I suddenly broke out in a sweat. Here I was talking to a roomful of strangers considering a criminal prosecution against my friend because of her sex life with the President."

While Neysa, Ashley Raines, Debra Finerman, and others were all obliged to tell the truth, whatever harm it might do Monica, about their conversations with her, for Catherine Allday Davis the situation was further complicated by the fact that at that time she was still living in Tokyo. Not only was she subpoenaed, but so was the computer she had used to send e-mails to Monica and receive her answers when her friend was working at the Pentagon. In mid-March, while the FBI unearthed the contents of her hard-disk drive, Catherine was flown from Tokyo to Washington appear before the Grand Jury on March 17; she had to testify against her friend. She found the experience as embarrassing as it was humiliating. "It was awful—I'm no prude, but they wanted very, very specific details about their sexual relationship. I felt I was violating her. I thought it was so wrong and quite disgusting to have to talk about another woman in front of a bunch of complete strangers.

"Worse than that was the feeling that they were trying to use me to catch her, to squeeze her into submitting, to prove that she had lied in her affidavit. That was terrible. They wanted to prosecute her and have her squeal on the President. There were moments during my testimony where I was thinking, "My God, I'm here to help these people screw the President of the United States.'"

Just as defiling was the cavalier way the OIC printed out all the e-mails from her subpoenaed computer, without regard for their relevance to the case. Yet it did not necessarily help Starr's investigators, for while she had deleted some information, Catherine had sensibly—and fortunately—saved correspondence relating to Vernon Jordan and Monica's job search. These e-mails showed that the attorney had been involved in that search long before the Paula Jones case swept Monica up under subpoena. Unforgivably, ignoring the protests of Catherine and her attorney, Starr's deputies published private correspondence about members of her family, including her feelings about her husband, Chris, which appeared in the Special Prosecutor's report to Congress.

The effect on Catherine was devastating. "I have never been so angry in my life," she says. "It was so violating to have your personal thoughts published for the world to read. I find this hard to deal with, and I hate this government for what they have done to people in this case. I couldn't bring myself to vote last time. As my father is British, I am seriously considering renouncing my American citizenship." Chris, a company executive, feels equally strongly about what he considers to be an "outrageous" invasion of their privacy. "We were side-players in this whole drama, had absolutely nothing to do with it at all. Yet our rights as citizens were trampled over by this bizarre political process," he says.

Interestingly, through the experiences of Monica, Catherine and others, computer users worldwide have learned from Starr's investigation that Big Brother is always watching. Many companies now instruct their staff to compose and word confidential e-mails as though someone were standing at their shoulder reading what they write.

It is significant that those who entered "Starr country" soon saw the dark side of the American dream. Monica's friends and family are white, affluent, middle-class, liberal-minded, law-abiding people who came to understand the hard realities of untramelled power, be it of the government, the judiciary or the mass media. Marcia Lewis, for example, through her friendship with Billy Martin, her stalwart African-American lawyer, saw just how the other half lived, the constant fear and routine repression faced by ethnic minorities in America, particularly the black community. "I would walk down the road in the 'hood' [the neighborhood] with Billy and people would come up and give me a hug and say, 'You are one of us,'" she remembers. Clearly, while neither the media nor most of affluent America saw her as a victim, that society's other victims did.

Indeed, the moment the story broke on January 21 it was, for its chief victim, Monica, as though she had been instantly transported to another world, a land where time stood still and darkness and Dan Rather reigned supreme. Each day she would get up about eight, breakfast—keeping to her diet of half a bagel, cream cheese and coffee—and watch the news on CNN or surf the Internet, when at her father's, afraid of missing anything about her story.

At lunchtime she would tune in to the legal show *Burden of Truth*, which at that time invariably focused on issues surrounding the Starr inquiry, while she walked on her treadmill before having a Weight-Watchers lunch. "I didn't have the patience to read books, I just couldn't focus. Most of the time I spent obsessing about the case, constantly ruminating on the legal issues. I really got a crash course in the law."

In the evening she surfed TV stations, watching shows such as *Larry King Live* and *Geraldo* which constantly pursued fresh lines of legal inquiry whose true significance only she knew. Her new lifestyle was an unnecessary form of masochism, a reflection of her personality, her need to be in control of her life while at the same time punishing herself as she helplessly watched her life being cruelly dissected.

In her daily search for scraps of information, she heard the TV pundits denigrate her lifestyle, her clothes and her morality. "In their eyes I was this sad, pathetic loser who loved the limelight and made up a relationship with the President." Certainly, Monica would not have suffered so much anguish and torment if she had left her legal team to do their job and kept the television off. That, however, is not her way. More constructively, from mid-March, she traveled to Nate Speights's office downtown and helped with organizing the case, filing and researching material. It was work as therapeutic as it was vital.

If making herself useful was one consolation, another was the avalanche of mail that well-wishers sent—about seven out of ten of her correspondents were sympathetic—although she was legally barred from replying. One letter in particular had caught her eye. It was from an actress, Sheri Densuk, living in New York, who was worried because she had been contacted by the Office of the Independent Counsel and didn't know what to do. She said that she had never had an affair with the President, although she had had illicit relationships with other famous men; she wondered whether Monica's attorney, Bill Ginsburg, would represent her. Both Monica and her mother thought this amusing, assuming that here was an actress trying to hit the headlines by employing the man who was, at that time, America's most famous lawyer.

Several weeks later, in early March, Monica received another letter from Ms. Densuk, this time enclosing a copy of her subpoena from Starr. Feeling sorry for her, Monica, against the wishes of her mother, passed the letter on to her attorney, Nate Speights, who in turn gave it to a Washington, DC, lawyer friend, Keith Watters. There the matter lay—for the time being at least.

At about the same time, Monica was hit by a double whammy which sent her spirits spiraling downwards. Bayani Nelvis, the White House Steward to President Clinton, was called to testify before the Grand Jury for the second time. As she watched him on TV, she noticed with horror that he was wearing the first tie she had given the President. She had two immediate reactions: first, that the President had insisted that "Nel" wore his tie as a signal to her to support him; the second that she meant so little to him that he had given her tie away. Given her natural melancholia, she inclined to the latter view.

The second incident, a few days later, had a more sinister flavor. Her hairdresser, Ishmael Demir, called and gave her the astonishing news that Linda Tripp had been to see him. He had become briefly famous earlier when Monica had gone to him to have her hair cut shorter—she had been followed by a posse of media types who had filmed and photographed the event through the salon window. Tripp made an appointment at Toka salon under a false name, with the result that Ishmael was forced to tend to her—otherwise she could sue him for breaking the appointment. On learning of Tripp's visit, Monica's lawyers advised Monica that she could no longer use the hairdresser, whom she liked enormously, without placing him in legal jeopardy. It may seem a trivial loss, but Monica felt it deeply, for in a world where every piece of her was now owned by others, be they journalists or the judiciary, Ishmael had been one person who was still part of her former, happier, existence.

Nor was this the first time that her nemesis had deliberately stalked Monica. On her first public appearance after the scandal broke in January, Tripp had worn a coat Monica had given her, while on the day in June when she appeared before the Grand Jury she sported a fake Chanel handbag that Monica had brought back for her from her trip to Korea with the Department of Defense. More recently, shortly after it was announced in October 1998 that Monica was to give her first TV interview to Barbara Walters, Tripp approached the show's producers and tried to secure her own time in the media spotlight.

On the evening of Thursday, 12 March, while she was still brooding on these events, Monica went out to a Washington steakhouse, Sam and Harry's, for dinner with her legal team. They were joined by Keith Watters, the lawyer who was by then representing Sheri Densuk. As they tucked into steak and fries, Nate Speights leaned over the table and conspiratorially told Monica that Densuk was "Jane Doe Number 7"—the girl after her in the Paula Jones case.

This was Monica's worst nightmare come true, for it meant that the President had been seeing another woman at the same time as he was conducting a relationship with her. She had been duped. She rushed to the bathroom, where she burst into uncontrollable sobbing. "If there was a Jane Doe Number 7," she says, "it meant that everything he had ever said to me was bullshit, that I meant nothing to him and that the whole two-year relationship was a farce. After having gone through so much pain already, having cared so much and risked so much, I tormented myself with the idea that she could have meant more to him, that he liked her more, that they had had sex—maybe he even said that he loved her."

Still in tears, she returned to the table and asked to be taken home. The lawyers refused to leave until they had finished eating, Ginsburg brusquely telling the sobbing girl to stop making a scene. As she sat there in misery, she made up her mind that this was the end: she had finally and absolutely reached the end of her rope. "I had decided that I was going to go home and kill myself. That was it. I'm out."

When she got back to her apartment, she debated whether to take an overdose of pills or to slit her wrists. She weighed up the options, and then decided to call her therapist, Dr. Susan. "I was hysterical and that night she saved my life. I have never been that close to committing suicide in my whole life. I didn't know how to function anymore but she calmed me down. At that time I had just a toehold on life but she pulled me back into the land of the living.

"Certainly if I had killed myself it would have been because of my unrequited love for the President of the United States. I felt that my life was over; I didn't feel that there was any piece of me left. What was the point of living, anyway? There was nothing more here."

After talking to Dr. Susan, Monica went to bed. When she woke the next morning, she found that she had gained a fresh perspective on life. She now knew that, come what may, she was going to get through this, and that, though she might have been down, she was far from being out. She had reached a turning point of sorts. Moreover, the whole incident had a more or less happy ending, for it later emerged not only that Sheri Densuk had been wrongly subpoenaed, but that there was in fact no Jane Doe Number 7. Monica had contemplated killing herself over a misunderstanding.

For once, though, she had no chance to brood. After two months, the prisoner of the Watergate was allowed her first visitor, her closest friend, Catherine Allday Davis, who had just testified before the Grand Jury. Monica had implored her lawyers to let her meet her friend afterwards. The lawyers were worried about the legal consequences, but had eventually relented—though they gave Monica strict instructions that the two women must not talk about the case. Typically, Monica spent the time before Catherine arrived in an anxious ecstasy of expectation, not knowing if, after her March 17 Grand Jury ordeal, her friend would still want to know her. She need not have worried.

Fearing that her apartment was bugged, they met in a conference room in the Watergate, It was an emotional reunion, neither girl sure how the other would behave. Catherine was worried that her friend would feel betrayed because she had been compelled to testify, while Monica was anxious because she could not recall whether, in her casual conversations with Linda Tripp, she had made any catty comments about her best friend. If she had, they would, of course, have been recorded and so would very likely appear among Starr's evidence.

Catherine remembers their meeting vividly. "As soon as we saw each other we knew that everything was going to be all right. We cried and hugged each other and we talked about our emotions, our experiences with the media and so on. We both were expressing shock about how the media had latched on to her and wouldn't let her go, and that the Monica that was out there was not the real Monica. We just laughed at the absurdity of it all."

As for Monica, "Seeing Catherine that day was a great morale boost for me. I knew now that I had at least one friend in the world and that there was still a piece of me that existed, that there was someone out there who still loved the real me. If Dr. Susan had preserved my physical life, then Catherine saved my soul. From that day on I knew I would survive."

When Monica woke the next morning, her face was really painful. She realized that she had smiled so much when she saw her friend that it had made her cheek muscles ache. It was the first time in two months that she had had something to smile about.

April brought cause both for tears and for more smiles. The tears were occasioned by the fact that she couldn't go to her mother's wedding to Peter Straus in New York that month. Had she done so, she knew, the ceremony would have been turned into feeding time in the media piranha pool, and Marcia and Peter's special day would have been ruined.

To escape from her Washington prison for a time, Monica again visited with Bernie and Barbara in Los Angeles. Besides being able to live a life of at least partial normality there, she was able to mend more fences with her father. "It was a very powerful time for my dad and me," she says. "I came to understand my dad and Barbara much better, and they came to appreciate me as well. For the first time, they were in the front line, following every twist and turn in the story, so it became as intense for them as it was for me."

Stepmother and stepdaughter became almost inseparable. Barbara taught Monica to knit, and encouraged her to take up sewing again. She made bags and scarves for friends, tacking onto each item a red-and-white cotton label that read, "Made Especially for you by Monica." "It was very therapeutic," she says, "and reminded me that since I had been living in Washington I had allowed my creative skills to wither."

Barbara's family, the Lerners, were also good to Monica. Indeed, they were more supportive than some of Bernie's family, who not only kept their distance but wrote to Monica in censorious tones, something that hurt Bernie almost as much as his daughter. (He also had to listen in helpless, silent indignation as local Orthodox Jewish elders discussed the possibility of using religious law to cast Monica out from the faith.) However, Bernie's younger sister Hanna and her family were supportive.

It was not only Monica's mind and emotions that were nourished by her stay in Los Angeles. The fitness guru Kacy Duke was spending a month in the city, and brisk workouts with her whipped Monica's body into shape. "C'mon, girl," Kacy would say in her distinctive New York accent, as she took Monica for a bike ride or a timed walk on the beach. "C'mon, girl, you have to be 'scrong', you need 'scrength'." The success of the workouts was amply demonstrated when Monica took a German cousin, Natalie, on a sightseeing tour of Venice Beach. The girl whose face had launched a thousand headlines was approached by a woman in a store and told, "You look just like Monica Lewinsky, only thinner."

This battle, at least, she had a chance of winning.

• •

CHAPTER FOURTEEN

The Avuncular Mr. Ginsburg

*S*UDDENLY, the media had a new superstar. Within weeks of arriving in Washington, Bill Ginsburg had been transformed from an obscure Californian medical-malpractice attorney into a national figure, his beard, bow ties, hats and deep voice, like that of a sober W.C. Fields, making him instantly recognized by millions of Americans.

He enjoyed his stardom and when, in March 1998, he was asked to a glittering black-tie dinner to celebrate seventy years of *Time* magazine—it was billed as the celebrity dinner of the year—he accepted with alacrity. Both he and the guest of honor, President Clinton, he told Monica, would be speaking. His client was upset, not only because she herself could not possibly, under any circumstances, see her "Handsome" but also because Ginsburg had been invited only as a result of her miserable situation.

Yet the following day she was anxious to hear what had happened, and to know whether he had seen the President. Ginsburg was full of himself: "Yeah, I saw him, and he said, 'I wish her all the best,' and winked at me." Monica was elated, pleased that the man she had striven so valiantly to protect still cared about her enough to send a fond message. It was only about a month later that she discovered that Ginsburg had been pulling her leg.

The incident characterized Monica's tumultuous relationship with her showman attorney. He saw himself as her surrogate father, yet he never understood the depth of her feelings for the President, or the way in which his own inappropriate, and often sexual, comments added to her private pain and public humiliation. At the same time, the fact that he drove a wedge between members of the Lewinsky family showed another side of the self-styled "avuncular Mr Ginsburg." Just as Kenneth Starr was the enemy without, so after a few weeks Bill Ginsburg came to be seen by Monica and her family as the enemy within, legally, emotionally and financially. Peter Straus, typically, pinpoints the lawyer's chief weakness: "With hindsight he was a terrible choice. The fact that he loved showbiz and razzmatazz only served to reinforce the image of Monica as a Beverly Hills girl who was over the top."

While Monica watched her family disintegrate under the strain, her attorney relished his new life in the limelight. Every day a gaggle of reporters gathered outside the Cosmos Club, Ginsburg's Washington quarters, and waited for him to hold forth on the issue of the day. It made great copy, but the new king of the soundbites caused eyebrows to be raised even in the media. Breakfast-TV-show host Katie Couric mentioned the fact that Ginsburg had boasted of appearing on five TV talk shows in a single day.

When Monica complained, he would shrug his shoulders and say, "If you don't feed the [media] bear, it'll eat you because it's hungry. If you feed the bear too much, it'll crap all over you. But if you feed the bear just enough, it'll leave you alone." Unfortunately, Bill Ginsburg just couldn't stop feeding the bear, no matter how often it chewed his hand, whether he was making off-the-cuff remarks at a high-powered *Washington Post* editorial meeting, or thinking on his feet in a TV studio.

The way he courted coverage, tipping off photographers and reporters each time he and Monica went out to a restaurant or other public place, added to the pressure on her, and often resulted in her being labeled a media junkie. In early April 1998, for example, Ginsburg was due to address the American Bar Association in Philadelphia (the invitation itself a product of his startling climb to fame, if not notoriety), and took Monica along to give her a break from the four walls of her Washington apartment. He promised that, after they had checked into their hotel, he would take her to see the famous Liberty Bell, the symbol of America's freedom.

She was taken aback, when they arrived at their hotel, to see camera crews, reporters and photographers massed outside. She had supposed that she and Ginsburg would be incognito, but he, she found, had other ideas: a journalist from CNN walked up and asked him what time they were going to see the Liberty Bell. Monica was furious with her lawyer. "I just looked at him in disbelief. I was so angry that I had to walk away." They were followed by a dozen or so newshounds, photographers snapping away as lawyer and client stood in line to look around Independence Hall, where the bell with its celebrated crack is housed.

The media's presence encouraged other tourists to take notice, and they certainly did: so much so that a parade celebrating Greece's Independence Day was disrupted, to the annoyance of the organizers. The center of all this attention was mortified. "I felt like an exhibit in a traveling freak show," she says. "It was so unnecessary and all because Bill loved the limelight."

Ginsburg did not always have it his way, however. In early April, Monica and her family put their foot down when he threatened to attend the annual White House correspondents' dinner, at which the President and First Lady are traditionally the guests of honor. It was the kind of occasion which, under normal circumstances, Monica would have loved to attend, but even though she was invited, she well knew that as things were it would be folly even to consider going. Her parents backed her, her father agreeing that if Ginsburg, in the face of their objections, accepted the invitation, they should look for a new attorney. In the end he backed down, but it was a battle that Monica and her parents considered should never have taken place. "It was," she admits, "very frustrating, always trying to keep my lawyer's ego in check."

More distressing than Ginsburg's penchant for playing the clown in public was the way in which he insinuated himself into the private dynamic of the Lewinsky family, pitting its members against one another. For example, in an interview with *Time* magazine in March, he had talked warmly about Bernie Lewinsky but commented on the "aggressive" behavior of Marcia Lewis, remarks which went far beyond his brief as family attorney.

The truth is that Ginsburg saw his role as being much more than just that of a lawyer, boasting often of his unique position as Monica's surrogate father. He maintained that he had kissed her inner thighs when she was just six days old—"Look at those little pulkes," he claimed he had said of the newborn Monica—even though in reality he did not meet her until she was in her early twenties. Given the sexual overtones of the case, these remarks were wildly inappropriate, as well as fanciful. More offensive to Monica, however, was when he described her as being like a "caged dog with her twenty-four-year-old libido," a description that was duly printed in *Time*.

He was even more crass in private. During a dinner party at his home in Los Angeles for Bernie and Barbara Lewinsky, he remarked that the President only liked women with dark pubic hair—an obvious reference to Monica. His wife, Laura, was so disgusted by his vulgarity that she walked out of the room. Monica also found it disturbing that Ginsburg, a happily married father of two teenagers, wanted to know graphic details of her affair with the President, displaying a degree of interest that went far beyond the normal attorney–client relationship.

Certainly he took his self-imposed role as surrogate father to extremes. On one occasion in April, when father and daughter were talking together in Dr. Lewinsky's Brentwood home, Ginsburg put his arms around them and said, "We don't want you two getting too close, do we?" Ginsburg had dropped by with Barbara Walters, who had interviewed her father a few weeks earlier. As they chatted, Monica explained to Walters that when she was a growing up she was basically a good kid who kept herself out of trouble; she never smoked or took drugs, always got good grades and never shoplifted like other children. Without missing a beat, Walters said drily, "Next time, shoplift."

While the two women were talking in one room, Dr. Lewinsky and Bill Ginsburg were engaged in a more serious conversation elsewhere. In the course of their conversation, the lawyer emphasized a point he had frequently made during their long-distance phone calls. "You know, Bern," he said, "she is really angry at you. Did you know that Monica hates your guts?" If true, his comments were an intolerable intrusion into their lives; if false, they were unforgivable.

Monica was devastated when she learned what he had said. "Here's my dad—his heart is breaking, his wallet is busting, he's nervous and despairing, and he's got Bill Ginsburg telling him that his daughter, for whom he's going through all this pain, hates his guts. I love my father. He and Barbara have been wonderful during this whole crisis. Of course I have issues and problems with my dad, but who doesn't? They are our business." To this, her father adds, in his usual understated way, "Bill Ginsburg got involved in the family dynamic in a way that was inappropriate. His comments only added to the angst and stress that we were all feeling."

Ginsburg's policy of divide and conquer came into the open over the sensitive issue of money. For months he had claimed that Monica insisted on being taken everywhere in a chauffeur-driven limousine, and had sent hefty bills which reflected that wish. "Now you are going to have to be patient with Monica," he told Bernie in his deep voice. "I'm trying to wean her off the limos." In fact, Monica normally took a taxi or walked during her infrequent covert excursions from the Watergate apartment. The truth emerged only when she noticed her father signing yet another large check to Ginsburg, to pay a bill which included $5,000 for limos for "Monica's security."

Ginsburg again overstepped the mark when, during casual conversations with his friends, he told them that Monica had contemplated suicide. She discovered this indiscretion in March when one of his female friends approached her and said consolingly, "Bill told me how upset you were the other night, and I just want you to know no one is worth killing yourself over." Her words were meant kindly, but the incident did little to improve Monica's confidence in Ginsburg's judgment or discretion.

Reluctantly, the rest of the family came to share her view of her attorney after the furor that blew up over a set of glamorous photographs of Monica which were published in the summer of 1998 in the glossy monthly, *Vanity Fair*. One shot in particular raised the blood pressure of many patriots: it showed Monica posing with the Stars and Stripes on the beach at Malibu in California.

The idea of Monica modeling for a set of pictures arose quite by chance when, in March, she and Bill Ginsburg attended a launch in Washington for a book by CNN TV host Larry King. It was one of the very few times that Monica had ventured outside her apartment, and it was only after some hesitation that she had decided to go along. As she chatted to various media folk at the party, a writer for *Vanity Fair* suggested that she have a set of portraits taken. Not unnaturally, the idea appealed, not least because all the photos of her that had thus far appeared in the media had been taken by stalking paparazzi when Monica was off-guard. At a time when everything in her life was out of control, including her image, it was a chance to take back some command.

So in April she flew out to Los Angeles for the photo shoot with the acclaimed photographer Herb Ritts. She remembers. "As I have always been concerned about my weight I was very nervous." Besides worrying about the pictures themselves, Monica had discussed with Ginsburg issues of final approval, confidentiality and so on, expecting him to ensure that they would keep ultimate control over what was published. In his usual fashion, he became angry when she asked about the legal issues, and told her that, if she didn't like the way he had organized matters, they could call the whole thing off. Unsurprisingly, Monica, intoxicated by the thought of being out in the open air and sunshine after months of virtual imprisonment in Washington, wouldn't hear of it.

As she puts it, the shoot "was champagne for the soul. For the last four months I had been constantly ridiculed and criticized . . . it really energized me." Also, she enjoyed working with Herb Ritts, posing for him in a variety of outfits which gave her something of the look of the young Elizabeth Taylor. She had her own hairdresser, make-up artist and other attendants, including a security guard watching over $600,000 worth of diamond jewelery she wore for the photos. This time, she truly was "queen for a day."

When her father, himself a keen photographer, and Barbara arrived, they were greeted by the surreal sight of Monica in a blue chiffon dress, holding a pink poodle. Some of the gilt was rubbed off the occasion, however, when Ginsburg made yet another of his crude remarks. "The President," he told Bernie, "is going to cream his pants when he sees this."

Monica remains ambivalent about that day in Malibu. She treasures the friendships she made, and the memory of an experience that made her feel like a whole human being once more. With hindsight, she would not pose with the American flag again, simply to avoid the inevitable fuss, but that is as far as her regret goes. She is not, and never has been, disloyal to her country, and sees no reason to feel ashamed of being seen with its most emotive symbol.

In fact, even before the *Vanity Fair* furor, Marcia had become concerned that Ginsburg was seriously mishandling the media, to her daughter's detriment. She had too often seen Monica in tears because of an off-color, inaccurate or exaggerated remark by her attorney. It was bad enough that she had acquired an image as a fantasizing publicity-seeker; the last thing she needed was Ginsburg contributing to the hype.

After discussing the vexed issue of media relations with her attorney, Billy Martin, and with her sister, Debra, Marcia decided to enlist a public-relations expert, freeing the legal team to concentrate on the court battles. Martin, who was a tower of strength not only to Marcia, but to the whole family, suggested a long-time colleague, Judy Smith, a seasoned publicist and attorney who had worked in public relations at the White House and for the NBC TV network. They discussed the idea with Monica, who, aware that Kenneth Starr had hired his own public-relations advisor, thought it made sense. Luckily, she was immediately impressed by Judy Smith, finding her sharp, sassy and focused, and, most important, prepared to work *pro bono*.

The next hurdle was to convince Ginsburg that he should concentrate on the courtroom, rather than carousing with correspondents from CBS, CNN and the other TV networks. In late April, therefore, a full-scale family meeting was convened at Bernie and Barbara's house in Los Angeles, to which the lawyer also came. That conference awakened deep-seated emotions in Monica. It was a double first—the first time for years that her parents had been in the same room together, and the first time ever that her father and Barbara met Marcia's new husband, Peter Straus. "Everyone got along famously," she recalls. "I really felt the most loved ever, and to sit down at dinner with both my parents and to see them getting along was a really wonderful feeling."

The only fly in the ointment was Bill Ginsburg. When Monica, who chaired the gathering, outlined her case for bringing Judy Smith on board, he ostentatiously doodled on his pad, making it clear that he took little interest in the proceedings. Monica had prepared a three-page brief clearly outlining her reasons for dividing media and legal matters into separate portfolios. "We have," she argued, "reached a turning point in this case. First and foremost, Starr has said he is in for the long haul, and has hired a media consultant. This makes our team the only one which does not include someone whose sole responsibility and expertise is the media."

Although she promised that she would not respond personally to attacks on her integrity, she felt that she badly needed someone who would put her case more effectively. "My reputation is that of a stupid '90210 Valley girl' who services men. This is not acceptable because that is not what I am." Predictably, despite the cogency of her arguments, Ginsburg opposed the plan, arguing that he should remain in sole control of the family's affairs. Only very reluctantly did he agree to relinquish his grip on Monica's public image.

Shortly afterwards Judy Smith joined them and "Team Lewinsky" was born. Judy and Monica worked in harness to generate public support, and to make it clear that Starr had no case against her. At another family pow-wow in May it was a very subdued Bill Ginsburg who faced the media when the family group walked out of the Park Hyatt Hotel in Los Angeles after lunch on May 17, where the issue had at last been settled. As one reporter noted, "In contrast to the family's bright mood, the lawyers were straight-faced."

Not that Monica had much to cheer about. Two days earlier a Federal appeal court had declined to become involved in her long-running dispute with Kenneth Starr over whether or not she was immune from prosecution. Ever since February, when the Independent Counsel had rejected the immunity agreement, Monica's legal team had been at war with him, sniping at his methods and questioning his integrity. Now, not content with filing a motion to enforce legally the written immunity agreement, Ginsburg asked the Attorney General, Janet Reno, to launch an official inquiry into alleged leaks from Starr's office of facts relating to the case. He also demanded that the Attorney General order lie-detector tests to be conducted on Starr and his various deputies to establish whether they had leaked privileged information to reporters.

This echoed a formal complaint made by the President's private lawyer David Kendall, who in early February had filed a motion accusing Starr of contempt of court and calling for the Independent Counsel's office to be investigated, again for alleged leaks about testimony given to the Grand Jury. A judicial inquiry was instituted, and found twenty-four possible leaks of Grand Jury information, in violation of federal law. The judge ordered an investigation.

While Kendall had stuck to the courtroom, Ginsburg had continued to conduct his case on the studio floor, endlessly berating Starr in a non-stop round of talk shows, and once even declaring the Special Prosecutor to be a "menace . . . a nonconstitutional monster." His remarks, justified or not, made wonderful headlines, but he was becoming more of a TV talking head than an advocate for Monica.

Nor did his tactics did sit well with Judge Norma Holloway Johnson, a Washington district judge known for her disapproval of flashy lawyers. When arbitrating on the vexed question of whether the written immunity agreement between Monica and the OIC was legally binding, she had made it clear that she did not like her cases to be tried in the media, a barbed reference to Ginsburg's daily punditry. His partner, Nate Speights, had urged him to stop "feeding the bear," since to continue doing so would be bound to harm their case, but as soon as a microphone was poked in his direction Ginsburg had to talk.

For all his public huffing and puffing, Ginsburg, a Washington outsider, was faced with a tenacious Beltway bruiser in Starr. While he might have behaved like a confused, if enthusiastic, bloodhound, he kept the bite on

Monica. By late March, with a constant parade of witnesses appearing before the Grand Jury, and Congress voting $1.3 million for a possible impeachment probe, it had seemed that the Independent Counsel held all the aces.

The Lewinsky family were playing against high rollers in this legal poker game and they were rapidly running out of stake money. In desperation, Bernie set up a defense fund, and appeared on the *The Larry King Show* and other TV programs to raise money to pay the spiraling legal bills. His performances attracted around $35,000 from well-wishers, but Bill Ginsburg was unhappy, and made sure that he appeared on the same shows soon afterwards, to demonstrate that he was still the media star. As Bernie says, "When I went on TV, he saw it as taking his power away. He didn't want [Monica's] dad to play a role."

A ray of sunshine briefly illuminated this gloomy legal scenario when, on April 1, Judge Susan Webber Wright dismissed Paula Jones's case against President Clinton, ruling that his "alleged conduct does not constitute sexual assault." After that verdict the nation, canvassed by opinion poll, declared by a margin of almost two to one that Kenneth Starr should abandon his inquiry as well. He, however, had no intention of stepping aside, and declared that Judge Wright's ruling "doesn't affect our case." As for Monica, though she was pleased for the President, her joy was tinged with sorrow that she would not be able to share his reaction to the news. "It made me miss him deep down in my heart," she says. "I felt very lonely. I wanted to see the look on his face when he heard the good news."

In truth, she had more than enough to worry about without pining over the President: it was she, not he, who was facing jail. In a warning shot across the bows of Monica's legal craft, it was made clear that the more hawkish prosecutors in Starr's team were keen to indict her for perjury if Judge Johnson found in their favor—that is, ruled that the original immunity agreement from February was not binding upon the OIC. The very least Starr expected in exchange for any future immunity agreement was for Monica to make a more forthcoming proffer—a promise that she would testify under oath that President Clinton had had sex with her and then tried to cover it up.

Both her attorneys were confident that they would win the day against Starr. They were wrong. In late April, Judge Johnson rejected Ginsburg's arguments that the immunity deal was legally binding. Ginsburg now changed his tune, and said he had expected to lose in front of the District Judge but was confident that they would win on appeal. Moreover, if that failed he was looking forward to a trial and the chance to cross-examine Linda Tripp in the witness box. In fairness, and for all his shortcomings, Ginsburg is an excellent trial attorney.

Nor is he easily downhearted. Every new defeat and setback was greeted with his now immortal phrase, "We're right where we want to be" (a maxim which today the Lewinsky family mock mercilessly). Just over two weeks later, when the Court of Appeals for the District of Columbia refused to become involved in the dispute, Monica found herself right where she didn't want to be—facing indictment and a possible jail sentence for perjury and other crimes. As one media wag commented, "It's time for Monica to decide if she wants to see how she looks in an orange prison jumpsuit."

For Monica and her family, this was very, very far from a joke. Her fear that she might spend as long as twenty-seven years in prison had subsided, but she still often woke up with a start in the middle of the night, consumed by fear of being shackled and handcuffed like Susan McDougal. Her anxiety was shared by her father, who suffered a recurrent nightmare in which he saw himself escorting her to jail in chains. "I could not fathom the notion of Monica in shackles," he says.

Until she was granted immunity, Monica lived in constant fear of arrest. On one occasion she and Judy Smith were in a cab on their way to the train station when they were pulled over by an unmarked police car; such cars are also used by the FBI. A plain-clothes detective got out, walked over and flashed his silver badge. Monica's heart started beating faster, her mouth went dry and she began to sweat. It turned out that he had stopped the cab driver for a driving infringement, but the incident revived in Monica the paralyzing fear she had felt in Room 1012. "I thought they were going to arrest and indict me there and then," she remembers with a shudder. "I had nightmares for days afterwards."

In her new life of notoriety, the main enemy was the mob of photographers who hung around the Watergate apartment and stalked her every move. Even other journalists were shocked by the way she was hounded. One tabloid TV commentator who had been consistently bitchy about Monica on the air, bumped into her at the hairdresser they both used and was horrified to see massed TV crews and photographers on the sidewalk outside, taking pictures through the glass as Monica had her hair done. (One of the reasons why she now wears her hair short is so that she can tend to it at home, rather than having to run the gauntlet of the paparazzi.)

To give the enemy the illusion that she never left without their knowing, Monica seldom used the main exit from the Watergate building. By using other exits, she could avoid the media pack and thus move around Washington incognito. Wearing dark sunglasses, and with her hair pulled back and pushed under a straw hat, she was able, at least for a time, to escape her tormentors. (On one occasion she was walking around fashionable Georgetown when the presidential motorcade roared by. She did not catch so much as a glimpse of "Handsome.") Most Sundays, Walter

Ellerbee, a private investigator working on business for Billy Martin, phoned her at her apartment and asked cryptically, "Is the package ready for pick-up?" He and Shawn Wright would then call for her and take her for a drive in the countryside to "air her out."

For the rest of the time, Monica assumed she was always followed. She came to live by the maxim, "Just because you're paranoid, it doesn't mean that someone's not watching you." Her suspicions were apparently borne out in June, when she and Judy flew to Los Angeles: also on the plane was Mike Emmick, the Starr deputy who had interrogated Monica in Room 1012.

Shades of the prison house began to close around her in earnest after the Appeals Court denied her immunity plea on May 15. Within days, the Independent Counsel subpoenaed her to appear at the federal courthouse in Los Angeles for fingerprinting. As she had often been warned by her attorneys, this was the first stage in the indictment process, a procedure that would eventually culminate in a visit to the prison where she would be sent if convicted.

On May 28 Monica, accompanied by her father, Bill Ginsburg and another attorney, Todd Theodora, ran the gauntlet of reporters waiting outside the Federal Building on Wilshire Boulevard, where her prints were to be formally taken and logged. In response to a shouted question, Bernie said, "My daughter is being used as a pawn by two powerful men. This is un-American." Inside the gloomy building, Monica had to face a continuation of the subtle and not so subtle intimidation she had resisted in Room 1012 more than four months earlier. The party was made to use the full-body jail turnstile before being led past the mug-shot room to the fingerprint room. It was no coincidence, Monica believed, that Agent Fallon, the FBI man who had tried to frighten her by showing her his gun and handcuffs, had flown out to accompany her.

The fingerprinting was as long and drawn-out as it was humiliating. Besides the usual fingertip impressions, the prosecutors wanted prints of the fronts, sides and palms of her hands. In all, it took thirty minutes— Bernie Lewinsky knows, because he timed it. "I was crying when I watched them do this to her," he confesses. "It was scary and it was unnecessary—after all, she had one of the highest security clearances at the Pentagon. It was all done deliberately to intimidate her, treating her as if she had committed mass murder."

Starr's deputies did not want voice prints or samples from her, but they did want comprehensive specimens of her handwriting; she had to write with various pens in different styles. Distrustful of the OIC prosecutors, she objected when they tried to get her to sign checks and to copy out a letter she had sent to the President. It was a wearying process, made all the more stressful because Bill Ginsburg, who, not being a criminal lawyer, was unfamiliar with the procedure, had to keep calling his colleague, Nate Speights, who does practice criminal law, for guidance. Monica remembers that "I was very stoical and quiet, but inside I was scared stiff."

Agitated and distressed by this legal performance, Monica left the building with her attorneys and, flanked by police, they walked through the media crowd like avenging sheriffs in a Western movie. By now, though, Monica was gunning for only one man: Bill Ginsburg. Two days earlier, an article by him entitled "An Open Letter to Kenneth Starr" had appeared in *California Lawyer* magazine. In it, he virtually admitted that Monica and the President had had sexual relations. Given that, at this time, she was still standing by her false affidavit, it seemed to cut the legal ground from under her, causing a furor in the media and consternation in legal circles.

Ginsburg also charged Starr with trampling over Monica's right to privacy and turning her into a "virtual prisoner." "Congratulations Mr Starr!" he wrote. "As a result of your callous disregard for cherished constitutional rights, you *may* have succeeded in unmasking a sexual relationship between two consenting adults. In doing so, of course, you've also ruined the lives of several people, including Monica and her family, whilst costing them $1,000s in legal fees to protect themselves from the abuses of your office."

Even the respected attorney and legal scholar Alan Dershowitz, who in his book *Sexual McCarthyism* later savagely criticized Starr for turning a "tawdry series of Oval Office encounters into a constitutional crisis," was alarmed. He said that, however justified Ginsburg's criticism might be, he had gone too far. Dershowitz publicly called on the Lewinskys to ditch Ginsburg and "start from scratch" with an experienced Washington attorney. Bernie Lewinsky reluctantly—"It was," he says, "very embarrassing"—recognized that his legal friend had outlived his usefulness.

In fact, Ginsburg's indiscretions might have been a great deal worse. On the weekend of the *Vanity Fair* shoot, he had called Monica to say that *California Lawyer* had commissioned him to write the article. She had been worried about it, feeling that yet more publicity would only hurt her chances of being granted immunity. When Ginsburg read her a draft of the piece, her worst fears were confirmed. "Now Mr Starr," he had written, "thanks to you, we will know if another's lips aside from the First Lady's have kissed the President's penis."

Monica was aghast. "Bill, you cannot say that! Over my dead body! It is the crudest, most appalling thing I have heard in my entire life." Not much chastened, but recognizing the sense of what she said, he promised to tone down the article and to inform Judy Smith when the article was due to appear. However, the story about his article leaked prematurely.

With Monica now facing the prospect of imminent indictment and her attorney an object of ridicule, action had to be taken quickly. Another family conference was convened, and it was decided that Billy Martin should be deputed to put together a short list of lawyers who were prepared to take over the case. The consensus was that the new team members must be seasoned attorneys who could operate shrewdly inside the brutal Beltway ring. Bernie knew of no one, but Marcia had read a flattering profile of Jake Stein, himself a former Independent Counsel, in *The New Yorker*. Martin contacted both Stein and another respected figure, Plato Cacheris, both of whom he had known for fifteen years, and the two men signaled their interest in taking on the case—with the proviso that they would not work with Bill Ginsburg.

After lining up two other lawyers, Billy Martin hired a conference room at the discreet Washington Court Hotel for Monday, June 1. He planned a daylong "beauty contest," during which Monica could meet her prospective attorneys, see whom she liked and then make her choice.

There remained one major problem for the newly re-formed "Team Lewinsky": how to smuggle Monica, who was still in Los Angeles, to Washington without the media or—more importantly—Bill Ginsburg finding out. Subterfuge was called for. Monica and Judy Smith caught the red-eye to Washington, where they were picked up at the airport by Walter Ellerbee and whisked off to their hotel. Thus, while Ginsburg, who was still in LA, believed that Monica was at some California beach with her brother, in fact she, Judy Smith and Billy Martin were listening to Jake Stein, Plato Cacheris and two other attorneys outline their legal strategies.

Stein, a low-key, silver-haired, courtly character, was first on the list. He told Monica he believed that, in spite of the setback at the Appeals Court, he could win her immunity. Next up was Plato Cacheris, an affable but bright attorney, who made it clear that, if what they wanted was a plea bargain in return for a measure of immunity, he was not their man. He was not prepared to enter the ring unless they were going either to fight for full immunity, or else to make an aggressive defense at trial. He felt that this was the best and only approach to take, basing his decision, not without justification, on the fact that that he had obtained immunity for another famous defendant, Fawn Hall, Oliver North's secretary, during the investigation into the Iran–Contra scandal of the nineteen-eighties.

Monica was impressed with both men, but by the end of the day, after meeting and considering other attorneys, she was punch-drunk from listening to their various plans to fight Starr. She had phoned her father that morning to tell him that she felt Stein and Cacheris were the men for her, and he advised her to stick with her initial instincts. So, at eleven that night, Martin called the two lawyers and asked if they would be prepared to work on Monica's case together. It turned out that they had already informally discussed that idea, and had agreed that they would be more effective working in harness.

On the following day, June 2, they met again, this time with Marcia present and Bernie connected via a conference call. The latter told Stein and Cacheris, "All I want is to make sure that my daughter is taken care of," a sentiment with which everyone agreed. After some discussion about fees, the two lawyers left, so that the family and their advisors could talk over the decision and make sure that everyone was comfortable with it. Shortly afterwards, Billy Martin called Monica's new attorneys and formally asked them to be her new legal "dream team."

Immediately on being engaged, Stein thought it prudent to call Kenneth Starr; he was anxious to let the Independent Counsel know what was happening before the media got wind of the new arrangements. When Starr failed to return his call, Cacheris phoned one of his deputies, Bob Bittman, and informed him that he and Stein were now representing Monica.

Meanwhile Judy Smith, who was still pretending to be in Los Angeles, was on the phone to Ginsburg. For the last few days he had been threatening to quit, angered by the mounting media criticism as well as by his deteriorating relationship with Monica. When Judy talked to him, he returned to this theme, but she gave no hint of the new arrangements, afraid that he would immediately leak it to the media, but say that he had resigned, rather than been fired.

Just half an hour before they made the public announcement on June 2, Judy and Monica spoke to Ginsburg in a long-distance conference call, and told him his services were no longer required. He was furious. He accused Monica of being ungrateful for all the work he had done, and threatened, ominously if unspecifically, to do what he had to do to protect himself, his family and his practice. Judy asked him to "take the high road" and join them in their press release, which stated that this had been a mutually agreeable decision. Ginsburg, however, slammed the phone down and then angrily called Bernie to vent his anger at the way he had been discarded. Bernie stood firm: "I thanked him for his efforts and the sacrifices made by himself and his family." Generously, he adds, "We will never forget that in the early days he did come to our rescue."

The final word on the "avuncular Mr. Ginsburg" may perhaps be left to Marcia, whose views, though less generous than Bernie's, are typically clear-eyed. "He was an advocate seduced by the media attention that engulfed his role as attorney. It was more important for him to fan the media flames than to look after Monica. The goal was always immunity, because it was clear that Monica was simply the sacrificial lamb as far as both sides were concerned. In his hatred for Starr he lost sight of that goal.

[239]

The final straw was the open letter he wrote to Starr that virtually stated that Monica had a physical affair with the President. It was an untenable position."

The change of attorneys—Nate Speights did remain, however—had been smooth, professional and, for once, leak-free. With Monica standing silently in the background, Stein and Cacheris made the announcement in a brief sidewalk conference, news that made headlines nationwide. Yet, though she had acquired a pair of savvy guides who knew their way around the Washington jungle, there was still no certainty that they would bring her safely home. Wandering in the legal jungle, every day facing the prospect of indictment and jail, she would need much help to sustain her on this uncertain journey.

The people who had betrayed Monica during the past few months were people she knew, trusted and loved. In biting contrast, people whom she hardly knew, or had taken for granted, displayed a shining integrity: the Watergate doorman who refused to let journalists rummage through her trash; the garage attendant who turned down $5000 offered by a newspaper if he would tip off its reporters about Monica's movements. She is profoundly grateful for such decency. "One lesson I've learned from this affair is never to judge people too hastily. All the people who worked at the Watergate were offered thousands of dollars. Instead [of taking the money], they protected and respected me as another human being, and I will always be grateful to them and the manager, Chris Hueple, for that."

Even complete strangers showed great sympathy and understanding— she received thousands of letters of support and encouragement from people around the world. A 101-year-old lady, who wrote that Monica was not to blame for the scandal, brought her much comfort. And a man in Sweden seemed genuinely to understand the profound fear felt by her and her family. "There is nothing more chilling," he wrote, "than to know that you are facing the awesome power of the State." Hearteningly, such kindnesses continue, even as the scandal rumbles on. On the last day of 1998, at King's Road café, a young man gave Monica a small bouquet, saying, "Happy New Year. You deserve them."

Perhaps the most touching message of all came in a package sent to Monica in April. Inside were two letters, one for her, the other for her father, and a packet. In the first letter the anonymous author, a woman, talked about her own experiences, which she felt were reminiscent of the difficulties Monica was enduring. Her father's parcel contained a beautiful and valuable diamond and sapphire ring in an elegant Limoges box, which the sender asked Bernie to place on Monica's finger to remind her of how special she was. Her reason for sending the ring, she wrote, was that, in an equally trying time in her life, she had been sent a similar ring with the same message. "The generosity of a complete stranger who wanted to share this lovely gift with me was very moving," recalls Monica. She tracked down the woman's address through the parcel company and sent her an effusive and heartfelt letter of thanks.

Some public figures, too, showed their support. One such was comedienne Kathy Buckley, who was born deaf but, because her condition was not diagnosed until she was in her mid-twenties, was sent to a school for the mentally handicapped. In her one-woman show she has her audience crying and laughing by turns, as she tells them about the trials and tribulations of her life—she has been run over by a lifeguard truck, and has had to overcome breast cancer; to cap it all she can't pronounce the letter "f."

In June 1998, Kathy was playing in a Los Angeles theater. Back in LA after signing up Stein and Cacheris, Monica, Bernie and Barbara went to see her, and laughed through their tears as she talked about the criticism and hostility she had faced. At the end of the show, she aimed a verbal kick at all the people who had attacked her in the past: "Don't buck with me." As she said those words, she winked at Monica and blew her a kiss.

After the performance Kathy came out to greet her public and made a beeline for Monica. Giving the girl an affectionate hug, she told her that she had often prayed for her, at which point both women shed tears. Then she put her hands on her shoulders, looked her in the eye and said with a smile, "Do what I do, Monica. Just turn a deaf ear."

CHAPTER FIFTEEN

• •

"An Utterly Preposterous Document"

*W*HEN MONICA WOKE UP on the morning of July 23, 1998, at her father's house in Los Angeles, for once she felt expectant and excited. It was her twenty-fifth birthday, a milestone in her personal calendar and one that she looked forward to celebrating with her friends and family. Catherine Allday Davis had flown in specially from Portland, and her mother and Peter Straus had traveled from New York to be with her.

As she mulled over her plans for the day—she fretted that Catherine and her friend Neysa DeMann Erbland, who had never met before, might not get along—she received a call from Plato Cacheris. Ominously, he told her that he wanted a conference call with her father before he would give any details about the matter in hand. But Bernie was operating on a patient, and they had to wait for over an hour before he could come to the phone.

During that anxious wait, Monica's first instinct was to assume that Starr had deliberately held off until her birthday before deciding to indict her. Since the fingerprinting session in May, the chance of being charged with a criminal offense had seemed greater; the threat was ever present at the back of her mind. It seemed that even the deployment of her new "dream team" of lawyers, Jake Stein and Plato Cacheris, would not be able to stave off the apparently inevitable indictment. Now, while she waited for Bernie to come out of surgery, she had plenty of time to review the legal twists and turns in her case over the last few weeks.

Early in June she had undergone a five-day debriefing by her new legal team. It convinced them that she was an eminently credible and forthright witness, smart if unworldly, a far cry from the almost universal image of her as a predatory opportunist. So far, however, they had not been able to convince Starr. At a meeting on June 9 between the Office of Independent Counsel and Monica's attorneys, Starr's deputy, Bob Bittman, had emphasized that the case against her for perjury and obstruction of justice was very strong. He had followed up that point in a letter which stated that the Office of Independent Counsel would have to interview Monica before any decision could be made about a possible immunity deal.

In mid-June, Bernie had flown to Washington to join Monica, her mother, Judy Smith and the legal team for a meeting at her Watergate apartment. By then, all the smoke signals coming from Starr indicated that it was more, rather than less, likely that he would indict Monica. The nightmare of her mother, her aunt, her closest friends and her former White House colleagues being obliged to testify against her in a criminal case, rather than just to a Grand Jury, had seemed ever nearer.

There had been one moment of unalloyed pleasure for Monica and her family in the course of this waiting game, when it was announced that the Maryland State Attorney was opening an investigation into whether Linda Tripp had broken state laws in taping Monica without her consent. The Lewinskys were delighted at the news. "Everyone in our family wants Linda Tripp to lie awake at night worrying about going to jail," says Monica, "because that's what happened to us. I was thrilled, literally jumping for joy. There was a feeling that, somehow, justice would prevail."

As Monica and her new team waited on the Office of Independent Counsel's next moves, it had became clear that time was at a premium for the Special Prosecutor. On July 17 Starr had made history by issuing the President with a subpoena ordering him to testify to the Grand Jury. Now he needed all the information he could gather from his potential star witness, before he examined the most powerful man in the world.

Four days later, Starr had called Stein and Cacheris and asked if they would care to meet him for breakfast at the Maryland home of his ethical advisor, Sam Dash, on July 23, Monica's birthday. At that meeting it became clear that Starr was very keen to interview Monica. What was more, it seemed that, after six months of toing and froing, he was prepared to offer her an immunity agreement. Far from having her worst fears confirmed, she was about to have her best hopes realized.

Those negotiations completed, Plato Cacheris returned to his Washington office to deliver Starr's birthday present to Monica. Now, in the conference call with her and her father, he said that he and Stein believed Starr was ready to offer her transactional immunity—that is, full immunity from prosecution on any aspect from the case—but that they wanted to make her what is known as a "queen for a day" proffer, under which the witness tells the prosecutor everything he or she knows without fear of prosecution, so that they could assess her credibility. Cacheris also explained that Sam Dash, a distinguished Democrat, was involved, a factor which immediately made everyone much more comfortable. In the light of all this, the lawyer asked Monica to fly to New York for a meeting with Starr's deputies and Dash on Monday, July 27. He emphasized that this had to be kept absolutely secret. For her part Monica insisted that Starr keep away those of his deputies who had browbeaten her in Room 1012.

As though that news were not reason enough to celebrate, Cacheris called again later and gave her another birthday present. He had had a message from the attorney representing Ashley Raines, passing on birthday wishes and telling Monica that she loved her. "That was the best birthday surprise I could have imagined," Monica says. "I had expected her to hate me because of all the trouble this had caused her at the White House. It was wonderful that she was still my friend."

Monica did as her attorney had said, smiling broadly but saying not a word to her friends about the upcoming meeting in New York. Before they left Judy Smith, who was in charge of what they called "covert operations," bought Monica a blonde, Pamela Anderson-style wig as a disguise. To complete the transformation, Monica boarded the plane on Sunday morning wearing not only the wig but also a baseball hat, a pair of reading glasses and no make-up. The subterfuge worked: no one gave them a second glance on the five-hour flight to New York.

That afternoon they met with Plato Cacheris, Jake Stein and Sydney Hoffmann, a female associate of Cacheris's who had been engaged to help with the case, in a small apartment off Fifth Avenue. Monica felt very comfortable with Hoffmann, who during their meeting led her sensitively and professionally through the more embarrassing aspects of her story. Hoffmann was and is impressed by Monica: "She is an incredibly intelligent, sharp and analytical young woman who has been very impressive throughout this oppressive and politically motivated investigation."

Despite the benefits of the meeting with her legal team, Monica spent a nervous, sleepless night, knowing that the next day's meeting was make or break. In the morning she met her three lawyers again. They decided that Sydney Hoffmann should question her for the first thirty minutes, taking her through major topics such as the details of her affair, her false affidavit, her search for a job, the "Talking Points" memo and the President's gifts to her. Then they took a short taxi ride to the elegant penthouse apartment of Starr's mother-in-law, which overlooked the East river—a fitting setting for Monica to be queen for a day. There she was introduced to Starr's legal team, which included Sam Dash, Mary Anne Wirth, Solomon Wisenberg and Bob Bittman.

As agreed, Sydney Hoffmann began the questioning. When she finished it was time for Starr's deputies to take over. Monica made an inauspicious start, bursting into tears when Mary Anne Wirth asked her what the President had said to let her know that he cared for her. It touched a very raw nerve, and she needed some minutes to compose herself.

Once she was calm again, they focused on less emotional matters, mostly times, dates and places, repeatedly asking about the role of Vernon Jordan and the origins of the "Talking Points." Monica made it clear that, if they looked at events during the critical weeks of December 1997 within the overall context of her two-year relationship with the President, matters which might otherwise seem suspicious, notably Vernon Jordan's involvement in her job search and the "Talking Points," were perfectly explicable.

After a sandwich lunch, the questioning resumed; it continued until late in the afternoon. Monica's legal team was quietly confident that she had performed well, but their satisfaction was short-lived. When, back at the apartment, she switched on the television, to her horror she heard NBC correspondent Lisa Myers announce that Monica Lewinsky had met with Starr's deputies and had admitted to having had a sexual relationship with the President. How could NBC have got the story so quickly? Only through a deliberate leak—and Monica knew it had not come from her side. She was "very upset, most concerned that some nut would try and kill me because I had turned on the President. It was very disturbing and selfish." Moreover, the delicate situation in which she was now poised was in danger of being compromised, for at that time no deal had been finalized: Starr's team had indicated that they would make a decision on the following day. With a final turn of the screw, the media reported that Starr wanted Monica to take a lie-detector test, an idea that Plato Cacheris had no truck with.

Worried now about her safety, and aware that the media would be watching the airports and train stations for her return to Washington, Monica and Judy Smith decided to drive back. So Walter Ellerbee flew into town, rented a car and drove them through the night to Washington.

That day, Tuesday, July 28, 1998, was one of high emotion for Monica. When her attorneys arrived back at their downtown office following an earlier meeting with Starr, they brought with them a watertight agreement, signed by the Independent Counsel. Monica and her parents now had full immunity from prosecution in connection with the Office of Independent Counsel's investigation. In return, she agreed to testify truthfully before the Grand Jury, telling the OIC everything about her relationship with the President. Not surprisingly, Stein and Cacheris expected her to be pleased. They were taken aback when, instead, she burst into tears.

"They didn't understand my emotional outburst," she says. "It was knowing that I was turning against someone with whom I had wanted to spend the rest of my life, someone I wanted to wake up with each day, someone that I loved. Even though he called me 'that woman' and hurt me so much, I still loved him. The last few months had stripped away the obsessive quality of my relationship with him, but the fundamental deep, quiet love was still there."

She was crying so much that she found it very difficult to sign the immunity agreement. When Stein and Cacheris went outside to announce the deal to the waiting media, Monica was still in the bathroom, trying to wash away the tearstains. In any case, she simply did not want to face the media. She was worried that if she did, they might make it appear that she was reveling in the fact that she was going to testify, and make her seem little better than the "despicable" Linda Tripp. By that time Tripp had completed her Grand Jury testimony. After completeing her testimony she had made a nervous—and subsequently ridiculed—statement in which she had told the American people, "I am you," before going on to say that if she had to betray Monica again, she would not hesitate to do so. Sanctimoniously, she had also urged her former friend to tell the truth when she appeared before the Grand Jury.

As Monica, accompanied by Judy Smith and Billy Martin, left her attorneys' offices, she took some small comfort from the news that the President's response to the immunity deal, according to his press secretary, Mike McCurry, was that he was glad things were working out for her. She took his words with a large pinch of salt, though. She strongly suspected that, now she had agreed to cooperate with Starr, the White House attack dogs would be let loose on her. Sure enough, within days the *National Enquirer* was questioning both her honesty and her sanity, citing a White House insider who had described her as a "virtual psychopath" who stalked the President.

Knowing what lay in store for her, at Billy Martin's house that night Monica, Judy Smith and Martin had a rather subdued celebration dinner which he had picked up from his favorite restaurant. But if their joy was muted by forebodings, Monica's family were naturally relieved that she was now out of danger of going to prison. That day, as Monica was leaving for her lawyers' offices to sign the immunity agreement, her grandmother, Bernice, had said, "At last I can sleep at night."

A few weeks later, in her grandmother's apartment Monica came across a zip-up bag stuffed with little pieces of paper covered in scribbled jottings. While watching the endless analysis of the scandal on television, Bernice had made notes she thought might be relevant to any future legal case in which Monica might be caught up. "She had kept that pain and fear to herself," Monica reflects. "It symbolized to me exactly what everyone in the family had been going through. We could all now breathe a sigh of relief."

Such relief, however, carried a very high price. Though she had been spared a possible prison sentence, Monica now suffered a punishment much more cruel and relentless. A methodical legal process was set in train which stripped her, layer by deliberate layer, of her dignity and her sense of self. By the end she had become arguably the most humiliated woman in history.

The degradation of Monica Lewinsky began on July 29, when she had to hand over all the gifts from the President that the FBI had missed in their original sweep of the Watergate apartment. They also confiscated the Christmas presents the President had given her at their last meeting; Monica had not told Tripp about them, so they are not mentioned on the tapes. Most significantly of all, she handed over the blue Gap dress she had worn for that fateful encounter with "Handsome" on February 28, 1997. Unbeknownst to her mother at the time, it had been in her apartment in New York when the scandal broke in January, but had been returned to Monica's Washington apartment in May. It was to go to the FBI laboratory for DNA testing, testing which later proved conclusively, and independently of other evidence, that the President had been sexually involved with Monica Lewinsky.

Many observers have wondered why on earth Monica did not destroy the dress, or at least have it cleaned, before she made her immunity deal. "It has been one of the most humiliating things, having to hand in the dress," she says. "I struggled long and hard about giving it over to the prosecutors. I had thought of washing it and saying, 'Here is the dress but it has been cleaned,' but I was so paranoid that I was being watched. It was possible that I would have had to take a lie-detector test and so they would know that I had broken the law by tampering with evidence. Then I would have been accused of obstruction of justice and lost my immunity."

As has been explained, Monica never intended to keep the dress as any kind of trophy, as Linda Tripp—displaying her usual disregard for the truth—has said. For one thing, she was by no means certain what the tiny stains were. They could have been guacamole, which she had had for dinner the evening of her meeting with the President. She was so unsure that she told Mike Emmick, when she gave him the dress, not to release the news that she had done so until the Office of Independent Counsel knew exactly what the stains were. True to form, within thirty minutes of her handing over the dress, the media reported that the prosecutors now had it. No wonder that when the debriefing process began, in a room in the Watergate Hotel, Monica's trust of Starr's deputies had fallen to a new nadir: she feared that her every remark would be leaked to the media almost before it was uttered.

The debriefing sessions were long, tedious and cruelly embarrassing, particularly when she was questioned about intimate acts between herself and the President. A couple of days into the process the humiliation began in earnest when the two female prosecutors, Karin Immergut and Mary

Anne Wirth, asked very detailed questions about the sexual aspect of the relationship. When she was asked if the President had masturbated her when he put his hand down her trousers, Monica broke down in tears and had to leave the room to compose herself. Her memories of this cross-examining are as raw as they are painful. "It was too violating and humiliating to talk about such private issues with a roomful of strangers, most of them men. It was very difficult to talk openly about a private sexual moment. Quite frankly, I thought the level of detail they wanted was sick."

It was equally upsetting when the prosecutors asked her to tell them what questions would surprise the President, throw him off balance by making him feel that they knew every detail, however trivial, about his life. Monica found it difficult to answer. She would tell them the truth, she said, but in no way would she help them in their attempts to impeach the President. "I don't want to be a part of helping you trap him," she told them. "I am not Linda Tripp. I am not reveling in this process."

After a grueling week of debriefing, Monica was scheduled to appear before the Grand Jury on August 6. Monica, worrying about what she was going to say in court, scarcely slept the night before she was due to appear before the Grand Jury. As a witness for the Special Prosecutor—and an exceptionally prominent one, at that—she would be accompanied by an agent from the FBI, but she was determined not to arrive at the court-house in an FBI vehicle, as Linda Tripp had done: Monica wanted the world to see that, although she had been granted immunity, she was not the OIC's stool pigeon. At the same time she and her family were concerned about her safety, knowing that there were people who hated her because she was effectively testifying against the President. Once again Billy Martin, long since dubbed the family's "Minister of Defense," came up with a solution: Monica would use her own car, driven by the ever-loyal Walter Ellerbee, but would be accompanied by an FBI agent.

When Monica Lewinsky arrived outside the Federal Courthouse on Washington's Constitution Avenue to give evidence, she was stunned by the size of the media contingent waiting outside the courthouse. However, Monica was now a pro with the cameras, and no longer needed to bite her cheek to stop herself laughing nervously as she ran the gauntlet of flashbulbs, microphones and shouted questions. That was just as well because, even in her stress and anxiety there was much to smile at. With their coolers filled with beer and sandwiches, canopies over their heads to shade them from the fierce August sun, their boom boxes, and striped lawn chairs, the massed ranks of the media at "Monica Beach" looked for all the world as if they were covering a county fair.

Once past the media hurdle and inside the building, she had to compose herself for her long day in court. She was very tense, so much so that her whole body began shaking when she was called to testify, and was worried that she would say something wrong or would not perform as well as Starr wanted, thus giving him an excuse to nullify her immunity. She was deeply thankful not to be wholly deprived of help and comfort. The presiding judge, Norma Holloway Johnson, had indicated that she did not want Monica's parents present, so the full "Team Lewinsky" was there in their stead, to give Monica moral support. Judy Smith ensured that cookies, chocolates and soft drinks were waiting when there was a rest break, and Stein, Cacheris, Preston Burton, Hoffmann and Bob Bredhoff were all on hand to offer advice and encouragement.

When she appeared before the twenty-three grand jurors, Monica talked at length about her affair with the President, as well as detailing Vernon Jordan's involvement in her search for a job. Inevitably, though, it was the intimate details of her relationship with Bill Clinton—the reason why the Grand Jury had been convened in the first place—that riveted the court. For the jury's benefit, and also to save Monica from having to go into intimate sexual detail during her testimony, the OIC's prosecutors had prepared a chart of significant events. It was divided into sections, and in one, the "sex box," they had written "oral sex" against the dates on which she and the President had been physically intimate with each other at the White House.

The experience was as distressing as it was humiliating, for the stark wording on the chart completely traduced the feelings that had underpinned the affair. "One of the frustrating things," says Monica, "is that everyone from the prosecutors, the media and the public, has focused on the oral sex as if was the main part of the relationship. There was never a time when I went to the Oval Office and just performed oral sex. It was always more passionate and loving than that stark phrase. I'm very sensitive to that narrow response to our relationship."

As she gave her evidence, Monica tried to make eye contact with the jurors, hoping to engage them in her story. For a girl who always wants everyone, even Starr's prosecutors, to like her, one of the most difficult aspects of that day was seeing the hostility on the faces of some of the jurors. It seemed, though, that she was not the only one trying to make contact with others—it was possible that someone was attempting to send her a signal. At the end of the session, the prosecutors told her that they thought the President was that day wearing one of the ties she had given him; they had not wanted to tell her while she was testifying, as they had felt it might upset her.

It was a weary and emotionally drained Monica who arrived home at the Watergate; by way of consolation for not being able to attend the court, her anxious mother had bought her favorite Chinese dish, chicken chow mein. Monica switched on the television news to check the presidential neckwear, and there he was, indeed wearing one of her ties. To her, this was a clear signal of support and friendship. "I thought he might wear one of my ties to pull on my heartstrings the day before I testified. I would stake my life on it that he did it deliberately, no matter how much he denied it in his own testimony."

That testimony had finally come to the forefront, for now that Monica had given evidence to the Grand Jury, the pressure was very much on the President. Some days after her court appearance it became clear not only that he was going to be questioned before the Grand Jury, via a video link to the White House, but that he was scheduled to speak to the nation afterwards.

In her heart, Monica wished that he had admitted to the affair months ago. She believed that the pressure would have been taken off both of them if he had confessed and apologized. He had chosen not to do so, however, and would therefore have to face the consequences. Now that Monica was working with the Office of the Independent Counsel, and as a result saw how much evidence against the President they had collected, she was even more concerned about him. "My immunity agreement meant that I had to tell the truth, come what may. So whatever exonerated him, exonerated him, but whatever implicated him, implicated him. I could no longer protect him."

Monica waited anxiously through the hours before he spoke to the nation on August 17, wondering whether his testimony before the Grand Jury, given earlier that day and then still secret, would chime with her own recollections. Neysa DeMann Erbland, who was visiting New York with her scriptwriter husband, Chris, tried to take her mind off the President's upcoming speech, but with little success.

That evening, in common with the majority of Americans, Monica was profoundly disappointed by the words of the man she had once wanted to marry. Tired and agitated after more than four hours of sparring with Starr and his six deputies before the Grand Jury, the President, whose greatest talent is his ability to persuade, gave the impression that he was not so much sorry for his behavior as sorry that he had been caught. Many viewers sensed that he felt little genuine regret that he had lied, and none at all for the way Monica had been treated.

In his broadcast, the only sitting President ever to testify before a Grand Jury investigating him admitted, for the first time, that he had indeed misled the public, although he emphasized that his testimony in the Paula Jones case had been "legally accurate." He confessed that he had had a relationship that was "not appropriate" with Monica Lewinsky, and said, "I know that my public comments and my silence about this matter gave a false impression. I misled people, including even my wife. I deeply regret that." Yet his four-minute speech was less an apology, mixing candor with contrition, than an irritated attempt at self-justification for his behavior. It was only toward the end that any of the fire of sincerity crept in—when he condemned Kenneth Starr for investigating his private life and called for the Special Prosecutor's four-year inquiry to be wound up.

His speech, which she insisted on watching alone, reduced Monica to tears. He was all politician and President; she saw nothing of Bill Clinton the man—the man she had come to love so much. "I was very hurt and angered by his speech," she says. "I felt like a piece of trash."

Of her treatment at the hands of the President, she says now, "I wondered how I could have ever cared about this man. He was so self-righteous and self-centered. I was hoping that he would give me some kind of stamp of approval, tell the world that I was a good, intelligent person, and stop everyone from being so mean to me. I felt, too, that he should have acknowledged my family—after all, there are plenty of fathers who would have been far more vocal in their criticism of Clinton's behavior. My dad had too much respect for the presidency to do that."

Even given her views on her former lover, she could not wholly expunge the memory of what, once, he had meant to her. On the following day, August 18, the Clinton family flew to Martha's Vineyard for their annual holiday. As Monica watched Bill, Hillary and Chelsea Clinton walk hand in hand to the waiting helicopter she "felt terrible for Chelsea, because no young person wants to think of their parents in terms of intimate sexual acts. I felt very, very sorry for her."

She spent the next couple of days at the OIC, being debriefed by Starr's deputies. During this time she formed the impression, from reading reports in the media, that in his (still secret) Grand Jury testimony the President had indicated that she meant nothing to him. She said as much when she appeared before the Grand Jury for the second time on August 20. "It's my understanding that this was a service contract, that all I did was perform oral sex on him and that's all this relationship was," she told the jurors. "And it was a lot more than that to me and I thought it was a lot more than that [to him]." In fact, her fears were groundless. When the President's testimony was released a month later, it became apparent that, far from belittling Monica, he had acknowledged her as "a good young woman with a good heart and a good mind." He did add, "I think she is burdened by some unfortunate conditions of her upbringing but she is basically a good person."

During her second Grand Jury appearance—she had been summoned to answer jurors' questions, rather than to challenge the President's testimony—Monica was much more relaxed, finding the experience curiously uplifting. By now the faces and the routine were familiar to her; furthermore, she had developed the ability to compartmentalize her emotions.

When she arrived at the courthouse she once again had to run the media gauntlet. Even her method for dealing with that was now practiced, however: straighten skirt, suck in stomach and slide out of car. As she passed the next gaggle of reporters waiting inside the courthouse, she was caught by surprise when one yelled, "Monica, do you think the President should have apologized to you the other night?" While she had a fleeting vision of herself turning round and saying "Yes," she did what she had done for the last seven months and ignored the question.

She had waited on tenterhooks for this court appearance, knowing that every question and answer brought her nearer to the moment when she would win her life back. Yet no matter how she tried to steel herself, nothing could have prepared her for the sheer humiliation of the day's events, as her sexuality, her character and morals, indeed, her very mind, were laid bare before twenty-three strangers. Every foible, every failing, every silly remark was on parade. The questions were as remorseless as they were agonizingly embarrassing. Did the President ever use a cigar in a sexual way? Did he touch her on the breast or in the genital area? Was it through her clothes or in direct contact with the skin? At times, Monica had to close her eyes, in a futile attempt to retain a shred of self-respect, as she answered.

At the same time, she was asked a number of pertinent, sometimes even poignant, questions which went to the heart of the relationship, forcing her to address her often contradictory responses to him. Asked whether she still loved the President, she replied that before his August 17 broadcast to the nation she would have said "Yes"; after it, she was not so sure.

More disconcerting than questions about her private sex life was being forced under oath to address her flaws and weaknesses, character failings that she has struggled with for years. The juror of whom Monica was most nervous was a middle-aged African-American woman, who seemed strongly disapproving. In a telling question she asked how Monica could talk about truth and honesty in her relationship with the President, when the affair was based on lies; indeed, it was a mirror image of her relationship with Andy Bleiler. "You're young, you're vibrant," the juror continued, "I can't figure out why you keep going after things that aren't free, that aren't obtainable."

Monica found it both very difficult and very painful to answer. She admitted that she had to work on herself, and said she particularly regretted that she had an affair with a married man. Yet this response, though truthful as far as it went, did not begin to address Monica's unresolved conflict between her heart, whose dynamics derived largely from her childhood response to her parents' divorce, and her head. Smart woman, stupid choices. "It was the toughest question I faced," she admits now. "I felt as if I were standing naked in front of the whole world, all my weaknesses exposed for everyone to look at."

The jury then moved on to ask her about another harrowing experience, the day of the sting at the Ritz-Carlton Hotel in Pentagon City. At that point Monica requested that Mike Emmick, the Starr prosecutor who had been with her in Room 1012, leave the courtroom, before taking them through the worst day of her life. She and some of the jurors broke down in tears as she relived the fear, the guilt and the pain of those long and agonizing hours. Typical of Monica, she wanted the jury to have some sense of the real her, asking them to call her "Monica." One female juror said, "But you'll always be Miss Lewinsky." Monica replied: "Not if I get married!"

As the questioning drew to a close, the jurors asked if she had anything that she wanted to share with them. Monica, who realized that this would be her first opportunity to make a statement as well as an apology to the representatives of the country as a whole, had given the matter some thought. Now she said, "I would just like to say that no one ever asked me to lie and I was never promised a job for my silence. And that I'm sorry. I'm really sorry for everything that's happened." Once more she burst into tears, just managing to blurt out the words, "And I hate Linda Tripp."

As frightening and demeaning as the process had been, Monica's honesty and openness had clearly touched the strangers sitting opposite her. The juror who had asked such penetrating questions told her that she had won her forgiveness, and several others urged her to forget Linda Tripp and move on with her life. Finally, the forewoman took the floor and, speaking on behalf of the whole Grand Jury, told the unhappy girl, "We wanted to offer you a bouquet of good wishes that includes luck, success, happiness and blessings." Once more Monica struggled to stem her tears, deeply moved by these generous words. Even Starr's deputies were impressed; prosecutor Karin Immergut told their prime witness, "I've never seen a lovefest like it."

Monica felt vindicated, not by the fact that the President, after seven months of evasion, had finally admitted to a relationship with her, but by the response of the jurors, who had set aside their preconceptions and prejudices and opened up their hearts and minds to a vulnerable yet honest young woman. But she could not help wondering whether, if she had turned down the immunity deal, the Grand Jury would have indicted her. It was a sorrowful moment, made worse by the feeling that somehow she might have been able to protect the President and save herself the humiliation and pain of the last few weeks. Her only consolation was that, like the rest of "Team Lewinsky," she believed she was now free of the Special Prosecutor, the Grand Jury and the FBI.

She had a rude awakening. The Office of the Independent Counsel told her that, because of what the President had said in his testimony to the Grand Jury, she must make a deposition, under oath, about the sexual aspect of the relationship. Not only that, but Special Prosecutor Starr wanted the cameras rolling as Monica answered detailed questions about how, when, where and why she had performed oral sex on the President, and talked about other intimate details of their sexual relationship. This, it seems, is what his four-year investigation had come down to—making, in the name of the American people, a video as verbally explicit as a pornographic movie.

Ostensibly, the rationale behind the idea was that it would spare Monica the ordeal of talking about these matters in front of the Grand Jury. Video-taped evidence is used in court cases involving young children, especially in cases of rape or sexual abuse. In those instances, however, the video evidence is shown in closed court and remains absolutely confidential. Yet when, on September 9, Starr submitted to Congress his report and eighteen boxes of supporting material, almost every detail was published.

The idea that Starr's sex video itself might also be released to the public—and undoubtedly it would have been a best-seller—filled Monica with the deepest dread. Not even her impressive reserves of courage and resilience could have coped with such an intrusion. "It would have been the complete and utter destruction of my soul," she says. "I don't think I would have ever been able to recover from that. I try not to think about it much; the only way I have been able to deal with it is to put it aside. As my step-uncle Jeff says, denial is underrated."

When the videotape idea was first mooted, she had consulted her attorney Plato Cacheris. At first, he told her that he didn't see a real problem with videotaped evidence. He then had second thoughts, however, feeling that the process was unnecessary. By contrast, Bernie Lewinsky had had not a moment's hesitation in condemning the proposal when they told him of it. "I said that, speaking as her father, I thought this was salacious and wrong," he says. "It was sick."

Though the video idea was dropped, Monica still had to go through each sexual encounter in detail with two female prosecutors, Karin Immergut and Mary Anne Wirth. What angers her most of all about the taking of her deposition, which she considered to be fundamentally misogynistic, was that the OIC justified it by claiming that the President's testimony concerning their sexual relationship differed substantially from Monica's. Yet when his testimony became public, it was clear that his account was based on a strict legal definition of sexual relations, conforming to his defense in the Paula Jones case, and performing semantic acrobatics to sidestep the admission of a sexual relationship with Monica. In any case, since she had already answered the Grand Jury's questions about the sexual side of their affair, Monica felt that this further deposition was superfluous.

August 26, the day on which she made her deposition at the Office of the Independent Counsel on Pennsylvania Avenue, was perhaps the most degrading of all. At one point, compelled to talk about performing oral sex on the President, Monica said to the two prosecutors, "I can't believe my dad is going to have to hear this one day." They assured her that her evidence would not necessarily be made public. Then the questioning continued—"Who unzipped whose zipper?" "Did he touch you under the bra or over the bra?" "Did he have his mouth on your breast or over your bra?" and so on—for two agonizing hours. When it was all over, Monica went home and took a long, hot shower, trying to wash away her shame and humiliation. "I felt so dirty, like I had been emotionally raped. It was really disgusting."

She was desperate to get out of Washington, the city that had defiled her, as soon as possible. Starr's deputies were reluctant to let her leave, however, in case they needed her to go over Linda Tripp's tapes. When they eventually agreed that she might go away for a few days, they demanded to know where she would be. Monica thought it was none of their business and refused to tell them. In the end they gave in, but they said they just wanted to know if she was going anywhere near Martha's Vineyard, where the Clintons were on holiday. At this Cacheris broke in, saying with a chuckle, "Yes, she's going to see Vernon Jordan about a job."

In fact, she did go to New England—though not to Martha's Vineyard—where she spent precious time with her mother and Peter Straus's family at their holiday home. After just four days, however, Plato Cacheris called to say that the OIC had ordered her to return to Washington to listen to the Linda Tripp tapes. "This was the moment I had been dreading all along," she says. "I didn't know how I would handle it. The whole thing made me very nervous and apprehensive. Next to going to jail, publication of the Tripp tapes was my worst nightmare."

On September 3, Monica and her attorney Sydney Hoffmann arrived at the offices of the Independent Counsel in Washington and began the "tortuous" process of listening to twenty hours of conversation between herself and Tripp. It took three full days, which were spent sitting in a windowless, airless room, listening to duplicates of the tapes while correcting the transcripts and highlighting personal comments they wanted deleted or edited. For Monica, "It was humiliating, it was painful and it really opened up the well of hatred and anger I feel for Linda Tripp. It awakened my disbelief at myself and the stupid things I said. There was so much more bullshit there than substance—half the conversations were about diet, shopping, being fat and other stupid stuff. Even the material about the President was just me whinging away." At one point she began to laugh, and told Karin Immergut, the prosecutor listening with them, that she could not believe the investigation had been based on such trivial nonsense.

One person was taking it very seriously, though. While Monica sat listening to herself complain to Tripp about the "Big Creep," the President told a press conference in Ireland, "I made a big mistake. It is indefensible and I am sorry." It was his first true apology and Monica missed it, of course, because she was carefully screening the tapes.

The more she heard, the more clearly she realized that, when Linda Tripp had first approached the Special Prosecutor's office in January, she had given them a highly colored and only partial account of the events of October, November and December 1997. A number of significant conversations—notably talks about Vernon Jordan's involvement with her job search, which clearly demonstrated that the attorney had been helping Monica before she was caught up in the Paula Jones case—were not there.

The fact that key conversations appeared to have been omitted led her to suspect that Tripp may have doctored the tapes, leaving out certain key conversations specifically in order to make Monica's surviving comments seem more dramatic and conspiratorial. Monica believes "with my heart and soul that Linda Tripp misled them when she saw Starr. I read it in her testimony. She just twisted everything, making it seem more sinister than it was."

As she listened to the tapes, what also both startled and annoyed her was how little incriminating evidence there was about Vernon Jordan, and how very often Tripp's sentiments—those concerning Kathleen Willey, for instance—neatly dovetailed with the "Talking Points." She thought that Starr and his deputies should have realized, simply from listening to the tapes, that the issues discussed in the "Talking Points" memo were reflected in her conversations with Tripp, and that no third party, let alone a lawyer, had ever been involved.

What concerned Monica most of all, however, was that she had said some hurtful things about members of her own family, and she was frantic at the thought they might learn of them. Indeed, she felt so wretched and ashamed of herself that, as the process continued, she no longer wanted to see or even to speak to those close to her. "I felt so horrible—I couldn't believe my language and the stupid, cruel things I said about people I love. I was so worried that I was going to ruin everybody's lives." To a lesser extent, she was also worried by the way her personality came across on the tapes: even the prosecutor could not believe that the woman sitting with her in the room was the woman on the tapes.

The lowest point in those three days was when she was forced to listen to herself sobbing over the line to Tripp. "I burst into tears," she admits. "I had forgotten how much pain I'd been in with this relationship. I just couldn't believe the cruelty of someone who would deliberately tape that pain."

Besides having to deal with the raw emotions provoked by listening to the tapes, Monica was confronted with documents taken by the prosecutors from the hard-disk drive of her computer. These were letters, most of them never sent, which she had written to the President during the tumultuous period before Christmas 1997. Not content with snatching her body, Starr's deputies were now invading her mind. They had exposed her sex life and dissected her personality; now they wanted to scrutinize her very soul. It was an intrusion too far. Monica started to cry, and then screamed at Immergut: "This is so *wrong*! Do you not understand that no one else is supposed to read this?" Her attorney Sydney Hoffman was equally outraged. Faced with this display of fury, Immergut assured them that the documents would be placed under lock and key, and indicated that they might not appear in the final report.

The issue of publication had preyed on Monica's mind ever since she had won immunity. Even on the day she signed the agreement she had wanted written confirmation from Starr that they would agree to "redact"—that is, edit—or delete personal material, particularly comments about her family, which was not relevant to the inquiry. Although no such confirmation was forthcoming, Monica's attorney assured her that there would be no problem over the issue.

In the light of all the leaks there had been, she had no faith in Immergut's assurances, so when she came to make her "sex" deposition on August 26, she saw it as her last bargaining chip with which to extract from the OIC a written agreement ensuring that her family's privacy— what little remained of it—should not be violated. Her family were equally anxious. Marcia wrote to Starr, begging that his published material should respect the family's privacy. He did not deign to reply. Neither did Republican Senator Henry Hyde, Chairman of the House Judiciary Committee, to whom she wrote in similar vein before the committee's decision to release the Tripp tapes into the public domain. (Ironically, Congress was so stunned by the public backlash resulting from the sensational, prurient, almost pornographic nature of the Starr Report, that the Judiciary Committee ordered the Tripp tapes to be heavily censored before releasing them.)

In the end, on September 9, the day Starr submitted his report to Congress, the prosecutors and Monica's attorneys met to discuss any mutually agreeable deletions. For example, Starr had wanted to name all Monica's lovers so as to establish her credibility in relation to the President's testimony, but in the end, Congress deleted their names.

Like everyone else involved in the case, Monica was a helpless spectator as the Starr Report and its accompanying eighteen boxes of information—"guilt by volume," as one wit noted—which the Special Prosecutor had accumulated during his four-year investigation were delivered to the House of Representatives by uniformed police officers. The Whitewater land-deal scandal, which Starr was originally deputed to investigate, was mentioned only four times in his 453-page report. He concentrated his fire almost exclusively on the President's relationship with Monica Lewinsky. In all, the report listed eleven possible grounds for impeachment, including perjury, witness tampering, obstruction of justice and abuse of power. The test for impeaching the President under the US Constitution was whether Clinton had actually committed "treason, bribery or other high crimes and misdemeanors." It was left to Congress to decide whether the Independent Counsel had made a compelling case for implementing that process.

Almost immediately, the President's attorney, David Kendall, hit back at the report, saying, "This is personal and not impeachable. The salacious allegations in this referral are simply intended to humiliate, embarrass and politically damage the President." Naturally, this view did not wash with Kenneth Starr, who had written in his report, "In view of the enormous trust and responsibility attendant to his high Office, the President has a manifest duty to ensure that his conduct at all times complies with the law of the land." Perjury and obstruction, he continued, "are profoundly serious matters. When such acts are committed by the President of the United States, we believe those acts 'may constitute grounds for impeachment.'"

As the nation watched the drama unfold, the President once again donned sackcloth and ashes, telling an audience in Florida on that same day, September 9, "I let you down. I let my family down. I let this country down. But I'm trying to make it right. I'm determined to never let anything like that happen again." Two days later, after the House of Representatives voted to release the report on the Internet, a contrite Clinton spoke at a prayer breakfast in Washington, at which he said, "I don't think there is a fancy way to say that I have sinned." He did, however, use the occasion to apologize, not only to his own family, friends and colleagues, but also, and for the first time, to Monica and her family. "It is important to me." he said, "that everybody who has been hurt knows that the sorrow I feel is genuine: first and most important, my family, also my friends, my staff, my Cabinet, Monica Lewinsky and her family, and all the American people. I have asked all for their forgiveness."

He had come a long way from the dark days of January, when he had told senior aides that Monica was hardly more than an infatuated stalker whose claims to have had a relationship with him had little basis in reality. Understandably, Monica considered his tardy apology "a day late, and a dollar short," although "I was pleased he did acknowledge the anguish felt by myself and my family."

That he did indeed understand something of what they had been through became clear when his video testimony to the Grand Jury was released on September 21. Watching it, Monica was surprised and even "shocked" by the extent of his support for her. "I was shocked because for once it was not just the politician talking. There were glimpses of the Bill Clinton I had always known. It was a refreshing change." In that testimony, she believes, he was speaking as a man, not a president, when he criticized the way Starr's prosecutors had treated her: as if she were a "serious felon." He accused Linda Tripp of "stabbing her in the back," and added that "it broke my heart" that she had become involved in the Paula Jones case, which he described as a bogus lawsuit funded by his political enemies.

As a politician, however, he was far more circumspect in acknowledging both the sexual and romantic dimensions of his relationship with Monica. He did not, he said, attach any significance to the ties she had given him, and, though he admitted to "inappropriate intimate conduct and sexual banter" with her, he refuted the notion that his behavior had constituted sexual relations as he understood the term. It was this contention, parsing sentences and wriggling around definitions of the words "is" and "alone," which left most people incredulous. It also gave comedians a field day.

The President's support for her, and his contrition, were balm for Monica's soul, but nothing and no one could heal the emotional wound gouged in her by the Starr Report. Monica was in New York with her mother when the text became available on the Internet. When she saw it, she voiced her alarm, commenting on passages as she surfed the document. Her mother asked her to read out loud what Starr had said, but Monica was too embarrassed. "The whole world is reading about my daughter," Marcia remarked in amazement, "and yet you can't tell your mother?"

Monica's embarrassment is wholly understandable. The report makes vile reading, both because of the extent of sexual detail, including the incident with the cigar, and because of its use of even the most deeply personal and private material. Her unsent letters to "Handsome," which Karin Immergut had indicated might be omitted, were printed in all their sentimental, self-indulgent glory. Furthermore, although she did not know it then, her "sex" deposition, another supposedly confidential interview, was to be published in full a few weeks later.

Then, too, the report contained a number of errors. Monica had pointed them out but, because of the haste with which it had been written and hustled into Congress, they were never corrected. For instance, her friend Catherine called her in puzzlement, wondering why she had never said that she had been on medication since 1995, as the Starr Report stated. Monica explained that this was a typing error; she had only started medication after the scandal erupted in January 1998. Such errors may seem trivial, but in fact they were sometimes extremely important: some Democratic politicians later argued, wholly erroneously, that Monica's testimony differed from the President's because she had been on anti-depression drugs for three years. In *Vanity Fair* journalist Renata Adler publicly expressed contempt for the Independent Counsel's magnum opus: "The six-volume report by Kenneth W. Starr . . . is in many ways an utterly preposterous document: inaccurate, mindless, biased, disorganized, unprofessional and corrupt."

During his investigation, Kenneth Starr had not once met Monica Lewinsky, and yet she felt that he had defiled and molested her—not physically, but by using his legal and constitutional power to strip away every last vestige of her dignity and her humanity. "As a result of his report I felt very violated. I really felt raped and physically ill with myself, as if anybody who looked at me would only think about me performing oral sex. I just felt that the world looked at me as a whore.

"It was very painful and humiliating. It confirmed to me even more that no one cared for me as a person, no one saw me as a human being. I was just a pawn used to get the President."

She was virtually inconsolable in the first few days after the report's publication on the Internet. Her mother and stepfather, anxious to help, took her to dinner in New York with Rabbi Mark Gollub, who spent a few minutes talking with her privately, offering her spiritual counseling. She needed a great deal of help and guidance during the next few weeks, especially as it seemed that Congress was intent on releasing not only the transcripts of Linda Tripp tapes, but also the audio version. Ever since she had heard the recordings of herself sobbing and swearing over the phone, this was what she had dreaded most.

Monica wanted to make a statement before the tapes were released, publicly apologizing to her family, to the President, to Hillary and Chelsea Clinton, and to the American people for the trouble she had caused—at least then people would be able to hear her voice when she was in control of what she was saying. But the plan was dropped because the Office of the Independent Counsel wanted to approve her words.

Surprisingly, the tapes were not released by the House Judiciary Committee until after the November 3 elections to Congress and the Senate. It had been widely expected that the voting would reflect the scandal's adverse effect on the Democratic Party—in September, Democratic Senator Joseph Lieberman, although a Clinton supporter, had earned a standing ovation in the Senate when he attacked the President's behavior as "disgraceful and immoral." In fact the elections resulted in a remarkable reversal for the Republicans and the subsequent resignation of the flamboyant Speaker of the House of Representatives, Newt Gingrich; a fierce long-term opponent of Clinton, Gingrich was also a member of the House Judiciary Committee.

Knowing that the tapes were about to be made public, and distraught at the knowledge of how much hurt they would cause, Monica had intended to take a sleeping pill and spend the day in bed. In the event, her friend

Neysa came to her emotional rescue, treating her to a day out in order to take her mind off the inevitable publicity.

As she had feared, the very people about whom Monica cared the most about were those most deeply hurt, not just by Starr's report, but also by Tripp's tapes. One of the saddest results was that the divisions between father and daughter, which had seemed healed, were reopened. Bernie had vowed never again to read or listen to anything about his daughter, but whenever he turned on the TV or radio he could not help hearing more distressing details. Especially painful for him was the recording of a conversation during which Monica had told Tripp about learning to lie to her father when she was growing up. "She said things about the family," he says, "that I hope I will never hear in full. What bits I have heard have shocked me, and I am still very distraught at some of the things that she said."

Marcia is less judgmental, for she had been so worn down by the constant carping criticism of Monica and her family that there was little on the tapes that could upset her. "I know Monica and I know how much she loves her family. The kinds of things that hurt very deeply six months ago now have less effect because I have given up expecting humanity from anyone. The lack of privacy has been so total and so violating that today there is nothing that anyone could say or reveal about our family that would shock me."

One passage on the tapes, in which when she heard Monica crying, she did find distressing, however, because it reminded her of those awful days in the fall of 1997 when her daughter's world was falling apart. "It is," she acknowledges, "something that few people know or care about. I know, her friends and family know, how much pain she suffered. This whole episode in her life caused her so much torment, some intentionally inflicted by others, some of it self-inflicted in that she invested so much into something she should not have done."

The passing of the days did little to dim Monica's guilt and anguish. Sometimes she was caught unprepared, and then the pain burned afresh. Over breakfast one morning, she heard popular psychologist Dr. Joyce Brothers, who was talking about the Starr Report on the *Today* TV show, ask the viewers, "Can you imagine a young man bringing home Monica Lewinsky to his parents and saying, 'I'm going to marry Monica Lewinsky'?" This scathing comment was too much for Monica. She collapsed into hysterical sobs, inconsolable.

Over the last year her privacy, her sexuality, her mind and her soul had been explored and exploited by Kenneth Starr, by the White House, and by the mass media. Listening to Dr. Brothers, she realized with near-despair that even her future had been taken away from her.

CONCLUSION

• •

Girl on a Swing

*A*s I write, it is just over a year since Monica Lewinsky last met with the President, and yet he still haunts her nights and her waking hours. Indeed, he appears frequently in her dreams, ever present yet always elusive. "I wake up some mornings and I have an instant moment where I miss him with every ounce of my being, my head, heart and body," she says. "I miss the way he used to hold me, so much."

He generates a kaleidoscope of emotions ranging from tenderness and longing, to remorse, guilt and anger. "There was a moment recently," she admits, "when I closed my eyes real tight and imagined myself back in my little office in the East Wing of the White House. The phone rang I held my breath and sure enough, it was that voice, a voice so familiar to many but private to me, a voice suffused with longing, sadness and hunger.

"It was so strange. My heart was beating loudly and I felt like I was really there. Sometimes I miss the joy that I felt as I walked towards the Oval Office after I got 'the call.' My pulse would race and my face would be flushed; I got excited just thinking about his smell, his touch and the warmth of his body when he was close to mine. I couldn't wait for that first moment of a delicious kiss from my 'Handsome.'

"I cannot believe that my relationship with the President is over. The soft touches and strong hugs are gone for ever. I still miss the adoring look in his eye, and that broad grin that always greeted me."

Yet her sentimental musings upon Clinton the man easily give way to anger against the President who jabbed his finger and told the world that he had never had sexual relations with "that woman." This is Monica's paradox, an inner battle that leads her to say, "While there are some days when I miss his presence there are others when I never want to see him again, times when I have to turn off the TV because I feel sick looking at him." Yet however torn she may be emotionally, these days Monica sees Clinton far more as a politician than as a man, a politician, moreover, who lied to her and the nation. She says: "I always knew he wasn't a very truthful person but the events of the last year have shown him to be a much bigger liar than I ever thought. Now I see him as a selfish man who lies all the time. That makes me very angry and resentful."

This sense of outrage is, understandably, shared by her family and close friends. Thus one of the rare sources of dispute between Monica and Catherine Allday Davis is the fact that while Bill Clinton was Monica's boyfriend, he was also her President. Catherine is unforgiving, declaring: "He's my President, twice her age with a daughter almost the same age, and I cannot excuse his behavior."

Throughout the scandal, Monica's father resolutely refused to criticize the President, stonewalling TV-show hosts Barbara Walters, Larry King, and Katie Couric when he appeared on their programs. Since the publication of the Starr Report and the release of the Tripp tapes, however, he has hardened his heart. Today he states unequivocally: "I hate his guts for what he did. I find it difficult to call the President of the United States a louse, but that is what he is. I'm very angry about what he did to my daughter, who is just few years older than Chelsea. I don't think he would enjoy anybody doing that to his daughter. His cover up was cowardly, not having the guts to take responsibility for what he did."

Just as Monica is deeply angered by the way the President abandoned her in her hour of need, so she feels a profound loathing for Linda Tripp and her cohorts, the people who betrayed her and the President. "I have a lot of anger to go round," she says ruefully, her ruefulness an acknowledgment that until she puts those feelings aside she will never move on as a whole person. So while she considers suing Linda Tripp for illegally taping their conversations, she also knows that such a case would involve reliving the past, a past she is trying to put behind her, a past that constantly overwhelms her present, denying her the chance of a purposeful future.

Hand in hand with her sense of anger is her overwhelming feeling of guilt, shame for the trouble and anguish she has caused not only her family and friends, but the President and his family, and particularly Chelsea Clinton. She still cannot quite believe, and far less accept, that what started as an exciting, if furtive, fling three years ago has ended with the first ever impeachment of an elected President of the United States.

When, in mid-December 1998, Congress voted by a narrow partisan majority to impeach Clinton, Monica put herself on trial. "I felt really, really bad for him," she says. "I cried so hard, I felt so wretched, I just couldn't believe it was happening." She blamed herself for the President's woes, telling herself that if she had never confided in Linda Tripp, then the whole disastrous sequence of events would never have come about. Her argument is, as the lawmakers on Capitol Hill like to say, a "hypothetical," the President himself contributing to his own downfall by dint of his testimony in the Paula Jones case and before Starr's Grand Jury.

While an inconsolable Monica spent the day in bed, unable to bear the news, the American people reacted in bemused horror as the House of Representatives elected to impeach the President even while that official, as Commander-in-Chief, had engaged the nation's armed forces, with those of Britain, in a major bombing operation against Iraq.

The whole partisan affair bore the hallmark of the political show trials that marked Stalin's regime in Communist Russia; state prosecutors launching a reign of terror, pitting mother against daughter, lover against lover, relative against relative, friend against friend, in a case where the verdict was known before the evidence was heard. More charitably, other observers have compared it to Lewis Carroll's *Alice's Adventures in Wonderland*, in which the Queen of Hearts cries, "No, no! . . . Sentence first—verdict afterwards."

By any standards, the impeachment debate was surreal, a trial that managed to be both the high-water mark of the American legal system and, arguably, the nadir of natural justice, the triumph of the system over common sense. For Congress, which voted on party lines, decided to impeach the President on the ghost-written report of a man who had not even met, let alone interviewed, the key witnesses. In turn, that report was based on testimony before a one-sided Grand Jury. Yet, as they like to point out in legal circles, a smart prosecutor could "indict a cheese sandwich" before a grand jury.

Any such reservations were cast aside, however, when Congress voted that the President should be impeached on two articles; namely, that he perjured himself before the Grand Jury, and that he obstructed the administration of justice. These "articles of impeachment" were then sent from the lower legislative chamber—that is, the House of Representatives—to the Senate, where a full trial began on January 7, 1999. The senators, all one hundred of them, were sworn in as jurors, of whom just over two thirds needed to accept the House's case in order to remove the President from office. As the Republican Party does not have the requisite majority in the Senate, this was seen by many observers as a pointless, indeed absurd, exercise that would serve only to damage the country.

For Monica, the historic trial of President Clinton in the Senate provoked not only anxiety and guilt, but also resentment as the upper house of Congress debated whether witnesses were to be called, something for which the Republican prosecutors and Clinton's opponents devoutly wished. Every day she waited in trepidation to see if she would be called as a witness, and thus to be grilled before the Senate live on prime-time television. She kept a bottle of vodka on ice to drown her sorrows if she were called, and a bottle of her favourite Veuve Clicquot champagne to celebrate if the Senate simply voted not to have witnesses called.

At the same time, she felt a deep hostility towards the way in which a private relationship had been turned into a political vendetta. "This was my love—my spirit and my body—[and it] has been turned into this vile political creation," she laments.

It is this progression from illicit affair to full-scale impeachment proceedings that is perhaps the most striking feature of the whole saga. At root, it is a human story of love and betrayal, guilt and remorse, and yet it has been explained almost entirely in legal terms, the debate conducted by journalists, lawyers and politicians, professions defined by an adversarial rather than a conciliatory philosophy. Sentiment and romance do not figure high on their agendas.

After compelling judicial arguments by managers from the House of Representatives and the White House legal team, it was left to a member of that team, Dale Bumpers, a former Senator and Governor of Arkansas and a close friend of the Clinton family, to remind the house, and the nation, of the scale of this human tragedy.

In his ninety-minute closing address, Bumpers spoke of the five years of sleepless nights suffered by the Clintons since the start of Starr's Whitewater inquiry, of the huge legal bills, and above all of the emotional fallout since the Lewinsky scandal had broken. The investigation, he said, had put a huge strain on "the relationship between husband and wife, father and child," adding that the President's rapport with his daughter Chelsea had been all but destroyed. "There is a total lack of proportionality, of balance in this thing," he concluded. "The charges and the punishment are totally out of sync."

It is not only the legislators' sense of proportion that is out of kilter, however, for when all is said and done, what has riveted the world for the past year is the microscopic analysis of an office romance between a very junior employee and her boss. It was Monica's folly—and, one might add, her bad luck—to fall in love with a powerful man whose enemies are both zealous and unforgiving. In any other circumstances, after the affair had ended she would have been allowed to pack her bags and move on.

In any other circumstances, maybe—but, as her mother sees only too clearly, "If she had not been such a caring, romantic and vulnerable young woman, it would have been a very different story. In the normal course of events this would have been one of those lessons in life that women learn privately in the process of growing up. Instead, her private pain became entertainment for the masses, and this was the cruelest, cruelest thing. What enormous crime did she commit that made it necessary to destroy her, to strip away every last vestige of dignity and privacy from this young person's life?"

Thrown into the political piranha tank, Monica's personality was quickly picked clean in a media feeding frenzy, every imperfection and shortcoming stripped bare by columnists, photographers, comedians and amateur psychologists. Just as Dale Bumpers reminded the nation that the Clintons were human beings, so too, in a lesser arena, Monica's father let a major California radio station know that its airing of off-color remarks about his daughter was hurting not just her, but her entire family.

It is only in the last few months—now that the world realizes that she had not been living in a world of make-believe and that her testimony was a fair record of her relationship with the President—that the unbridled hostility towards her has diminished. Many now recognize that she is a woman who has been cruelly traduced, by Linda Tripp, by Kenneth Starr, by Bill Clinton, and by the world's media. In a tale already rich in ironies, it is an abidingly rich, if uncomfortable, one to consider the moral code of the former intern against those of the three people who have betrayed, denied or used her.

Writing in the *New York Times*, Andrew Sullivan has observed: "For a very long time she did all she could to avoid betraying her lover, even to the point of signing an affidavit that denied the affair. Once cornered, she resolved to tell the whole truth. The most stunning aspect of the Starr Report is how far this young woman was prepared to go to abide by the law, even to the extent of opening herself up to grotesque public scrutiny. What a contrast with the President. If this morality tale is essentially about honesty, then Ms. Lewinsky is its heroine."

Yet she has paid a very high price—too high—for that honesty and openness. In the weeks I spent talking to her, the one question to which Monica could not find an adequate answer concerned the humiliation she has endured throughout the scandal. "For the last ten months I have seen the Special Prosecutor, the press, the White House and the public ripping apart layer upon layer of my soul. I don't know what I did to deserve that humiliation. Certainly I made mistakes and foolish judgments, but did they warrant this level of abuse? Yes, I probably am the most humiliated woman in the world, but I just can't deal with that thought. I have to block it out because it is too much to handle."

For just as the O.J. Simpson trial exposed the racial fault line running through American society, so the Monica Lewinsky saga has spotlighted the underlying misogyny that still permeates American life, and particularly the media. Clinton the adulterer and liar is a forgiven man; Monica Lewinsky the temptress is a scorned woman, derided by feminists and conservatives alike. Her loyalty, her honesty and her silence are qualities deemed to be without merit. As far as modern moral America is concerned, for her to be female, young, confident, well groomed, at ease with her sexuality—and loved—constitutes some sort of crime. What is far worse, however, she has committed the greatest sin of all: she is overweight.

Her punishment is to be followed by paparazzi who jostle and harass her, calling her vile names in an attempt to reduce her to tears and thereby win a more saleable picture. Once the photographers have snared her, the columnists and editors take over, subjecting her to a verbal lashing. Described as "the portly pepperpot," and worse, by the tabloids, she was then routinely berated by columnists like Maureen Dowd of the *New York Times*. As one British commentator, Anne McElvoy, wrote: "Monica must do what America expects, indeed demands. She must lose weight. Monica's increased size is a sign of her moral laxity or divine punishment." Lest non-American journalists become too self-congratulatory, however, it is worth noting another report, printed in a leading British newspaper. On 26 January, under the portentous sub-heading "Trial of the President— Day 9", the *Guardian* had this to report: "Ms Lewinsky had two pancakes and orange juice, a witness said, and was dressed in a dark trouser suit." Diet and dress sense, it seems, were as important as her evidence in the impeachment debate.

In her own willfully principled way, Monica has tried to take the moral high road ever since the scandal broke, rejecting, for example, a five-million-dollar offer from Fox TV, a tabloid network, for interviews, a book and a hair commercial. Even though there were many who advised her to take the money and run, she did not want to become involved with the "sleaze merchants" who had made her life a misery for the last year. Instead, although she considered an offer from TV superstar Oprah Winfrey, she decided to give her first television interview to Barbara Walters—for free.

With the passage of time, what was initially notoriety has inevitably mutated into an unwanted celebrity. "I don't want to make a career out of being Monica Lewinsky," she says, adding, "I haven't done anything to be proud of." Much as she resents this cloak of fame, it is now a fact of her life, as her stepfather Peter Straus, a former director of Voice of America, has explained to her. He is, he says, "leaning on her hard to develop a thicker skin, not to read the tabloids in the morning." There are upsides, however. Certainly it amused Monica and her family—and this author— when, in the *New York Times* in December 1998, a Gallup poll of the ten women Americans most admired ranked her alongside Queen Elizabeth II of Great Britain.

Besides the price she has paid emotionally, and in the utter disruption of her life, fame has also come at a savage cost in financial terms, not just for her but for her family and friends. It is a price they are still paying. Over the last year this $40,000-a-year office worker has been landed with a million dollars' worth of legal bills, as well as being forced to watch in helpless silence as the lives of her family and friends have been ravaged and exploited.

It has been her fate to be a pawn in a power struggle between two mighty foes, President Clinton and Judge Starr. One broke her heart, the other tried to break her spirit, and it is the latter of whom she is most wary. Even today, Monica lives in dread of the Special Prosecutor, fearing that at any moment he will revoke her immunity and send her to jail. Certainly he keeps her on a remorselessly tight rein.

The events of 1998 have made Monica and others closely associated with the scandal far more skeptical and critical of the nature of government in America. "Justice in this country is a joke," she maintains, adding, "Our tabloid TV has now spawned tabloid government." Her mother, who has been almost equally battered by the scandal, sees all too clearly the damage not just to her daughter, but to her innocent friends, many of whom have faced unnecessary legal bills, unwanted media harassment, and even investigation by the FBI. There is a sorrowful weariness to Marcia Lewis's view of America now: "Before all this happened I thought of the government as a friend, never as my enemy, but I now realize it has the power to frighten and to threaten. I don't think I will ever look at my country, my homeland, in quite the same way again." She adds, of the President and the Special Prosecutor, the twin causes of most of her daughter's troubles: "I hate Starr and the others for what they did to my daughter, for the threats and fear and how they have ruined her life. It was they who made her go through this living hell. That does not for a moment excuse President Clinton for the way he behaved."

Indeed, the implications of this whole sorry saga reverberate way beyond those of a simple sex scandal. As David Remick commented in *The New Yorker*: "Monica is the woman of secrets who no longer has any. Her eyes are not windows but mirrors, and what we see in them is awful. Yet we go on staring."

It is an episode in American history that, as far as Billy Martin is concerned, reflects badly on the legal system he has worked inside for more than twenty years. As he says: "At the moment I am not proud of the law in my country that can allow this miscarriage of justice, where an Independent Counsel can be appointed to prosecute matters that would not be worthy of prosecution by the US Department of Justice."

His colleague Sydney Hoffmann, who watched Monica being subjected to days of humiliating questions by middle-aged men, echoes the feelings of the First Lady, who described the process as a "right-wing conspiracy," Hoffmann says: "This investigation was politically motivated. This whole scandal is not the stuff of a criminal case."

Although Monica's indomitable will, helped by her gallows sense of humor, has enabled her to survive the most tumultuous year of her life, the feisty young woman who dared call the President of the United States "Butthead" has been chastened and bruised by the experience. Her friend Lenore Reese, who saw her last fall for the first time since their days at college, remembers from their meeting that "there was a sadness about her; she was nervous and far more cautious because for the last year her freedom has been taken away. One of the most attractive things about her was her light-hearted spirit, but this whole episode has ended her innocence."

Neysa DeMann Erbland, who has frequently picked Monica out of the emotional troughs during the last few months, has also seen the changes in her friend. "She sounds like an older woman, a weary woman, a woman who has had her heart destroyed, along with her reputation, on prime-time TV. She is twenty-five, an age that should be filled with the delicious discomfort of finding oneself. Instead, Monica spends her time knitting scarves and sweaters. She dreams of a time when she can have the privately tumultuous life of a twenty-something again. She wants her life back."

Emotionally exhausted she may be, but much of the pre-scandal Monica, with all her flaws and foibles, remains. She is still the impatient, headstrong, self-willed and fiercely loyal young women her friends know and love; moreover, she is still, in spite of everything, surprisingly trusting and naive. Yet those same qualities that gave her the strength to survive the onslaught of Starr and the media, make it more difficult for her to cope with her current life in limbo. "She is not a patient person and her life now means that she has to learn patience," Catherine Allday Davis remarks.

The unresolved emotional problems Monica faced before the scandal, issues linked to her weight and her relationships with men, have only been exacerbated by the attention she has attracted. Until the media caravan moves on—presumably after the end of the Clinton presidency—Monica will remain in the limelight, waiting for the time when, in Barbara Lewinsky's words, "the name Lewinsky doesn't make people jump out of the swimming pool."

For someone by nature impatient, this period in purdah merely compounds the difficulty of fulfilling her rather prosaic ambitions; to find a loving partner, start a family, begin a useful career. She has talked about returning to graduate school to take a PhD in forensic psychology, or a degree in law—she has certainly had a crash course in that during the last year—and even of undertaking volunteer work with disadvantaged children, teaching them reading skills.

Undoubtedly her ability to marshal cogent arguments, her capacious memory and her analytical mind make Monica eminently suited to a career as an attorney. Even so, she feels very strongly that, if anything good is going to come out of this horror, then she should attach her name to a worthwhile cause, especially one that concerns children. "Maybe if I do good, good will come to me one day," she says. Yet the truth is that, whatever her friends and family suggest, she has still to overcome the trauma of the recent past before she can rationally consider a way forward. Her father has no doubts about her most pressing needs: "My initial fear for Monica was the prospect of jail. Now I worry about where she goes from here. Certainly she will need long-term counseling to get over the post-traumatic depression that is inevitable as she faces up to the full horror of the last year. She also needs to have healthy relationships with single guys."

The last recommendation is easier said than done, however. As a girl who has always had problems reading the road map of romance, the way forward is filled with all kinds of false trails. Until she can break the emotional cycle that has led her into two dead end relationships with married men, she will find it difficult to choose the path to lasting happiness. These days, she needs her emotional compass, never previously a particularly reliable mechanism, to guide her as never before. Her problem is that she is now an uncertain witness to her own perceptions, the betrayals of the last year by lovers and by others whom she trusted making her as unsure of her own instincts as she is now wary of others' motives.

Surprisingly, however, she has recently enjoyed the companionship of a young single man. It is a relationship that she has allowed to develop at its own pace, something helped by the fact that, for a while at least, she was able to keep his name out of the headlines. For her, the friendship has been both a revelation and a reassurance, a first step into the real world of male–female relationships.

These are her first faltering steps on a very long road to recovery, an emotional convalescence that will have to resolve the issues of her family life and discard the emotional detritus, the hurt, the humiliation and the anger, of the past year.

Her life in limbo, her future uncertain, Monica is anxious to move on, to find a companion and start a family. Understandably, she wonders: "When will all this be over? I want my life back and at the same time I'm scared I will never be able to have the life I dream of—a full, rich life with a loving, tender husband, the laughter and joys of children and maybe, just maybe, contentment."

On a warm November night in 1998, Monica is gently swaying to and fro on a swing in Holmby Park playground, near her apartment in Los Angeles, where she and her brother Michael played when they were young. Ever since she was a child she has enjoyed swings and tonight is no different. As she sways gently in the moonlight she talks wistfully about what might have been; her dreams of marrying by the time she was twenty-four, and of having a brood of children before she was thirty.

For whatever her professional ambitions, her personal goals are thoroughly old-fashioned: to find a husband and have children. She will make a loving mother, and one who, Marcia Lewis believes, will be able face her own children and tell them her story without embarrassment, admitting her mistakes but emphasizing that she betrayed no one as she was betrayed.

Monica's dreams remain unfulfilled, however, for this essentially traditional, middle-class American girl is today reduced to hiding in the shadows, a fugitive in her own land. As a result, she exists in a modern-day Orwellian nightmare that has become, for her, a daily reality. Each move she makes is monitored, either by the paparazzi or the FBI, her diet is picked over by pundits, her every purchase becomes a matter for international reportage.

Above everything, though, stands the moon-faced figure of Kenneth Starr, the man who has effectively made himself the puppet-master of her life. When he pulls the legal strings, she is forced to dance to his command. The bland, tightly-smiling, face of the Special Prosecutor is almost a personification of the "Big Brother" of Orwell's future, a no longer fanciful scenario in which the state can search a person's thoughts and soul as easily as their house and computer. Monica, her family and her friends know that all too well.

Earlier that night in November 1998, the face of the man Monica at once fears and reviles had filled the television screen in her apartment. Feeling she had to escape his eye, she left her apartment like an escaping prisoner, giving her "guards," the ever present paparazzi, the slip. Donning a baseball cap as a disguise, she roared off in her leased four-wheel-drive, nervously checking the rear-view mirror in case she were being tailed by the photographic predators who pursue her everywhere. So it came about that, at nine in the evening, she was able to escape the Special Prosecutor and the media, and enjoy a few furtive moments of freedom, swinging in the night air and dreaming of what might have been.

This, then, is the fate of Monica Lewinsky, a child-woman searching for a future and trying to obliterate a past, an obliging, intelligent, well-mannered girl who could be anybody's sister, anybody's daughter. She is a prisoner in the land of the free, every move she makes served up for the masses. And so it will remain until, one day, the media circus moves on.

POSTSCRIPT

"Sometimes I Miss Him So Much"

$\mathcal{I}$ THOUGHT I had written the last chapter of this book. Then, on Friday, January 22, 1999, I received an anxious, middle-of-the-night phone call from Monica Lewinsky. She was frightened, more frightened than I have ever heard her sound, her soft girlish voice filled with fear.

She told me that Kenneth Starr had obtained a court order forcing her to fly from Los Angeles to Washington, there to be interviewed by the House Republican managers prosecuting the case for impeachment against the President in the Senate. If she failed to do his bidding, she could end up in jail.

Over the last few months I have become used to reading the varying inflections in her voice; the barely controlled anger when she speaks of Linda Tripp, the sentimental tone she uses when she talks about the President, and the flinch of fear that infects her speech when she refers to Starr and the Office of the Independent Counsel. The nearest comparison to the relationship between Starr and Lewinsky is the reaction of an abused child in the presence of the abuser, or that of a badly-beaten animal to its bullying owner.

"All of a sudden this whole impeachment thing is back on my shoulders," she said, "I am anxious that Starr thinks I'm going to turn this around for him, which I don't want to do and can't do. It's not my fault that there's not really a case here. So I'm nervous about what he will do to me if he doesn't get what he wants."

Ever since the Senate trial had begun in early January, Monica had taken only a passing interest in the day-to-day events, preferring to ignore the arguments in the Chamber as a way of keeping up her own spirits. When we had discussed the possibility of her being called as a witness it had been in the context of her being examined along with Betty Currie, Vernon Jordan and several others. Now she had been ordered to go on her own.

The move was seen by the Democrats as the last throw of the dice by House Republican prosecutors, who had consistently demanded that witnesses be called to testify before the Senate—a move which the White House legal team bitterly opposed. All that week the prosecutors had seen their arguments for impeachment dissected and diminished with forensic skill and precision by the White House lawyers, of whom Cheryl Mills, a young attorney, perfectly complemented the leader of Clinton's legal team, the seasoned Charles Ruff.

In desperation, the prosecution used Starr to ask a Federal judge, Norma Holloway Johnson, to grant an emergency order forcing Monica to cooperate with them, although the phrase employed was that she was to "allow herself to be debriefed." The decision caused an uproar, Democrats and the White House attorneys attacking the way the House Republican prosecutors had singled out Monica because she was legally beholden to Ken Starr by virtue of her immunity deal with the OIC. Other potential witnesses who had no need of immunity, like Jordan, had refused to become involved with the trial unless or until the Senate itself voted to call witnesses.

Essentially, the House Republican prosecutors, fearing that they were losing the argument to call witnesses, used Starr to strongarm Monica Lewinsky by threatening her with jail if she failed to comply. Yet on the floor of the Senate they spoke in beguilingly genial terms about having a friendly chat with the former intern, simply so that she could get to know them and they could find out what she had to say.

The reality was very different, however. Not only was Monica obliged to cooperate, but under the same order her family and friends were banned from speaking out in her behalf. As her attorney Plato Cacheris said, "This was the low point for us. She should not have been required to go through this yet again. While Monica did a very good job, it was burdensome and traumatic for her." Monica's father, Dr. Lewinsky, became so distressed at the news that his blood pressure, for which he already needs medication in order to keep it stable, rose to such dangerous levels that he almost had to go to the hospital for attention. "I am finding it very hard to get my anger under control," he said. "This latest episode will prove to the whole world that Monica is nothing more than a pawn in a vicious political struggle. It is scary how much power Starr now has in this country."

For Monica herself, all the fear and agony of the last year—emotions that had been gradually subsiding—came flooding back; her deep terror and suspicion of Starr, her guilt about betraying the President, and her dread that she was being watched and bugged by the FBI. As an extra irony, at the time her father was attending the same annual conference on cancer as he had been when he first heard about the sting operation against Monica.

Having been told by her attorney, Plato Cacheris, that she was obliged to follow Starr's orders, Monica found it difficult to sleep that night, so consumed was she by anger and fear. Her father got up at four the following morning to take her to Los Angeles airport to catch the seven o'clock United Airlines flight to Washington. As they tearfully hugged, he told her to be strong for the ordeal that lay ahead. To add insult to injury, while Starr's office had booked her flight, they had not paid for it, leaving Monica to pick up the tab for the ticket.

There were scenes of mayhem at the airport in Washington and later at the hotel, as security men hustled Monica, who was wearing a baseball cap advertising the independent film company, The Shooting Gallery, where her friend Jonathan Marshall works, through the media throng to the safety of her room. She wrestled her way past the cameras to find that her mother, Peter and Aunt Debra and Uncle Bill had all arrived to support her. Marcia was especially proud of the way her daughter handled herself amidst the frantic media attention and under Starr's pressure, remarking, "She was a Daniel thrown into the lions' den and she came out strong and truthful." One benefit of the media attention was that her baseball hat became a hot fashion item, Marshall's company ordering thousands more to cope with the demand, giving a portion of the profits to charity.

Once in the $200-a-night hotel, Monica immediately changed her room, assuming it had been bugged, and from then on conducted all sensitive conversations with the shower in the bathroom running. Almost the only light moment came when she read an article in a tabloid, *The National Enquirer*, which stated that she was pregnant; among the potential fathers the magazine listed was her female fitness instructor Kacy Duke. "I've got bad news for you, Andrew," she joked to me when I called her. "You're not on the list."

She was nervous about meeting the House Republican managers, and more so about seeing Starr's deputies again, resolving that she would stick to her sworn testimony. After all, more than two thousand pages comprising her testimony and the transcripts of the Linda Tripp tapes had been published in the Starr Report, and the House Republican prosecutors themselves had commended her for her fine mind and her capacity for remembering details. Why then, if they believed she had such a remarkable memory, did they need to see her in the first place?

In the blaze of TV lights three House Republican prosecutors, Asa Hutchinson, Bill McCollum and Ed Bryant, as well as Starr's deputies, including Mike Emmick, arrived at the Mayflower Hotel to meet Monica and her legal advisors, Plato Cacheris, Preston Burton and Sydney Hoffmann. In the event, she was pleasantly surprised. She had expected them to be aggressive and confrontational; instead the meeting was cordial and friendly, everyone sipping coffee in casual conversation. She even joked to

Emmick, once her tormentor-in-chief, "We should stop meeting in hotel rooms like this."

Not every outcome of the meeting, which lasted an hour and three-quarters, was so funny, however. While the House managers went away suitably impressed by her poised and intelligent demeanor, Monica was distinctly underwhelmed. Not only had she been forced to run the media gauntlet yet again, but her weekend in Washington had cost her around $15,000 in legal fees, quite apart from what she had spent in upgrading her air ticket and on hotel and security expenses.

So Monica, a woman of modest means, was being forced to fund the Republicans' case against the man she had once loved, at a cost of about two hundred dollars for every question they put to her. Nor was it as though they had asked anything incisive, or followed any new and un-explored line of questioning. Instead, among other incidentals, they quizzed her about when she had started as an intern, and went over the same ground about the President's gifts, wanting to know just whose call to whom had led to Betty Currie coming to Monica's Watergate apartment to collect the boxed-up presents. She had, too, answered all their other specific questions before, either during her Grand Jury testimony or in her FBI statements, leading her attorney, Plato Cacheris, to say afterwards that she had "added nothing to the record that is already sitting before the Senate."

Nor were her responses to a series of hypothetical questions particularly encouraging for the Republican cause; for example, she did not, she said, know how she would react if President Clinton were sitting in the Senate if she was called as a witness. When they asked her how, in her opinion, the trial should be concluded, her answer reflected the views of more than 70 per cent of Americans. She told them that she thought Clinton was an "incredible" President who should not be removed from office, arguing that his behavior could not be construed as "high crimes and mis-demeanors."

For the next couple of days Monica remained in her hotel room, spending long hours knitting and watching the trial of the President on television. The fact that the media continued to mill around in the lobby was an all too painful reminder of the months she had spent as a virtual prisoner when the scandal first broke; "It makes me feel very scared and agitated," she admitted, before turning her thoughts to one of the constant themes of her life, commenting, only half in jest, "How am I going to find a boyfriend with all this going on?"

Briefly reprieved from Starr's attentions, she was allowed to return to Los Angeles, only to learn that she was required to testify to the Senate yet again, via video cameras, on Monday, February 1. Before her ordeal she did manage a night out with Jonathan Marshall and his friends when she flew back to LA later in the week. There she was a guest at a dinner party—which included British actor Julian Sands, star of the Merchant-Ivory movie *A Room With A View*—and was pleased, if disconcerted, when the assembled throng raised a glass to wish her well in the trial that lay ahead.

Once again, at 4.30 in the morning on Saturday, January 30, her father, feeling rather helpless that he was unable to protect his daughter, took her to the airport to catch the early-morning flight to Washington. It seemed that the bonhomie of the night before when Jonathan's friends had wished her well signified a sea change in the national mood towards Monica. At long last people were realizing that she was the victim in this political fight, a young woman who had shown remarkable reserves of strength in her battle with Starr and her degradation by the media.

The flight steward handed her a touching note, telling her how his own teenage daughters had learned lessons from Monica's story. "You could be like Princess Diana and do good in the world," he told her. A woman passenger gave her another good luck message while fellow travelers wished her well and hoped that her ordeal would be over soon.

Even when she arrived at the Mayflower Hotel and ran the media gauntlet she emerged into the lobby to find guests lining up and applauding her. "I was embarrassed, but flattered," she remarked. For a girl who likens her life to a movie, the last reel was hinting at, if not a happy ending, at least a new beginning.

The final showdown came on Monday, February 1, or MON day as several TV shows called it. She was due to meet the House prosecutors, the White House legal team and a Senator from each party and spend the day going over her affair with the President.

There had been endless speculation in the media about what she would say and whether she would provide the 'smoking gun' that would spell High Noon for President Clinton. In reality she intended to stay as closely as possible to the testimony she gave under oath, principally to the Grand Jury. She spent the day before reading through her testimony, going back over events she has spoken about twenty-two times in either FBI depositions or sworn statements. As she said: "Nothing puts you to sleep faster than reading your own testimony."

While her legal team took her through some of the key events that she was bound to be quizzed on—the affidavit, the gifts and job search—Monica was so nervous the night before that she couldn't eat dinner which, as she jokes, is a sign of just how scared she was. She barely slept, waking at seven in the morning and dressing with care, wearing a formal navy blue blazer, navy skirt and pearls.

Her father had suggested that she eat protein for breakfast so she sat down with her legal team and tucked into a mozzarella cheese and mushroom omelette. Then at 9.00 sharp, they took the elevator to the tenth floor of the hotel where, appropriately, the Presidential suite had been prepared for the deposition.

Monica sat at one end of a starched-white-clothed mahogany table, the video camera crew facing her. On her left were her inquisitors for the day, Republican Congressmen Ed Bryant and Jim Rogan, on her right the White House team, David Kendall, Nicole Seligman and Cheryl Mills, the young lawyer much admired by Monica for the way she argued Clinton's case. The two Senate referees were Republican Mike DeWine and Democrat Patrick Leahy— during one of the breaks Monica told Leahy that she hoped his planned legislation to give parent-child privilege, like attorney-client privilege, would one day be approved so that no family would have to undergo the torment that Starr had put her mother through.

Outside the hotel was Monica's fan club, including a man from Cincinnati who called himself the "Naked Cowboy," striding up and down Connecticut Avenue in nothing but a pair of briefs, cowboy boots and hat, playing his guitar.

While the mood ouside was jovial, inside, Monica's three-hour-and-twenty-minute questioning was rather more serious, the former intern very much aware that her every utterance could have deadly consequences for the President. "I was so nervous, I had knots in my stomach," she told me later.

Monica had warned the House Republican prosecutors the previous week that she could parse a sentence as well as the President and she was as good as her word, considering every utterance before she replied. "I had to pay much more attention to my answers than in the Grand Jury," she says. "I felt that the whole world was watching."

On occasion Bryant became peeved with her answers, rather testy when she stuck to her Grand Jury testimony about the disposal of the gifts from the President. Nor was she simply accepting of everything thrown at her. When Bryant characterized the first sexual encounter between the President and Monica in November 1995 as 'salacious' she determinedly pointed out that she didn't see it that way.

As her lawyers predicted, the majority of the questioning concerned the job search, the gifts and the affidavit, Monica sticking pretty much to the sentiments in her Grand Jury testimony. "I think I gave them more of a flavor of the human dimension of the relationship," she says. "People will see that the President hurt me but that he wasn't committing a crime, he was committing adultery."

Her attorney Plato Cacheris, who sat with her during her deposition, described her testimony as a textbook example of how to behave as a witness. He said: "It was a difficult and stressful situation and she came across as articulate, poised and intelligent, yet vulnerable." Most people who saw her evidence televised on February 5 agreed wih his verdict.

The questioning, which ended in the mid-afternoon, was not entirely sober, Monica's comments occasionally lightening the atmosphere. She says: "You know me, I can't be serious for too long." As the questioning began she was assured that her body mike would pick up her every remark. "Oh, the Linda Tripp version," she quipped. When she was asked if she considered the President to be an intelligent man she replied that she thought him an intelligent President, a response which earned guffaws from the assembled politicians. Her growing assurance was shown when prosecutor Bryant retracted a question he was asking her. "See, I'm making my own objections," he said. "Sustained," joked Monica, to much laughter.

After Bryant finished quizzing her, the White House legal team indicated that they had no questions for Monica, Nicole Seligman reading out a short statement that went straight to her heart. "On behalf of the President we want to let you know that he is very, very sorry for what happened."

When she told me about the proceedings, for the first time in all our months of interviews, Monica wept openly as she spoke of her "mixed feelings" for him. "It was so hard, it was an emotional day and with his statement I was hit by the fact that I don't have him in my life anymore. I felt his spirit was with me and it's hard to know that it's all gone.

"At the end I felt like crying because it was hard to talk about the relationship, especially in a roomful of strangers some of whom want to harm the President. I feel that for the last year everyone has spent so much time on my relationship, my emotions, my love and I'm tired of everybody picking it apart. It has been taken away from me by these people.

"I just miss him so much right now."

Even though there will always be a small room in Monica's heart for "Handsome," she no longer opens that door frequently. This evening was one of those occasions. As she admits, however, compared to how she used to see him as a man and a president, she now sees him as all politician, all of the time.

The impeachment trial, for all the antics of the House Republican prosecutors, was winding down, and it was clear that the Republicans could not muster enough votes to remove the President from office. Monica did not provide the "bombshell" the prosecutors needed; the trial was ending, to quote her beloved T.S. Eliot, "not with a bang but a whimper."

The nation was moving on, and so was Monica Lewinsky.

Index